CW00665469

From Fields Fountains

The Story of Bloomsbury's Russell Square

Ricci de Freitas

Ricci deF / Nov '2019.

© Marchmont Association

Acknowledgements:

Special thanks are due to the
Marchmont Association Committee
for their consistent support and encouragement,
to Ivor Kamlish for his excellent design work,
to Roz Perrott for her generous proofreading,
and to David Hayes for his supplementary
historical research.

The Illustrations

The following organisations and individuals
have generously given their permission
to reproduce illustrations free of charge:

Camden Local Studies Library
and Archives Centre (CLSAC)
National Portrait Gallery, London
Wellcome Library, London
Brian Girling
British History Online
British Museum
The University of London
Imperial London Hotels Ltd (ILHL)
PH Hotels (Hotel Russell)
The Picture Research Association (PRA)

The author has made every effort
to identify copyright holders of all illustrations
and to obtain permission
to include images in this book.

Any omissions are unintentional.

This book is dedicated to all who have lived,
worked and played in Russell Square
during the past 200 years.

Published by the Marchmont Association, 2016
(marchmontassociation.org.uk)

Designed by Ivor Kamlish
Printed by Holywell Press Ltd

British Library Cataloguing in Publication Data.
A catalogue record for this book is available
from the British Library.

All rights reserved.
ISBN 978 1 871438 68 0

Contents

Introduction

The Right Honourable John Wilson Croker (1780-1857) in a parliamentary debate in 1825, *"solemnly propounded the question… Where is Russell Square?"* (*Hansard*, 28th March 1825). Although spoken in jest in the heat of debate, his comments reflected the prevailing view among the upper echelons of society that any place located between the City and Mayfair was unworthy of knowing, let alone visiting.

The Morning Chronicle, 25th October 1826, put the record straight in its survey of Bloomsbury, stating that its former fields had been, *"…covered with spacious and even magnificent houses, and laid out in squares and streets not surpassed, if they are equalled by any portion of the metropolis…Russell-square, known to everyone, except that knowing personage, Mr Croker, has for several years stood pre-eminent in size and rank."*

Rowland Dobie's scholarly observations recorded in his *History of St Giles in the Fields*, 1829, provided a more measured assessment of the worth of Russell Square:

"In taking more minute notice of the improvements in Bloomsbury, Russell Square demands our attention. This has a magnificent appearance…It is so extensive as to decide a common observer, that it vies in that respect with Lincoln's Inn Fields Square; nor is it far behind it when compared. It has, from its first formation, been a favourite residence of the highest legal characters; and here merchants and bankers have seated themselves and families, the air and situation uniting to render it a pleasant retreat from the cares of business."

Controversy has continued to punctuate the history of Russell Square from that momentous day on 24th June 1800 when the Duke of Bedford and James Burton signed building agreements signalling the demolition of the Duke's London home, Bedford House, and the creation of new formal architectural compositions in the manner of the Piazza in Covent Garden and Bedford Square (i.e., imposing houses set in uniform terraces) on the sprawling fields to the north.

This book maps the development of the square from its origins during the Napoleonic Wars to the present day, focussing on the lives of the square's many interesting early residents and the momentous events which have altered its character and physical appearance over the past two centuries.

The first two chapters describe the history of the square and its gardens, respectively. The remaining chapters are devoted to the lives of the square's most notable early residents and other interesting occupants, who are revealed house-by-house in an anti-clockwise journey round the square, interrupted by stories of the squares most historically significant buildings, including the Imperial Hotel, Baltimore/Bolton House, Hotel Russell and the University of London's Senate House.

It is my hope that this book will inform you, and occasionally amuse and amaze you.

All proceeds from the sale of this book will be used to support the Marchmont Association's on-going work to improve the area.

Ricci de Freitas

Chapter 1

From Fields to Fountains - the Origins and Development of Russell Square

The Bedford Estate

Thomas, Lord Wriothesley, later the 1st Earl of Southampton, purchased the manor of Bloomsbury from the Crown in 1545. Charles II granted the 4th Earl a licence to build on his land in 1661, beginning with Bloomsbury Square and Southampton House (later Bedford House) on the north side of the Square. The Russell family then acquired the Bloomsbury Estate in 1669 by the marriage of Lord William Russell (1616-1700), second son of the 5th Earl (and 1st Duke) of Bedford, to Rachel, Lady Vaughan (c.1636-1723), the widow of Francis, Lord Vaughan, daughter and co-heir of the 4th Earl of Southampton, who had died in 1667 leaving three daughters but no sons. Lady Rachel ruled her grand house for forty years until William was implicated in the Rye House plot against the throne in 1683 and executed in Lincoln's Inn Fields, where a bronze tablet commemorates the event. Bedford House, as it was now called, enjoyed its heyday under John, the business-like and politically active 4th Duke of Bedford (1710-1771). He was succeeded by his five-year-old grandson, Francis Russell (1765-1802), 5th Duke of Bedford, with the estate being held in trust due to his tender age. The dominant trustee was his grandmother, Gertrude Leveson Gower, the dowager Duchess of Bedford and driving force behind the creation of Bedford Square, the only intact 18th-century square surviving in London today. Prior to 1776, development of the estate had been confined to the area south of Great Russell Street, when this street was *"…inhabited by the Nobility and Gentry, especially the North side, as having Gardens behind the Houses; and the prospect of the pleasant fields up to Hamsted and Highgate. Insomuch that this Place by Physicians is esteemed the most healthful of any in London."* (Strype's *Survey of London*, 1720). The poet Thomas Gray (1716-1771), whose *Elegy in a Country Churchyard* had already made him famous by the time he came to pursue his antiquarian interests in the newly-founded British Museum in 1759, took lodgings in a house at the north end of Southampton Row, which later became the east side of Russell Square, *"…in order to enjoy the pure air and the clear view northwards to Hampstead."*

Rachel, Lady Russell

John Russell, 4th Duke of Bedford by John Gainsborough
© National Portrait Gallery, London

Francis Russell, 5th Duke of Bedford by William Grimaldi
© National Portrait Gallery, London

Gertrude Leveson Gower,
the dowager Duchess of Bedford

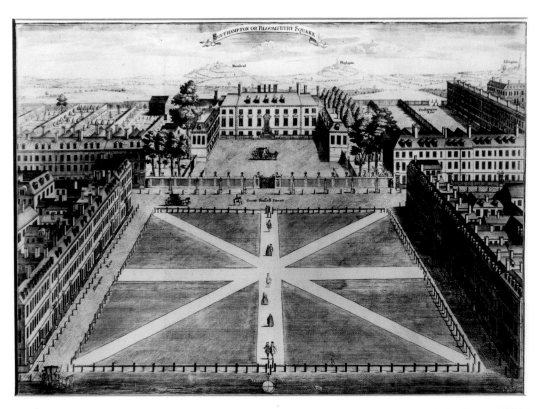

| View north of Bloomsbury Square with Bedford House and the hills of Hampstead and Highgate in the distance, 1720-28

Thomas Gray by John Giles Eccardt (1747-1748)
© National Portrait Gallery, London

Long Fields

The open fields which extended northwards from Bedford House were originally known as Southampton Fields and later Long Fields. Macaulay's *History of England*, 1685, refers to the fields as "…a vast area renowned…for peaches and snipes." It was a favoured spot for duellists as well as the more innocent pastime of kite flying, and in the 1790s the Royal Toxophilite Society (founded in 1781 by Sir Ashton Lever with the Prince of Wales, the future

King George IV, as its patron) rented the land which now lies between Birkbeck College and the School of Oriental and African Studies, using it for archery practice with long bows. They were to move to Regent's Park when Russell Square was developed for housing.

From as early as 1693 and for much of the 18th century the fields were farmed by the Cappers, a prominent local family, although the fields were criss-crossed by footpaths and heavily used for recreation. According to the *Public Advertiser* in 1764, Long Fields was regarded as a place of unruly behaviour, most notably by "…*swarms of loose, idle and disorderly people who daily assemble… to play cricket, tossing up & c which usually terminates in broils and is the cause of various kinds of mischief.*" The two Misses Capper were said to have taken direct action to deal with this behaviour – one of them by cutting the strings of boys' kites with shears whilst riding her grey mare, and the other by taking the clothing discarded by the boys who had gone to the fields to bathe in the miscellaneous ponds which periodically formed in clay pits filled by rainwater or leakage from the New River Company's raised pipes which traversed the fields. Christopher Capper's farmhouse was sited behind Heal's on Tottenham Court Road until 1913, when it was pulled down to make way for a new Heal's bedding factory and other buildings. It had

Capper's farmhouse

Act of Parliament for building Fifty New Churches, and the sixth and final London church designed by the leading architect of the English Baroque, Nicholas Hawksmoor). The grand carriage on the Duke's Road passes several people who are either working or taking leisure in the fields. The remnants of the Civil War fortifications built in 1643 are clearly visible, running along the back wall of the Bedford House garden, which was roughly aligned with the houses to be built along the south side of Russell Square. The fortifications are labelled "11" in the key to Vertue's map, 1738. The position from which Malton painted this scene would have been close to the site of another substantial mansion named Baltimore House, which was built by the 7th and last Lord Baltimore in 1759-63, not long after the completion of London's first by-pass, the 'New Road', in 1756, now known at this point as Euston Road (see map). Thomas Gray recalls that the only other building in the Long Fields at this time was a small chimney-sweep's cottage located some distance north of Baltimore House, which is labelled "D. of Bolton" on John Cary's map, 1795, being then occupied by the Duke of Bolton. Long Fields stretches from Bedford House to New Road, with only one diagonal path indicated. The Duke of Bedford's Road denotes the boundary between the

provided accommodation for Heal's staff until then. Christopher Capper's widow died in 1739, and his daughters, Esther Capper, and Mary Booth were in occupation until 1768. The idyllic view south across Long Fields painted by Thomas Malton in the late 18th century shows Bedford House on the left, Montagu House on the right and the distinctive steeple of St George's Church in the background (Note: St George's Church, Bloomsbury, is one of the twelve new churches designed and paid for under the 1711

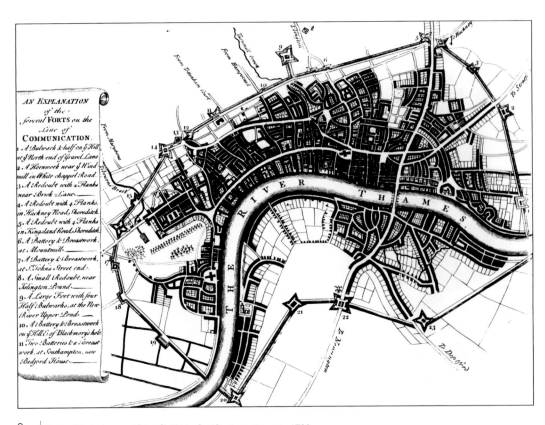

| Part of Vertue's map of the Civil War fortifications, drawn in 1738

Long Fields viewed south towards Southampton/Bedford House (centre), Montagu House (right)
and the distinctive spire of St George's church, Bloomsbury c.1740 by Thomas Malton - Country Life 19.10.1967

Bedford Estate and the Foundling Hospital Estate to the east.

Rowland Dobie (*The History of the United Parishes of St Giles in the Fields and St George Bloomsbury,* 1829) provides an equally unflattering but intriguing view of Long Fields: "*…in 1800 these fields lay waste and useless…the resort of depraved wretches, whose amusements consisted chiefly in fighting pitched battles,*

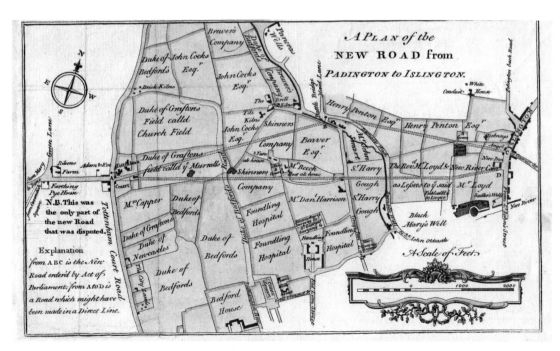

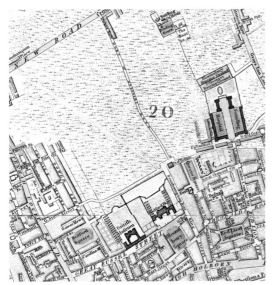

John Cary's map, 1795

James Burton

and other disorderly sports, especially on the Sabbath day… *Tradition had given to the superstitious of that period, a legendary story of remote times, of two brothers who fought in this field so ferociously as to destroy each other; since which, their footsteps, formed from the vengeful struggle, were said to remain, with the indentations produced where these forty footsteps were*

thus displayed. This extraordinary arena was said to be at the extreme termination of the north-east end of upper Montague Street; and, profiting by the fiction, the Miss Porters have recently written and published an ingenious romance thereon, entitled, 'Coming Out, or the Forty Footsteps'.

Dobie goes on to tell of Colonel James Burton's 1,000-strong *The Loyal British Artificers* mustering for exercises on these fields in preparation for the day Napoleon Bonaparte would invade England. By 1795, the rapid development of the adjacent Foundling Estate by a prolific speculative builder, the same James Burton, had inspired the Duke to consider developing the Long Fields, with Bedford House and its grounds to be retained at the heart of the development and the uninterrupted views of the hills of Hampstead and Highgate preserved for the continuing benefit of the occupants of Bedford House. The fields were to be landscaped and made an ornamental pleasure ground, flanked on two sides by terraces of houses in a similar way to John Nash's more elaborate later plans for Regent's Park.

This 'vision' was reflected in a covenant contained in the building agreements for Southampton Terrace, which would face the Long Fields from the east, the effect of which was to prevent any buildings being erected thereon, "…*except ornamental or other buildings for the use of the ground, during the said term of ninety-nine years.*" The houses on the east side of Southampton Row, extending into the proposed development site, had no such protection. They are numbered 24 and 25 on Richard Horwood's map, 1792-99, and became 61 and 62 Russell Square,

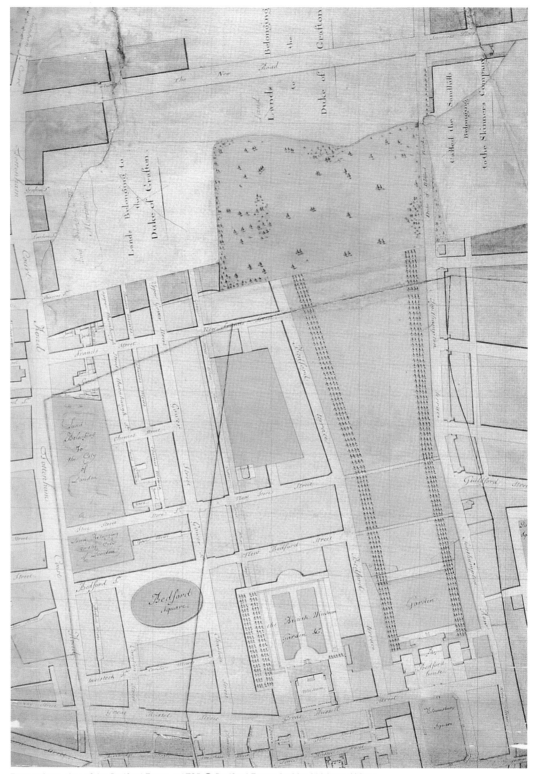

Extract from plan of the Bedford Estate, c.1795 © Bedford Estate Archive, Woburn Abbey

respectively. Bolton House is the large isolated house on the corner of Southampton Row and Upper Guilford Street, with the distinctive bow-shaped frontages on its west and north sides.

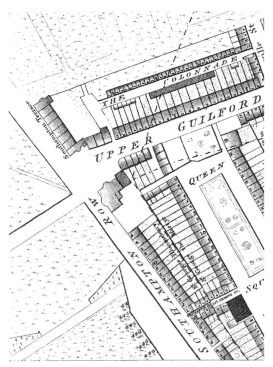

Richard Horwood's map, 1792-99

James Burton develops the Duke's estate (1800-1804)

By 1799, the Duke had abandoned the 1795 plan in favour of a new scheme which he commissioned Burton to put into effect from 1800. This entailed the immediate demolition of Bedford House, for which Burton had offered the Duke a 5,000 guineas 'sweetener' for the materials and furniture, with a large quantity of pictures and statues being sold on the spot by James Christie on 7th May 1800. The site of Bedford House was to be covered with houses (Bedford Place) and the Long Fields with a succession of wide and regular streets and two new garden squares, one of which, Russell Square, would be the focal point for the development and the second largest square in London after Lincoln's Inn Fields. "A Plan of the intended Improvements on the Estate of his Grace the DUKE OF BEDFORD 1800" would have been issued by James Gubbins, the Duke's surveyor, although James Burton is cited as the person from whom further particulars may be obtained, suggesting that the plan was most probably produced for the benefit of prospective contractors.

Donald J. Olsen (Town Planning in London, 1982) proffers an explanation for the Duke's radical change of heart: "By 1800 the detached mansion had become an anachronism in London. Most of the big seventeenth-century houses in Piccadilly, like the sixteenth-century

palaces in the Strand, had long been pulled down, and their sites taken by speculative builders. Yet even they had not been set in grounds as extensive as the portion of the Long Fields which the 1795 plan had marked for preservation. The potential value as building land of so large an area was obviously too great for the Duke to ignore... Quite apart from consideration of estate management, Bloomsbury had ceased to be a fashionable address for a duke, and even the view of Hampstead and Highgate could not wholly compensate for such a situation. In 1800 the Duke moved not only out of Bedford House but off his own estate, and transferred his town residence to Arlington Street, St James's." Burton, for his part, was only too aware of the value of the fields as land for development, not least because of the presence of the same brick earth, clay and gravel which had been readily available for use in his development of the adjacent Foundling Estate.

The building agreements signed by the Duke of Bedford and James Burton on 24th June 1800 specified that the squares and more important streets should be formal architectural compositions in the manner of the Piazza in Covent Garden and Bedford Square - i.e., imposing houses set in uniform terraces. However, the existing terraces of houses built earlier by Burton and fellow builder Henry Scrimshaw on the east side of the proposed square were exempt from these agreements, which covered the north side of Bloomsbury Square, both sections of Bedford Place, the south side of Russell Square, the west side of Southampton Row for a distance of 559 feet southwards from Russell Square, and along the east side of Montague Street for a distance of 519 feet from Russell Square. Burton's designs for the south side of the square were exhibited at the Royal Academy in 1800, contrary to his often understated credentials as an architect. Burton later contracted to build the west side of Russell Square and Montague Street southward from New Bedford Street (now Montague Place) for 465 feet. He also agreed to enclose and plant an area in the centre of the square, either according to his own plan or according to the more elaborate plan of James Gubbins, the Duke's surveyor, and to build the necessary sewers at 12 shillings a foot. The Estate, according to Burton's proposals, would pay him for the cost of the enclosure and the sewers, while the Commissioners of the intended Russell Square Act would reimburse the Estate for the cost of the enclosure and the residents would eventually pay for the sewers (see chapter 2 for more details of the central enclosure/gardens). Under the provisions of a Paving Act obtained by the Bedford Estate in 1801 (39 & 40 George III.

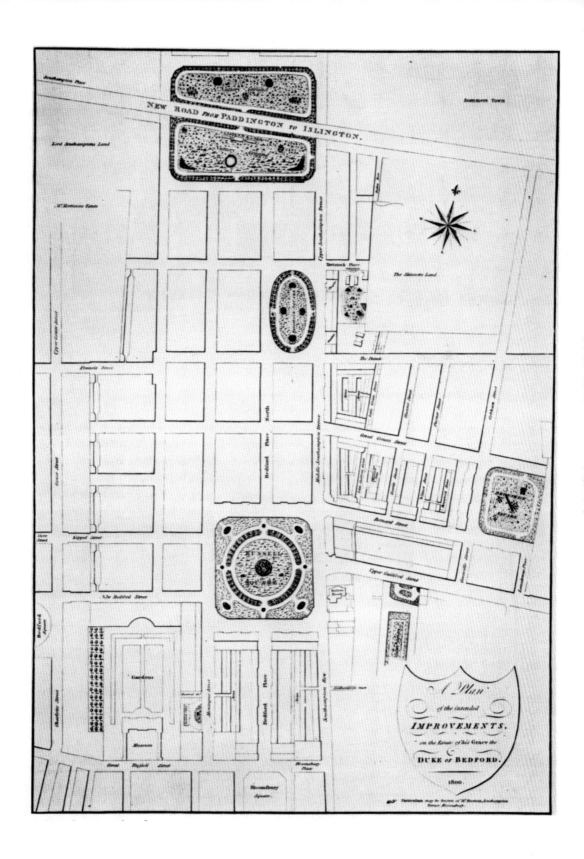

"A Plan of the intended Improvements on the Estate of his Grace the DUKE OF BEDFORD 1800"

South side of Russell Square, between Montague Street and Bedford Place, c.1905 © Brian Girling;

cap. 50 [sic]) the "… *owner of the fee-simple in the Square, together with certain other specified persons, was appointed for five years to carry out the Act; and afterwards the owner of the land and the occupiers of the houses in the Square were appointed Commissioners for regulating the central gardens, &c., the exclusive use of which is vested in the owner and the aforesaid occupiers. Towards the formation of the garden the Commissioners were empowered to levy a rate upon the houses not exceeding 1s. in the £ per annum on the yearly rentals or values of the houses, and for its maintenance a further rate not exceeding 6d. in the £ per annum."* (From information provided to E. Beresford Chancellor [*The History of the Squares of London, Topographical and Historical*, 1907] by A.R.O. Stutfield Esq., Steward to

East side of Montague Street, built by James Burton c.1801

West side of Russell Square and Montague Street viewed south from New Bedford Street, now Montague Place

17-20 Russell Square (r-l) prior to 1899 terracotta adornments – Olsen, p.55, © Trustees of Bedford Estate

the Duke of Bedford.) Sadly, the Duke did not live to witness the fruits of his deliberations, dying at Woburn on 2nd March 1802 at the relatively young age of 36. A grand statue of the Duke stands today on the south side of Russell Square Gardens (see chapter 2 for more details).

Although Burton designed the house façades, the overall appearance of the square was the responsibility of Gubbins and the estate office, who instructed the contractors for the north side of the square – Henry Scrimshaw, David Alston, Jr. and Thomas Lewis - to mirror Burton's designs for the south side (see photo of 17-20 Russell Square prior to 1899 terracotta adornments). *The Building Act* of 1774 prescribed minimum construction standards for four categories of house, with those in Russell Square all falling into the *"first class".* With the east side of the square having been built prior to 1800, the opportunity was grasped to build *"…one of the largest and most handsome houses in London…"* (John Britton's *Picture of London,* 1826) on the west side of the square, with a central pediment and Iconic pilasters on the central and end houses, infilled with grand houses similar to the style of the largely intact buildings to be found at the northern and southern ends of the west side today. Nos. 31 to 36 were designated a *"Clearance site"* by the London County Council after World War II, but the houses remained standing until the University of London began the construction of Stewart House, which opened in 1982 (see chapter 5).

In praise of Burton

Burton had his detractors, but Dobie reminds us *"…that this vast speculation of Mr Burton's was begun and finished during a long disastrous war, most unfavourable to such an undertaking, yet he sternly persevered, and in spite of predictions to the contrary, succeeded and prospered to an extent far beyond his expectation… The fields where robberies and murders had been committed, the scene of depravity and wickedness the most hideous for centuries, became, chiefly under his auspices, rapidly metamorphosed into splendid squares and spacious streets, receptacles of civil and polished society."* J.P. Malcolm, in *Londinium Redivivum,* 1803, whilst lamenting the demise of Bedford House, also found much to admire in the development of the Bedford Estate. *"Squares and spacious streets of the first respectability are rising in every direction; and the north side of the parish will, in a few years, contain an immense accumulation of riches, attracted by the general structures in Russell Square now almost complete… Perhaps, in these times of difficulty and distress no plan has a more beneficial effect than thus employing so many hands, which would have otherwise been idle. When the excessive price of every article of necessity is considered, what heart is there but must rejoice at the busy scene this neighbourhood presents, and bless the proprietors?"*

31-36 Russell Square (r-l) c.1963

RHUBARB!

Russell Square

RHUBARB!

Craig del.   Published April 23 1804 by Richard Phillips 71 S.t Pauls Church Yard.

The 1804 cartoon of a Turkish street vendor of *RHUBARB!* was drawn at the corner of Guilford Street outside Bolton House (formerly Baltimore House) looking towards Nos. 41-38 (left to right) on the west side of the square, with the south terrace of Montague Place to their right. Note also the ornate gas lamp holder on the garden railings and the established shrubs inside. The caption under the cartoon reads: *"The Turk, whose portrait is accurately given in the Plate, has sold Rhubarb in the streets of the metropolis for many years. He constantly appears in his turban trowsers and mustachios, and deals in no other article. As his drug has been found to be of the most genuine quality, the sale affords him a comfortable livelihood."* The boom in house building on the Foundling and Bedford Estates had effectively ended by 1804, leaving the marshy northern section of Long Fields in a forlorn state until the impressive Thomas Cubitt (best known for creating Belgravia and Pimlico) turned his attention to developing this land from 1820, but not before Burton had built the east side of Tavistock Square, along with most of the houses on the Skinners' Estate to the east.

Tavistock Square, east terrace, c.1904

"Where is Russell Square?" (1805-1850)

William Faden's 1813 revision of Richard Horwood's map of London, 1792-99, shows the completed square with houses numbered anti-clockwise from Guilford Street (No. 1) to Southampton Row

Row and Guilford Street. These are numbered 61 to 67 in later maps, although Bolton House is already shown as two separate buildings, with the land on the corner of Guilford Street already marked out for development (see chapter 3 for more details on the development of the east side). William Faden was chosen by the Ordnance Survey to print their first map of Kent in 1801, the same year he published his map of the country twenty-five miles round London, which had been copied and re-engraved by the French War Department in preparation for an invasion of England, such was his international reputation as a cartographer. He also published maps of the West Indies, India and France and was involved in producing maps of America at the time of the Wars of Independence, including some showing troop movements and battle plans. His *North American Atlas*, dated 1776, is now a prized collector's item, as is his *United States of North America*, 1785.

Rowland Dobie wrote of the early development of Russell Square in 1829: "*In taking more minute notice of the improvements in Bloomsbury, Russell Square demands our attention. This has a magnificent appearance… It is so extensive as to decide a common observer, that it vies in that respect with Lincoln's Inn Fields Square; nor is it far behind it when compared. It has, from its first formation, been a favourite residence of the highest legal characters; and here merchants and bankers have seated themselves and families, the air and situation uniting to render it a pleasant retreat from the cares of business.*"

William Faden's 1813 map showing house numbers

(No. 60), as well as the central enclosure, as laid out by Humphry Repton (see chapter 2). Note the uncertain numbering of the original houses on the east side of the square between Southampton

However, the reputation of Russell Square had been much maligned by the Right Honourable John Wilson Croker (1780-1857) in a parliamentary debate in March 1825 in which he "*…solemnly propounded the question… Where is Russell Square?*"

Although intended in irony, this phrase reflected

John Wilson Croker by William Owen

The Morning Chronicle of 25th October 1826 remarked, in its survey of Bloomsbury, that its former fields had been "...covered with spacious and even magnificent houses, and laid out in squares and streets not surpassed, if they are equalled by any portion of the metropolis... Russell-square, known to every one, except that knowing personage, Mr Croker, has for several years stood pre-eminent in size and rank". "But the die was cast by Croker's joke. It was quoted and embellished by a host of commentators and writers until it became one of the phrases of the century." (Rosemary Ashton, Victorian Bloomsbury, 2012). Ashton puts the record straight: "As for Russell Square in its role as representative of Bloomsbury at large, it had been the remote area of Hook's and Croker's mischievous imaginings. In the years immediately following their jokes, both the physical development of Bloomsbury and its colonising by cultural institutions gained it national significance in matters of education and culture... By 1900 the Museum, Russell Square, and Bloomsbury in general were indisputably 'central'."

Russell Square was not only the largest square in Bloomsbury, but also the 'top' square in the early 1800s, with a pocket companion to London published in 1811 describing the "...principal squares..." of the area, declaring Russell Square "...remarkable for the elegance of its houses..." and its "...ornamental area...". Cruchley's Picture of London (1835) describes Russell Square as "...the largest and most uniform square in London...", praising the "...great taste and variety..." of its interior layout and the airiness of the situation. "But it is Thackeray himself who definitively established Russell Square as the home of vulgar upstarts, the newly rich merchants who want a grand house still convenient to the City." (Ashton, 2012). In his best known novel Vanity Fair (1847-8), William Makepeace Thackeray (1811-1863) deliberately placed his upwardly mobile principal characters, the Osbornes and Sedleys, in large comfortable family houses in the Square in 1815, alongside the fictional lawyers and judges and other respectable, professional, middle class families leading comfortable lives, which mirrored the lives of the first non-fictional inhabitants of James Burton's houses. Vanity Fair was to set a trend for novels based on upwardly mobile characters who made their homes in the square, including journalist and author Edmund Yates (1831-94), who had quarrelled with Thackeray early in his career and wrote a satirical novel of an artist whose father was "...a merchant-prince—a Russell Square man—a person of fabulous wealth, who...lived but for his money, his dinners, and his position in the City; a fat, pompous, thick-headed man, with a red face, a loud voice, a portly presence, and overwhelming watch-chain..." (Edmund

the prevailing view among the upper echelons of society that any place located between the City and Mayfair was unworthy of knowing or visiting. The debate in question was about the proposed location of the National Gallery. Robert Peel had asserted that "...if the national gallery were banished to the neighbourhood of St Giles's and Russell-square it would much lessen the value of the collection...", which led Croker to argue that the Dulwich Picture Gallery, established in Dulwich in 1811, was "...quite as distant as Russell Square; though he did not profess to know exactly where Russell-square was [a laugh]!" (Hansard, 28th March 1825). The Tory satirist Theodore Hook perpetuated this negative view of Russell Square in his novels at the time in which he locates Russell Square (and the British Museum) in some distant wilderness. Others were keen to defend the reputation of the Square, including Thomas Denman, the wealthy lawyer and resident of No. 50, on the south side of Russell Square, who made the following point in May 1825, during a parliamentary debate about judges' salaries: "...at the head of people of middling fortune, which was better than being at the foot of the higher order; and, though some aristocratical gentlemen in that House had treated their usual residence with so much contempt as to profess they did not know where Russell-square was, he thought they were much more respected in that quarter than they would be were they to intrude themselves amongst the wealthy inhabitants of Grosvenor-square." (Hansard, 16th May 1825).

Yates, *The Business of Pleasure*, 1879). The article titled
"EXTRAORDINARY ATTEMPT TO STEAL A DEAD BODY",
which appeared in *The Times* on 7th April 1827,
provides a revealing insight into life in Bloomsbury
and London when wealthy and 'respectable'
Londoners lived cheek by jowl with the poor
and criminal classes, and newspapers were the
predominant 'social media' outlet.

William Makepeace Thackeray

Edmund Yates, 1865

EXTRAORDINARY ATTEMPT TO STEAL A DEAD BODY.

On Wednesday morning last, a gentleman of very respectable appearance was proceeding through Russell-square, when he was seized with a fit of apoplexy, which caused him to fall down in a state of insensibility. A crown of persons immediately surrounded him, and rendered every assistance, and ultimately conveyed him to the house of a medical gentleman in the neighbourhood, where, on examination, he was found to be quite dead. The body was conveyed to St. Giles's workhouse, where, on being searched, a pair of silver spectacles and 9s. in silver were found in the pockets, but nothing whatever to lead to a discovery of who or what he was. The parish officers instantly forwarded information of the circumstance to Mr. Stirling, the Coroner, to hold an inquest, and caused bills to be printed and circulated, giving an accurate description of the deceased's dress and person, in order that it might be claimed by his friends. Mr. Stirling attended yesterday morning, and the jury, after investigating the matter, returned a verdict of "Died by the visitation of God."

Immediately after the inquest, a female of respectable demeanour called at the workhouse in a state of the most anxious agitation, and requested to have a sight of the deceased's body, stating that she felt assured that it was her uncle, who had been missing from his home since Wednesday morning last. Her request was of course immediately granted, and on entering the dead house where the body lay, on beholding the countenance she gave a shriek, and exclaimed, "My uncle, my dear uncle," and embracing the body, she caressed it repeatedly, and appeared to be almost heart-broken with grief. Indeed, the officers had considerable difficulty in causing her to quit the place, prior to doing which she steadfastly gazed on the remains of her "dear uncle," and at length was obliged to be supported from the place. When in the governor's room she with the most urgent entreaties requested that the body might be sent home immediately, as his family were in the utmost distress on account of the melancholy circumstance. This, however, was prudently avoided until proper inquiries were made, and on being asked for the address of the deceased, she said, "Mr. Williams, 24, Blackfriars-road." Previous to her leaving the place, a young man who had to transact some business at the workhouse, entered the place, and hearing that the lady had made application for a dead body in the workhouse, his mind was instantly struck with suspicion, as he identified her as the person whom he had seen a short time before conversing at the corner of Belton-street, Long-acre, with as notorious a resurrection-man as any in London; and he intimated his suspicions to the parish officers, who determined upon being on the alert. Bartlett, the beadle, and the young man who made the discovery, repaired to No. 24, Blackfriars-road, when, on making inquiry, they found that it was kept by an honest blacksmith, who knew nothing at all of Mr. Williams, or the death of any of his relations. They, however, traced the applicant to a brothel in Dawson-street, Kent-road, and ascertained that she was a complete adept in such practices, and was connected with a gang of resurrection-men, and that her husband had been transported. This information they imagined to be sufficiently strong to warrant the detention of the woman, and she is now in St. Giles's workhouse, until the matter be thoroughly investigated, as it is anticipated that she can be traced so as to link her with an organized gang of "body-snatchers," who have indulged in similar practices with impunity, through the medium of her assistance. In the course of yesterday several well-known resurrection-men were observed lurking about the neighbourhood, no doubt waiting to ascertain the result of their fair colleague's application, and on being spoken to upon the subject by one of the beadles, they attacked him with the most violent abuse. It is presumed that had she gained her point with the parish-officers, by having their consent to take the body away, she would have called in her companions, who were in readiness, and the body would have been consigned *instanter* to one of the dissecting rooms of a celebrated anatomist, not far distant from St. Giles's, at the west-end of the town.

"Extraordinary attempt to steal a dead body",
The Times, 7th April 1827

A favoured place for public assembly

Although Russell Square was never favoured by 'high society', it was a highly favoured place for public assembly in the 19th century. *The Times* dutifully provided very detailed and respectful accounts of these mass gatherings in an age without television or radio, not to mention social media. Two such articles illustrate the broad range of participants in these significant social gatherings. *The Times*, 11th April 1848, elaborately describes the Chartists' rally: *"One body of the Chartists, forming what was called the western division, was appointed to meet in Russell-square, and by 9 o'clock a considerable crowd had assembled to witness the start. Soon after, small parties of men, intending to join in the procession, marched into the square under leaders, and a few of them bearing banners with devices and mottoes suited to the occasion. The greater portion of them appeared to have mustered in connexion with the following trades: - Cordwainers, tailors, and bricklayers, to which must be added two 'brigades' of the Irish Confederation. The cordwainers were preceded by a banner bearing the words, 'Liberty, equality, fraternity, - no surrender.' So far as we could observe, the tailors unfurled no banner on the occasion; but the bricklayers, who turned out in great strength, could boast of two – one of them of beautiful white silk, with the inscription, 'The People's Charter, and no surrender'; the other bearing the following:- 'Every man is born free. God has given men equal rights and liberties; may it please God to give man the knowledge to assert these rights, and to let no tyrannical faction withhold them from the people.' The 'Irish Confederates', however, made by far the finest display; one body of them bore a banner of crimson, white, and green silk, with the words, 'Emmett brigade of the Irish Confederation', and the motto, 'What is life without liberty?' Another party had an orange and green banner, on which was inscribed, 'Let every man have his own country'. Shortly before 10 o'clock the various bodies were placed in order, and marched out of the square seven and eight abreast. The number of persons in the procession at this moment was as near as possible 1,000, but they augmented as they passed along, and ultimately amounted to about 2,000 people....The great majority of the persons forming the procession were in their holyday dress; many wore rosettes in their breasts, and had all the appearance of respectable working men. The bricklayers, with whom were mixed a considerable number of men having the appearance of 'navvies', must, however, be named as an exception so far as dress goes. The procession passed along the streets in a very quiet and orderly manner, and though a considerable crowd accompanied them* on their march, little obstruction to the ordinary traffic in the streets was experienced." *The Times*, 15th August 1854, describes a much larger gathering, the *"GREAT TEMPERANCE DEMONSTRATION"*, in a similarly detailed and respectful fashion: *"Several thousands of teetotallers congregated yesterday morning in Russell-square for the purpose of paying their fourth annual visit to the Surrey Zoological Gardens. Every part of London and its suburbs contributed its quota to the general mass; and by the time the procession was ready to start it was found that Russell-square, capacious as it is, would not hold it, and large bodies of persons had to move down the adjoining streets in order to give the leaders an opportunity of making a dignified exit. Every description of vehicle which could be begged or borrowed was brought into requisition to convey the enthusiastic teetotallers, and the procession was made of omnibuses, cabs, clarences, broughams, gigs, &c., headed by bands of music, the vigour of which must have taken the aristocratic residents of Russell-square and its neighbourhood not a little by surprise. Shortly after 11 o'clock the procession made a start, amid the deafening cheers of the persons who composed it, some hundreds of whom were children, designed the 'Band of Hope', who are bound by a solemn league and covenant never to take alcoholic liquors themselves, and to discourage the practice in others. Mr. Gough, the well-known temperance orator, whose sudden and remarkable conversion from excess to total abstinence is well known, headed the procession, which moved along Tottenham-court-road, Oxford-street…to Surrey-gardens, where a grand fête took place."*

Arresting the decline of the square (1850s-1890s)

The Bedford Estate strived to preserve the social exclusivity of Bloomsbury, firstly by gating the entrances to squares to prevent through traffic, secondly by fencing and gating the gardens to restrict their use to bona fide residents, and thirdly by inserting restrictive covenants in house leases which forbade any trade whatsoever in all the important streets and squares. However, these restrictions proved difficult to enforce, with many private family homes being discreetly converted into lodging houses by the 1850s. In the 1890s, the Estate took steps to stop the 'lodging-house rot' which was causing an exodus of the better-off residents. In Russell Square in 1899, with the original leases expiring, the Estate commissioned its surveyor, Charles Fitzroy Doll, to smarten up the Georgian house façades with Victorian terracotta ornamentation and fancy iron railings, *"…thus spoiling their Georgian character without*

South side today, between Bedford Place and Southampton Row, showing the late 19th-century terracotta adornments

Terracotta detail at 24 Russell Square

stopping the rot…", according to John Summerson (*Georgian London*, 1991). These 'improvements', which deliberately complemented Doll's opulent Hotel Russell, which opened on the east side of the square in 1900, are still visible today on the façades of the houses on the north and south sides of the square. Chancellor (1907) had previously observed that the east side of the square "…*has become altered in a very striking way, for quite half of that side has been absorbed in one of those vast hotels which appear to be springing up with the same frequency as new theatres, all over London… the sumptuous Hotel Russell… is constructed in terra-cotta, or brick which resembles it, and nearly all the houses on the north side and some in other parts of the Square have been refaced with the same material, which, perhaps artistically, carries out the scheme of the dominant building, but has not greatly conduced to the preservation of the otherwise Georgian appearance of the houses, and inevitably*

Four surviving original houses on the north side, with terracotta adornments

A typical form of public transport plying its trade through the east side of Russell Square in 1906. It is captured outside Hotel Russell next to Guilford Street

suggests the idea that the surplus material, after the erection of the hotel, has been thus carefully utilised." (See chapter 3.3 for more about Charles Fitzroy Doll and his two grand hotels.) One might be tempted to conclude that the houses on the west side of the square 'escaped' the terracotta cladding because they were not in such close visual proximity to Hotel Russell as the houses on the north and south sides. However, it was almost certainly due to the 'planning blight' caused by a combination of the 'imminent' development of the west side of the square by the expanding British Museum (affecting Nos. 38-43) and the early negotiations between the Government and the Bedford Estate over the relocation of the University of London to Bloomsbury (affecting Nos. 25-37). It is ironic how this combination of factors accidentally led to the west side of the square retaining much of its original Georgian character, notwithstanding the merits of the Neo-Georgian Stewart House (Nos. 31-36).

In 1878, St James's Magazine referred to the negative effect of through traffic on the otherwise pleasant atmosphere of the square: "Russell Square is, under ordinary circumstances, a very nice place to walk in. If those troublesome railway vans and goods wagons would not come lumbering and clattering, by way of Southampton Row, through the square, and up Guilford Street, on their way to King's Cross, 'La Place Roussell' would be as cosy and tranquil as 'La Place Royale' in

Paris. It has the vastness of Lincoln's Inn Fields without its dinginess." The decline continued as the eastern side of the square became a main thoroughfare following the passing of an Act of Parliament in 1890, which abolished all gates and barriers on private estates in London. By the end of the 19th century the Bedford Estate had become in large part institutionalised, with many of the original family homes being 'colonised' by reforming educational and medical institutions. This transformation was compounded by the falling in of the original 99-year leases, although Russell Square would appear to have bucked this trend, according to Charles Booth's Poverty Maps of 1889 and 1898-99, which show the houses in Russell Square still fully occupied by "Upper-middle and Upper classes. Wealthy" residents in 1889, with only the houses in the southern section on the west side showing a slight decline by 1898-99, being occupied by "Middle class. Well-to-do" residents. As late as 1907, Chancellor confidently asserted, "Many notable people still reside in Russell Square, which seems to be again resuming its position as a fashionable locality. The legal profession is still largely represented, and to the legal has been added the theatrical, a combination which has become traditional." However, the residential stability of Russell Square was to be short-lived, with the occupancy of buildings listed in the street directories over the next 30-year period switching dramatically from residential to organisations, institutions and businesses, with ratios of 47 to 3 in 1900, 23 to 32 in 1920, and 14 to 72 in 1930. It is during this period that the Bedford Estate, buoyed by the success of Hotel Russell, appears to

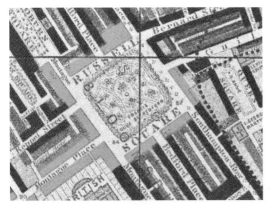

Charles Booth's Poverty Map, 1889

Charles Booth's Poverty Map, 1898-99

BLACK: Lowest class. Vicious, semi-criminal.

DARK BLUE: Very poor, casual. Chronic want.

LIGHT BLUE: Poor. 18s. to 21s. a week for a moderate family

PURPLE: Mixed. Some comfortable others poor

PINK: Fairly comfortable. Good ordinary earnings.

RED: Middle class. Well-to-do.

YELLOW: Upper-middle and Upper classes. Wealthy.

Key to Affluence

The University of London makes an indelible impression on the square (1930s)

have given in to market forces and granted permission to Henry Walduck to build another grand hotel, the Imperial, a few doors away from the Russell, with the dependable Charles Fitzroy Doll as its architect (see chapter 3, part I for details). The east side of the square was totally devoid of residents by 1930.

Following the seismic impact of the two Victorian hotels on the east side of the square, the Georgian character of the other three sides of the square remained largely intact, that is until the dramatic arrival of the University of London in the 1930s, when it relocated its headquarters to Bloomsbury. A bizarre series of transactions had begun in 1920 with the proposed University site on the west side of the square being purchased by the Government from the Duke of Bedford for £425,000, and sold back to the Duke six years later, then sold again to the University following the dramatic intervention of Sir William

Hotel Russell and the Imperial Hotel (left and centre) dominated the east side of Russell Square in 1929

Beveridge, vice-chancellor of the University. Although the physical presence of the towering Senate House made an indelible impression on the square, the front elevations of the original Georgian houses, which the University had acquired for its own use, remained largely unaltered until the 1980s, when Stewart House replaced the middle terrace (Nos. 31-36), even though this site had been designated a *"Clearance site"* on the London County Council's Bomb Damage Map, 1939-45 (No. 37 had been demolished the year before to enable Montague Place to be widened).

The full story of Senate House and the University's ill-fated master plan for the wider area is told in chapter 5, with bomb damage to other parts of the Square being referred to in the respective chapters. Suffice to say, the Square was relatively unscathed in comparison to the wholesale destruction inflicted on the City of London and much of Holborn Borough lying to the south of the Square, particularly on the night of 29th/30th December 1940, when the Luftwaffe dropped 24,000 high explosive bombs and 100,000 incendiary bombs, creating what has become known as the 'Second Great Fire of London'. The street directories during World War II show very little change in occupancy of the buildings in Russell Square, which remained largely occupied by established businesses, organisations and institutions.

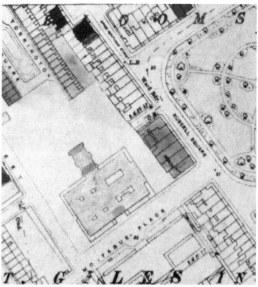

Bomb Damage map showing Nos. 31-36 as a *"Clearance area"* (light blue) and Senate House's *"Blast damage, minor in nature"* (yellow)

1930s traffic gyratory heralds eight decades of motor vehicle domination

In the 1930s, the Ministry of Transport introduced one-way traffic in a clock-wise direction on the south, west and north sides of the Square, with two-way traffic being retained on the east side between Woburn Place and Southampton Row, accompanied by the introduction of *"traffic light signals"*. This traffic gyratory had the effect of turning Russell Square into a race-track where pedestrians feared for their lives, and triangular islands on the north-west and south-west corners filtered traffic into and out of the Square with minimum speed constraints (See 1938 Ordnance Survey map). The footways on the south-east and north-east perimeter of the gardens were also extended at this time to provide more pedestrian space opposite the Imperial Hotel and Hotel Russell, respectively, with ornamental fountains and flower beds being inserted in the 1950s. The extended footway and fountain opposite the Imperial Hotel, which can be seen in the photograph, were removed in the early 1960s when the east side was made one-way, and all north-bound traffic from Southampton Row joined the 'race-track' round the entire Square. A large railed triangular pedestrian refuge, introduced at this time, is shown on the 1965 Ordnance Survey map and can be seen in the classic 1966 photograph of the Imperial Hotel in chapter 3.1. An alternative view north along the east side of the square shows the effect of the traffic gyratory in 1979. The refuge was dissected by a bus lane in c.2001, and the island colonised by layers of forbidding railings, as seen in the photograph taken shortly before the major public realm improvements were introduced in time for the 2012 Olympics. The fountain opposite the Hotel Russell survived until 1984 when it was decommissioned by Camden Council. An earlier ambitious proposal (1931) to install three subway entrances on the corners of Russell Square, Woburn Place and Bernard Street, connecting to a reconstructed Russell Square station in the style of Piccadilly Circus, was never implemented. All that remains of this aborted scheme is the tall London Underground roundel which is 'stranded' outside HSBC Bank at 1 Woburn Place, and has puzzled visitors to the area ever since.

1938 Ordnance Survey map showing triangular islands in the NW and SW corners

Ornamental fountain opposite the Imperial Hotel in the 1960s © CLSAC

1965 Ordnance Survey map showing large triangular pedestrian refuge opposite the Imperial Hotel

Bus Lane introduced on the east side of Russell Square in c.2001

Progress and conservation collide (the 1960s)

Traffic gyratory, 1979 - EH

Donald J. Olsen, in his scholarly 1964 edition of *Town Planning in London*, observed: *"Bloomsbury was built for a less exalted kind of life than were the Adam houses in Mayfair and Marylebone, but that life, too, came to an end. When the English middle classes stopped being able or willing to lead the kind of life which Bloomsbury and Bayswater and Kensington were made to house, their town houses were converted into private hotels, solicitors' offices, student hostels, and self-contained flats. The square gardens are either beautiful but unused – like Bedford Square – or, like Bloomsbury and Russell Squares, turned into public 'amenities', parodies of their original selves. The Georgian and Victorian estates of London are today neither what their planners intended them to be nor wholly satisfactory environments for life in the 1960s. The street pattern is ill suited to modern traffic, the houses are ill suited to an age without servants."*

The controversial replacement of Fitzroy Doll's extravagantly styled Imperial Hotel in the 1960s with the 'geometrical' concrete and glass structure we see today heralded the unveiling of Sir Leslie Martin's planned mixed-use development for the University of London, which proposed the destruction of *"…much of the existing Georgian landscape…"* to create a *"…larger secluded university precinct that could rival the spacious out-of-town sites"*. This proposal, along with the Bedford Estate's *"…comprehensive redevelopment…"* scheme (1963-68), which would have seen the rebuilding of large stretches of the frontages at both Bloomsbury and Russell Squares, was rejected in 1969. The perceived emasculation of Russell Square's Georgian character moved Nicholas Pevsner to present his controversial evidence to a planning inquiry in 1973, in which he argued against the preservation of the historic frontages, in the face of opposition from a powerful conservation lobby, which included the Georgian Group, the Royal Fine Art Commission, the Society for the Protection of Ancient Buildings, the Victorian Society and the Garden History Society, and which had been effective at reducing the impact of these major development plans. The buildings within the Square today are largely what existed at the time of this inquiry, with the notable exception of the Neo-Georgian Stewart House, with its façade mimicking Burton's surviving

| 'Stranded' London Underground roundel outside HSBC Bank

Aerial view of Russell Square, c.1963, with the original Imperial Hotel standing proudly on the east side next to the recently opened President Hotel, with its glass and concrete exterior glistening in the sunshine © CLSAC

houses at Nos. 38-43. The bomb-damaged houses at Nos. 17-19, on the corner of Bedford Way, were eventually replaced by Lasdun's Queen's Award-winning Institute of Education in 1971-6. All of the surviving original houses in the Square, along with Hotel Russell, appear in Historic England's National Heritage List for England (NHLE), the official database of nationally designated heritage assets maintained by Historic England on behalf of the Government. Also listed is the historic cabmen's shelter, which was installed in the north-west corner of the Square in 1987, following the repeal in 1980 of the *Bloomsbury Square Act (1806)*, which forbade Hackney coaches from standing in the Square or within 300 feet of it. The shelter was originally erected in Leicester Square in 1897, and was funded by Victorian theatre impresario Sir Squire Bancroft, who dedicated it in 1901 "...for the benefit of Theatreland". It is one of 13

surviving shelters of the 61 original structures installed at key cab pick-up points in central London in the late 18th century to provide cabmen with "wholesome" food, but mainly to keep them out of the pubs. They were originally conceived by Captain G.C. Armstrong of St John's Wood, and provided by the Cabmen's Shelter Fund, which was largely financed by the Earl of Shaftesbury in 1874. Cabmen were required by police to take up no more space than a horse and cab and could not leave the shelter while their cab was parked outside. Rules for cabmen also included no swearing or drinking. Many of these shelters were removed in the 1960s and 70s, but those that survive were Grade II listed by English Heritage in order to protect them. The shelter was carefully repositioned by Camden Council from the triangular traffic island in the NW corner to a nearby position when they remodelled the highways around the Square in 2010-11.

Plaques on the door of the cabmen's shelter

Inside a typical cabmen's shelter in 1875

Cabmen's shelter on the north-west traffic island in 2006

Cabmen's shelter in its present position

Mixed fortunes in the early 21st century

Major improvements were made to Russell Square in 2002, when Camden Council commissioned Land Use Consultants to refurbish Russell Square Gardens with funds provided by the Heritage Lottery Fund's Urban Parks Programme. Arguably the most distinctive features of this scheme for the casual visitor will be

View of the central plaza fountain with pleached-lime pathway and restaurant in the middle distance

the high-tech fountain in the central plaza with an alleged vertical reach of 30 feet, the partial restoration of Repton's pleached-lime horse-shoe path and the new restaurant building. Further details of the transformation works can be found in chapter 2.

A dark cloud descended over the square on 7th July 2005 (often referred to as 7/7) when central London's public transport system was devastated by a series of co-ordinated suicide bomb attacks during the morning rush hour. It was the day after London had won its bid to host the 2012 Olympic Games, which had specifically highlighted the city's multicultural population. Four Islamist extremists separately detonated three bombs in quick succession aboard London Underground

Emergency services outside Russell Square station on 7th July 2005

Police cordon at the entrance to Bernard Street

Triangular railed pedestrian refuge in the south-east corner of the Square prior to the 2011 improvements

This 'maze' of railings outside Hotel Russell was purged in 2011 under a major highways improvement scheme

The relatively traffic-free south side of Russell Square

| The frequently grid-locked north side of Russell Square

trains across the city and, later, a fourth on a double-decker bus in Tavistock Square. Fifty-two civilians were killed and over 700 more were injured in the attacks, making it the UK's worst terrorist incident since the 1988 Lockerbie bombing, as well as the country's first ever suicide-attack. Russell Square and neighbouring streets were brought to a standstill as the police cordoned off the area after declaring it a crime scene. Ambulances and fire appliances filled nearby Bernard Street and Tavistock Place, as the dead and injured in the Piccadilly line train, which had been hit by an explosion between King's Cross and Russell Square stations, were brought to the surface at Russell Square station. Russell Square and Tavistock Square in particular experienced intense global news coverage on the day and for some time after the incidents, such was the impact of the day's events. A tree was planted in Russell Square Gardens, where a multi-faith memorial service was attended by the families of victims, politicians, faith group representatives and the local community.

Meanwhile a consortium of London boroughs, including Camden, had formed the Cross River Partnership (CRP) as a joint venture to improve linkages between boroughs north and south of the River Thames. One such project was the ill-fated Cross River Tram, which was intended to link 'up-and-coming' Brixton town centre with trendy Camden Town via the Thames and Russell Square.

Funds were secured from a combination of Transport for London and the European High Speed Train Integration fund (HST4i) to widen the footways along the south side of Bernard Street in order to improve pedestrian connectivity and increase the capacity of the footway in advance of the anticipated extra pedestrian footfall between the planned tram stop in Russell Square and the tube station. Although these works were implemented in 2006-07, the Cross River Tram project was aborted.

Russell Square itself was eventually given a much needed lift in 2011, when Camden Council, financially assisted by Transport for London, set about reversing decades of through traffic dominating the Square by substantially extending the footways surrounding the gardens and changing the traffic gyratory to two-way working, with a consequent reduction in vehicle speeds on three of the Square's sides. The jury is still out as to whether these changes have resulted in a reduction in air-pollution, which is measured with scientific equipment located on the east side of the gardens. Whereas the south side of the Square is generally congestion free, the north side is frequently grid-locked with traffic, as illustrated in the photographs. Other improvements included the eradication of footway 'clutter', including the maze of pedestrian safety barriers on, or adjacent to, key crossing points, such as those illustrated in the photographs taken outside the Imperial Hotel and Hotel Russell, respectively. The works were completed in good time for the Square to serve as the transport hub for the world's press attending the London 2012 Olympics, when severe restrictions were placed on through traffic and vehicles were severely restricted from using the Square.

"Russell Square, one might argue, due to its immense generosity of layout has stood up to the surrounding behemoths extremely well. It is still the centrepiece of Bloomsbury and represents in its juxtaposition of university, commercial and domestic buildings the balance of interests that characterise and control the area." (Birkbeck, *FCE Occasional Paper No. 5*, 2004)

View towards Russell Square from the Centre Point viewing gallery prior to its closure in 2015

Chapter 2

From Private Enclosure to Public Amenity – the Story of Russell Square Gardens

In the beginning…

Under the terms of the Building Agreement signed by Francis, 5th Duke of Bedford, and James Burton on 24th June 1800, Burton agreed to enclose and plant an area in the centre of Russell Square, either according to his own plan or according to the more elaborate plan of James Gubbins, the Duke's surveyor. The 1800 Estate plan (See chapter 1) and the 1806 plan are virtually identical and both refer to *"Mr Burton, Southampton Terrace Bloomsbury"* as their source for further particulars. The Estate, according to Burton's proposals, would pay him for the cost of the enclosure, while the Commissioners of the intended *Russell Square Act* would reimburse the Estate for the cost of the enclosure. *"An Act for enclosing and embellishing the Centre or Area of a certain Square, intended to be called Russell Square, purposed to be made in the Parish of Saint George Bloomsbury, in the County of Middlesex, and for forming and making the same into a Pleasure Ground, and for continuing and keeping the same in Repair"*, was presented to Parliament by the Duke and passed on 20th June 1800 (*George III. cap. 50*).

Although Burton was contracted to set out and plant Bloomsbury and Russell Squares, he had been in discussions for some time with Humphry Repton, England's foremost landscape designer, before appointing him in 1805 to design and plant both Squares, his fee for Russell Square being a very reasonable £2,750 (equivalent to £283,250 in 2016). It is clear that Burton had already carried out some preparatory works in Russell Square, as evidenced by the *Rhubarb!* print, dated 1804 (See chapter 1), and Repton's opening remarks in *An Enquiry into the Changes of Taste in Landscape Gardening* (1806), in which he bemoans the fact that the ground had already been laid out flat at considerable expense, so it could not be changed, and that *"…the great size of this square is, in a manner, lost by this insipid shape"*. He went on to outline his ideas, listing the pre-requisites for achieving a degree of *"…perfection of Modern Gardening."*… *"First, it must display the natural beauties, and hide the natural defects of every situation; Secondly, it should give the appearance of extent and*

HUMPHRY REPTON.

London Published June 1st 1802, by J. Taylor, High Holborn.

Humphry Repton, 1802

freedom, by carefully disguising or hiding the boundary; Thirdly, it must studiously conceal every interference of art, however expensive, by which the natural scenery is improved; making the whole appear the production of nature only; and fourthly, all objects of mere convenience or comfort, if incapable of being ornamental, or becoming proper parts of the general scenery must be removed or concealed. The interior, moreover, wants to be perfectly secluded; somewhere between a garden and a park." Repton referred to statues and other art work as *"…eye traps (which) …tend to lessen the apparent greatness of a place; for one can seldom lose sight of so conspicuous a landmark; we are in a manner tethered to the same object."* True to his principles, when instructed to incorporate a large statue of Francis Russell, 5th Duke of Bedford, into Russell Square Gardens, Repton deliberately positioned it outside the main body of the gardens, where it would eventually be shielded from the gaze of garden users by a grove of trees. Lithographs printed in 1817 and 1829 show

Statue of the Duke of Bedford, 1817 © CLSAC

Russell Square, and Statue of the Duke of Bedford, drawn by Thos. H. Shepherd, 1829-31 © CLSAC

34

The Duke of Bedford's statue remains an integral part of the streetscape today

the extent to which the trees and shrubs had grown to obscure the view of the statue from the gardens, thus rendering it integral to the streetscape, as it remains today.

The 1817 print also portrays Southampton Terrace on the right and the eastern arm of the north terrace on the left, whilst the 1829 print features the pre-Burton houses on the right, with only a glimpse of Southampton Terrace through the more established garden trees.

Repton could conceivably have been influenced by Thomas Fairchild (1667–1729), so-called 'Gardener of Hoxton', who in 1722 wrote emphatically in his book *The City Gardener* "…*by no Means on the Outside of such a Square, should be planted any Trees that rise higher than the Wall or Pale-side, because they will break the Prospect; which by no Means should be interrupt'd next to the Houses, by which the whole is maintained.*" Nothing, he insisted, "…*must stand in our Way, and resist our Sight, and so rob the Gentleman of that View which they have by their Expence endeavour'd to gain.*" This principle is fully reflected in Russell Square, where no trees have been planted outside the garden perimeter fence to this day

Repton's designs for Russell Square ran into the hundreds, but the general shape and design

Thomas Fairchild

35

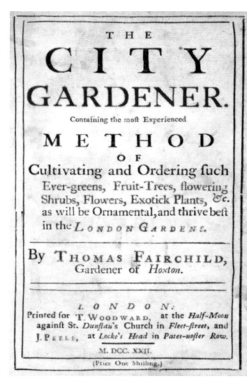

Frontispiece of Fairchild's *The City Gardener*, 1722

The Duke of Bedford's statue showing 'agricultural adornments'

consisted of a broad perimeter gravel walk with privet and hornbeam hedge, clipped to six feet to screen the walk from the street. A large area of lawn was intersected by a horse-shoe shaped broad walk under two rows of lime trees, to be clipped to form a *"cloister-like walk"* which started and ended at Sir Richard Westmacott's nine-foot high bronze statue of the Duke, on an eighteen-foot high Scottish granite plinth. Although this statue was planned by 1806, it was not completed and unveiled until 1809. The Duke is shown as a Roman senator, or *"...one of those illustrious statesmen of ancient Rome, whose time was divided between the labours of the Senate and those of their Sabine farms"* (Walford, *Old and New London*, vol. iv), surrounded by groups of allegorical figures connected with agriculture and four figures representing the seasons, celebrating his achievements as an agricultural 'improver' on his estate at Woburn.

Charles James Fox and the 5th Duke of Bedford facing each other down Bedford Way

He is facing southwards down Bedford Place towards Bloomsbury Square, where a statue of his good friend, Charles James Fox (also by Westmacott), was erected in 1816, with the two men deliberately facing each other.

Two narrower walks intersected the gardens, bow-shaped and leading from the north-east to south-east corner and the north-west to south-west corner, with the centre of the gardens divided into four compartments, which Repton treated in different ways: a grove of trees near the statue, flowers and shrubs in different arrangements in the other three. A shelter, called a *"Reposoir"* by Repton, was at the centre of the Square with four low covered

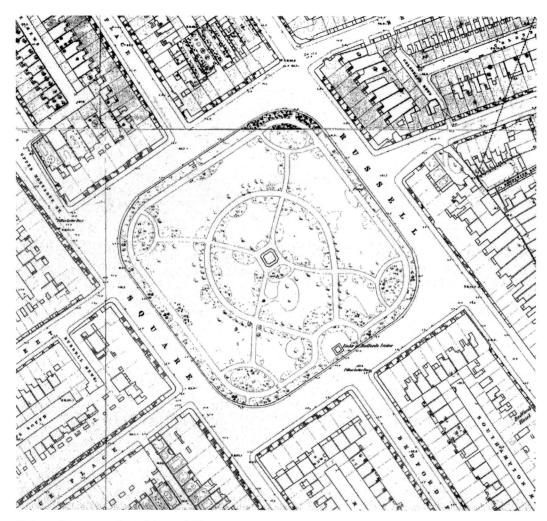

Ordnance Survey map of Russell Square, 1871

seats and four open seats covered with trellis and climbing plants, the seats concealing a gardener's shed in a courtyard. Loudon was to later describe the *"Reposoir"* as a *"...centrical covered seat and retreat"*. Outside the centre were lawns. This design is clearly visible on Horwood's map, updated by Faden, 1813 (See chapter 1). Repton envisioned *"A few years hence, when the present patches of shrubs shall have become an umbrageous avenue, and the children now in their nurses' arms shall have become the parents or grandsires of future generations, this square may serve to record that the art of landscape gardening in the beginning of the 19th century was not directed by whim or caprice, but founded on due consideration of utility as well as beauty."*

Rowland Dobie (1829) refers to the north and west sides of the Square having a higher elevation than the others, which, besides giving a bad

architectural effect, *"...renders the carriage pavements so unequal, that no art can prevent it overflowing with wet in various parts, at certain seasons of the year"*. Dobie lists the precise dimensions of the Square (meaning the gardens) as: north side - 655 feet 6 inches; south side - 665 feet 3 inches; west side - 672 feet 7 inches; and east side - 667 feet 1 inch. This variation in the lengths of each side is noticeable in the first (1871) and subsequent Ordnance Survey maps, which clearly show that the Square is not technically square at all. It may also be of interest to the purist that the 1813 map shows only four entrances into the gardens (north side, west side, east side and north-east corner), which by 1871 had become seven (additions being on the south side, south-west corner and an extra entrance on the east side which was most probably to provide access to the pump indicated on the map).

Repton's design for Russell Square Gardens set the benchmark for other London squares, and he continued his association with the 6th Duke of Bedford at Woburn Abbey. However, the realisation of Repton's vision for Russell Square was to be short-lived, when one of his protagonists, John Claudius Loudon (1783-1843) - Scottish botanist, garden designer, cemetery designer, author and garden magazine editor - was invited to intervene in the 1830s after many of Repton's lime trees had died or were dying because of heavy pollution. Loudon's solution was to introduce the London Planes in the horseshoe and on the perimeter, which proved to be tougher and more resilient, as evidenced by the magnificent specimens which survive today. Only four of the trees in the Square today survive from Repton's era..

John Claudius Loudon, 1845
© National Portrait Gallery, London

The management and financing of the gardens

The 1800 Act made the following provisions for the future management and financing of the gardens: the *"...owner of the fee-simple in the Square, together with certain other specified persons, was appointed for five years to carry out the Act; and afterwards the owner of the land and the occupiers of the houses in the Square were appointed Commissioners for regulating the central gardens, &c., the exclusive use of which is vested in the owner and the aforesaid occupiers. Towards the formation of the garden the Commissioners were empowered to levy a rate upon the houses not exceeding 1s. in the £ per annum on the yearly rentals or values of the houses, and for its maintenance a further rate not exceeding 6d. in the £ per annum."* (From information provided to E. Beresford Chancellor by A.R.O. Stutfield Esq. in *The History of the Squares of London, Topographical and Historical*, 1907). Commissioners could also impose fines of between 10 shillings and £5 on anyone found committing theft in, or vandalising the Square, and they continue to have a partial role today as a result of the renewal of leases on the gardens from that time to the present.

The Act ensured that the gardens were well maintained in the early years, as evidenced by a document in the Bedford Estate's archives, dated 5th September 1823: *"An estimate for painting works*

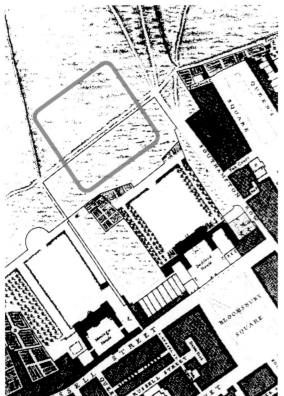

| The approximate position of Russell Square Gardens on John Rocque's 1746 map

to be carried out in Russell Square: *Paint all the iron rails round the pleasure ground and the statue and the Watch Boxes and the Pump twice in oil Lead colour. Paint the roof, sides, and seats of the eight alcoves in the centre of the pleasure grounds, and all the seats in the pleasure ground twice in oil green. Paint the stucco walls at the back of the alcoves for times in oil stone colour. The whole to be done for the sum of eighty eight (sic) pounds.*" However, in 1860, the Duke was so disturbed by the "*…unsightly state of the trees and plants in the gardens of several squares*" on the Bedford Estate that he hired a certain Mr Mann (who looked after Kensington Palace Gardens) to inspect them, resulting in the Duke spending the princely sum of £447 in 1861-62 (equivalent to £49,170 in 2016) on drainage, the renewal of the soil "*…and re-planting and carrying the character of the garden*".

The Bloomsbury Flower Show

The following year, the gardens played host to the first *Bloomsbury Flower Show*, which was deliberately intended to "*…encourage the taste for cultivating flowers among people of the working class*". This was seen as a startling innovation, being the first time the working classes had been allowed into one of the large, private London squares: "*…thrown open for the recreation of the masses*" was how the event's organiser, the Revd. Samuel Hadden Parkes, senior curate of St George's Bloomsbury, put it, describing the event as a "*…working man's flower show*". The *City Press* expressed its dismay: "*The inhabitants of Russell Square have consented to allow the exhibition to be held in their garden, which sounds as if the end of the world was near at hand.*" The event, which was attended by the Earl of Shaftesbury, featured in the *Penny Illustrated News* on 18th July 1863, titled *Working Men's Flower Show*. It was so successful that it was repeated the following two years, with reports in the *Holborn and Bloomsbury Journal* describing the events as inclusive, with as many women as men involved, and with entries from schools and domestic servants. The events were loosely based on the traditional summer fêtes hosted by householders of squares for their friends and neighbours, with the addition of a large marquee filled with a wide variety of flowers grown by local people. Charles Dickens was particularly enamoured with the August 1864 event, named the *Bloomsbury Bouquets Flower Show*. He wrote: "*Outside the tent a police band, all the members in blue coats and oilskin-topped hats; numberless young ladies in the*

The 1864 Flower Show as featured in the *Illustrated London News*

most delightful summer costumes, with young gentlemen to match, behaving as the youth of both sexes do under such circumstances; numberless rich old people, bored and stupid; numberless poor old people, wondering and dazed 'which how they can wear them bonnets on the tops of their 'eads, and such rolls of 'air be'ind, good gracious!' numberless poor children; save those who were evidently exhibitors, there did not appear to be many poor people of middle age, they were mostly veterans or children, interspersed among the promenaders. And it was one of the curious sights of the day, to witness how thoroughly at home the children made themselves, and how, in blessed ignorance of childhood, they utterly ignored any deference to the powers that were." Dickens was particularly moved by the way in which the event demonstrated that "the great arts of fighting against adverse circumstances, and of suffering and being strong, were practised among a certain portion of the poor with an exemplary patience worthy of emulation." (Dickens, Bloomsbury Bouquets, 1864). A full feature, titled The Bloomsbury Flower Show in Russell-Square Inclosure, appeared in the Illustrated London News, 23rd July 1864, together with an engraving of a view of the event.

Hadden Parkes was pleased to note that "… upwards of 3,000 persons, rich and poor together" attended, while the Illustrated London News welcomed the show as an "observable" sign that "…amidst [London's] rush of utilitarianism there is pleasing approach to sentimentalism".

The Illustrated London News article provides a meticulous insight into the nature of London society at the time: "We give an Illustration of the annual flower show held in the gardens of Russell-square with a view to encourage the taste for cultivating flowers among people of the working class in the parish of St George's, Bloomsbury. This pleasing exhibition took place on Wednesday week. A large tent, as shown in our Engraving, had been erected in the grounds, and this was abundantly decorated with fuchsias, geraniums, annuals, and various other flowers and plants. The company consisted, for the most part, of the poorer inhabitants of the parish; but among the more distinguished visitors were the Earl of Shaftesbury, Sir S. Morton Peto, Bart., M.P., Mr. Payne, the Hon. Arthur Kinnaird, M.P., Miss Twining, the Hon. Misses Ashley, Mr. W. Hawes, and the Rev. Emilius Bayley, Rector. All present seemed to enter most heartily into the pleasures of the scene; and the laudable arrangement which caused the customary barriers of exclusiveness to be thrown down for the time, and the gardens to be opened to the poorest parishioners, was evidently much appreciated. It appears that the system of exhibiting flowers under the present circumstances has rapidly increased in public favour; and whereas in the first year only 140 plants were

entered, nearly 800 were now registered, and 400 persons had given in their names. The prizes, varying from 1s. to 10s., were distributed by the Earl of Shaftesbury, who delivered an address expressing the delight he felt at the character of the exhibition and pointing out the many advantages that must arise from it. But it was not alone for the best display of flowers that prizes were awarded. The owners of clean and tidy rooms were also honoured, and these competitors received rewards varying from 10s. to £2. Lord Shaftesbury, in presenting them, congratulated the parishioners on the progress they had made in adopting measures for the preservation of their own health, and for the extension of a salutary example to others. For the prizes in respect to the possession of clean and tidy rooms, 800 names were entered, and the Rev. Mr. Bayley and his curate had paid no less than 600 visits in the space of six weeks, in order to ascertain who amongst the occupants were best deserving of rewards. The competition was confined exclusively to the inhabitants of the parish, both as regarded the exhibition of flowers and the prizes for clean and tidy rooms. It should be observed that none of the flowers were cultivated in conservatories or elaborately-trimmed gardens, but in bow-pots and wooden boxes fixed on the window-sils (sic) of the humblest parishioners. Two bands of music were in attendance—that of the E division of the Metropolitan Police, and that of the 37th Middlesex volunteers—and when the distribution of prizes had been completed many of the younger part of the company amused themselves with dancing."

Interest in the flower show continued for a few years, with Bloomsbury Square playing host in 1865 and the Foundling Hospital in 1866. After an apparent interlude of two years, "…the committee of Russell-square" (again) "generously accorded the use of their garden" to the Bloomsbury Flower Show "under Lord Shaftesbury's presidency", possibly for the last time, although the idea caught on in other towns and cities across Britain, largely as a result of the influence of Hadden Parkes's Window Gardens for the People, and Clean and Tidy Rooms; Being an Experiment to Improve the Lives of the London Poor, 1864.

The actress and writer, Fanny Kemble, recalls in her Records of a Girlhood (1878), that when staying in Great Russell Street she had a key of this garden given her, and how with a book in her hand, generally Shakespeare, she used to mechanically pace the gravel walks, and ever after associated certain readings of Othello and Macbeth with that place. Another resident of Great Russell Street, Lady (Georgiana) Burne-Jones, in her Memorials of Burne-Jones, recalls "…the garden of Russell Square furnished the marigolds that fill the space in the foreground beneath the wayside shrine".

Fanny Kemble

Lady (Georgiana) Burne-Jones, c1882, by Frederick Hollyer

Signs of unrest

By the 1880s, residents of the Square were becoming disgruntled with their perceived neglect of the gardens. A certain Humphry Ward, husband of Mary Ward, wrote a letter to the Bedford Estate in January 1884 on behalf of the Garden Committee in which he explained that the Committee had used up all its funds obtained by the levy on householders, leaving no funds to repair or renew the plant house which they described as being *"in a ruinous condition"*. Another letter from Frederick McPocter (Treasurer) dated 24th March 1887 refers to the Committee having spent £790.12 (equivalent to £93,220 in 2016) on repair works to the Square and railings.

By the 1890s, the general public, on the other hand, were beginning to show their resentment that London's great squares were still barred to through traffic and their gardens remained the exclusive domain of square residents. The London County Council secured a parliamentary Act in 1890 which led to the abolition of gates and barriers, allowing traffic to pass through Russell Square for the first time. This was followed in 1906 by the *Open Spaces Act*, which gave Commissioners the right to vote squares into the control of the Local Authority (i.e. the power to lease out the square). In 1931, the *London Squares Preservation Act* imposed significant restrictions on the development of Russell Square (and many other Bloomsbury squares and gardens), although it failed to address the management or neglect of squares or the negative impact of vehicular traffic, including noise, pollution and parking, which were detrimental to the appearance and ambience of London's garden squares. There was also a growing tension between garden users who wanted to obscure the view and negative effect of traffic with dense hedging and trees and those who believed the lush vegetation was smothering the open spaces and obscuring views to the surrounding architecture. The 1914 photograph of the group of British Association of Rotary Clubs members posing opposite Hotel Russell and the charming photograph of the Artists Corps learning signalling, c.1914, both illustrate how rustic the gardens were at that time. Regardless of the liberating and protective measures being introduced across London, Russell Square Gardens remained resolutely private, that is until the onset of World War II (1939-45), when the Government decreed on 10th November 1941 that all iron railings should be removed from public squares to be melted down for munitions. Hastings Russell, 12th Duke of Bedford, strongly protested about the removal of the railings from Russell Square Gardens, but the Government went ahead with their removal. In October 1943, indignant protesters, denouncing the Duke as unpatriotic, daubed slogans in yellow paint on the base of his grandfather's statue (i.e., the 5th Duke) under the cover of the night-time blackout. They read: *"Grandfather of a Quisling! Down with traitor 1941 and his railings – Down with the Duke!"* (Philip Zeigler, *London at War 1939-1945*, 2002).

British Association of Rotary Clubs members posing opposite Hotel Russell in the rustic setting of Russell Square Gardens, 1914 – EH

Artists Corps learning signalling in Russell Square Gardens, c.1914

The 'democratisation' of the gardens

The loss of the railings inadvertently provided free access to the gardens for the general public, who began to use them for recreation and as convenient pedestrian routes through the area. This accidental 'democratisation' of the gardens led inevitably to a change in their status from private to public open space in September 1943, when an agreement between the Duke of Bedford, the Commissioners and Holborn Borough Council transferred their maintenance and management to the local authority for a period of seven years. In that same year, Russell Square Gardens hosted one of the best-documented events in the national *Holidays at Home Programme*, which was intended by the Ministry of Information (based in Senate House) to provide relaxation for

war workers without throwing too much strain on transport. The *War Fair, Holiday at Home Fête in Russell Square* saw the still private gardens transformed into a public pleasure ground, decorated with bunting, pennants and Union flags, and filled with a variety of fairground attractions and civil defence stalls.

However, the 'feel good' effect engendered by this event was to be seriously undermined on 23rd June 1944, when Repton's much maligned *"Reposoir"* suffered a direct hit from a V1 bomb, which also destroyed many of the surrounding trees and injured nine people.

During the period of austerity following the end of the War, Holborn Borough Council maintained the gardens as best it could. A scheme devised by landscape consultant, H.F. Clark, and published in a report to the Council on 19th September 1946, titled *The Proposed Improvements to Russell Square and*

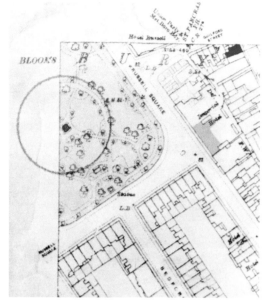

Bomb Damage map, indicating the V1 bomb with a large circle and the *"Reposoir"* at its centre

Railings being removed from Russell Square Gardens in 1942
© Imperial War Museum

Local people enjoying the *War Fair, Holiday at Home Fête in Russell Square*

Bloomsbury Square, was never implemented. Meanwhile, the Council continued using the garden as a means of raising the spirits of the local populace, organising regular summertime concerts to entertain the public. One such concert was organised on 22nd July 1949 to celebrate Poland's National Day and Chopin's centenary year. It was arranged by the British Polish Society, in co-operation with the Polish Cultural Institute and Holborn Borough Council and consisted of a piano recital by Julius Isserlis, which was entirely devoted to the works of Chopin. A local newspaper published an enthusiastic review of the event under the bold heading *"CHOPIN IN RUSSELL SQUARE",* adding, perhaps with a sense of irony, *"The distant hum of traffic, though undoubtedly to a certain extent distracting to both artist and public, was not sufficient to mar the peaceful attention of the audience."* The local authority's regular concerts were lower-key events, with their 'pop-up' summer bandstand being wheeled in through a gap on the north side of the gardens, where it was diligently erected and minimally decorated by Council staff, who also provided a few rows of municipal chairs for the comfort of the small but appreciative audiences.

Repton's *"Reposoir"* or Central Pavilion as it looked prior to V1 bomb destroying it in 1944 © CLSAC

The Central Pavilion and surrounding trees damaged by the V1 bomb on the night of 22-23.6.44 © CLSAC

Officials inspecting the Central Pavilion on 23.6.44, the day after the V1 bomb was dropped, injuring 9 people © CLSAC

Holborn Borough Council gardeners scything the lawns, August 1948 - viewed west from the north lawn

CHOPIN IN RUSSELL SQUARE

"Chopin in Russell Square", 1949

Holborn Borough Council's 'pop-up' summer stage arrives in style via a gap in the fence on the north side of the gardens
© CLSAC

A jazz quartet plays to an appreciative audience © CLSAC

The gardens receive a 'make-over'

The 1943 lease was extended on 25th December 1949 for a term of fifty years, with an annual payment of £10.00, to be paid each Christmas Day thereafter. Under the terms of the lease the Council undertook to maintain the Square as an open space and garden for public use and for the following types of entertainment: open-air band concerts, dramatic performances, charity fetes and pageants but not funfairs – no doubt influenced by feedback from residents of the Square in response to the post-war programme of events staged in the gardens. Apart from a shelter for gardeners and a small canteen for the public, the Council could make "...no material alteration in the layout of the Square garden...nor shall any trees be felled pollarded or substantially lopped... without the written consent of the Duke" It comes as no surprise, therefore, that little change took place in the landscape of the gardens until 1957-60, when

the Borough Architect, S.A. Cooke, redesigned the gardens for their future use as a public space, following which the Council carried out extensive replanting and introduced a central paved area with three, large circular 'Festival of Britain' commemorative fountains and a tea house in the north-east quadrant. The fountains bore this 'it does what is says on the can' inscription: "During the years 1959-60 the square (sic) was replanned and the fountains and tea house constructed by Holborn Borough Council for the enjoyment of the citizens of the Borough and those who succeed them". Other changes included reshaping trees and felling of those damaged by shrapnel, new paths related to desire lines and the replacement of the railings removed during the War, albeit with a less robust and modernistic version, as illustrated in the photograph taken on 17th April 1957 at the official inauguration of the railings by the Duke of Bedford and Mayoress of Holborn, Mrs Reed. The ceremony was equivalent to laying the foundation stone of a new building and was considered significant enough to warrant an article in *The Times* on 18th April 1957 under the intriguing heading *"HISTORY REPEATED IN RUSSELL SQUARE"*. The article alludes to the history of the Square and the Russell family's associations with it, and the fact that, *"In 1900, the 11th Duke of Bedford became the first Mayor of Holborn, and in 1931 he was made the first freeman of the borough. Since then, the relationship between Holborn and its squires has lapsed in all but the formal sense, until yesterday, when, to the evident pleasure of the councillors of Holborn, the present head of the Russell family went as their guest to help install the first new railings for the square. After the Duke of Bedford and the Mayor of Holborn, Mr. G.B.M. Reed, had gone through the motions of bolting two sets of railings together with ceremonial chromium-plated spanners for the benefit of photographers and the entertainment of lunch-hour-strollers in the square, the Duke recalled that his family built the first fences and houses in the district at their own expense. He remarked dryly that he felt privileged to have been invited to repeat the process at the expense of the borough."* We must be grateful to *The Times* for showing so much interest in the detail of this three-year programme of works, which was to cost the Borough £15,000 to implement (equivalent to £339K in 2016). The article continues: *"Lack of fencing round the gardens has encouraged their use as a short-cut and as a paradise for the rowdy pleasures of small boys. By redevelopment, the Council hope to transform the square (sic) into a more restful place. The railings, embedded in a new granite chip base to replace the present dilapidated foundation, will be painted green and set closely against* a hedge of flowering shrubs 6ft. high, to keep out noise and dust. There will be four entrances, one at each corner, with gravel paths converging at the centre of the square on a paved court with a fountain in the middle." The artist's impression for this scheme shows the Duke of Bedford's statue being reintegrated into the gardens with the removal of Repton's hedge screen. However, a low hedge can just be seen in the photograph taken

The Duke of Bedford & Mayoress Mrs Reed at the inauguration of the Russell Square railings in 1957

View towards Guilford Street, with the Premier Hotel on the right and circular bench around the London Plane tree, c.1950 © CLSAC

Artist's impression of the intended improvements to Russell Square Gardens completed in 1958 © CLSAC

| The central area with hexagonal theme and commemorative fountains in the 1960s © CLSAC

South side of Russell Square Gardens in 1958
after the installation of the new railings

The layout of Russell Square Gardens, as shown
on the 1965 Ordnance Survey maps (joined up)

after the completion of the works, as well
as the new railings, which were missing
from the artist's impression. A children's
sand-pit was added in 1963, on the north
side of the gardens. This can be seen in
the 1965 Ordnance Survey map, as well
as the three artesian fountains in the
central area and the café building with
gardener's depot to the rear. Also shown
is the ornamental fountain on the north-
east perimeter of the gardens.

Ornamental fountain on the north-east corner of the square in 1956 © CLSAC

Famous Liverpudlian's send Russell Square Gardens global

The Beatles posed in the gardens for publicity photographs taken by Dezo Hoffmann on 2nd July 1963, when they were staying at the recently completed President Hotel, on the corner of Guilford Street and Russell Square. Although Hoffmann was taking the photographs for the *Liverpool Echo*, they also appeared in the British music press, the London *Evening Standard*, fan magazines, posters and publications worldwide. The photograph of the Beatles posing behind the hexagonal flower containers with obligatory municipal geraniums, was used as the cover of an extended play (EP) record, and the shot of them posing by the commemorative fountain was one of their most popular early 'pin-up' posters. Another famous Liverpudlian, Cilla Black, was photographed in 1964 in a typically ebullient mood on the lawn opposite the original Imperial Hotel, which would soon be razed to the ground.

BOYS • CHAINS • LOVE ME DO • BABY IT'S YOU

The Beatles EP cover, 1963

Cilla Black in Russell Square Gardens, 1964

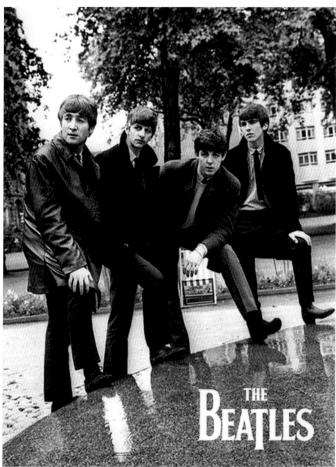

The famous Beatles poster, 1963

The Millennium make-over

The 'Great Storm' of 1987, which wreaked havoc on several of Russell Square's larger London Plane trees (and much of southern England for that matter), may have been a blessing in disguise, having thinned out the dense tree canopy which had long starved the lawns of direct sunlight.

At the time of the storm, Camden Council was operating a *"Camden Heritage/Tourism Information Centre"* in the gardens, housed in a *"24ft X 8ft...*

'Great Storm' aftermath, 1987

prefabricated building", which the Council granted itself planning permission to install in 1986. Undeterred by the storm, the Council obtained conditional permission to extend its stay in the gardens. The Director of Planning and Transport's decision letter of 14th November 1988 to the Chief Executive of Camden read: *"The limited period for the retention of the structure shall be until 31st January 1991 by which date the structure shall be removed."* The reason given for this restriction was, *"The type of building is not such as the Council is prepared to approve, other than for a limited period, in view of its appearance."* It is ironic that whilst Camden Council was actively promoting the heritage value of the borough, it needed to be reminded by its own planners of the need to avoid inflicting an entirely inappropriate building on one of its greatest heritage assets, Russell Square Gardens. The Council sought to make amends for its apparent neglect of this heritage asset in the late 1990s, as the 1949 lease came up for renewal, when it decided to apply to the Heritage Lottery Fund (HLF) for a grant to restore the gardens to their *"...original splendour closely following Humphry Repton's plans of c.1805."* (A quote from the two interpretive boards installed in the gardens). The Bedford Estate, who were not initially aware of the Council's plans, responded by resurrecting their 1971 proposal to install an underground car park, as they had done previously in Bloomsbury Square. It is worth mentioning here that whilst the Commissioners controlled what went on in the gardens above ground, the Bedford estate retained control of the space below. The Friends of Russell Square (FoRS) was formed in 1994 to partner the Commissioners and Council, who commissioned Land Use Consultants (LUC) to develop a landscape

strategy and proposals for the restoration of the gardens. The Friends' group was a prerequisite of grant-aid. The role of the Commissioners, which had effectively lapsed since the 1949 transfer of the Square to Holborn Borough Council, was similarly revived in accordance with HLF's requirements. A new lease, also required by HLF, was agreed for 25 years (expiring on 22nd December 2024) at £5,000 per annum, to be paid to the Commissioners by Camden, largely under the same terms as the 1949 lease, with an additional undertaking to carry out the HLF-funded restoration works. The HLF awarded a grant of £1.4 million under its Urban Parks Programme in September 2001, with the works being undertaken by LUC and completed in April 2002.

Although *"Russell Square has been warmly praised as a good example of the comprehensive refurbishments brought about by the Campaign for London Squares"* (Todd Longstaffffe-Gowan, *The London Square*, 2012), the scheme had its detractors, including representatives of the gay men who had been using the gardens as a night-time 'cruising zone' for some years. However, consultation had revealed that the general public's deepest concern had been personal safety, which led to 75% of the perimeter shrubberies being removed to open up views into the gardens from the surrounding streets. The higher railings were designed, in tandem with the removal of much of this shrubbery, to deter gay men from using the gardens at night, when they would in future be locked. John Beeson of the pressure group OutRage! argued that, *"If local people don't like gay sex in Russell Square, they should stay away. No one is forcing them to go there. They can use Bedford Square or Coram's Fields instead. In any case, what are these heterosexual whingers doing* wandering around Russell Square at 2 a.m.? They should be at home looking after their children." (For the record, Bedford Square is a private garden and adults may only enter the uniquely wonderful Coram's Fields if accompanied by a child.) Martin Stanton, the Parks Service Manager at the time, said that Camden Council had been concerned for some time about the regular incidents of gay men being attacked in the gardens overnight, some quite savagely. He added that they were also concerned that if this violence continued after their 'flag-ship' gardens had re-opened, it could undermine the reputation of the gardens and all the effort and money that had been invested in them. Martin said that despite the overnight locking of the gates, some gay men continued to climb over the fences for a short while after. An area to be designated for dogs only and another area for Muslims to pray in were both rejected, along with what appears to have been a compromise proposal for an area to be set aside exclusively for the use of gay men. Other critics bemoaned the loss of the three 'artesian fountains' which occupied the central plaza since the 1950s (see above), even though they had been out of action intermittently for many years, just like the fountain which stood outside the gardens in the north-east corner of the square.

Notwithstanding these local pressures, the design brief was, by their own admission, a challenge for LUC, who "…sought to conserve Humphrey Repton's design for the Square whilst introducing facilities for the 21st century." LUC also "…sought to actively conserve and enhance the Square's finest features", so it was clearly a 'no-brainer' that the surviving London Plane trees introduced by Loudon after Repton's lime trees had failed, should be fully retained and be given "…sensitive arboricultural surgery to extend the lifespan of the magnificent set of mature Plane trees" (LUC), even

though they were not part of Repton's 'original vision' for the gardens. LUC originally wanted to remove more vegetation, describing anything that wasn't a plane tree as a shrub, but this was apparently resisted by the Commissioners. "Using archive plans and archaeological trial pits, the original intricate path layout was reinstated" (LUC), although the original planting scheme within the loops of the paths was given over to lawn, which LUC refused to have planted with daffodils, although this was subsequently over-ridden by Camden Council in response to public demand, with each spring heralding a glorious display of daffodils throughout the gardens.

Notwithstanding the raised height of the railings, "Using archive photographs, the original railing, finial and gate designs were faithfully recreated, and remnant sections of the perimeter stone plinth provided the template for new moulds to be made." (LUC). Repton's "Reposoir" was substituted with the 'dancing' fountains, which now provide a new focal point for the garden, contrary to Repton's design principles, which specifically forbade the use of such "eye traps". The Duchess of Bedford, fiercely opposed the proposed fountain, proclaiming "Over my dead body!", but she was out-voted by the Commissioners, who were keen to replace the defunct former fountains with a more impressive fountain framed by York stone paving, which would also serve as "a performance and events space" for the restored gardens. There is no doubt that the fountains, which are computer-controlled to regulate their height and frequency, give much pleasure to garden users all year round.

The refurbishment also included an enlarged and redesigned café, restoration of the statue of the Duke of Bedford, and the pergola and path layout echoing Repton's design, while not replicating it entirely. The LUC scheme planned to complete the arch

The central fountain gives great pleasure to people of all ages

of pleached limes (presently confined to the north section) around Repton's 'horse-shoe' path *"in future decades as the existing mature trees die back."* The timber-slatted benches, which line the paths at intervals and are grouped around the central fountain, were reproduced from a 19th-century design.

An inevitable change to Repton's layout, the reduction of the original four corner flower beds to two, was designed to connect the so-called 'Celebratory Gateways' (LUC) in the north-east and south-west corners in acknowledgement of *"… the importance of the 20th century desire line from the Underground to the British Museum"* (LUC). A proposal to create an opening in the west side of the railings as a means of improving pedestrian connectivity to and from the British Museum, was made by Camden Council in 2009, based on a recommendation in Farrell Associates' *Bloomsbury – A Strategic Vision*, 2007. However, this was withdrawn due to conservation concerns, despite a path and entrance being clearly indicated in the intended position on Faden's 1813 map (see above).

The arch of pleached limes has provided a perfect setting for art installations at the annual Bloomsbury Festival

'Celebratory Gateway', north-east corner

'Celebratory Gateway', south-west corner

All of the above might help to explain why English Heritage somewh at begrudgingly described the refurbishment as "…*loosely based on the original scheme by Repton*" in their entry for the Grade II listed gardens in the *National Register of Historic Parks and Gardens of Special Historic Interest*. As was pointed out by the Birkbeck study (2004), there are various errors in the opening text on the two interpretive sign boards telling the story of *"The Restoration of RUSSELL SQUARE GARDEN"*. The quality of the historical images on the boards also leaves a lot to be desired. It is therefore regrettable that such an excellent scheme is shown in such a poor light, although the saving grace is that the boards are positioned adjacent to the least busy entrances and will consequently be missed by most visitors to the gardens. They are now also out-dated, in as much as they are referring to a specific scheme implemented at a particular point in time, when what would be of greater interest to the visitor is the story of Russell Square and its rich social history, as depicted by the interpretive boards in some other Bloomsbury garden squares.

The Friends of Russell Square (FoRS) continues to play an active part in the on-going maintenance and improvement of the gardens in partnership with Camden Council. FoRS is also an active member of the Association of Bloomsbury Squares and Gardens, which was established in 2012 as a forum for all stakeholders in Bloomsbury's gardens, sharing news and information about activities, events and issues of concern. The gardens have continued to provide equal pleasure for residents, students, office workers and the throngs of visitors to Bloomsbury's many attractions, whilst also providing an ideal setting for a range of community events and 'happenings'.

Camden Youth Orchestra perform
at an Open Garden Squares Weekend 2007

Pagan Pride procession, May 2010

Patchwork tree 'skirt' at the Bloomsbury Festival 2011

Chilling out at the Bloomsbury Festival 2010

Thought-provoking art installation
at the Bloomsbury Festival 2011

London Tweed Run 2014 participants
resting awhile in Russell Square Gardens

SOAS World Music stage at the Bloomsbury Festival 2013

On location for the popular TV series, *Sherlock*

The future?

In addition to being listed for its special historic interest under the *Historic Buildings and Ancient Monuments Act 1953* within the *Register of Historic Parks and Gardens* held now by Historic England, the gardens are protected under the *London Squares Preservation Act 1931*. The freehold of the Square is still owned by the Bedford Estate in the names of the Honourable Charles William Cayzer, James Fitzroy Dean, Edmond Connolly Mahony and Robert Waley-Cohen, and leased to Camden Council until 2024. The prospect of ever-diminishing budgets led Camden Council in 2015 to explore alternative options for managing and financing the upkeep of the gardens under their so called Bloomsbury Squared project. Their investigations included setting up a Business Improvement District for Bloomsbury

Garden Squares, which was ruled out, due to lack of support from local businesses. They then investigated the feasibility of establishing a Development Trust for all Bloomsbury Garden Squares, including those owned and managed by the University of London. Reviving the role of the Commissioners of Russell Square was considered to be integral to this process, so a special meeting of eligible residents and organisations was convened by the University of London on 26th January 2015 with a view to taking this forward. Russell Square Gardens have survived more than two centuries of momentous events. There is every reason to believe that it will continue to play its important role as the heart (and lungs) of Bloomsbury for centuries to come.

Epilogue

Russell Square Restored

The Duke of Bedford, then the fifth,
had land enough to spare,
and thought he'd build some properties
around a garden square.

So handsome piles in Georgian style
were put up for the rich,
while railings strong kept out the throng
as sure as any ditch.

In later democratic days,
with populace empowered,
the Square was opened up to all
to walk in gardens flowered.

With railings gone to help the fight
in time of war and strife
no gates were safely locked at night
and wickedness was rife.

Request went to the lottery
to ask that work be funded
to make the Square as it had been
in time of 1800.

The garden closed, the work was done,
the squirrels lived in peace,
but missed their nuts from passers-by
until the workmen ceased.

Now fountains play, in modern style,
the kind they call 'surprise',
for when you think to pass dry-shod
fierce spouts of water rise.

In Russell Square today you'll see
all nations passing through,
as tourists, students, old and young
enjoy the rural view.

Jennifer Tanner February 2005
(Jennifer is a local resident and a retired primary
school teacher)

Summer in Russell Square Gardens

Introduction to Chapters 3-6

The lives of the most notable early occupants of Russell Square are revealed house-by-house in an anti-clockwise journey round the square which begins at the site of one of the oldest houses, No. 61 - the most southerly house on the east side - and ends at the most easterly house on the south side, No. 60.

The east side (chapter 3) is divided into three sections, corresponding to the sites of three historically significant buildings - the Imperial Hotel, Baltimore/Bolton House and Hotel Russell, in that order. The north side (chapter 4) is divided into its east and west terraces, respectively. The west side (chapter 5) is divided into three terraces, plus a section devoted to the University of London's Senate House. The south side (chapter 6) is divided into its west and east terraces, respectively.

The original Russell Square house numbers, which have been superimposed on the first Ordnance Survey map of 1871, still apply today.

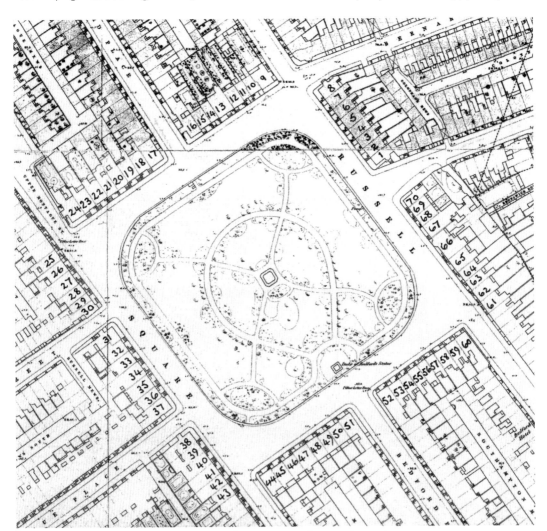

Ordnance Survey map, 1871, with the original Russell Square house numbers superimposed

Explanatory note: Various historical street directories (Kelly's, Post Office, etc.) and Court guides, inspected mainly at Camden Local Studies Library and Archives Centre, are predominantly referred to throughout the book in the following abbreviated forms:

Street Directory	– SD
Boyle's Court Guide	– BCG
Royal Blue Book	– RBB
ABC Court Guide	– ABCCG
Webster's Royal Book	– WRB

Boyle's Fashionable Court & Country Guide, and Town Visiting Directory, in short Boyle's Court Guide, was established in 1792 and continued to be published for 140 years until it was absorbed by Webster's Royal Book.

Chapter 3

The East Side

The original houses on the east side of Russell Square pre-dated the houses built by James Burton under the agreement he signed with the Duke of Bedford on 24th June 1800. The first house to appear on the site of what was to become Russell Square was Baltimore House, which was built in 1759-63 as the London residence of Frederick Calvert, the 6th and final Lord Baltimore. The 18th-century poet, Thomas Gray, recalled that, apart from the chimney-sweep's cottage in the distant fields to the north, Baltimore House remained the only building to the north of Southampton House (later renamed Bedford House) until the 1790s, when the terrace on the east side of Southampton Row (named after the 1st Earl of Southampton, Henry VIII's Chancellor) was extended northwards to form what would later become the east side of Russell Square. Gray was excluding the two houses numbered 24 and

25 Southampton Row on the extract from Richard Horwood's map of London, 1792-99, which would become 61 and 62 Russell Square, respectively. The gap between No. 62 and former Baltimore House (renamed Bolton House in 1770) was in-filled with three houses by 1813, along with the eight houses that formed Southampton Terrace, stretching north from Upper Guilford Street (named after Lord North of Guil[d]ford, who was president of the Foundling Hospital). These houses were the work of several speculative builders, most notably James Burton and Henry Scrimshaw (see chapter 3, section 3). Southampton Terrace, numbered 1 to 8 on William Faden's 1813 revision of Horwood's map, was entirely replaced by Charles Fitzroy Doll's Hotel Russell at the end of the 19th century, with Doll's Imperial Hotel replacing Nos. 61-66 a few years later (see Imperial Hotel item, below). The Premier

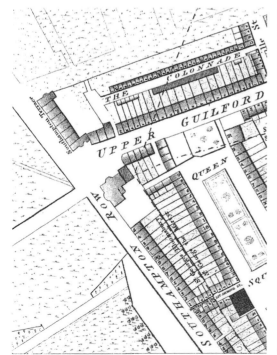

Richard Horwood's map, 1792-99, showing the bow-fronted Bolton House and other houses pre-dating the creation of Russell Square

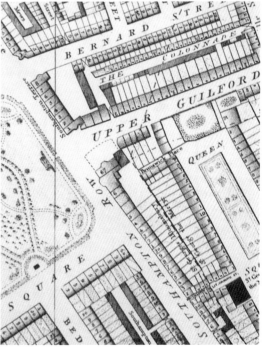

William Faden's 1813 revision of Horwood's 1792-99 map, after the creation of Russell Square

Hotel occupied Nos. 67-68 in 1918, expanding into Nos. 69-70 by 1922, only to be replaced by the President Hotel in the 1960s, thus completing the eradication of the original Georgian houses on the east side of the square (see chapter 3, section 2). The c.1905 photograph, which appears in Brian Girling's *Bloomsbury and Fitzrovia Through Time* (2012), shows Nos. 65-70 (r-l) prior to the construction and expansion of the Imperial Hotel in 1907 and 1911, respectively. No. 65 displays a tablet commemorating the residence of Sir Thomas Lawrence, and Nos. 66 and 67 (with the bow front and porticoed entrance, and tablet to the left of it commemorating the residence of Lord Loughborough) comprise the former Baltimore/Bolton House (see chapter 3, section 2). The imposing Hotel Russell is in the middle-distance, with the terraced houses of Woburn Place beyond. These were replaced by the imposing 'Art Deco' Russell Court in 1937 (designed by Lieut. Colonel Val Myer).

Russell Square, east side, c.1905 © Brian Girling

The site of the Imperial Hotel – Nos. 61-65

61 - Mary Augusta (Mrs Humphry) Ward (1851-1920), author and reformer, lived here from 1881, the year her author and journalist husband Thomas Humphry Ward (1845-1926), joined *The Times*. They lived here with their three young children until 1891. *"Thomas Humphry Ward"* is listed in the SDs, 1886-90. No. 61 was also the birthplace in 1887 of Mary's nephew, scientist **Sir Julian Sorell Huxley** FRS (1887-1975), who was born while his father was attending the jubilee celebrations of Queen Victoria. Huxley was an evolutionary biologist, eugenicist, philosopher, author and internationalist. He was a proponent of natural selection, and a leading figure in the mid-twentieth century evolutionary synthesis. He was also secretary of the Zoological Society of London (1935–1942), the first Director of UNESCO, a founding member of the World Wildlife Fund and the first President of the British Humanist Association.

The Wards' daughter, Janet Penrose Trevelyan, recalled the house in her book *The Life of Mrs Humphry Ward* (1923): *"…in that comfortable Bloomsbury region, which was then innocent of big hotels and offices, and where the houses in Russell Square had not yet suffered embellishment in the form of pink terra-cotta facings to their windows. They found that the oldest house in the Square, no. 61, was to let, and in spite of the dirt of years with which it was encrusted, perceived its possibilities at once, and came to an agreement with its owner. A charming old house, built in 1745, its prettiest feature was a small square entrance-hall, with eighteenth-century stucco-work on the walls, from which a wide staircase ascended to the drawing-room, giving an impression of space rare in a bourgeois London house. At the back was a good-sized strip of garden shaded by tall old plane-trees and running down to meet the gardens of Queen Square, for no. 61 stood on the east side of [Russell] square and adjoined the first house of Southampton Row."* The diminutive size of the house compared to the adjacent houses is reflected in the photograph which appeared in *Pictorial London* in 1896, three years prior to the terracotta adornments being installed on the houses on the right of the photograph. No. 61 appears to have been either remodelled or rebuilt with lavish terracotta adornments and individual bow windows by the time the 1903 photograph was taken,

Mary Augusta (Mrs Humphry) Ward

Julian Huxley in 1964

presumably around the time that the Bedford Estate 'improved' the exteriors of the houses on the north and south sides of the square in 1899. According to the SDs, the house was occupied by George Earle Buckle (see below) until 1896, and vacant in 1897, with Edward Tyas Cooke occupying the 'new' house from 1898 to 1904 (he was knighted in 1912 – see below), when it was demolished to make way for the construction of the original Imperial Hotel.

The house served as the headquarters of Mary Ward's educational projects for the Wards' ten-year occupation, but first she published articles, translations and fiction including her best-selling second novel *Robert Elsmere* (1888). This caused a sensation by asserting the primacy of the social gospel over evangelising in Christianity's order of priorities. It sold half a million copies in America within a year and in Britain "…*an edition of 5000 copies*

No. 61 in 1903, with terracotta adornments and bow windows © CLSAC

| View east along the south side of Russell Square, 1896, showing Nos. 61-63 (r-l) - *Pictorial London*

"The House in Russell Square" from *Writings of Mrs Humphry Ward* Vol II Houghton Mifflin ed., 1911

a fortnight was the rule for many months after the one-volume edition appeared" (Ward 1918). It was whilst living at No.61 that she opened the University Settlement in Gordon Square, based on the model of Toynbee Hall in east London, with the intention of bringing educational and recreational opportunities to the poor of the area through a number of *"Residents"* at the Hall, young professional men, mainly lawyers, who would give lectures and lead activities in return for board and lodging. Copeland Bowie, who attended a meeting of social reformers in Mary's dining room at No.61 in February 1890, recalled that *"Mrs Ward was the moving and executive force; the rest of us were simply admiring and sympathetic spectators of her enterprise and zeal. It is delightful to recall her abounding activity and enthusiasm."* Mary also occupied the Marchmont Hall behind 94 Marchmont Street. Both were replaced in 1897/8 by the imposing Mary Ward Settlement in Tavistock Place, which was financed by the great philanthropist John Passmore Edwards (1823-1911) and built to the Arts & Crafts designs of Smith and Brewer - praised by Pevsner as *"...one of the most charming pieces of architecture designed at that time in England".*

Mary Ward House, 5 Tavistock Place

Mary managed the Settlement with energy, pioneering play centres for poor children left on the streets after school and before their parents finished work, and offering activities for both children and parents in the evenings and on Saturdays. In February 1899, she opened the first school for disabled children in the building, and in July 1902 she started the first Vacation School for children. Mary was strangely a significant campaigner against women getting the vote, becoming the founding president of the Women's National Anti-Suffrage League and creating and editing the *Anti-Suffrage Review*. She published a large number of articles on the subject, while two of her novels, *The Testing of Diana Mallory* and *Delia Blanchflower*, were used as platforms to criticise the suffragettes. In a 1909 article in *The Times*, Ward wrote that constitutional, legal, financial, military, and international problems were problems only men could solve, although she came to promote the idea of women having a voice in local government and other rights that the men's anti-suffrage movement would not tolerate. She wrote under the pen name Mrs Humphry Ward. After Mary's death in 1921, the Passmore Edwards Settlement was renamed the Mary Ward Settlement in her honour, Passmore Edwards having died in 1911.

Sir Oliver Joseph Lodge, FRS (1851-1940), was a British physicist and writer involved in the development of, and holder of key patents for, radio. He identified electromagnetic radiation independent of Hertz' proof and at his 1894 Royal Institution lectures (*"The Work of Hertz and Some of His Successors"*), Lodge demonstrated an early radio-wave detector he named the *"coherer"*. In 1898, he was awarded the *"syntonic"* (or tuning) patent by the United States Patent Office. Lodge was Principal of the University of Birmingham from 1900 to 1920. He is listed at No. 61 as *"Oliver Lodge"* in the ABCCG, 1871, and SD, 1878, living here whilst attending the University of London, where he obtained a Bachelor of Science degree in 1875 and a Doctor of Science in 1877. University College London Special Collections hold 1,991 items of Sir Oliver Lodge's correspondence between 1871 and 1938. The Science Museum in London holds an early notebook of Oliver Lodge's dated 1880, correspondence dating from 1894 to 1913 and a paper on atomic theory. There are many other institutions holding items of his work. He also wrote more than 40 books, about the afterlife, aether, relativity, and electromagnetic theory. The author of his obituary in *The Times* wrote: *"Always an impressive figure, tall and slender with a pleasing voice and charming manner, he enjoyed the affection and respect of a very large circle... Lodge's gifts as an expounder of knowledge were of a high order, and few scientific men have been able to set forth abstruse facts in a more lucid or engaging form... Those who heard him on a great occasion, as when he gave his Romanes lecture at Oxford or his British Association presidential address at Birmingham, were charmed by his alluring personality as well as impressed by the orderly development of his thesis. But he was even better in informal debate, and when*

he rose, the audience, however perplexed or jaded, settled down in a pleased expectation that was never disappointed."

Sir Oliver Joseph Lodge

George Earle Buckle (1854-1935), editor of *The Times* (1884-1911) and biographer, is listed at No. 61 in the SDs, 1892-96. As editor, he did little to alter either the appearance or the policies of the paper, which endeavoured to present the news irrespective of bias or interest, with an editorial practice aimed at serving the public interest, which in effect meant supporting whichever government was in power at the time. After retiring from *The Times*, George worked for the next eight years to produce the final four volumes (of six) of the *Life of Benjamin Disraeli*. After its completion in 1920, he was asked to take on another ongoing project, the editing of *Queen Victoria's Letters*, covering Victoria's letters from 1861 until her death. Buckle's final project was organizing a multi-volume history of *The Times*, the first volume of which was published before he died in 1935.

George Earle Buckle

Sir Edward Tyas Cook (1857-1919), journalist, biographer and man of letters, is listed at No. 61 in the SDs, 1898-1904. Whilst at Oxford he was president of the Union and of the Palmerston club and, on coming to London as secretary for the extension of university teaching, he became a contributor to the *Pall Mall Gazette*. He was later assistant editor under W.T. Stead and editor from 1890 till 1892, when the paper passed into the hands of Mr W.W. (afterwards Lord) Astor and changed its politics. Cook then resigned, but a year later became first editor of the newly founded liberal evening paper, the *Westminster Gazette*. In 1896 he gave this up to take the editorship of the *Daily News*, which he held until 1901, whilst living at No. 61. His departure was precipitated when David Lloyd George organized a consortium of Liberal businessmen to purchase the paper, declaring that the paper would adopt a stance of neutrality on the war. A strong imperialist, Cook was unable to remain under these circumstances, and was replaced. He then worked as a leader writer for the *Daily Chronicle* until 1910, whilst also editing the writings of Ruskin. During World War I, conjointly with Sir Frank Swettenham, he directed the official Press Bureau. He was knighted in 1912, and created KBE in 1917 on the inauguration of the Order of the British Empire. He was a lover of art and of gardening. He published *Studies in Ruskin* (1891), edited the works of Ruskin (1903-7), published in 39 volumes, and wrote the authoritative *Life of Ruskin* (1912), also producing handbooks to the National Gallery and the Tate Gallery, and to the Greek and Roman antiquities in the British Museum. His book on *The Rights and Wrongs of the Transvaal War* ran into several editions, and he wrote *Life of Florence Nightingale* (1913) and *Delane of the Times* (1915), as well as two volumes of *Literary Recollections* (1918 and 1919). He died at South Stoke, Goring on 30th September 1919.

Sir Edward Tyas Cook, c.1916 © National Portrait Gallery, London

Other early occupants of No. 61 include:
Mrs Jackson (BCG, 1808); Mrs Wilson (BCGs, 1820-44, and SD, 1841, but only Miss Wilson in 1842); W.J. Whyte, solicitor (BCGs, 1846-57, plus Albert Cohen in 1857, both joined by W.R. Turner, solicitor, in the RBB, 1858); William Collison and William John Whyte, solicitors (SDs, 1861-62); there are no further entries for No.61, because it was demolished along with Nos. 62-64 to make way for the *"Imperial Family Hotel, Harold Walduck"*, which is listed for the first time in 1907, joined by No. 65 in 1909 and No. 66 in 1910.

62 - William Cowper (1731-1800), poet and hymnodist, lived at No. 62 when he was at Westminster School (which he attended from 1742), according to E. Beresford Chancellor, 1907: *"Mr Swan Sonnenschein, who informs me of this, bought it in 1887. It was demolished in 1905."* One of the most popular poets of his time and a forerunner of Romantic poetry, Cowper (pronounced Cooper) was also a chronic depressive, although he is ironically best known for his comical account of the efforts of John Gilpin (1782), *"a linen-draper bold"* of Cheapside, to control a bolting horse. Hazlitt commented on the style of Cowper's letters that *"...he shakes hands with nature with a pair of fashionable gloves on"*. Cowper's negative perception of himself lead him to declare, *"I have no more right to the name of poet than a maker of mousetraps has to that of an engineer."* Samuel Taylor Coleridge called him *"the best modern poet"*, whilst William Wordsworth particularly admired his poem Yardley-Oak. His poem *Light Shining out of Darkness* gave Christians the phrase: *"God moves in a mysterious way/His wonders to perform."* He is represented with fifteen hymns in *The Church Hymn book*, 1872. He also wrote a number of anti-slavery poems and his friendship with curate John Newton, an avid anti-slavery campaigner (who wrote the hymn *Amazing Grace*), resulted in Cowper being asked to write in support of the Abolitionist campaign. Cowper wrote a poem called *The Negro's Complaint* (1788) which rapidly became very famous, and was often quoted by Dr Martin Luther King, Jr during the 20th-century civil rights movement. He also wrote several other less well known poems on slavery in the 1780s, many of which attacked the idea that slavery was economically viable. Cowper was seized with dropsy in the spring of 1800 and died. A window in Westminster Abbey honours him.

William Cowper

No. 62 in 1903 © CLSAC

The William Cowper window in St George's Chapel, Westminster Abbey

Thomas Gray (1716-71), poet, letter-writer and scholar, lodged *"next door to Cowper"* (not certain whether it was No. 61 or 63), praising the location for its *"air and sunshine and quiet"*. He was the fifth of twelve children of Philip and Dorothy Antrobus Gray and the only one to survive infancy. Although he was regarded as the foremost English-language poet of the mid-18th century, being offered the post of Poet Laureate in 1757 (which he turned down), he was so self-critical and fearful of failure that he published only thirteen poems during his lifetime. His *Elegy in a Country Churchyard* had become a literary sensation by the time he came to live in Russell Square in 1759,

primarily to pursue his antiquarian interests in the newly founded British Museum.

"In July 1759 Gray took up residence in London, in lodgings formerly occupied by his friend Wharton in Southampton Row. For the next two years his principal occupation was historical research in the manuscript holdings of the recently opened British Museum, some of it by way of assisting Walpole in his historical projects. In November 1761, having read enough at the museum, Gray returned to his rooms at Pembroke." (Oxford Dictionary of National Biography [ODNB]) The Walpole referred to was Horace Walpole (1717–1797), youngest son of Sir Robert Walpole, then Prime Minister. A letter written by Gray to a Mr Walpole on 24th July 1759 begins: *"I am now settled in my new territories commanding Bedford Gardens, and all the fields as far as Highgate and Hampstead, with such a concourse of moving pictures as would astonish you. So rus-in-urbe-ish, that I believe I shall stay here, except little excursions and vagaries, for a year to come. What though I am separated from the fashionable world by St Giles's and many a dirty court and alley, yet here is air and sunshine and quiet, to comfort you: I confess that I am basking with heat all the summer, and I suppose shall be blown down all the winter, besides being robbed every night; I trust, however, that the Mus um (sic), with all its manuscripts and rarities by the cart-load, will make ample amends for all the aforesaid inconveniences."* Letters written by Gray to Dr Wharton from Southampton Row, dated 22nd October and 13th November 1761, and to Mr Walpole, 28th February 1762, indicate that he remained there until at least March of that year. 1759 was also the same year that General James Wolfe, campaigning in Canada, famously declared to his troops with regard to Gray's Elegy, *"I would rather have written that poem, gentlemen, than take Quebec"*. The next day he took Quebec but died in the act. Gray died on 30th July 1771 in Cambridge, and was buried beside his mother in the churchyard of Stoke Poges, the setting for his famous Elegy.

Thomas Gray by John Giles Eccart, 1747/48

Gertrude Barbara Rich Tennant [née Collier]
(1819–1918), society hostess, lived with her husband,
Charles, at No. 62 from c.1847 to 1862. Her paternal
grandfather was Rear-Admiral Sir George Collier
(1738–1795), Admiral Sir Francis Collier was her
uncle, and on her maternal side she was descended
from Oliver Cromwell. Her father lost his savings in
a bank collapse, and in 1825 moved the family to
France, where they lived in genteel poverty among
the English expatriate community in Paris. Gertrude
attended children's balls at the courts of Charles
X and Louis-Philippe, and was sent to a finishing
school. She taught herself to speak fluent French and
became widely read in English and French literature.
She was invited to many *"brilliant salons"*, where she
met society hostesses and her idol Victor Hugo. Over
several years Gustave Flaubert was a regular visitor
to the Collier family's apartment on the Rond Point
of the Champs Elysées. After the death in 1846 of
Flaubert's sister, Gertrude Collier returned to England,
determined to remake herself as *"a respectable
Englishwoman"* (Waller, 108). In that spirit she
married, at Ryde on 11th September 1847,

Charles Tennant (1796–1873), attorney, landowner
and politician. Charles was born in Bloomsbury on
1st July 1796 and was unusually still a bachelor, aged
51, when he married Gertrude, although they had
first met in Boulogne in 1834. Charles's father,

George Tennant (c.1766-1832), attorney,
landowner and constructor of the Tennant's Canal in
South Wales (1817-24), is listed at No. 62 in BCGs,
1821-29. Mrs Tennant (presumed to be Charles's
mother) and Charles Tennant are listed in BCGs,
1834-44, and SDs, 1841-4. They are joined in BCG,
1845 by Henry Tennant (Charles's older brother),
but only Charles Tennant is listed thereafter in
BCGs, 1846-57, the RBB, 1858, and SDs, 1861-62.
Gertrude and Charles's married life at No. 62 was
overshadowed by the deaths of two of their five
daughters (they also had one son), money worries,
and litigation with members of Charles's family.
He, like his father, appears to have struggled, not for
want of trying, to make his mark in his parliamentary
career, and redirected his energies towards poetry:
*"In 1834, the seemingly shameless Tennant inflicted on
the world a truly execrable epic poem on* The State of
Man, *in which he sought to 'exhibit, in a concise form,
a view of the Divine purpose in the creation of Man'.
(Conciseness is by no means its leading characteristic,
as it runs to 4,026 turgid lines.)"* (David R. Fisher –
History of Parliament Online). His remaining energies
were reserved for preserving the prospects of his
inherited canal from competition from the railways,
which saw the canal continuing to carry commercial
traffic right up until 1934. His most substantial
contribution to *"the cause of rational improvement"*
was his treatise of 1857 on taxation, *The People's Blue
Book*, but between 1856 and 1869 he published at
least nine other works on the Bank of England and
decimal coinage, national defences, the American
and Irish questions, Utilitarianism, railways, and
the franchise. When the title to Charles's family
properties in south Wales was finally secured, he and
Gertrude moved from Bloomsbury to 2 Richmond
Terrace, Whitehall, in 1868. At the same time Charles
retired from his legal practice. Widowed in 1873,
at the age of fifty-three, Gertrude Tennant came
into her own. Financially independent, she devoted
her life to recreating the salon culture that she had
enjoyed as a young woman growing up in Paris. She
made her mission in life to bring together the great
men of the world, and to find husbands for her
daughters Eveleen (Evie) and Dorothy (Dolly) [see
below], beautiful and eligible young women who
were sitters for portraits by Watts and Millais. She
herself never remarried, but in 1878 was reunited
with her youthful flame Gustave Flaubert during
a visit to Paris.

The eldest daughter, Alice (1848–1930), suffered
learning disorders. Gertrude Tennant encouraged her
two other daughters to develop their artistic talents,
and both achieved distinction. The second daughter,

Dorothy (Dolly) Stanley (*née* Tennant) (1855–1926), painter and illustrator, was born at No. 62 on 22nd March 1855, and was educated at home by tutors. Dorothy Tennant had become interested as a child in the *"ragamuffin"* children she encountered on the capital's streets, and these became her principal subject. Her drawings of London street children impressed Ruskin in 1879. In 1890, she married the explorer of Africa, Henry Morton Stanley, and became known as Lady Stanley. She edited her husband's autobiography, reportedly removing any references to other women in Stanley's life. The third daughter, **Eveleen Myers** (*née* Tennant), (1856–1937), photographer, was also born at No. 62, on 21st November 1856.

William Swan Sonnenschein (1855-1931) was a scholarly London publisher. He is listed at No. 62 in the SDs from 1888 to 1904, when the house was demolished to make way for the original Imperial

Gertrude Barbara Rich Tennant (née Collier), 1890s
© National Portrait Gallery, London

Lady Dorothy Stanley, by George Frederick Watts

Charles Tennant, 1890s
© National Portrait Gallery, London

Dorothy (Dolly) Stanley as a child

Hotel. His name reappears at No. 58 in the SDs, 1905-11. As a young man, William was apprenticed to the firm of Williams and Norgate where he gained experience of second-hand bookselling before founding his own company, W. Swan Sonnenschein & Allen, with the first of several partners, J. Archibald Allen, in 1878. This partnership was dissolved in 1882 when William married and the firm's name changed to W. Swan Sonnenschein & Co. The firm published general literature and periodicals, but specialised in sociology and politics. He was also involved with the Ethical Society and published their literature. In 1895 Swan Sonnenschein became a limited liability company, and in 1902, William left to work at George Routledge & Sons and later at Kegan Paul. Swan Sonnenschein was amalgamated with George Allen & Co in 1911. Among his firm's early publications were radical works by Marx and Shaw, although intellectual eclecticism marked its handbooks in philosophy and the social sciences. In the light of the hostility towards Germans during the First World War, William changed his surname to Stallybrass in 1917, and used that name for the remainder of his life, as did some, but not all of his family, including his only son **William Teulon Swan Stallybrass** (1883–1948), jurist and university administrator. Despite a distinguished academic career, William's poor eyesight ruled him out of military service in the First World War, and he entered the Ministry of Munitions, where his work was recognized by the award of the O.B.E. He rose to the position of Vice-Chancellor of Brasenose College, Oxford in 1948, but tragically fell to his death at Iver, Buckinghamshire, as he was returning to Oxford from London on the midnight train on 28th October 1948.

Other early occupants of No. 62 include:
Edmund Thomas Walters (BCG, 1820); John Barnard (ABCCG, 1871); David Jewell (SDs, 1878-87).

63 – (John George) Henry Pownall (1792-1880), JP, magistrate, landed proprietor and philanthropist, lived at No. 63 from at least 1821 until 1829, according to BCG, which intriguingly lists *"Mrs Fish"* at No. 63 in 1820, and *"Mrs Fish"* and *"Henry Pownall"* from 1821 to 1829. A certain Charles Slater Fowler is listed in BCGs, 1834-40, with Henry back again with Henry Pownall, Jr and J. Fish Pownall in 1842-46, and although a certain *"James Punch"* is listed alone in 1857 and in the RBB, 1858, John Fish Pownall and Henry Pownall are again listed in the SDs up to the time of Henry's death in 1880, with Henry Harrison Pownall again listed from 1900 to 1904, when the house was demolished to make way for the Imperial

Family Hotel. Henry Senior married Amelia Sophia Waterhouse in Bloomsbury on 13th June 1816. They had four sons and two daughters: John Fish (born Bloomsbury, 13th May 1817); Henry William (born Epsom, 24th June 1821); George Purves (born Bloomsbury, 27th December 1822); Ann Fish (born Epsom, 1824); Amelia Jane (born Bloomsbury, 28th April 1827); and Frederick Hyde (born 22nd August 1831). Amelia died in 1860. Mrs Ann Fish, sometimes spelt 'Fysh', was apparently a cousin of Henry's wife. An investigation of Mrs Fish revealed that up to the time of her death in 1834 she was also the owner of 63, Russell Square, and, judging by her will, a very wealthy woman indeed. Her husband was John Fish, an owner of many properties in London and Middlesex (Harlington, Harmondsworth, West Drayton, for example), who died in 1815. She bequeathed much of her substantial estate to Henry, all of which accounts for him being listed in the 1873 return of *Owners of Land* as having 310 acres in Middlesex, with an annual rental income of £951 (about £80,000 today), and 11 acres in Southampton. Henry was strongly anti-Roman Catholic and financially supported Wilberforce in the campaign against slavery. He failed twice to secure a parliamentary seat 9.25*which the attempt to rescue the Fenian prisoners, Burke and Casey, from the House of Detention, were defeated. For this he received the thanks*

(John George) Henry Pownall, 1859
© Hounslow Local Library Collection

Mrs Amelia Pownall

Ann Fish Pownall

of both the Home Office and of the Court of Quarter Sessions… At the time of his death he was the senior treasurer of the Corporation of the Sons of the Clergy, having been for upwards of 40 years one of the governors - an office to which he was appointed mainly through the influence of Bishop Blomfield, and which he was enabled to render most efficient service in augmenting the annual income available for the relief of distressed clergy. He retained to the last his generous interest in the work in which he had borne so energetic a part."

A briefer and more parochial obituary in the Illustrated London News of 17th April 1880 reads: "… he took an active part in the management of the Middlesex County lunatic asylum at Hanwell and was an active promoter of improvements in the metropolitan prisons. He was mainly instrumental in inducing the bench to set aside the Westminster House of Correction for female delinquents, whereby the county effected a saving of £12,000 per annum. So far back as 1846 he presented a report from a committee appointed by the county magistrates to enquire into the state of juvenile crime, which led to an act of parliament being obtained in 1854 for the erection of the Middlesex industrial schools at Feltham… Mr Pownall has also taken an active part in the formation of the Royal Horticultural Society, South Kensington, and is one of the council conducting its proceedings." Additionally, in 1828, he had founded

a national newspaper called The Record. Pownall Road and Pownall Gardens in Hounslow are both named after him in recognition of his local contribution. He also had strong connections with Epsom, Surrey, where he wrote Some Particulars Relating to the History of Epsom, c.1825, which is apparently still 'essential' reading. "Henry Harrison Pownall", the son of John Fish Pownall, John George Henry Pownall's eldest son, is listed in the SDs, 1900-04, prior to the house being demolished to make way for the construction of the original Imperial Hotel.

Frederick Hyde Pownall (1832-1907), Henry's youngest son, was the architect of the second Middlesex Guildhall and Wandsworth Prison.

John Fish Pownall (1817-1898), FRGS, Middlesex County Magistrate and first born son of John George Henry Pownall, lived at No. 63 from at least 1842 (BCG) and certainly in the 1880s (Charles Dickens (Jr), Dickens's Dictionary of London 1888: An Unconventional Handbook, 1888), until 1898 (SD). Being born in Bloomsbury in 1817, he probably lived here most of his life, barring

John Fish Pownall

his stint at Cambridge University where he gained an MA. He was certainly living here when he was a barrister in Lincolns Inn from 1843 (BCG). He was also a magistrate and became Deputy Lieutenant of Middlesex in 1863. He died on 7th February 1898 at No. 63.

Ralph Waldo Emerson (1803-1882), New England preacher, essayist, lecturer, poet, and philosopher, lodged at No. 63 (according to *Mystery Reader's Walking Guide* – Alzina Stone Dale, Barbara Sloan-Hendershott, 2004) when he first visited England in 1832/3. Here he met Thomas Carlyle, Samuel Taylor Coleridge and William Wordsworth. Carlyle, the Scottish-born English writer, was famous for his explosive attacks on hypocrisy and materialism, his distrust of democracy, and his highly romantic belief in the power of the individual. Emerson's friendship with Carlyle was both lasting and significant, with Carlyle's insights helping Emerson formulate his own philosophy. According to the Poetry Foundation, Emerson "… *was one of the most influential writers and thinkers of the nineteenth century in the United States. Emerson was also the first major American literary and intellectual figure to widely explore, write seriously about, and seek to broaden the domestic audience for classical Asian and Middle Eastern works. He not only gave countless readers their first exposure to non-Western modes of thinking, metaphysical concepts, and sacred mythologies; he also shaped the way subsequent generations of American writers and thinkers approached the vast cultural resources of Asia and the Middle East."*

Ralph Waldo Emerson

Emerson led the Transcendentalist movement of the mid-19th century and was seen as a champion of individualism. His first book, *Nature* (1836), is perhaps the best expression of his Transcendentalism, the belief that everything in our world—even a drop of dew—is a microcosm of the universe. His concept of the Over-Soul—a Supreme Mind that every man and woman share—allowed Transcendentalists to disregard external authority and to rely instead on direct experience.

Nos. 63-64 (r-l) in 1903 © CLSAC

Other early occupants of No. 63 include:
Charles Slater Fowler (BCGs, 1834-40);
James Punch (BCG, 1857, and RBB, 1858).

64 - Dr William Adams (1772–1851), lawyer
and diplomatist, lived at No. 64 with his wife, the
Hon. Mary Anne Cockayne. He is listed at No. 64
as *"Dr Adams"* in BCGs, 1821-34. He was educated
at Tonbridge School, and in 1787 entered Trinity Hall,
Cambridge, of which he later became a fellow. At
the tender age of twenty-five he began to attend the
courts at Doctors' Commons, also called the College
of Civilians, being a society of lawyers practising civil
law in London. Like the Inns of Court of the common
lawyers, the society had buildings with rooms where
its members lived and worked, and a large library.
Court proceedings of the civil law courts were also
held in Doctors' Commons. In 1799 he took the
degree of LLD, and in November of the same year
he was admitted into the College of Advocates. With
a high reputation for business capacity and mastery
of legal details, Adams served on several important
commissions, including that appointed in 1811 to
regulate the practice of the vice-admiralty courts
abroad, and the commission of 1815–24 inquiring
into the duties, offices, and salaries of the courts of
justice and the ecclesiastical courts of England. His
chief claim to distinction, however, was his role in the
negotiations for a treaty with the United States in
1814 after the capture of Washington. He was one of
the three commissioners sent to represent England,
and was entrusted with the sole preparation of the
dispatches relating to maritime law, the most delicate
and important part of the negotiation. In 1815, he
was also named one of the three plenipotentiaries
sent to conclude a convention of commerce between
Great Britain and the United States, which was
signed on 3rd July. William was married twice, first to
Sarah Scott from 1803 until her death in 1806 and
second, in 1811, to the Hon. Mary Anne Cockayne
(d. 1873), with whom he had four sons, including
George Edward Cokayne (sic), and four daughters.
In 1820 he was named as one of the counsel for
the Bill of Divorce against Queen Caroline. The hard
work he put into this case had serious effects on his
health, which led to his enforced retirement from
professional life in 1825. He spent his last years at
Thorpe in Surrey, where he died on 11th June 1851.
He was survived by his second wife.
Their son, **George Edward Cokayne (Adams)**
(1825-1911), genealogist, was born at No. 64 on 29th
April 1825. On 15th August 1873, he assumed the
name and arms of Cokayne (minus the 'c') by royal
warrant, in accordance with his mother's testamentary

directions. On 2nd December 1856 he married Mary
Dorothea, third and youngest daughter of George
Henry Gibbs of Aldenham Park, Hertfordshire,
and sister of Henry Hucks Gibbs (afterwards Lord
Aldenham). She predeceased him on 11th March
1906. They had eight children, of whom two sons
and two daughters survived them. He was admitted
a student of Lincoln's Inn in 1850, and called to the
bar in 1853. Entering the College of Arms in 1859,
he held successively the offices of Rouge Dragon
Pursuivant-of-Arms (1859–70) and Lancaster Herald
(1870–82). In his heraldic capacity, George was
attached to the Garter missions to Portugal (1865),
Russia (1867), Italy (1868), Spain (1881), and Saxony
(1882). Appointed Norroy King of Arms in 1882, he
succeeded to the post of Clarenceux King of Arms
in 1894. He was an active member of the Society of
Antiquaries, being elected fellow on 22nd February
1866. He died of a heart attack at his residence,
Exeter House, Roehampton, on 6th August 1911.
George published much on genealogy and the last
part of his life was devoted to his major works, *The
Complete Peerage* (8 vols., 1887–98; 2nd edn., rev. and
enlarged by V. Gibbs and others, 13 vols., 1910–59),
and *The Complete Baronetage* (5 vols., 1900–06; index
vol., 1909). *"The Complete Peerage was (and is) unique
in that it gave a full historical and genealogical account
of all peerages created in the whole of the British Isles
(including Ireland) from the conquest to the date of
publication. The Complete Peerage therefore quickly won
the author general recognition as a genealogist of the*

George Edward Cokayne

first authority, and both it and the Baronetage (written on similar principles) have taken their place as primary authorities on their subjects… Cokayne was modest, industrious, and scholarly, with a great kindness and courtesy of manner." (ODNB)

Sir Francis Cowley Burnand

(1836-1917), usually known as F. C. Burnand (he is listed as such in the SDs, 1878-79, but with his full name until 1884), was an

F.C. Burnand in the 1870s

English comic writer and prolific playwright, best known as the librettist of Arthur Sullivan's opera *Cox and Box* and for being the editor of *Punch* magazine. The son of a prosperous family, he was educated at Eton and Cambridge, and was expected to follow a conventional career in the law or in the church, but he concluded that his vocation was the theatre. From his schooldays he had written comic plays, and from 1860 until the end of the 19th century, he produced a series of more than 200 Victorian burlesques, farces, pantomimes and other stage works. His early

successes included the burlesques *Ixion, or the Man at the Wheel* (1863) and *The Latest Edition of Black-Eyed See-Susan; or, the Little Bill that Was Taken Up* (1866). Also in 1866, he adapted the popular farce *Box and Cox* as a comic opera, *Cox and Box*, with music by Sullivan. The piece became a popular favourite and was later frequently used by the D'Oyly Carte Opera Company as a curtain raiser - it is still regularly performed today. By the 1870s, Burnand was generating a prodigious output of plays as well as comic pieces and illustrations for the humour magazine *Punch*. Among his 55 stage works during the decade was another frequently revived hit, *Betsy* (1879). For *Punch*, among other things, he wrote the popular column *"Happy Thoughts"*, in which the narrator recorded the difficulties and distractions of everyday life. Also admired were his burlesques of other writers' works. Burnand was a contributor to *Punch* for 45 years and its editor from 1880 until 1906 and is credited with adding much to the popularity and prosperity of the magazine. His editorship of the original publication of *The Diary of a Nobody* by the brothers George and Weedon Grossmith was a high point of his tenure in 1888–89. Many of his articles were collected and published in book form. His stage successes in the 1890s included his English-language versions of two Edmond Audran operettas, titled *La Cigale* and *Miss Decima* (both in 1891). His last works included collaborations on pantomimes of *Cinderella* (1905) and *Aladdin* (1909). Known generally for his genial wit and good humor, Burnand was nevertheless intensely envious of his contemporary W. S. Gilbert but was unable to emulate his rival's success as a comic opera librettist. In other forms of theatre Burnand was outstandingly

Royal Princess' Theatre

NICOLSON STREET.

F. C. BURNAND'S BURLESQUE OF

BLACK EYED SEE-USAN.

EVERY EVENING.

Mr. Burnand has done many bold things. He has caricatured Shakespeare.

Black Eyed See-Usan poster © Weir Collection   F.C. Burnand caricatures Shakespeare

successful, with his works receiving London runs of up to 550 performances and extensive tours in the British provinces and the US. He published several humorous books and memoirs and was knighted in 1902 for his work on *Punch*.

Other early occupants of No. 64 include: Robert Butler (BCG, 1820); William Newton (BCGs, 1840-44, and SDs, 1841-42); Miss Portal (BCG, 1857, RBB, 1858, SDs, 1861-76, and ABCCG, 1871); Mrs Haines (SDs, 1886-90); George Watson Haines (SDs, 1892-1903, and WRB, 1897). He was a Member of the Board of Works for St Giles District, Commissioner for Public Libraries and member of the Works Committee (1897-1900) – ref: Wellcome Library.

65 - Sir Thomas Lawrence (1769-1830), courtly painter and President of the Royal Academy – *"The outstanding English portrait painter of his generation."* (*The Oxford Dictionary of Art and Artists*) - lived at No. 65 from at least 1813 until his sudden death here in 1830 (*ODNB &*

An early drawing of Sir Thomas Lawrence's house

| Sir Thomas Lawrence's studio, 1824

Sir Thomas Lawrence by Richard Evans, c.1825
© National Portrait Gallery, London

Self-Portrait, 1788, by Sir Thomas Lawrence © PRA

UCL Project), although Chancellor (1907) confidently informs us that *"Sir Thomas Lawrence is more closely connected with Russell Square than any of the notable people who have dwelt in it; for he lived here, at No. 65, during the last twenty-five years of his busy life, from 1805 to 1830."* Chancellor's assertion is supported by *Old and New London: Volume 4* (Originally published by Cassell, Petter & Galpin, London, 1878) accessed via British History On-line: *"...Sir Thomas Lawrence, the courtly painter, and President of the Royal Academy, resided at No. 65 for a quarter of a century. He died there in 1830, after a very short illness."* He is listed in BCGs, 1820-29.

Lawrence was a child prodigy, supporting his family with his pastel portraits at the age of ten. At 18, he went to London (1787) and soon established his reputation as a portrait painter in oils, receiving his first royal commission, a portrait of Queen Charlotte and Princess Amelia, in 1790. Self-taught, he was a brilliant draughtsman and known for his gift of capturing a likeness, as well as his virtuoso handling of paint. He became an associate of the Royal Academy in 1791, aged 21 (half Constable's age at admission), a full member in 1794, and President in 1820. In 1792, on the death of Sir Joshua Reynolds, King George III appointed Lawrence *"painter-in-ordinary to his majesty"*. In 1810, he acquired the generous patronage of the Prince Regent and was sent abroad to paint portraits of allied leaders for the Waterloo chamber at Windsor Castle, for which he is particularly remembered as the *"Pictorial chronicler*

of the Regency" (Levey, 2005). By the time the Prince of Wales was made Regent in 1814, Lawrence was acknowledged as the foremost portrait painter in the country. As well as portraits of himself, the

Lawrence's portrait of Count Matvei Ivanovich Plato

"Two mounted Cossacks in full uniform stood as sentries"

of the heart" (Chancellor) at No. 65, aged 60, on 7th January 1830, at which time he was the most fashionable portrait painter in Europe. *The Times,* 11th January 1830 carried an article *"From the Literary Gazette",* which reads: *"The fine arts have, with awful rapidity, sustained a great and heavy loss, in the President of the Royal Academy; Sir Thomas Lawrence died about nine o'clock on Thursday evening, at his house in Russell-square. This sad event took place without any of those distant intimations which so often tell man to prepare for death. Sir Thomas Lawrence was in such perfect health that he dined on Saturday, with a distinguished party, at M. Peel's, where he became suddenly, but not alarmingly, indisposed. Inflammatory symptoms appearing, however, he was bled; and this operation produced to good an effect, that on Monday, Tuesday, and Wednesday, he was able to go out as usual. On the Wednesday… On reaching home in the afternoon, his complaint (an inflammation of the bowels) returned with such violence, that he survived little more than 24 hours, his last words being addressed to his valet, who was attending him, "****, I am dying!!"* The notice continues incongruously by describing

Prince commissioned portraits of allied leaders: the Duke of Wellington, Field-Marshal von Blücher, and Count Matvei Ivanovich Platov (Russian General who commanded the Don Cossacks in the Napoleonic Wars), sat for Lawrence at his new house at No. 65. Chancellor (1907) refers to the visit of the Count as recalled by *"Mitford"* which *"…caused quite a stir in the square in 1818* (not least because of) *the Cossacks mounted on their small white horses, with their long spears grounded, standing sentinels at the door of this great painter, whilst he was taking the portrait of their general Platoff."* Platov died shortly after the portrait was painted. Lawrence assembled a hugely impressive collection of art at No. 65, including a substantial quantity of paintings purchased at the sale of Sir Joshua Reynold's effects and drawings by the Grand Masters, including *"…180 by Raphael, 100 by Michael Angelo, 75 by Leonardo, 150 by Rubens, 60 by Titian, 90 by Rembrandt, &c."* (Chancellor).

Lawrence's love affairs were not happy (his tortuous relationships with Sally and Maria Siddons became the subject of several books) and, in spite of his success, he spent most of life deeply in debt and never married - *"Always in love and always in debt…"* (Jennings, 1885). He stayed at the top of his profession until his sudden death from *"an ossification*

Sally Siddons by Thomas Lawrence

Sir Thomas's appearance as "…extremely graceful and gentlemanlike; his manners full of suavity; and his countenance so pleasing and handsome, that it might almost, if the word were not misapplied to the masculine sex, be called beautiful." An extract from The Spectator which featured in the same article, reads: "It may be interesting to know that he was employed on a splendid portrait of the King in his robes, and worked upon it on the Wednesday preceeding his death." Sir Thomas specified in his will that his collection should go to George IV and the Trustees of the British Museum at a sum of £18,000, they both refused the offer. The collection was eventually sold to "Messrs Woodburne", art dealers, for £20,000, which "…represented less than half what the pictures and drawings had originally cost the painter" (Chancellor). According to his agent, Smith, the "…splendid and inestimable collection of early Greek and Roman foliated ornaments liberally and tastefully displayed on the walls of the staircase and painting-rooms of Sir Thomas Lawrence, in his house in Russell Square", was sold at the house by Christie's on 6th July 1830 for the paltry sum of £732 10s. The aquatint (1830) shows Lawrence standing in his private sitting-room at No. 65, surrounded by casts of classical sculpture.

Chancellor concludes, from an entry in painter and diarist, Benjamin Haydon's Journal on 25th May 1832, that No. 65 "…appears to have remained unoccupied for a considerable time after the painter's death". The poignant entry reads: "I passed Lawrence's house. Nothing could be more melancholy or desolate. I knocked and was shown in. The passages were dusty, the paper torn, the parlours dark, the painting-room forlorn, the very paint on the door green with mildew. I went into the parlour which used to be instinct with life! 'Poor Sir Thomas, always in trouble,' said the woman who had the care of the house. 'Always something to worrit him.' I saw his bedroom, small; only a little bed; the mark of it was against the wall. Close to his bedroom was an immense room (divided), yet open over the partitions. It must have been five or six rooms turned into one large workshop.. His painting-room was a large back drawing room: his showroom a large front one. He occupied a parlour and a bedroom; all the rest of the house was turned to business. And this was the home of one of those whose patrons were 'kings and princes, and peers and peeresses his companions,' one whose acquaintance not a genius in England but reckoned a pleasure if not an honour!"

"Lawrence's reputation declined after his death, however, and has never revived to its former heights. In spite of his success he was constantly in debt and consequently took on too many commissions, so his work is uneven and sometimes careless (and like Reynolds he was a failure as a history painter), but at his best he has a feeling for paint that few British artists can rival. He was also a superb draughtsman, producing highly finished portrait drawings that rival those of Ingres in delicacy of touch and sensitivity of characterization (Mary Hamilton, 1789, BM, London)." (The Oxford Dictionary of Art and Artists). He played a part in founding the National Gallery and in securing the Elgin Marbles for the nation, and

The private sitting room of Sir Thomas Lawrence, 1830 © National Portrait Gallery, London

Lawrence's funeral in St Paul's Cathedral, by J.M.W. Turner from memory

was noted for the unselfish help he gave to young artists. Lawrence was buried on 21st January 1830 in the crypt of St Paul's Cathedral. Amongst the mourners was J. M. W. Turner who painted a sketch of the funeral from memory, which is held by Tate.

The Imperial Hotel now stands on the site of No. 65, with the commemorative plaque having been rescued from Lawrence's house and installed on the front elevation above the main entrance to the hotel, albeit where No. 61 once stood. The plaque can be seen in the c.1905 photograph at the beginning of this chapter, but not in the 1903 photograph below. It remained in place until the building was demolished in 1910 (see photograph in Imperial Hotel section, below).

Here is a broad cross-section of Lawrence's famous subjects, from royalty to local 'A-listers'.

George III, 1792
© Herbert Art Gallery & Museum

George IV, 1820
© University of Oxford

Caroline Amelia Elizabeth of Brunswick, 1815
© National Portrait Gallery, London

Arthur Wellesley, 1st Duke of Wellington,
c.1815-16 © The Wellington Collection,
Apsley House

Pope Pius VII
© Google Art Project

Sir Robert Peel -
Glynn Vivian Art Gallery

Sir John Soane, aged 76, 1828/9 -
Sir John Soane's Museum

John Nash -
Jesus College, University of Oxford;

Edward Jenner, 1809 -
Royal College of Physicians

No.65 in 1903 © CLSAC

Sir Thomas Henry Brooke-Hitching (1858-1926), businessman and local politician, is listed at No. 65 in the SD, 1902, and is listed with his *"Sir"* prefix in 1903, having been knighted the previous year.

He is described by the *Survey of London* as *"Playing Card Maker"*, although he appears to have a hand in building *"expensive and dignified"* (his words) Parkside in Knightsbridge. He served as Sheriff of the City of London (1902-3). Born in Halifax, Yorkshire, he was the son of John Walter Hitching. In 1878 he married Sarah Kossuth Brooke and assumed the surname Brooke-Hitching by royal licence. He entered business in 1881 as a manufacturer of perambulators and invalid carriages. He moved to Marylebone in London, becoming chairman of the vestry. In 1898, he unsuccessfully sought election to the London County Council as a Moderate Party candidate at Walworth. In 1900 he became a councillor in the newly-created St Marylebone Borough Council, and was Mayor of St Marylebone in 1906-07. Also in 1900 he was elected to the London School Board as one of the representatives of the City of London. In 1901, he made his second attempt to gain a seat on the county council. He again failed to be elected, on this occasion at Marylebone East. He was also a common councilman on the Corporation of London, and served as Sheriff of London in 1902-03, at which time he was knighted. In 1904, he made his third attempt to win a county council seat, and he was duly elected as one of four councillors representing the City of London, serving a single three-year term. At the 1906 general election he stood as Conservative Party candidate for the Yorkshire constituency of Elland without success. In 1912, he was elected as an alderman for the City of London ward of Farringdon Within. However a petition against his election was issued which appeared to show a conflict of interest between his business and local government activities. Although he strongly denied the claims, he was found to be *"not a person fit and proper.."* to hold the office, and he was unseated. Orders: Coronation Silver Medal; Officer of the Legion of Honour, France; Officer of Leopold II., Belgium; Grand Cross of St. Saba, Servia; Grand Cross Danillo, Montenegro.

Other early occupants of No. 65 include: Frederick Cowper JP, DL (1794-1881) - (BCGs, 1840-46, and SDs, 1841-42). He and his wife, Susannah Lydia, had 7 girls and 4 boys when they moved into No. 65, with their youngest daughter Emily being born here in 1838. The 1851 Census has them at 82 Harley Street with 5 servants, which had risen to 11 by 1861, so they were very well off. He left £160,000 in his Will; Joseph Oxford (RBB, 1858, and SDs, 1861-62); Benjamin Michael (ABCCG, 1871, and SD, 1878); Harris Mark Birnstine (SDs, 1886-95) - Harris Bernstein is listed in the records of the Central Synagogue, living at 65 Russell Square; David Sinclair (SDs, 1905-08). No. 65 was absorbed into the Imperial Family Hotel in 1909.

Sir Thomas Henry Brooke-Hitching and Lady Brooke-Hitching, née Sarah Kussuth Brooke - *The Court*, 13th March 1903 ©V&A

N.B. Nos. 66-71 are included in section 2 of this chapter (Baltimore/Bolton House site) and Nos. 1-8 are in section 3 (Hotel Russell site).

Imperial Hotel: Changing Bloomsbury

The original houses at Nos. 61-64 Russell Square were demolished in 1904 to make way for the construction of the Imperial Family Hotel, which was designed by the same architect as the earlier Hotel Russell, Charles Fitzroy Doll, at the invitation of Harold Walduck, who was desperate to meet the excess guest demand at his ever-expanding Bedford Hotel in nearby Southampton Row (see entry for Harold Walduck in chapter 4 – No. 14). Doll's original design for the hotel would have replaced the entire terrace of historic houses from Southampton Row to Guilford Street (Nos. 61 to 70), but it was decided to build it in phases, beginning with the sites of four houses, Nos. 61 to 64, the first of which opened in 1907, when it was first listed in the SD as *"Imperial Family Hotel, Harold Walduck"*.

Nos. 64-69 (r-l) prior to the construction of the first phase of the Imperial Hotel (64 was still occupied in 1904

Charles Fitzroy Doll's original design for the Imperial Hotel, which would have replaced Nos. 61-70

Postcard depicting a rare view of the Imperial Hotel prior to the 1910 extension

According to their promotional booklet, *THREE LONDON HOTELS* (1910), within one year of opening, the Imperial's 300 bedrooms were *"filled to overflowing"*, and it soon became one of the most popular hotels in London, due to its *"…up-to-date accommodation at so moderate a charge as no large Hotel had hitherto attempted."* The demand became

so great that it *"…became necessary to provide an overflow and in 1909 an adjacent block of flats was secured next door but one. This was converted into a Hotel with 150 rooms and was given the name of The Premier Hotel."* (The house in question was two doors south of the Imperial, now known as Premier House, 150 Southampton Row. See section 2 for more details.) Continuing guest demand led Harold Walduck, in 1910, to announce his acquisition of two more houses adjacent to the Imperial: *"Mr. Walduck has purchased the two Leaseholds, Nos. 65 and 66, Russell Square. These two houses, together with stabling in the rear, and two houses, Nos. 2 and 3, Queen Square Place, have been demolished, and upon these sites together with the garden of 20, Queen Square, a magnificent addition to 'The Imperial Hotel' is now in a forward state of construction. This building will contain over 380 Bedrooms besides handsome Reception Rooms. It will also contain a Turkish Bath, to which access can be had either by a separate entrance from Russell Square or from the Hotel itself, and pains are being taken to make this the finest bath in London. It is believed that the*

Promotional ashtray, early 1900s

RUSSELL SQUARE, LONDON, W. C.

Baths will meet a long-felt want of the neighbourhood, as there are at present no Turkish Baths in the Central District. It is inevitable that the march of modern improvements should obliterate much that is of interest to the antiquarian and the historian." The extension, which was then under construction, is labelled as such on the cover of the THREE LONDON HOTELS brochure, with No. 67, the surviving section of Bolton House to the left.

OF HOTELS." Whilst lamenting the loss of the historic houses, the editorial also revealed a morbid curiosity with and tacit acceptance of the relentless march of progress: "Unfortunately the historic side of Russell Square is called upon to suffer in the forward movement. North of the already huge Imperial Hotel one sees a whitewashed line to-day, indicating the handing over to the housebreakers of the two famous houses, numbers 65 and 66, Russell Square. When they are down their

THE IMPERIAL HOTEL, Russell Square. LONDON.

Cover of THREE LONDON HOTELS brochure, 1910, depicting the built design for the Imperial Hotel on the site of Nos. 61-66 © ILHL

This dramatic period of transition was encapsulated by The Daily Graphic on 13th September 1910, in a feature titled "Changing Bloomsbury", which centred on the relentless march of new hotels along Southampton Row (which it took to include the east side of Russell Square), and the demise of the historic houses, with particular reference to Nos. 65 and 66. The article was juxtaposed to a photo-montage titled "THE TRANSFORMATION OF RUSSELL SQUARE AND SOUTHAMPTON ROW", with the caption: "FAMOUS CENTRAL LONDON THOROUGHFARES, FROM WHICH THE OLD-WORLD HOUSES ARE FAST DISAPPEARING TO MAKE WAY FOR THE EVER-INCREASING NUMBER

ravished sites will be devoted to the extension northward of the Imperial. No. 65, marked by a tablet, is well known as the house in which Sir Thomas Lawrence lived, painted, and held court, for the last twenty-five years of his busy life – from 1805 to 1830. No. 66 is more full of interest than Sir Thomas Lawrence's house, if less well-known to the general public. It is a slice of the great Baltimore House, sometime Bolton House, built by the seventh Lord Baltimore, of ill fame, in 1763." (He was in fact the 6th Lord Baltimore.) Commemorative tablets to Sir Thomas Lawrence and Lord Loughborough can just about be made out on the front walls of Nos. 65 and 67, respectively.

View south towards Southampton Row, as featured in *The Daily Graphic*, 13th September 1910

As if to ameliorate the sense of loss expressed in *The Daily Graphic* article, the owners of the hotel announced: *"It has been possible, however, to preserve one supremely interesting relic of mediaeval London, and even to employ it in the service for which it was originally created, for, by a curious coincidence, the twentieth-century Turkish Bath of 'The Imperial Hotel' will draw water from the ancient Water Head which was built in the reign of King Henry the Third."* The conduit head was indeed rescued by Charles Fitzroy Doll during the demolition works, and the Devil's Conduit was moved to New River Head in 1927. The article added: *"Water is still obtained from this Water Head, and in olden days it was reputed to have aver'ed the Leprosy."* The owners further proclaimed: *"The Imperial Hotel, when its extension is opened early in 1912, will contain accommodation for more guests than any other Hotel in London*

Site of the Imperial Hotel extension, encompassing Nos. 65 and 66

and will embody and represent the latest word in Hotel construction. Its present fine Entrance Hall will be doubled in size; it will contain a magnificent new Dining Hall, 136 feet in length and of noble proportions; the 384 new Bedrooms will each contain a radiator and running hot and cold water; a Masonic Temple and private Banqueting Rooms will be distinguishing features; and a new range of Stock Rooms will provide ample facilities for business men." The SD for 1911 was the first time that Imperial Hotel was listed as occupying Nos. 65 and 66, with the National Union of Teachers still firmly entrenched at No. 67 (and in No. 71 at the rear). The 1916 SD lists it for the first time as "Imperial Hotel, Imperial London Hotels Limited", along with "Turkish baths" at No. 66. The hotel's extravagant exterior was matched by its luxuriant interior décor, as illustrated in the photographs taken shortly before the building was demolished in 1966.

Imperial Hotel postcard after the extension was completed, featuring pictures of the Dining Room and Winter Garden with Minstrels Gallery

Imperial Hotel Dining Room, 1966, with figurines atop the pillars

Imperial Hotel Lounge, 1966

A later promotional brochure claimed that the hotel's baths were the *"Finest in the World"*, being open to non-residents for three shillings and sixpence, with *"Gentlemen's Baths open Day and Night"*, and offering a wide range of treatments, including Russian vapour baths, Aix and Vichy douches, 'Alpine Sun Bath', electric light and ultraviolet ray baths and hydro-electric therapeutic treatments. The Imperial's other special draw was its spacious Winter Garden, where an orchestra played during afternoon tea, before adjourning to the new Dining Hall to play during dinner. In 1915 the Imperial was advertising 1,000 rooms *"…furnished and fitted throughout with every luxury and comfort that art, science, or experience can suggest, while the rates will bear favourable comparison with any hotel in the Metropolis."*

Turkish Bath Frigidarium, 1913, with figurines atop the pillars

Turkish baths in 1966

The Devil's or Chimney Conduit,
20 Queen Square 24.11.1910

Gorky cartoon

Gorky stays at the Imperial

When Vladimir Lenin (Vladimir Ilyich Ulyanov) and Maxim Gorky (Alexei Maximovich Peshkov) attended the second congress of the Latvian Social Democrats in London on 3rd to 7th June 1907, Gorky stayed at the Imperial Hotel. They had only met once previously, but consolidated their friendship during the congress, visiting the British Museum in their spare time. *"When Gorky stayed here he was visited by Lenin who, always suspicious of hotels, carefully inspected the bed clothes to make sure they were not damp."* (The London Encyclopaedia, 3rd edn., 2008).

The 1907 photograph of the front of the Imperial, on page 82, would have been available to guests at the time Gorky stayed there. The Imperial produced a range of postcards during its early years, some of which have become collectors' items, including the

Maxim Gorky, 1906

Lenin, 1920

88 | Imperial Hotel postcard, c.1915, using Russell Square Gardens as a selling point to guests

Imperial Hotel postcard, c.1915 (classic view)

evocative samples illustrated here, which were captured after the extension had been built. A letter from the Home Office dated 12th April 1911 gave permission for the word *"Imperial"* to be used in the company's name, provided it was only used for this hotel, and that is how it was listed in the SDs thereafter.

Momentous events of historical significance

The Balfour Declaration of 1917 was drafted at meetings held in the Imperial. It was a short letter by Arthur Balfour, the UK's Foreign Secretary, to arguably one of the most influential Jewish families – the Rothschilds. It was assumed that the letter gave the British Government's support to the creation of a Jewish homeland. The letter read:

"Foreign Office
November 2nd, 1917

Dear Lord Rothschild,
I have much pleasure in conveying to you on behalf of His Majesty's Government, the following declaration of sympathy with Jewish Zionist aspirations which has been submitted to, and approved, by the Cabinet:
His Majesty's Government view with favour the establishment in Palestine of a national home for the
Jewish people, and will use their best endeavours to facilitate the achievement of this object, it being clearly understood that nothing shall be done which may prejudice the civil and religious rights of existing non-Jewish communities in Palestine, or the rights and political status enjoyed by Jews in any other country. I should be grateful if you would bring this declaration to the knowledge of the Zionist Federation.
Yours,
Arthur James Balfour"

Other significant guests were the three signatories to the Anglo-Irish Treaty who stayed at the Imperial after they had signed The Treaty on 6th December 1921, including Arthur Griffith, Eamonn Duggan and Michael Collins. The Treaty was an agreement between the Government of the United Kingdom of Great Britain and Ireland and Irish representatives that concluded the Irish War of Independence. It provided for the establishment of the Irish Free State within a year as a self-governing dominion within the British Commonwealth of Nations (the first use by the UK government of this term, rather than 'British Empire', in an official document). It also provided Northern Ireland, which had been created by the Government of Ireland Act 1920, an option to opt out of the Irish Free State, which it exercised.

Michael Collins (seated) signs the Anglo-Irish Treaty in 1922

Imperial staff shocked
by stabbing and shooting incidents

The first half of 1928 was a traumatic period for the staff of the Imperial, with first a shooting then a stabbing featuring in The Times newspaper. The lead article on Tuesday 20th March 1928, headlined "MAN FOUND SHOT AT LONDON HOTEL", told of a mysterious visitor who had arrived at the hotel the previous Tuesday and had been "found shot in his room on Friday evening". The reporter's enquiries revealed that, "The man had taken elaborate precautions to conceal his identity. Letters found on the body had had the addresses carefully removed, and makers' marks had been cut off his clothing. The man was not seen about the hotel on Friday, and when his bedroom door was tried it was found to be locked. The door was forced and the man was found lying on the bed shot through the heart. When the eiderdown was removed a heavy calibre revolver fell to the floor. The man, who was well dressed in American style, was aged about 32 years, 5ft. 10in. in height, clean shaven and of dark complexion. No money was found. Luggage labels showed that the man had travelled as a first-class passenger." The Times also reported on the inquest the following day, when the dead man was named

as John Harry Mitchell, aged about 32. "At first it was thought that he was a New York businessman, but he was found to be an Englishman who had spent some time in America. Miss Lily Mitchell, a nurse, said the dead man was her brother and she identified a letter as being in his handwriting. The Coroner read from it the following passages:-'Forgive me this act. I feel I am going insane and just cannot face it. I cannot carry on.' Mrs Hilda Tragoning, wife of a commercial traveller, of Bayswater, said she had known Mitchell about two months, and last saw him on Wednesday night. He was rather depressed, and he told her he had his wallet stolen. He had told her a fortnight before that he had had bad news from America. He told her he had cabled to America for money, but could not get it. Returning a verdict that Mitchell had killed himself while of unsound mind, the CORONER said that a letter addressed to him stated: "Circumstances have broken me financially. My courage is equally broken. There is little choice than to end things in this rotten manner, much as I dislike the inconvenience it gives."

An arguably more traumatic event occurred about three months later when a total stranger entered the hall of the hotel and stabbed the hotel's manageress, Miss Marjorie O'Sullivan, in the left forearm with a pointed table knife, causing a serious injury. According to the court report in The Times on 7th July 1928, Dr Henry Gregory of Russell Square informed the

Magistrate at the *"Bow-street Police Court"* that *"…
an x-ray examination revealed that the point of the knife
was embedded in the bone of Miss O'Sullivan's arm.
An operation had been performed, but a piece
of the metal was still left in the bone."* Also, two eye-
witnesses described how they saw *"Ernest Benjamin
Bailey, 34, no occupation of Euston-square, NW"*, stab
Miss O'Sullivan several times, one saying that *"He
was quite calm, and there had been no trouble between
them."* And the other describing how *"He then walked
about the hall looking dazed, and did not appear to
realize what he had done."* Such was the severity of the
alleged offence that Bailey was referred to the Central
Criminal Court for trial, which took place on 18th July
1928. Bailey pleaded *"Not Guilty"*, but he was found
*"Guilty of the act charged, but that he was insane
at the time, and not responsible for his actions, and
Judge Atherly-Jones ordered him to be detailed during
his Majesty's pleasure."* (*The Times*, 19th July 1928).
The centre-fold of the Imperial Hotel group's *Nine
London Hotels 2,500 Rooms* promotional booklet,
published c.1928, depicts life in the square around
the time of these two incidents, with the obligatory
line of taxis waiting dutifully for the next well-heeled
guest to emerge from the Imperial.

World-renowned scientist chooses the Imperial for its baths

In 1933, Leo Szilard (1898-1964), a Hungarian
physicist who had been working in Berlin for the past
decade, fled Hitler's Germany and checked into the
Imperial Hotel with his two suitcases in April. It was
less costly than the Hotel Russell, where his fellow
exiled scientist, the 1918 Nobel Prize winner Fritz
Haber (1868-1934) was staying, but for Slizard, who
had once declared that *"There is no place as good to
think as a bathtub"*, what made the Imperial irresistible
was its famous Turkish baths. Politically, the nationalist
Haber and the socialist Szilard had little in common,
although they were both enthralled by the idea of
science as power. Neither had set out in their careers
intending to create new weapons, but they both
played key roles in developing a new generation of
scientific super weapons. Haber thought that chemical
weapons would make him the saviour of his country,
whilst Szilard, an internationalist fired by an idealistic
vision of how science should transform human life
and society for the better, wanted to save the world
with atomic energy and create Utopia. Also, in direct
contrast to Haber, who was at the end of his career
and with not much longer to live, Leo Szilard was a

Telegrams—
RUSIMP
LONDON **IMPERIAL HOTEL & TURKISH BATHS, RUSSELL SQUARE, LONDON** Telephone—
Terminus 3655
(25 lines)

(8) Hotel de Luxe at Popular Prices. Fully Licensed. Orchestra daily in Winter Gardens. Six Beautiful Public Rooms and Magnificent Suites for Receptions, Dinners, Dances, etc. Garage at rear. Snack Bar, Brasserie and Popular Restaurant. Finest Turkish Baths in the World.	Single Room with Central Heating. Running Hot and Cold Water, with Bath and Full Table d'hôte Breakfast. ... **9/6** Ditto. Double Room per person ... **8/3** Ditto. Bed Sitting Room, per person **10/6** (9)

Centre-fold of 'Nine London Hotels 2,500 Rooms' promotional booklet published c.1928 © ILHL

35-year-old, budding nuclear physicist, with energy to burn. Throughout 1933, Szilard worked tirelessly and selflessly (unpaid) on behalf of his fellow refugee academics running the Academic Assistance Council (later the Society for the Protection of Science and Learning), an organisation he had helped found which dedicated itself to helping academics fleeing from the Nazis. He was living off his earnings from patents which he held jointly with his close friend Albert Einstein, including a design for a safe refrigerator, which didn't materialize, although their invention of a liquid metal refrigeration system was

Leo Szilard

later used to cool nuclear reactors.

Slizard's daily routine at the Imperial began with breakfast in the plush restaurant, followed by a leisurely and extended soak in a bath – the only luxury the decidedly non-materialistic Szilard permitted himself. It was not uncommon for him to spend three hours in a tub, awaiting Archimedean inspiration. Late on the morning of 12th September 1933, Szilard was reading *The Times* in the hotel foyer when he came across an article that reported Ernest Rutherford's speech on how subatomic particles might be used to transmute atoms, which quoted Rutherford as saying, *"…anyone who looked for a source of power in the transformation of the atom was talking moonshine"*. Szilard frowned as he read these words. If there was one thing in science that made Szilard really angry, it was experts who said that something was impossible. On 12th September 1933, while crossing at the traffic lights on Southampton Row into Russell Square, Dr Slizard suddenly had an idea, which was to prove prophetic for ushering in the Atomic Age. In his memoirs he recalls this 'eureka' moment thus: *"As the light changed to green and I crossed the street, it suddenly occurred to me that if we could find an element which is split by neutrons and which could emit two neutrons when it absorbs one neutron, such an element if assembled in sufficiently large mass, could sustain a nuclear chain reaction… In certain circumstances it might be possible to liberate energy on an industrial scale, and construct atomic bombs."* Slizard's ideas culminated in the Americans exploding atomic bombs over the Japanese cities of Hiroshima and Nagasaki on 6th and 9th August 1945, respectively, causing immense devastation and bringing World War II to an abrupt end in the Far East. (Richard Rhodes, *The Making of the Atomic Bomb*, 1986).

1930s postcard illustrating the east side of Russell Square with the imposing Imperial Hotel

Stanislawa de Karlowska

Imperial Hotel by Stanislawa de Karlowska, 1930s

The Learie Constantine incident

A dark cloud descended over the Imperial Hotel in 1943 when an incident concerning the treatment of a certain hotel guest was reported in the national press. *The Spectator*, on 10th September 1943 published a letter with the bold heading *"COLOURED BRITISH CITIZENS"*: *"Sir, - Many of your readers must have listened sympathetically to last week's broadcast talk by Mr Learie Constantine, the eminent cricketer (now an official of the Ministry of Labour) on his life-struggle in that part of the Empire in which he was born and his experiences as a resident in this country. He tactfully did not allude to the fact that he and his family had just been asked to leave a London hotel, but that fact has been a good deal commented upon in the daily press. The following appeared in the Daily Telegraph, September 3rd: "Mr Harold Walduck, managing director of the Imperial Hotel, Russell Square, London, said yesterday: 'After certain suggestion had been made to me by other guests I suggested to Mr Constantine that he would be more comfortable in one of our smaller hotels. Mr Constantine readily agreed. There is no suggestion that he was turned out. There is not a colour ban. We prefer to cater for white people.' It may well be that Mr Constantine 'readily agreed'. We would most of us 'readily agree' to take our families away from the company of fellow-guests who showed that they resented our presence and who were supported in this by the manager of the house? But what a shocking thing it is that, in the very capital of the Empire, British citizens should be thus insulted. And the hotel in question, in this particular instance, is the Imperial!"* Constantine's 'celebrity' status no doubt heightened the level of media interest, with cartoonist David Low drawing one of his more famous cartoons attacking the hotel's treatment of Constantine, who as a professional cricketer for the West Indies, had travelled to London to play for the Dominions team against an England XI at Lord's.

the hotel manager, Harold Walduck, who informed them that they could stay one night and no more, on account of complaints received from the white US servicemen who were also staying at the hotel. O'Sullivan later said that she feared a quarrel between Constantine *"and the Americans and colonials"* and that she had *"no staff to quell it"*. Harold, for his part, appears to have done his best to ameliorate the distress to the Constantine family by unhesitatingly offering the family alternative accommodation in the older, smaller and quieter Bedford Hotel, only a hundred yards away, where Constantine later recalled they were treated very well. In an era when racism was widespread and not illegal, that might have been the end of it, but Constantine was not the kind of man to be bowed. Although outraged by his family being treated as outcasts, he was only able to lodge a claim for breach of contract, in accordance with the common law principle that innkeepers must not refuse accommodation to guests without just cause, there being no statute that expressly outlawed racial discrimination in Britain at that time. The case proceeded despite the hotel making a £5,000 payment into the court (equivalent to £212,500 in 2016), presumed to be in settlement of the case. A top barrister, Sir Patrick Hastings, was hired for what was seen as a test case whose outcome could influence the attitude of West Indians to the war effort. Constantine won the case and was duly awarded five guineas in damages. At this time, racial

'Imperial Welcome' by David Low (1891-1963) - *Evening Standard* 7.9.1943

He and his family had a reservation to stay at the Imperial Hotel and when making arrangements he had taken the precaution of asking if his colour would cause any problems and was assured it would not and that he and his family were welcome and would be treated with the utmost respect, even though large groups of white American servicemen regularly stayed at the hotel. Racial slurs were, he recalled, *"...an unpleasant part of living in Britain."* When Constantine arrived with his family on the evening of 30th July it was immediately apparent that they were not welcome and after a brusque exchange with Margaret O'Sullivan, the manageress, asked to see

segregation was the norm in many US states, and within their own military, and Britain was more than twenty years away from becoming a land of equal opportunities for all. Hotels clearly operate within the social context and legal framework which exists at any time. Coincidentally, Harold Walduck's younger son, Stanley, who had rushed to join the army at the outbreak of war, was barred entry to the Savoy Hotel dining room in November 1939 *"...because a private soldiers boots might damage the dance floor."* Constantine later explained: *"Had I been inclined to do so, I could probably have succeeded in a further action for defamation... But I was content to have drawn* the particular nature of the affront before the wider judgment of the British public in the hope that its sense of fair play might help protect the people of my colour in England in future. From the tone of the hundreds of letters of congratulation I received from all over the country, I think my object was attained." The ruling is described by Nick Rennison, author of *The London Plaque Guide*, 4th edition (2015), as *"…a landmark victory in the battle against racial discrimination."* Constantine (1901-1971) was appointed Member of the British Empire (MBE) in 1947, and went on to write the book *Colour Bar* in 1954, which ignited a debate about racial prejudice in Britain, although it took until 1965 for the Race Relations Act to become law. He was knighted in 1962 and became Britain's first black peer seven years later. In recent years, Richard Walduck, as a Patron of the Caribbean Women's Standing Conference, has hosted a number of their gatherings in the Imperial, which have been attended by Caribbean High Commissioners and their representatives and Baroness Doreen Lawrence.

Constantine at his investiture at the House of Lords in 1969

The 1960s re-development – 'out with the old and in with the new'

Charles Fitzroy Doll's opulent Imperial Hotel was unceremoniously demolished in November 1965, to make way for a brand new hotel building fit for the future. The Labour Prime Minister, Harold Wilson, announced a ban on new hotel buildings during the snap election which he called and won on 31st March 1966. This impending ban, combined with the real prospect of the building being listed by the Historic Buildings and Monuments Commission for England, precipitated the Imperial's untimely demise. However, the Wilson Government was to have a change of heart, introducing the Hotel Development Incentives scheme (HDI) in 1968, and reinforcing its provisions in the Development of Tourism Act, passed in 1969. *"The HDI scheme provided for a grant of up to £1,000 per bedroom for projects with more than 25 bedrooms and which provided an evening meal. The effect was dramatic - with 72 new hotels and 108 extensions built in London, creating 20,000 new rooms, a fifty per cent increase in supply… Another direct result of the 'rush' to develop under this scheme was that the Greater London Council (GLC) and London's local authorities adopted a more stringent attitude and policy approach to hotel development in London."* (Demand and Capacity for Hotels and Conference Centres in London, Report to the Greater London Authority, August 2002). The HDI *"…overspent by ten times what the government envisaged in 1968, as hoteliers rushed to take advantage of the money on offer … over 100,000 new bed spaces were grant aided in England by 1974…"* (British Tourism – The Remarkable Story of Growth, Victor T.C. Middleton with the late Leonard J. Lickorish, 2005). An unwelcome consequence of these grants was a substantial development of hotels in the wrong places, such as the one notoriously sited a few metres away from the A40 Westway flyover near Paddington. Richard Walduck, in a letter to the London *Evening Standard* dated 25th October 1995, clarified, for the benefit of a certain Paul Barker, that *"The Imperial Hotel preceded the £1,000 grant by some five years."* The loss of the Imperial caused quite a stir at the time, with those for and against the march of progress voicing diametrically opposed views in the national press. These were the days before historic buildings were generally regarded as being worthy of protection and listing in what is now the National Heritage List for England (NHLE), maintained by Historic England on behalf of the UK Government. Even if this mode of protection had been in place at the time, there was no guarantee that the Imperial would have been listed, because Victorian and

Edwardian buildings were generally not deemed to be ancient enough by the arbiters of worthiness whose views prevailed at the time (there was a covert snobbery towards Victorian buildings). They were also unlikely to have been considered to be of sufficient architectural merit, due to their eclectic 'theft' of styles from different periods, with the Imperial displaying an even more extravagant interpretation of the Gothic than its surviving predecessor, the Hotel Russell.

This is best illustrated by the attempt to demolish the wonderful Midland Grand Hotel at St Pancras station (see below). Another consideration was the exorbitant cost of restoring, repairing and maintaining these complex structures and the technical problems associated with modernising their facilities to meet the modern standards sought after by hotel guests in the 1960s. The hotel owner's point of view was, therefore, it had to go.

Although the demolition of the Imperial had caused a stir, the designs for its replacement generated a tidal-wave of protest and derision, with such views largely prevailing today. In an article headed "More Bad Buildings than Good in Academy Preview" (The Times, 2nd May 1960), their Architectural Correspondent referred disparagingly to the new Imperial Hotel as "... the depressingly undistinguished hotel in Russell Square by C. Lovett Gill and Partners". The Imperial was viewed as one of "...at least half-a-dozen designs... that make one's heart sink at the prospect of seeing them built." This negative criticism was continued in an article about the finished building on 16th March 1971, in which Charles Forte's hotel group, Trust House Forte, was praised for "conscientiously" restoring Hotel Russell (allegedly spending £1M on the listed façade). It states: "The tragedy is that the same course was not followed in the case of the Imperial Hotel, the even grander building that shared the east side of the square with the Russell. The Imperial was recently demolished and replaced by a modernistic hotel wholly without character or distinction."

"1966 - HOTEL DEVELOPMENTS"

"In Russell Square the demolition of the grandiose Imperial Hotel was a severe loss, especially as it was superseded by a building so inappropriate to the square, and hardly becoming to anywhere else. Doll's other hotel nearby, the Russell, demonstrates the quality of what was needlessly demolished." (The Annals of London, John Richardson, 2000)

"...the 60s and 70s brought the destruction not only of Bradford Exchange, but of the Imperial Hotel in Russell Square, an even more fabulously eclectic and flamboyant edifice than its slightly earlier and still surviving neighbour, the Russell Hotel." (Victorian Web)

"At the turn of the century, the splendid Russell and Imperial Hotels ...were opened in Russell Square; with the latter scandalously demolished in the 1960s." (An Economic History of London 1800-1914, by Professor Michael Ball, David T. Sunderland, 2002)

Fiona McCarthy, in her article headed "Imperial demolition" in The Guardian on 1st November 1966, wrote in less complimentary terms about Doll's Imperial Hotel, and as if celebrating the demise of Doll's work, begins her article with: "Edward VII and his lifesize queen (in stone) have already been torn down from their tall Imperial niches. The Rudest Clock in London, an old man who rolls his eyes and sticks out his tongue at the striking of each hour, stops this very Tuesday. The Imperial Hotel, most monstrous joke of Bloomsbury, is falling flat at last, and demolition men are busy disarranging Fitzroy Doll's high patriotic Edwardian façade." Rumor had it that the old man was sticking his tongue out at the Duke of Bedford. MCarthy rounds off her article with a damning critique of Doll's work, followed by an argument for moving with the times: "Historically, the building is belated, mixed-up, tedious; aesthetically, the experts' formal view of it is tripe. And practically, the tight-packed bedrooms, and general structural frailty is unfair to foreign tourists. How many of them want to sleep in a hexagon, seven floors high up a mock-Bavarian tower, when the bedrooms in the next hotel, the bland and shiny President, are modern and rectangular, well-equipped and sane? So in with the modern amenities: TV, multi-channel stereophonic radio, weighing scales and bidets and international razor sockets, making our visitors feel more or less at home. Away with eccentricities like statues of the king, weathercocks and turrets, and the bright Imperial sun."

Whilst waxing lyrical about the wonderful Hotel Russell, Gavin Stamp, in his book Lost Victorian Britain (2010), reminds us that the Imperial Hotel was an even more remarkable Charles Fitzroy Doll hotel, designed in a style Pevsner (1951) described as a "... vicious mixture of Art Nouveau Gothic and Art Nouveau Tudor". Stamp informs us that its demise was partly due to a lack of bathrooms - though the restoration of the St Pancras Midland (now Renaissance) Hotel shows what can be overcome if there is a will - and to the Greater London Council's declaration that "... the whole frame was so structurally unsound that there was no possibility of saving it if a preservation order had been placed on the building". However, Stamp suspects that its loss had more to do with changing tastes in architecture than its structural condition. James Stevens Curl (The Oxford Dictionary of Architecture, 3rd edn., 2015) suggests that Pevsner might have added "Bavarian spires" to his description of the Imperial, which he believes to have been "replaced with tawdry Modernist banalities."

Sir John Betjeman (1906-1984), who was a founding member of the Victorian Society and a passionate defender of Victorian architecture, and served as Britain's Poet Laureate from 1972 until he died, was invited to say a few words at a 'farewell to the Imperial' party arranged by the Victorian Society and held in the Winter Garden of the old Imperial. Betjeman had fought a spirited but unsuccessful campaign to save the Propylaeum, known commonly as the Euston Arch, and is considered instrumental in saving the Midland Grand

An artist captures the Imperial Hotel in its final days

Hotel at St Pancras railway station, where his contribution was commemorated with a statue when it became an international terminus for Eurostar in November 2007. At the time, he called the plan to demolish St Pancras a *"criminal folly"*, so it is surprising not to find any historical references to him opposing the demolition of the Imperial Hotel. In his speech at the launch of the new Imperial, he light-heartedly referred to the building as *"three-dimensional chartered accountancy"*. Forty-six years after the demise of the original Imperial Hotel, Gary Powell, in *"SQUARE LONDON – a social history of the iconic London square"* (2012), expressed his retrospective disappointment: *"The modern-day Imperial Hotel replacing the original late 19th-century hotel of the same name is an eyesore, resembling a badly designed council estate rather than a building overlooking one of London's most celebrated squares."* The *Oxford Index* simply describes the replacement for the original Imperial Hotel as *"banal"*.

The last word is reserved for Richard Walduck OBE, DL, the present Director of Imperial

Statue of Sir John Betjeman at St Pancras International station

'Classic' view of the Imperial Hotel taken in 1966, shortly before it was demolished © CLSAC

Remnants of the past rescued for posterity

London Hotels Ltd, who explained in a letter to the editor of the *Evening Standard*, dated 25th October 1995, that the 1966 replacement was *"…a product of the planning regulations of the period, proposed as a fine tower project to offset London University opposite, but compressed to fit the parameters of so many, often conflicting, requirements, plot ratios, height, traffic light etc … As my late father observed on replacing its sister, the Imperial that Charles Fitzroy Doll designed for my grandfather, "We strive to achieve 'the good building' but can only erect what planning permits."*

"The Turkish baths… were the subject of an early campaign by the Victorian Society, which failed and the baths were demolished, with the rest of the hotel, in 1966. But the statues were rescued and now sit in the courtyard of the new hotel…" (Bloomsbury Past – Richard Tames, 1993). The statues in question can be seen alongside the entrance to the underground car park, with the five bells rescued from the original clock tower now sitting proudly above the Casino. The larger statues (six of the nine muses which once occupied niches in the clock tower), are life-size, scantily clad allegorical women, two of whom are clutching books helpfully entitled *"Literature"* and *"Chemistry"*, and another holding a mask, signifying *"Theatre"*, but the other three are a mystery to the author, who would be pleased to be enlightened by any classical scholars reading this book. The 21 smaller statues, which were originally housed in the Turkish Baths and Restaurant (see photographs above), represent Tudor characters, six of them repeated. Other original items to be salvaged include the five different-sized bells and clock from the clock-tower, which can be seen above the Casino. The bells, in decreasing size, are embossed: United Kingdom MCMXII (1912), India, Canada, Australia and South Africa.

View west from the ninth floor of Imperial Hotel, with the Senate House tower that the hotel was originally proposing to emulate

The rescued statues

The clock and five bells rescued from the original clock tower

Hotelier and businessman Sir Reo Stakis (1913-2001), formerly Argyros Anastasis, obtained planning permission in January 1981 to introduce the Regency Casino to the Imperial Hotel. Stakis owned 23 hotels by 1972, and a chain of 22 casinos, including the Regency. The face and hands of the old clock are now electrically driven, but the bells have not been connected. According to a notice in a shiny, illuminated, wooden cabinet in the hotel foyer, the *"Going Train"* or works of the old clock lay discarded and forgotten for 30 years in the basement of the new building until 1993, when they were refurbished by the hotel's resident engineer, R. Milliken, complete with *"Remontoire"* movement, new hands and face in the old style and the same pendulum still driven by a 200lb weight. These are now proudly displayed in said cabinet, which we are helpfully informed was constructed using some of the original hotel's timber, by the

The *"Going Train"* displayed in the hotel foyer

hotel's resident carpenter, P. Efstathiou in 1994.
Two sculptures of scantily clad women welcome new arrivals to the hotel today. These have no historical significance, apart from having been 'salvaged' from the Café Royal in Regent Street and used to decorate the Royal Hotel in Woburn Place. They have since been painted gold to conceal the juvenile 'adornments' applied to specific body parts.

The original pavement mosaic sign, which enticed prospective customers to enter the Turkish baths, is still to be seen on the corner of Guilford Street and Russell Square, where it is no doubt the source of confusion and curiosity to visitors and passers-by.

Original mosaic sign on the corner
of Guilford Street and Russell Square

To their credit, the owners of the original Imperial Hotel also rescued the ornate, bronze commemorative plaque to Sir Thomas Lawrence, which had been installed on the front of his house at No. 65 a few years before it was replaced by the hotel. The plaque can now be seen above the vehicle entrance to the hotel, although the actual site of No. 65 was four houses to the north of this position.

Close-up of clock tower prior to its demolition

This winter view of the east side of Russell Square emphasises the dominance of the three hotels

The Site of Baltimore House; later Bolton House; later divided into Nos. 66 and 67, then extended to No. 71

Baltimore House

Frederick Calvert (1731-1771), author and libertine, commissioned John Vardy (1718-65) to build Baltimore House in 1759-1763, where it stood alone for many years overlooking the Duke of Bedford's Long Field, with only a distant chimney-sweep's cottage interrupting the splendid northerly view of the hills of Highgate and Hampstead. Frederick inherited the title 6th Duke of Baltimore, aged 20, when his father died on 24th April 1751. He also succeeded his father as Proprietary Governor of the Province of Maryland, becoming at once both a wealthy nobleman in England and a powerful figure in America. His inheritance included a substantial holding of stock in the Bank of England, an estate at Woodcote Park, Surrey and an annual income of £10,000 from taxes and rents, equivalent to £2.01M in 2016.

1767 map, labelled Ld. Baltimore

Frederick took little interest in Maryland, never setting foot there. Instead, he lived a life of leisure, writing verse and treating Maryland as no more than a source of revenue as he divided his time between England and continental Europe, especially Italy and, for a brief time, Constantinople, which he was forced to leave after being accused of keeping a private harem. Such was Frederick's fascination with the Ottoman Turks that in 1766, on his return to England, he pulled down part of his London house and rebuilt it in the style of a Turkish harem.

Frederick married Lady Diana Egerton (1731-58) in 1753, *"…but separated from her three years later on account of his rakish ways"* (ODNB), and they had no children. In 1758, Lady Diana *"…died from a hurt she received by a fall out of a Phaeton carriage"*, while accompanied by her husband, who was suspected of foul play, although no charges were ever brought. By 1763 he had built a grand mansion on the south side of Guilford Street where it was later joined by the houses in Southampton Row, which had originally terminated near Guilford Street.

Frederick Calvert, 6th Duke of Baltimore

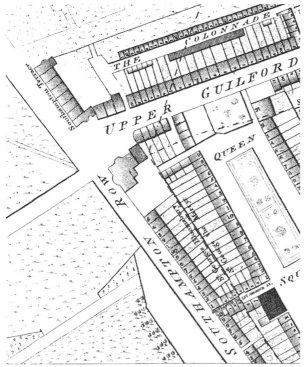

Richard Horwood's map, 1792-99, showing the double bow-fronted Bolton House and other houses pre-dating the formation of Russell Square

evidence to prove Woodcock's earlier complicity, he was eventually acquitted, but he left England after the trial. A detailed account of the events leading up to the trial, including the entrapment of Sarah Woodcock in Baltimore House by one of Frederick's 'agents' and her abduction to Woodcote Park, is given by E. Beresford Chancellor (1907). Following his acquittal, Frederick disposed of his property in England and returned to Italy to escape his disgrace, where he died three years later in Naples, *"…one of those worn-out beings, a hipped Englishman, who had lost all moral and physical taste"*, according to J. J. WinckelmannBefore being interred in the family vault at Epsom, Frederick's body lay in state at the Exeter Exchange in the Strand, London. Such was his unpopularity that, on its removal, the room was plundered by an angry crowd. According to *Gentleman's Quarterly*: *"His Lordship had injured his character in his life by seduction,*

Frederick unimaginatively named the property Baltimore House, which was described at the time as *"…a quaintly constructed solitary mansion standing on the outskirts of London amid rural scenery"*. It was to become part of the later Russell Square development. London topographer and author, John Noorthouck (1732-1816), later wrote, in 1773, that *"…it was either built without a plan, or else has had very whimsical owners; for the door has been shifted to different parts of the house,*

Sarah Woodcock being forcibly introduced to Lord Baltimore

until at last it is lost to all outward appearance, being now carried into the stable-yard." (Dobie)

Frederick's debauched lifestyle continued to attract critical attention until, in 1768, he was charged with raping Sarah Woodcock, a beautiful young Quaker milliner (with a shop in Tower Hill), at his country house at Epsom. Lurid details of the case, which was tried at Kingston Assizes on 26th March 1768, were discussed in numerous pamphlets. With sufficient

so that the populace paid no regard to his memory when dead, but plundered the room where his body lay the moment it was removed." Thomas Carlyle (one of the most important social commentators of his time) described Frederick as *"…something of a fool, to judge by the face of him in portraits, and by some of his doings in the world"*. Although he 'sired' five children by three different mothers, he died without a legitimate heir, and the title became extinct at his death.

Section for the Duke & Duchess of Bolton by Robert Adam
© Sir John Soane's Museum

Bolton House

**Admiral Harry Powlett
(aka Paulet)** (1720–1794),
6th Duke of Bolton, took up
the lease on Baltimore House
in 1770, promptly renaming it
Bolton House and employing
Robert Adam to make additions
and internal alterations.
*"The transformation of Vardy's
conventional Palladian house
into a stylish Neo-Classical one
took seven years to complete."*
(Sir John Soane's Museum).
*"It is surprising that Robert Adam's
splendid interiors for Bolton House
on Russell Square have hitherto
escaped attention. Though the
house is no longer there, his designs
are all preserved in Sir John Soane's
Museum and are among the most
attractive in the Adam collection.
Even more surprising, however, is
the discovery of parts of Bolton
House in New York City, in the
Center for Inter American Relations
on the corner of Park Avenue
and 68th Street."* (Robert Adam
on Park Avenue: The Interiors for
Bolton House, by Eileen Harris).
The house is indicated on
John Cary's 1795 map
of London as *"D. of Bolton"*.

Ceiling of the Duchess of Bolton's Dressing Room, designed by Robert Adam
© Sir John Soane's Museum

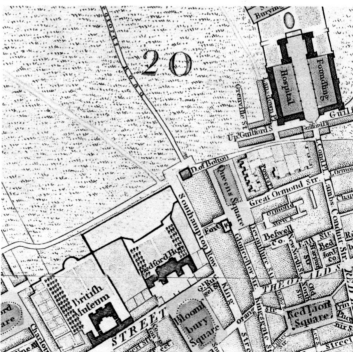

Cary 1795, showing house labelled "D. of Bolton"

This Duke of Bolton, who inherited the title from his elder brother Charles (the 5th Duke) after he committed suicide in July 1765, is often confused with the scandalised 3rd Duke of Bolton who, in 1751, married a former child prostitute Lavinia Fenton, with whom he first became besotted in 1726 when she portrayed Polly Peachum in John Gay's hugely popular *The Beggar's Opera*. Although Lavinia was unflatteringly described at the time by poet, playwright and clergyman Edward Young as *"no more than a greedy and grasping harlot"*, her pictures were in great demand, verses were written to her, and books published about her. She was probably the most talked-of person in London. Hogarth captured the essence of their relationship in his painting of a scene from the opera, dated 1731, now held in the Tate Britain collection, together with his portrait of Lavinia painted in 1745 *"in her later, riper years"* (Tate). The Duke perversely bought the theatre box from which he had watched Lavinia perform and installed it in

his church. He also became a Governor of the Foundling Hospital in 1739, no doubt strongly influenced by Lavinia with her first-hand experience of abandoned children and the workhouse.

Returning to our primary subject, Harry Powlett, he first came to public attention as the naval officer

Lavinia Fenton, later Duchess of Bolton, by William Hogarth, 1745 © Tate Britain

who brought charges of misconduct against his commander-in-chief, Admiral Griffin, for failing to engage eight French ships in 1748. Griffin, who was found guilty of negligence, and temporarily suspended from his rank, regarded Powlett's action as *"…the inveterate malice of a capricious turbulent young man"* (Rodger, 249). He retaliated by bringing Powlett to a court martial for cowardice and other serious charges. In spite of Powlett's attempts to avoid the proceedings by going on half-pay, the court martial assembled on 1st September 1752. But after five years, Griffin could produce no witnesses to support his accusations, the charge failed for want of evidence, and Powlett was acquitted. The incident produced a volley of pamphlets on both sides, and ultimately resulted in a duel between the two

A scene from The Beggar's Opera VI, 1731, by William Hogarth © Tate Britain

John Gay (1685-1732)

officers on Blackheath in 1756. Powlett went on to make meteoric progress in the navy due to family influence, being promoted to captain only four months after being made lieutenant, while his father was at the Admiralty. In 1756 he was duly promoted Rear-Admiral and, in 1758, Vice-Admiral of the White, despite being court martialled in 1755 for separating from the fleet and returning to port unjustifiably - charges for which he was acquitted and admonished, respectively. He was nicknamed Captain (later Admiral) Stern-post and widely regarded as the subject behind Captain Whiffle in Smollett's *Roderick Random* (1748). He was MP for Winchester from 1762 to 1765 and went on to be Lord-Lieutenant of Hampshire and Governor of the Isle of Wight from 1782 to 1791. He had previously been Governor from 1766 to 1770, MP for Christchurch, Hampshire, from 1751 to 1754, and he represented the family seat of Lymington from 1755 to 1761.

Admiral Harry Paulet, 6th Duke of Bolton, by Francis Cotes
© Metropolitan Museum of Art, New York

Lord Loughborough, 1785, by Sir Joshua Reynolds

Powlett died on 25th December 1794, with his reputation as a naval officer irrevocably tarnished by the Stern-post incident. Nor had he shone in politics.

Horace Walpole thought him *"...a silly, brutal, proud man, yet whose valour was ... problematical"* (GEC, Peerage, 2.215). The laudatory but disingenuous inscription on his monument in St Mary's Church, Basing, refers to his *"...excellent understanding and firm persevering disinterested attachement to the liberty of his country"*. At his death the Dukedom became extinct.

Alexander Wedderburn, first Earl of Rosslyn,
better known as **Lord Loughborough** (1733-1805), acquired the lease on Bolton House after the death of the 6th Duke of Bolton in 1794, and renamed it **Rosslyn House** for the period of his residency. Wedderburn was Solicitor-General in 1771, Attorney General in 1778, Lord Chief Justice of the Common Pleas from 1780 to 1793 and Lord Chancellor from 1793 to 1801. He was a very distinguished (and not at all eccentric) lawyer and politician, who was elected a Fellow of the Royal Society in 1787 and accepted an honorary vice-presidency at the Foundling Hospital in 1799.

"Wedderburn's struggle to establish himself in English practice was a difficult one, and at a time of pervasive English mistrust of Scots on the make, the transition from representing Anglicization as cultural improvement in Scotland to making professional progress as a Scottish lawyer and politician in England marked Wedderburn for life." (ODNB). Nevertheless, he effectively paved the way for Russell Square to become the favoured place of residence of the legal profession, which later earned Bloomsbury the nick-name 'Judgeland'. *"He became a valued government speaker in the House of Commons during the difficult years of the American War of Independence..."* (ODNB).

One incident is indelibly written in English history. Dr Benjamin Franklin obtained in 1773, by means of some unknown Member of Parliament, certain letters from crown officials in Massachusetts, written before the outbreak of hostilities and recommending the employment of a military force for the suppression of the discontent which prevailed in America. These letters he sent to the Speaker of the House of Assembly, and that body thereupon prayed for the recall of the officials. The application came before a committee of the Privy Council, known as 'the cockpit', when Wedderburn, as Solicitor General, took the role of Franklin's designated inquisitor. In a controlled tirade that lasted for well over an hour and which Franklin later likened to *"bull-baiting"*, Wedderburn gave Franklin a public and humiliating dressing-down, accusing him of being the *"mover and prime conductor"* of a conspiracy against the royal government in Massachusetts. He labelled Franklin a common thief, who had *"forfeited all the respect* of societies and of men", comparing *"the coolness and apathy of the wily New Englander"* with the *"revengeful temper of the negro Zanga"* in Dr Young's play of the *Revenge*. Pounding on the table, Wedderburn claimed that Franklin, far from being a servant of the colonial governments of Pennsylvania and Massachusetts, was instead behaving like *"…the minister of a foreign independent state"*, all with the intent of moving forward *"…the idea of a Great American Republic."* As Wedderburn continued his verbal assault, the crowd of British courtiers packed into the cockpit cheered the Solicitor General and mocked Franklin. The American, dressed in a simple velvet suit, kept his emotions firmly under control. As one of those present observed, *"…the Doctor… stood conspicuously erect, without the smallest movement of any part of his body. The muscles of his face had been previously composed as to afford a placid tranquil expression of countenance, and he did not suffer the slightest alteration of it to appear."* Wedderburn's conduct during this hearing would appear to be out of character with the Wedderburn known by Brougham who wrote of him: *"…his manners were courteous and even noble, polite in his demeanour, elegant, and dignified in his habits."* (*Statesmen of Time of George III.*, first series). Wedderburn's political career appears to have been hampered by his personal loyalty to George III as King rather than to a political party or an individual politician, which may explain why he was referred to in *The Letters of Junius*, as having *"…something about him which even treachery cannot trust"*

(GEC, Peerage, 11.174). He was also caricatured in the popular press at the time.

His special relationship with the King saw Bolton House being honoured by a royal visit on 21st June 1799, when the King was accompanied by Queen Charlotte and other members of the royal family.

Lord Loughborough caricature
© National Portrait Gallery, London

Franklin's 'interrogation' by Wedderburn

Following a lavish reception, the royal entourage proceeded to the Foundling Hospital, incorporating a great review of London's corps of volunteers. An account of the occasion in George III: His Court and Family, vol. ii refers to the spectators in the Foundling Chapel being *"affected, even to tears of loyal joy"* by the singing of the National Anthem, while the King was so pleased with the parade put on by the corps of volunteers that he commanded the Duke of York *"…to express the heartfelt satisfaction which every part of the conduct of those patriotic troops had excited in his mind."*

Wedderburn only remained a few years longer in Bolton House, before moving to St James's Square in 1803 and dying at Windsor in 1805, with the King uttering the words, *"Then he has not left a greater rogue behind him."* This was a barbed reference to Wedderburn's role in the Regency Bill, which led to the Regency Act of 1811, allowing George, Prince of Wales, to act as Regent while his father, King George III, was incapacitated (popularly known as the madness of King George). George ruled as the Prince Regent until his father's death, when he ascended the throne as King George IV. Wedderburn was nevertheless buried with full honours in St Paul's Cathedral and a commemorative tablet was installed in his memory on the front of No. 67 c.1905, which can just be made out in the two photographs of the east side of Russell Square featured in the first section of this chapter. The tablet disappeared when the building was incorporated into the Premier Hotel, with a shop front replacing the ground-floor wall where the plaque was positioned, unlike the equivalent tablet to Sir Thomas Lawrence (also visible in the photographs), which was 'rescued' from No. 65 when the original Imperial Hotel was extended and installed on the front of the current Imperial Hotel more than fifty years later. Wedderburn's impressive coat of arms displays the motto: *Illæso lumine solem,* which translates as 'To behold the sun with sight unhurt', which seems to resonate with the way he led his life.

Baron Loughborough's coat of arms

Bolton House was subsequently occupied by two distinguished 'pillars of the establishment', both of them judges and politicians:

Sir John Nicholl (1759-1838), judge and politician, was the next prominent person to occupy Bolton House. He was a Welsh MP and judge, noted *"...for inflexible impartiality and great strength and soundness of judgement"* (Sir John Nicholl, *The National Library of Wales* online). Nicholl was appointed King's Advocate in 1798, for which he was knighted, in accordance with tradition. He was elected MP for Penryn, Cornwall in 1802. After a brief period as MP for Hastings from 1806 to 1807, he was elected to the seat of Great Bedwyn and remained their MP until the Reform Act of 1832, when he retired. He was a staunch Tory throughout his political career and consistently opposed parliamentary reform and Roman Catholic emancipation. Sir William Holdsworth's *History of English Law* testifies to Nicholl's outstanding contribution as an ecclesiastical and Admiralty court judge. He died at Merthyr Mawr on 26th August 1838, where he was buried in the parish church. He had purchased the Merthyr Mawr estate in 1804 and rebuilt the residence. He also founded a national school at Bridgend in 1812, followed in 1817 by a savings bank.

Sir John Nicholl, by William Owen
© Oxford College Anon II, University of Oxford

Sir Vicary Gibbs, KC (1751-1820), was the last prominent person to occupy Bolton House, although it had been divided into two houses by the time of his death in 1820. He was an English judge and politician whose *"...incivility, condescension, and sarcasm earned him the nickname Vinegar Gibbs."* (R.A. Melikan, *ODNB*). He held legal office for the Prince of Wales from 1795 until 1805, the year he was made Solicitor General and knighted. The second Portland government in 1807 saw him made Attorney General. In the House of Commons, his most significant activity occurred in 1809, during the inquiry into military corruption and the activities of Mary Anne Clarke, mistress of Prince Frederick, Duke of York, who was commemorated in 2014 by a Marchmont Association blue plaque on the site of her former home in nearby Tavistock Place, where she was 'visited' by the Duke c.1803. Mary Anne's adroit response to Gibbs's examination delighted the attendant press, many of whom had suffered from his vitriolic attacks. His caustic tongue also didn't endear him to the House of Commons. In May 1812 he resigned his post to become a puisne judge in the Court of Common Pleas. Henry Brougham regarded the move as an expression of personal anxiety, attributing the aggressive prosecutor's apparent loss of nerve to the assassination of Spencer Perceval. Nevertheless, in February 1814, another promotion made him Chief Justice of the Common Pleas. Gibbs died on 8th February 1820 at Bolton House.

Sir Vicary Gibbs © National Portrait Gallery, London

The division of Bolton House

It is not entirely certain as to when Bolton House ceased to exist as a single entity, with Mr John Thomas Smith asserting in *A Rainy Day*, 1845 and 1861 (2 editions), that the house was "… *subsequently demolished and several houses built upon its site*", and this assumption being corrected by Mr. Wifred Whiffen in the final 1905 edition, in which he asserts that the house was still standing, but had been divided into several smaller residences. John Timbs, FSA, in *Romance of London*, 1865, describes the original Bolton House as two separate houses:

"Now Nos. 66 and 67, still distinguished by handsome carved mantelpieces, and a ceiling said to have been painted by Angelica Kaufmann. No. 67 is now occupied by the National Union of Teachers, and No. 66 by the Royal Photographic Society, the Secretary of which has kindly given me this information … the unity of the house is still preserved in the pitch of the slated roof: one of the residences is named Bolton House and the corner of Guilford Street, Bolton Gardens." (Smith's childhood memory of Bolton House was in 1777, when he was on a sketching expedition with his father to Pancras Old Church, from where he recalls an uninterrupted view of Bolton House across swathes of uncultivated farmland). The situation is further confused by No. 67 continuing to bear the name Bolton House for some time after its division. The frequently updated BCG narrows down the date of the division by listing John Harrison at No. 66 and Captain Blackall at No. 67 in the 1808 edition. BCG also first listed No. 68 in 1846, with Nos. 69-71 all being listed in 1857.

66 - Sir John Hullock (1767–1829), lawyer, judge, and Baron of the Exchequer, was listed at No. 66 as *"Baron Hullock"* in BCG, 1829. *The Annual Biography & Obituary, 1830, Vol XIV*, carries a *"memoir"* of Sir John Hullock, Knight, Baron of the Exchequer, in which he is praised as *"…one of the soundest lawyers in Westminster Hall"*. He was appointed as Serjeant-at-law in 1816, during which service *"…he was retained by the government to assist in conducting some momentous proceedings arising out of the disturbed state of the north… He also presided, with great ability, on the Commission of Lunacy respecting the earl of Portsmouth."* He became one of the Barons of the Court of the Exchequer in 1823. He published *The Law of Costs*, 1792 and *The Law of Costs in Civil Actions and Criminal Proceedings*, in two volumes, 1797 and 1810. He died on 31st July 1829. His fellow judge and close friend Mr. Baron Vaughan was effusive in his praise for Sir John: *"As a Judge, he was, in every sense of the word, a loyal, a right, and a good man; a man of the most quick perceptions, of the most sound, accurate, and discriminating judgment; a man whose industry was indefatigable, and who was perfectly acquainted with those depths and shoals of the law which render the investigation of it so intricate and difficult. As a private man, he was everything that could be wished; he was generous, humane, and charitable, and the most stubborn and inflexible integrity."* His widow, Dame Mary Hullock, survived him many years, and died on 18th November 1852. They had no children.

Sir John Hullock

John Benjamin Heath © National Portrait Gallery, London

John Benjamin Heath, **1st Baron**, FRS, FSA, FRGS (1790-1879), merchant and banker, lived at No. 66 from at least 1834 (BCG) until 16th January 1879 (SDs and WRB, 1879), when he died at home (ODNB). He was the son of John Heath, merchant of Genoa, and a grandson of Benjamin Heath the great book collector. He was educated at Harrow School, where he is said to have 'fagged' for Lord Byron. A merchant and foreign banker in London, he also served as Consul General for the Kingdom of Sardinia 1817-61, and is so listed in BCG, 1834-57, and in the SDs up to 1861. He was also Consul General for the Kingdom of Italy 1861-79, with a corresponding change to his listing in the SDs, 1862-78, as well an expanded range of credentials (FRS, FSA, FRGS and "The Baron" prefix in 1878). During the years No. 66 served as a Consulate it was effectively foreign territory, with all the associated diplomatic rights and privileges. Heath was Director of the Bank of England 1823-1872, Deputy Governor 1843-1844, Governor 1846-47, and Master of the Grocer's Company in 1829. He was created Baron Heath of the Kingdom of Italy 26th May 1867. He was elected a Fellow of the Society of Antiquaries in 1832, and a Fellow of the Royal Society in 1843. His collection of autographs was sold by Sotheby, Wilkinson & Hodge, 24th April 1879, and part of the family library of Amédee John Heath, Baron Heath by Sotheby, Wilkinson & Hodge 7th November 1892. His book, *Some account of the Worshipful company of grocers of the City of London*, 1829, 1854 & 1869, was re-published in 2011, being a 'must read' for researchers of domestic and international law, government and politics, legal history, business and economics, criminology and much more.

Other early occupants of No. 66 include:
John Harrison (BCG, 1808); Anthony Brough (BCGs, 1820-24). He and Mrs Brough appear in the *List of Governors and Officers of the Asylum for the Support and Education of the Deaf and Dumb Children of the Poor*, 1817 & 1821. Patrons listed include the Duke and Duchess of Gloucester, and Vice-Presidents, the Duke of Bedford and William Wilberforce. Anthony is also listed in the Annual reports of the London Infirmary for Diseases of the Eye in 1821 and 1823 as Governors paying an annual subscription of one guinea. He also subscribed to the Philanthropic Society in 1816, which placed Anthony at No. 66 from that year at least, although this coincides with the time Sir Vicary Gibbs (above) lived at Bolton House; Harry Lobb, surgeon (SDs, 1882-1889); Michael Mary Brophy (SDs, 1890-96); Royal Photographic Society (SDs, 1902-09 – see photo). *"Imperial Family Hotel, Harold Walduck"* is extended from Nos. 61-65 to include No. 66 in the 1910 SD, although it is listed as *"Imperial London Hotels Ltd. Turkish baths"* from 1916. The feature titled *"THE TRANSFORMATION OF RUSSELL SQUARE AND SOUTHAMPTON ROW"* in *THE DAILY GRAPHIC*, 13th September 1910, was accompanied by photographs illustrating the *"OLD-WORLD HOUSES… FAST DISAPPEARING TO MAKE WAY FOR THE EVER-INCREASING NUMBER OF HOTELS"*. The editorial linked to this feature postures: *"Another great interest in No. 66 is the supposition, put forward by the DAILY GRAPHIC some years ago, and contested by Mr J.W. Garnett at that time, that the house was the home of Thackeray's Sedley family. It is the only house in Russell Square with big bow windows. George Osborne, coming up Southampton Row, could well have seen Amelia Sedley in one of those windows, which to-day have a fine view down to Holborn."*
(See photographs in previous section)

No. 66 in 1903, when it was home to the Royal Photographic Society © CLSAC

Richard Meux Benson

67 - Richard Meux Benson (1824–1915),

Church of England clergyman and theologian, *"was born on 6th July 1824 at Bolton House"* (ODNB). His father, *"Thomas Starling Benson"*, is listed at No. 67 in BCGs, 1823-24. Benson was the key figure in the movement to found an Anglican religious order for men, to which John Keble had given impetus in a sermon of July 1863. The Society of St John the Evangelist came into being when three priests made their life vows of poverty, celibacy, and obedience on 27th December and Benson was elected Superior.

Benson's loyalty to the Church of England was undeviating, but his critique of the entire system of Christendom that had been inaugurated under Constantine was very radical. He believed that a renewed apostolic Christian community could emerge only from the disintegration of Christendom, and criticized political schemes for disestablishment as partial and unrealistic. Much of his motivation for foreign mission stemmed from his hope that the younger churches could forge more authentic expressions of Christianity. In 1870 Benson went to the USA to establish a branch of the society in Boston. His work in India began in 1874 and in South Africa in 1883. The era of his leadership drew to a close in 1890 when he resigned as Superior. He left for a long mission tour in India and then Canada, finally settling in Boston in 1892, where he was to stay until recalled to Cowley in 1899. He continued to be active in preaching and the conducting of retreats for several years until the onset of blindness and crippling rheumatism curtailed his ministry. He died at the mission house in Oxford on 14th January 1915.

BENSON *of* Cowley

Benson of Cowley

Sir Charles Flower, 1st Baronet, wearing the robes of the Lord Mayor of London

Sir Charles Flower, 1st Baronet (1763 – 1834), was the next titled person to occupy Bolton House, by which time it had been multiple-occupied for more than twenty years. Although he is listed at No. 67 in BCGs, 1829-34, the house was still known as Bolton House, and had a more impressive frontage than No. 66. He was not a lawyer but a merchant who served as Lord Mayor of London in 1808, having been appointed alderman in the City of London's Cornhill ward in 1801 and as Sheriff of the City of London in 1799. Flower traded in salt-meat, butter and cheese and was described as having acquired *"an ample fortune"* by the time of his ascendency to the mayoralty. He was created a Baronet of the Flower Baronets in 1809. Flower was also a liveryman of the Worshipful Company of Framework Knitters.

Sir Thomas Noon Talfourd (1795-1854), barrister, playwright and politician, who became Judge of the Court of Common Pleas, first lived at 56 Russell Square. He is listed at No. 56 as *"Mr. Serjeant Talfourd"* in BCGs from at least 1840 to at least 1846. By Michaelmas 1850 the Rate Books indicate that *"Mr Justice Thomas Noon Talfourd"* has moved to No. 67. He was presumably still resident there when he died in Stafford in 1854, as the ratepayer on Lady Day 1855 is his widow *"Lady Talfourd"*. E. Beresford Chancellor (1907) confuses the issue by alluding to an entry in the great actor Macready's *Diary* of December 12th 1839, in which he refers to a dinner party at Talfourd's house at 67 Russell Square, when the Rate Book has him living at No. 56. His biography in the *ODNB* reads: *"In the early 1830s he became famous for the dinner parties which he and his wife gave in their home at 56 Russell Square, London. His dinners were remembered for their informality, conviviality, swarming children, and numerous cats."* (See the entry for No. 56 in the South Side chapter for further details).

An earlier portrait of Thomas Noon Talfourd

Best known as the author of the plays *Ion* and *Glencoe*, Talfourd was a good friend of Charles Dickens, who dedicated the September 1837 edition of *The Pickwick Papers* to him - Talfourd being universally recognized as the person on which Dickens based the character of Tommy Traddles. In 1846 Talfourd and his wife visited the Dickens's in Lausanne, Switzerland, and in 1849 Talfourd met Dickens at Bonchurch, a seaside visit to which Dickens alludes fondly in his final reminiscence of the kindly lawyer. Prevented by his family's poverty from attending university, Talfourd visited Henry Crabb Robinson (see entry for No. 30 in the west side chapter) on 23rd February 1813 to discuss his future. On the advice of Lord Brougham he decided on a legal career. Talfourd reported on legal cases for *The Times* and contributed essays to *The New Law Journey* and *The New Monthly Magazine*, including a graphic portrait of Lord Tenterden (see entry for No. 28 in the west side chapter) in February 1833. He also wrote articles about drama and literature in *The Edinburgh Review*. During this period he became friends with Charles Lamb, Douglas William Jerrold, William Makepeace Thackeray, William Macready, Daniel Maclise and John Forster. Dickens, was a regular visitor to the Talfourd home. He recalled: *"If there ever was a house… where every art was honoured for its own sake, and where every visitor was received for his own claims and merits, that house was his... Rendering all legitimate deference to rank and riches, there never was a man more composedly, unaffectedly, quietly, immovable by such considerations... On the other hand, nothing would have astonished him so much as the suggestion that he was anyone's patron."* Chancellor, who wrote warmly of Talfourd's human

qualities, relates an event which took place at No. 67 which was *"…graphically described in the great actor's Diary for December 12, 1839"*… *"It was while dining with Talfourd here, in company with Forster, that Macready found, to his delight, that an anonymous play called Glencoe, which had been submitted to him, was the work of his host."* Serjeant Ballantine also recalls the social gatherings that took place at Talfourd's, which *"…included not only those who had obtained eminence in their profession, but the young who were striving to do so."*

On 7th January, 1835, Talfourd was elected to represent Reading in the House of Commons. He was a leading campaigner for universal male suffrage and an end to the slave trade. He was also in favour of women's rights and was responsible for *The Infant Custody Act* (1839) that gave the court discretion to award custody of children under seven years of age to the mother in cases of separation or divorce, provided she was not guilty of adultery. Encouraged by writers such as Charles Dickens, William Makepeace Thackeray and William Wordsworth, he campaigned for a new Copyright Act. This was designed to enable the dependants of authors to profit from the sales of their writings after their deaths. Dickens was so pleased with his efforts that he dedicated *The Pickwick Papers* (1837) to Talfourd, who eventually persuaded Parliament to pass the 1842 Copyright Act.

Talfourd was seized with an apoplectic fit while addressing a Stafford jury from the judge's bench, and

Sir Thomas Noon Talfourd © National Portrait Gallery, London

died shortly afterward. Claire Tomalin summarised Talfourd's achievements: *"Although his name is hardly remembered now, Talfourd was an outstanding figure in his day, idealistic, hard-working and effective... He had protested against the Peterloo Massacre in 1819, supported universal male suffrage and the total abolition of slavery, steered through the bill giving divorced women custody of their young children, and saw through the 1842 Copyright Act that for the first time protected authors' earnings in England during their lifetimes and for a period after their death.*

Other early occupants of No. 67 include:

Captain Blackall (BCG, 1808); Bowen May, solicitor (BCG, 1857, *"James Bowen May, solicitor (Bolton House)"* appears in the RBB, 1858, and in the SDs, 1861-62. *"Augustus Wakeford Bowen, solicitor"* is listed in the SDs, 1878-86. Various Mays occupy the house until 1900, with WRB, 1897, listing *"Bolton House, Bowen May"*); Frank Walter Goldstone MP is

No. 67 Entrance hall, 1913 © CLSAC

listed at Nos. 67 & 71 in 1911-14; The National Union of Teachers (NUT) and various associated bodies are listed simultaneously at Nos. 67 and 71 from 1902 to 1914, both being parts of the former Bolton House. *"J.H. Yoxall Esq., MP, Secretary"* is listed alongside the NUT, and it is he who provides Chancellor (1907) with the opportunity to wax lyrical about the opulent interior of No. 67, with detailed descriptions of the historical features which had survived from the Duke of Bolton's era, including *"...the well staircase... the beautifully decorated ceilings, in the manner of Angelica Kaufmann... the classic elegance (the word must be*

No. 67 The Drawing Room, 1913, with the Adam Chimney-Piece now in the Percy Pyne House, New York © Greater London Photograph Library

No. 66 first floor front room fireplace, 1910 © CLSAC

No. 67 The Great Drawing Room, 1913 © Greater London Photograph Library

forgiven me because I am speaking of Georgian style)
of the cornices and ceilings, somewhat in the Adams
manner… Some of the Mantelpieces are extraordinarily
fine, one particularly noticeable representing on the
entablature the Death of Socrates…" - all of which
are illustrated in the selection of photographs
of the interior of former Bolton House in the
Holborn Society's Collection.

No. 67 in 1903 © CLSAC

Chancellor's link with the past is supported by entries
in the SDs, 1861-1878, in which No. 71 is listed as
"Bolton Gardens". However, all of this would soon be
lost forever by the march of progress as half of this
historical house (No. 66) was demolished for the
extension of the original Imperial Hotel in 1911,
with No. 67 being incorporated into the Premier
Hotel in 1918, together with No. 68.

Nos. 68-70 were built c.1845 onwards, according
to entries in BCG (see below), extending the terrace
beyond former Bolton House into Guilford Street,
where the road was duly narrowed to create space
for these new buildings. No. 71, which appeared at the
same time, was accessed via an entrance in Guilford
Street, briefly known as Bolton Gardens, being the
surviving rear wing of former Bolton House.

68 - Early occupants include: Alexander Prince
was the first occupant of the newly built house,
according to BCG, 1846; then came Abraham
Moses, of A. Moses, Sons & Co. (BCG, 1857, RBB,
1858, SDs, 1861-62, and ABCCG, 1871). A marriage
announcement in the *Jewish Chronicle*, 1869, read:
*"On 10th February, Jacob Moses, youngest son of
Abraham Moses of 68 Russell Sq., to Maria, fifth
daughter of Lewis J Jordan of 6 Bedford Sq."* His second
son was married at No. 68 in 1858, according to *The
Sydney Morning Herald*; Mark Marcus (SDs, 1882-87,
joined by Herbert John Marcus in 1886-95). Mark
Marcus died on 23rd February 1895. His executors
were Herbert John Marcus, solicitor, and Almosnino
Lindo Charles Marcus; J. Hutchison (WRB, 1897, listed
as *"James Hutcheson W.S."* in 1899). He is listed with
both spellings in the SDs, 1896-98; Martingale Senior
(SD, 1900); Alfred Raphael (SDs, 1902-05)

No. 68 in 1903 © CLSAC

John William Sherwell, Clerk of the Guild of Saddlers (SDs, 1906-13), author of *A Descriptive and Historical Account of the Guild of Saddlers of the City of London*, 1889; Danish Club (SDs, 1914-16); *"Imperial London Hotels Ltd. Premier Hotel"* was first listed in the SD in 1918, with Harker's outfitters occupying new ground floor commercial premises numbered 68 by 1929 and during World War II (see 1946 photograph of Premier Hotel, below).

69 - Lionel John Alexander Monckton (1861-1924),

songwriter and composer of musical theatre, who became Britain's most popular composer of Edwardian musical comedy in the early years of the 20th century, lived at No. 69 from 1904 to at least 1924 (SD listings). Monckton soon became a regular composer (and sometimes lyricist) of songs for the very successful series of frothy musical comedies performed at London's Gaiety Theatre, under the management of George Edwardes, which premiered throughout the 1890s and into the first decade of the 20th-century. At the same time, Monckton contributed songs for the musicals playing at Edwardes's Daly's Theatre, which tended more towards romantic comedies than the light musicals presented at the Gaiety. *The Arcadians* (1909), co-composed with his *Kitty Grey* colleague, Howard Talbot, was also the best Monckton musical - arguably the best musical of the whole Edwardian age - and it scored an enormous worldwide success. Edwardes purchased the lease of the Adelphi Theatre and began his productions there with another Monckton and Millar hit, *The Quaker Girl*, in 1910. Monckton's music remained popular in Britain until after World War II, when American musicals took over the stage, and even into the latter half of the 20th century, in the case of his most popular shows. Monckton died at No. 69 at the age of 62 and is buried in Brompton Cemetery. He left an estate valued at £79,518 (equivalent to £4.34M in 2016), having contributed materially to the success of a quarter of a century of musical shows. Principal shows and original runs in which Monckton was the principal composer include: the principal composer include:

A Country Girl (1902) – 729 performances
The Cingalee (1904) – 391 performances
The Spring Chicken (1905) – 401 performances
The Girls of Gottenberg (1907) – 303 performances
Our Miss Gibbs (1909) – 636 performances
The Arcadians (1909) – 809 performances
The Quaker Girl (1910) – 536 performances
The Boy (1917) – 801 performances

Other early occupants of No. 69 include:
John Henry Benbow, solicitor (BCG, 1857, RBB, 1858, SDs, 1861-78, and ABCCG, 1871); Mrs Bolton (SD, 1882); Dalton Thomas Miller (SDs, 1886-92); Thomas Ernest Wirgman (SDs, 1894-1903, and WRB, 1897); Librarie Internationale occupied the ground floor commercial premises at No. 69 from 1929/30, with B. Bright Bros Ltd, tobacconists, trading there during World War II.

Lionel Monckton

No. 69 in 1903 © CLSAC

70 - Early occupants of No. 70 include: Charles Turner Simpson, barrister (BCG, 1857, RBB, 1858, and SDs, 1861-62); George White, solicitor (ABCCG, 1871); Leon David (SD, 1878); Morris Davis (SDs, 1882-94); Edward Upton (SDs, 1895-97, WRB, 1897); James Arthur Brown, surgeon, and William Frederick Pedler, dentist (SD, 1899, but only James Arthur Browne, surgeon, from 1900 to 1908, when he is joined by Quintin Chalmers MD, who is listed alone from 1909 until at least 1921; Stanley Griffin Smith, trunk-maker, occupied the ground floor commercial premises from 1929/30 and during 1939-44.

71 - Richard D'Oyly Carte (1844-1901), was a theatrical impresario, talent agent, composer and hotelier during the latter half of the Victorian era.

Richard D'Oyly Carte

Rising from humble beginnings, Carte built two of London's theatres and a hotel empire, while also establishing an opera company that ran continuously for over a hundred years and a management agency representing some of the most important artists of the day. Though unlisted at No. 71 in SDs, the SGIF/SGB rate books show that D'Oyly Carte lived in Russell Square for around five years, his address being *"Bolton Gardens"*, not yet No. 71, but always listed immediately after No. 70. He first appears at Lady Day 1881, when his name - always given as *"Carte D'Oyley"* with a rogue second E - is inked in above that of the previous occupier (Miss Julia Anna Seed). From Michaelmas 1881 he is shown as the ratepayer. His last appearance is at Lady Day 1886 (the year after the death of his first wife). The address was also indicated on maps of the time as *"Bolton Gardens"*.

Chancellor writes, in a footnote linked to No. 71 in the main text on page 216, "*Mr. D'Oyly Carte is stated to have occupied this house when it was a separate tenement.*" Richard lived here during what was probably his most productive period before moving to Adelphi Terrace in 1886. His close friend and business partner, Michael Gunn, also lived at No. 45 while in London, being listed in the 1882-86 SDs. D'Oyly was not part of the family's surname, and

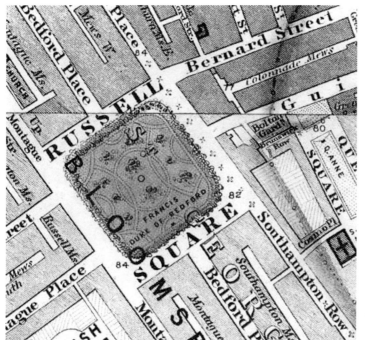

Stanford (Edward), Library Map of London and its suburbs (1862-1871) showing Bolton Gardens

that wholesome, well-crafted, family-friendly, English comic opera could be as popular as the risqué French works dominating the London musical stage in the 1870s. To that end, he brought together the dramatist W.S. Gilbert and composer Arthur Sullivan and, together with his wife Helen Carte, he nurtured their collaboration on a series of thirteen Savoy operas. He founded the D'Oyly Carte Opera Company and built the state-of-the-art Savoy Theatre to host the Gilbert and Sullivan operas. He also built the adjacent Savoy Hotel and acquired other luxury hotels.

He later built the Palace Theatre to house a new school of English grand opera, although he only ever produced one grand opera, *Ivanhoe*, by Sullivan. Nevertheless, his partnership with Gilbert and Sullivan, and his careful management of their operas and relationship, created a series of works whose success was unprecedented in the history of musical theatre. His opera company, later operated by his wife Helen and then by his son, Rupert, and granddaughter, Bridget, promoted those works for over a century, and they are still performed today.

No. 71, a.k.a. Bolton Gardens, in 1903 – © CLSAC

Richard D'Oyly Carte's parents and siblings were plain Cartes. Though Richard junior was given D'Oyly as his middle name, his brother was Henry W Carte. The D'Oyly middle name was passed on by Richard to his son Rupert (and possibly also his other son Lucas). Both were teenagers in 1881. David Hayes amusingly pointed out that if Richard's wife had been the ratepayer in Bolton Gardens, she would have been listed as Carte Blanche. Carte believed

Mr. W. S. Gilbert: "Well, D'Oyly, and when do you think you will want me again?"

Gilbert and Carte cartoon

121

Savoy Theatre in 1881

George Grossmith and D'Oyly Carte cartoon

At the unveiling of an English Heritage blue plaque in 2010, the Director Mike Leigh said of D'Oyly Carte: *"He was the first person in the country to have a lift installed in a private home, was a successful composer in his own right, and even was one of the first people in the country to take up jogging: he would be spotted running around Russell Square, where he lived, when this type of exercise was just not done."* Other eccentricities included fitting out a holiday home on an island in the Thames where he kept a pet crocodile. Mr Leigh added that in the cut-throat and risky world of theatre production, D'Oyly Carte quickly earned a reputation for never backing a dud. English Heritage historian Susan Skedd added: *"He was a shrewd businessman and an outstanding stage manager. He succeeded in maintaining his worldwide monopoly over Gilbert and Sullivan productions and set new standards in staging and singing in opera. He also proved to be an innovative hotelier and created the first luxury hotel in London… The Savoy was the first place to serve cocktails and have electric lights, for example… He was unrivalled in his day and is the first opera impresario to be honoured with a blue plaque."*

Savoy Theatre auditorium

D'Oyly Carte Opera Company poster

"Queen Victoria - I thought gags were things that were put by authority into people's mouths. D'Oyly Carte - These gags, your Majesty, are things that people put into their own mouths without authority" (Richard D'Oyly Carte).

Thomas Leverton Donaldson (1795-1885), architect, notable as a pioneer in architectural education, as a co-founder and President of the Royal Institute of British Architects, and as a winner of the RIBA Royal Gold Medal, is listed at No. 71 in BCG, 1857, and in the RBB, 1858, in which No. 71 is described as *"Bolton Gardens House"*. He is joined by James Smollet Donaldson, architect, in the SDs, 1861-63, with James alone being listed in 1864-65. Thomas was described by the Prince of Wales in 1879 as the father of the Royal Institute and of the profession. In 1841 he was appointed as University College London's first Chair in Architecture – one of the first in the UK, founding what later became the UCL Bartlett School of Architecture, which celebrated its 175th anniversary in 2016. He held this post until 1865. He reworked substantial sections of the Wilkins building at University College London (UCL), and designed its Flaxman Gallery and library buildings. He also designed Dr Williams's Library in Gordon Square, built in 1848-49 as University Hall to mark the passing of the Dissenters' Chapels Act in 1844. Thomas died at home at 21 Upper Bedford Place on 1st August 1885.

Other early occupants of No. 71 include:

Thomas Leverton Donaldson © Wellcome collection

Dr Williams's Library, Gordon Square

"Sir Frederick Perkins, MP, JP, FRGS (Bolton Gardens)" appears in the SDs, 1868-79, with his full collection of titles from 1875; No. 72 is not listed in 1880-6; The National Union of Teachers and its associated benevolent funds, provident society, all under the stewardship of its charismatic Secretary, James Henry Yoxall, MP, occupied No. 71 from 1890 to 1914; *"Evan Evans, motor car agent"* is listed in the 1930 SD, from where he ran his coach tour business from 1933 until 1941, after which he made the pragmatic switch to groceries for the remainder of World War II.

Evan Evans (1882–1965), coach tour operator and local politician, was a Welsh-born, self-made man who came to London in 1897, where he first worked for a cousin in his dairy off the Edgware Road, in Marylebone. By the time he was 22 he owned three dairies, but sold them to his brothers during the First World War, and turned to farming, renting a large arable farm near St Albans. When farming became unprofitable, he returned to London and opened Woburn Garages in the Colonnade mews to the east of Russell Square, where he started to deal in cars, with a showroom in Russell Square. In the late 1920s he opened a small hotel in Bloomsbury, and in the early 1930s bought the Celtic Hotel, 62 Guilford Street. Evans founded Evan Evans Tours in 1933 at 71 Russell Square. He was already hiring out chauffeur-driven cars, and saw the potential for using larger vehicles. Foreign agents subcontracted to Evan Evans Tours, which made all the transport arrangements and hotel reservations for private tours and provided vehicles for excursions out of London. The company also sold individual seats on tours through travel agents and hotels. At its peak the company operated over seventy vehicles, including coaches and chauffeur-driven cars. Based in London, it grew into one of the largest private hire coach operators in Britain. Evans became interested in local politics after the First

World War, and in 1922 was elected to St Pancras borough council, remaining a councillor until 1959 (except for 1945–9). A right-wing member of the Conservative Party, he was an alderman from 1935 to 1945, and mayor of St Pancras between 1939 and 1941. In 1928 he was elected chairman of the public health committee, and when he was re-elected to the council in 1949 he immediately resumed this position. As chairman of the emergency committee during World War II, he was responsible for providing shelter for those made homeless by the blitz, and in 1941, as mayor, he opened the St Pancras travelling library, the capital's first mobile library. He was also a member of the London County Council from 1931 to 1934. Elected a freeman of the City of London in 1946, he was a liveryman of the Loriners' and Carmen's companies. He served as a JP on the Pentonville prison bench justices committee. From his early days in London, Evans was closely involved in the Jewin Chapel in Clerkenwell, the oldest and largest Welsh chapel in London. He became a senior elder, and secretary from 1938 until his death, and was moderator of the Presbyterian Church of Wales from 1961 to 1962. After the Jewin Chapel was destroyed in 1940 Evans was instrumental in raising the money to rebuild it in 1961. He also served as president of the Cardiganshire Society in London and the London Welsh rugby football club. Evan Evans died on 24th July 1965 at his home in the Celtic Hotel, Guilford Street, a few metres from Russell Square. After his death his son, Dafydd Gwyn Evans, ran the family's coach and tour business until it was taken over by the Leeds-based company Wallace Arnold in 1969.

Premier Hotel

The original Premier Hotel was opened in 1910 on the site of present day Premier House at 150 Southampton Row, which was a private block of flats at the time. Henry Walduck acquired the building in 1909 with a view to converting it into a 180 room overflow for the nearby Imperial Hotel, where customer demand had far exceeded expectations.

The Premier Hotel, Southampton Row in 1910

Premier House, 150 Southampton Row today

The SDs confirm that the National Union of Teachers remained at Nos. 67 and 71 until 1914, and Nos. 68, 69 and 70 were still individual houses in 1916.

The Premier Hotel was trading at Nos. 67-68 from 1918, according to both the SDs and a promotional postcard of that year, which features the hotel's Queen Square elevation. In the 1922 photograph (p.125) of the east side of Russell Square, the Premier Hotel sign can just about be made out on the side of the former Bolton House entrance portico at No. 67, and no signs on the upper walls. The hotel was listed at Nos. 67-69 in 1925, with a certain Quintin Chalmers QC still occupying No. 70. This had changed by 1929, when the exterior of the four original houses had been homogenized by what appears to have been stone cladding, so as to create the impression of a single entity, which was reinforced by large PREMIER HOTEL signs on the Russell Square and Guilford Street elevations. The entrance to the hotel and official address was still No. 67, but the ground floor was entirely occupied by commercial premises and renumbered 67-73. The aerial view of the east side taken in 1921 shows (from left to right) the Morton Hotel, Hotel Russell, the original Georgian houses numbered 67-70 prior to them being subsumed into the Premier Hotel, and the completed Imperial Hotel. The hotel looks surprisingly 'worse for wear' in the c.1932 photograph (p.127), with new signs being the only visible improvement in the 1946 photograph (p.130). Also, note the bold sign at the rear of the hotel advertising rooms for 5 shillings a night at all of the Imperial Hotel Group's hotels. The 'Bohemian' Librarie Internationale, which was trading at No. 69 in 1930, had moved to the more advantageous corner premises by 1939, although Stanley Griffin Smith, trunk-maker, had retained his trading address at No. 70. All of the shops appear to be suffering from the post-war malaise that affected the entire city.

Aerial view of the east side of Russell Square, photographed in 1921

Premier Hotel postcard c.1918 © CLSAC

President Hotel

The Premier Hotel was demolished in the early 1960s, along with the adjacent buildings in Guilford Street, to make way for the construction of the **President Hotel**, which opened in spring 1963, with its entrance in Guilford Street. It was to be called the Premier Hotel after its predecessor, but Imperial Hotels Ltd decided to change the name to the President, in return for which they were on the receiving end of a flurry of abusive letters from objectors to this perceived Americanisation of London, even though President Kennedy of the United States was much admired in Britain at the time, especially by the younger generation. Another hotel sporting the name President Kennedy had been due to open near Euston station around the same time, triggering a swift intervention by the owners of the President, resulting in the owner of the Euston hotel dropping President from their name. President Kennedy was tragically assassinated on 22nd November 1963.

The President Hotel was opened by Raine Spencer, socialite, London politician, and daughter of Dame Barbara Cartland. Raine went on to marry Earl Spencer, thus becoming stepmother to Diana, Princess of Wales, and at 23 she became the youngest member of Westminster City Council. She also served on the Greater London Council for Richmond, with a special interest in environmental planning and ancient buildings, which is ironic considering the impending demise of the adjacent Imperial Hotel. Her three marriages accorded her five different titles: Honourable Mrs Gerald Legge, Viscountess (or Lady) Lewisham, Countess of Dartmouth, Countess Spencer and Comtesse de Chambrun. She officiated at the opening of the President Hotel as Lady Lewisham, and remained in politics for 17 years as Countess of Dartmouth. The opening also got a mention by David Frost on the popular satirical TV programme *That Was the Week That Was* (TW3).

| Premier Hotel and Guilford Street c.1932

Nos. 67-70 in 1922

Raine Spencer (left) and her mother,
Dame Barbara Cartland

The Beatles stayed at the spanking new President Hotel throughout the spring and summer of 1963, having previously stayed in the Royal Hotel in Woburn Place (also part of the Imperial Hotels group) on their first visit to London in 1961. They were photographed by Dezo Hoffmann in Guilford Street on 2nd July as they strolled past the front entrance of the hotel towards Russell Square. This was part of the now famous session called *A Day in the Life of The Beatles*, for which Hoffmann was commissioned by the *Liverpool Echo* newspaper. This iconic photograph appeared on posters and in magazines. *"Reproduced in countless publications all over the world, it remains one of the best and liveliest pictures of the group."* (*The Beatles in London*, 1994). Hoffman also photographed them in their hotel room, No. 114, and in the hotel foyer posing on luggage trolleys with four porters behind them. The day before, the 'Fab Four', as they were then known, had just finished recording *She Loves You* in Studio 2 at Abbey Road Studios. During their residence at the hotel many of their Liverpool musician friends also came to stay, including Cilla Black, Gerry and the Pacemakers, and their manager with the Midas touch, Brian Epstein. The Beatles were also visited by numerous journalists and photographers, including Robert Freeman and Norman Parkinson, who shot his classic wide-angled portrait of the group here, dubbed the 'shish kebab picture' by Parkinson. Hotel director Richard Walduck remembers, *"One morning in 1963 I suggested to four young guests that, in London, at that time, ties were worn at breakfast. The head porter, Kevin Napier, said, 'You can't speak to them like that. They're the Beatles.' I said, 'Who?'"*.

Premier Hotel occupying Nos. 67-73 in 1929

The Beatles, captured by Dezo Hoffmann as they strolled along Guilford Street on 2nd July 1961, and the same view today.

The President was considered state-of-the-art at the time of its opening, with its private baths and Philips television sets in every room, although today it carries a 3-star rating. The saw-tooth elevation above the Guilford Street entrance and on the Russell Square elevation was continued in the design of the adjacent Imperial hotel, completed in 1966, both of which Pevsner described as, *"…a tawdry affair… unworthy of [its] position…"* (see photo in section 1 of this chapter). An extra floor was added to the hotel c.1995 and the exterior was sensitively restored in 2015 to something approaching its original appearance.

Staged pillow-fight picture of The Beatles in Room 114

The Beatles outside Room 114

Norman Parkinson's 'shish kebab picture' of the 'Fab Four'

1903

| 1946

These photographs illustrate three stages in the
evolution of 68-70 Russel Square, from the original
four Georgian houses in the 1903 photograph, which
were remodelled in the 1930 to form the Premier
Hotel, as shown in the 1946 photograph. The 1960s
heralded the redevelopment of the site to form
the ultra-modern President Hotel, which has largely
retained its appearance (apart from the mansard
roof addition) in the contemporary photograph.

3.3

The Site of Hotel Russell - Nos. 1-8 (between Guilford Street and Bernard Street)

Nos. 1-8 Russell Square collectively formed Southampton Terrace, which was built around the same time that the houses on the east terrace of Southampton Row were extended northwards into what was to become Russell Square. Southampton Terrace is named on Richard Horwood's map of 1792-99, but the houses were not numbered until William Faden revised Horwood's map in 1813 (see maps in section 1 of this chapter). The terrace extends north from what was then Upper Guilford Street (the 'posh' end) to what became Bernard Street (named after Sir Thomas Bernard, who was Vice-President of the Foundling Hospital in 1806), both of which were developed by the prolific speculative builder, James Burton, on land belonging to the Foundling Hospital

Estate. Building leases for Nos. 1-4 Southampton Terrace were granted to Burton in 1796 and 1798. Henry Scrimshaw was granted leases on Nos. 5 and 8 in 1798 and 1797 respectively, with the leases on Nos. 6 and 7 being granted respectively to William Criswell and John Hunter in 1798. Southampton Terrace retained its house numbers when Russell Square was first developed, which explains why the numbering sequence, which survives today, begins at the mid-point of the east terrace rather than at one of the Square's corners, in the conventional manner. The photograph of former Southampton Terrace was taken in 1894, just before the houses were demolished by the Bedford Estate in July of that year. The site remained vacant for two years whilst the

One of the earliest photographs of Hotel Russell, published in the *Illustrated London News*, 16th June 1900

Hotel Russell viewed from Russell Square Gardens, winter 2015

11th Duke of Bedford considered proposals from some of London's leading architects, which included the construction of a Guild Hall. A building lease was finally granted to Frederick Hotels Limited on 24th April 1896, but not before the Duke had personally approved the architect's plans for their new hotel, which happened to have been drawn up by the Bedford Estate's own surveyor, Charles Fitzroy Doll. Letters exchanged between the Duke and Doll in March 1897 also reveal the decision to clad the building in its famous 'thé-au-lait' terracotta finish. The Duke no doubt also had a say in the naming of the hotel, which assumed the Bedford family name, Russell.

View down Bernard Street, c.1905, illustrating how Hotel Russell dwarfed the Georgian terrace

Rear view of 6-8 Southampton Terrace from Bernard Street, by the Duke of Bedford, c.1892

Charles Fitzroy Doll JP, FRIBA (1850–1929), was an English architect of the Victorian and Edwardian eras. He was educated in Germany, and on his return to Britain he trained as an architect under Sir Matthew Digby Wyatt, where he worked on drawings for the India Office, Whitehall, London (1866-1868). He was appointed Surveyor to the Bedford Estates in 1885, and designed the Hotel Russell in 1898, and later, the equally extravagant Imperial Hotel. His design for Grade II listed 42-56 Torrington Place (1907-08), now home to Waterstone's Bookshop, is described by the *Oxford Index* as *"…the exquisitely detailed Flemish Franco-Gothic terrace of shops with apartments over them"*. He also

Hotel Russell replaced these houses in Guilford Street – by the Duke of Bedford, c.1892

designed the relatively understated Headquarters building for the Express Dairy Company (1904) at nearby 15-17 Tavistock Place, which also served as Headquarters for the British Transport Police and now houses a faculty of the London School of Hygiene and Tropical Medicine. Although Doll resisted the use of terracotta adornments at Tavistock Place, he nevertheless created a decorative effect on the façades with the discreet use of different coloured bricks. His original design, partially illustrated by the historical artist's

Grade II listed 42-56 Torrington Place (1907-08)

Artist's impression of Charles Fitzroy Doll's original Express Dairy HQ in Tavistock Place

London School of Hygiene and Tropical Medicine, 15-17 Tavistock Place (1904)

impression, included three triangular pediments which were lost after the building sustained significant bomb damage in World War II. The left-hand section with the archway and ornate brick entrance in the surviving building was apparently not envisaged by the artist.

His reputation for elaborate architecture gave rise to the popular expression 'Dolled-up', which was typically used to describe any person making a special effort to look smart and attractive, usually for a special occasion, or to describe particularly plush surroundings. Doll was a member of Holborn Borough Council, and served as Mayor of Holborn in 1904–1905 and 1912–1913. He lived at Hadham Towers, Much Hadham, Hertfordshire, where he was a Justice of the Peace. His son, Christian Charles Tyler Doll (1880–1955), inherited his father's architectural practice and was partly responsible for reconstructing the grand staircase of the Palace of King Minos at Knossos in Crete.

A detailed account of Hotel Russell follows the entries (below) for each of the notable former residents of the Georgian houses which previously occupied the site:

1 - Joseph Robley (1742-1805), merchant, slave owner and colonial administrator in Tobago, is listed at No. 1 in BCG, 1808, even though he had died there on 9th September 1805, and his main residence was on the 'West Indian' island of Tobago. Let me explain, beginning with an extract from an entry in the *Annual Register*, 1805, which briefly alludes to his life and legacy: *"At the house of his nephew, John Robley, esq. in Russell-square, aged 63, Joseph Robley, esq. late of the island of Tobago, where he had filled the offices of governor and perpetual president… he first introduced the plough into the West Indies with effect, where, by his superior skill in the management of his plantations, he amassed the wealth of 30,000 l. per annum; 40,000 l. of which he has bequeathed among his relations and friends and the remainder to his aforesaid nephew and heir."* Joseph's will states that he left to John Robley three separate sugar plantations, each of about 400 acres, *"…with all the slaves thereon or belonging thereto, supposed to be around 900."* He also manumitted *"my mulatto woman named Betty and my negro woman named Peggy"* and left them four enslaved girls each. The explanation for this is that Joseph's wife and four children remained in Russell Square, while he formed two additional families on Tobago.

Tobago plantation scene

Joseph's time in Tobago was one of turmoil. In 1771 there was an insurrection by the slaves, which was put down ruthlessly, with seven slaves being executed, and their right arms being cut off before they were burned at the stake. Joseph's sugar estates were plagued with ants, which forced him to concentrate on cotton. From 1794 to 1795 Joseph enjoyed almost complete control of the affairs of the Colony while acting as Governor, but in 1796 he was seized whilst on a ship heading for Boston and imprisoned in Gaudeloupe. His release was secured by the British government after three months of ill treatment and he returned to Tobago. 1807/1808 was a most eventful time for the Robley family. Both father John Robley and Joseph Robley died within a very short space of time leaving the bulk of their estates to **John Robley Jnr** (1775-1821), merchant and slave owner, who for a long time had had power of attorney for all of Joseph's affairs in England. John almost immediately lobbied and obtained the support of the then British Foreign Secretary, Lord Castlereagh, who duly authorised his appointment to the governing Council in Tobago, where he went to live on the Golden Grove Estate. The Prerogative Court in Canterbury reported that John Robley *"quitted the country in 1808"*, leaving behind *"his wife Caroline Robley"*. By 1810, he was

well established in Tobago and becoming a very real power in the Assembly. However, he fell out with the Governor, Sir William Young, and there were questions about his financial probity – being an altogether less scrupulous person than his uncle. Although a codicil to John's will reveals that he did follow in his uncle's footsteps in one respect, by starting a second family in Tobago and having several fleeting relationships. His most important interracial relationship was with Eliza McKenzie, whom he described in 1812 as *"a free Mulatto woman residing with me as my housekeeper"*. Eliza was the mother of at least six of his children. He had a further daughter and son by two separate 'Tobago women'. He died in November 1821, leaving all of his mixed race children substantial sums in his will, along with his surname. Apart from the value of the thriving business he inherited from his father, John had placed a combined value of £100,000 on the Golden Grove and Friendship Estates, which will have been equivalent to £8.75M in 2016. In Tobago today there is a flourishing 'clan' of Robleys. *"Mrs Robley"*, presumed to be John Robley's wife, Caroline, is listed at No. 1 in BCGs, 1820-21, the house being one part of her substantial inheritance. The Slavery Abolition Act 1833, defined as *"An Act for the Abolition of Slavery throughout the British Colonies; for promoting the Industry of the manumitted Slaves; and for compensating the Persons hitherto entitled to the Services of such Slaves"*, put an end to slavery in the British Empire on 28th August 1834. On 1st August 1985, Trinidad and Tobago became the first country in the world to declare a national holiday to commemorate the abolition of slavery.

Other early occupants of No. 1 include:
George Anstey (BCG, April 1824). He and his wife Judith had four children. The family also lived at 35 and 39 Tavistock Square. George died on 22nd September 1826, with Harrow School giving his eldest son's address as 3 Upper Montague Street in 1825-26; William Metcalfe (BCG, 1834); John Foster (BCGs, 1840-43); John Entwisle (BCGs, 1844-57, RBB, 1858, SDs, 1861-76, with FRGS, FGS suffixes, and ABCCG, 1871); Mrs Francis (SD, 1879); Noah Davis (SDs, 1884-1894).

1a - Sir Francis Charles Oppenheimer (1870-1961), *"diplomatist"* (ODNB), was born at No. 1a in 1870. He was the oldest of seven children of Sir Charles Oppenheimer (1836-1900), City merchant and later British Consul-General at Frankfurt am Main, and Bertha (d. 1919), daughter of Leopold Goldbeck, a Frankfurt cloth merchant. Sir Charles is listed simply as Charles Oppenheimer in the SDs, 1865-71, with *"Mrs Oppenheimer"* alone being unconventionally listed in the ABCCG, 1871.

Sir Francis described himself as the *"Stranger within"* the Foreign Office (John McDermott, ODNB, 2007), having served in the Diplomatic Service before and during World War I, and succeeding his father as honorary British Consul to Frankfurt in 1900. David Lloyd George drew on Oppenheimer's memoranda on German social legislation when framing his own national insurance scheme, praising Sir Francis in October 1911 as *"one of the ablest consuls of the British empire…"* (The Times, 16th October 1911). However, this did not prevent him becoming the target of a press campaign against Britain's representatives in Germany, whose loyalty was impugned because of their German names. He took the unusual step of robustly defending himself in a letter to The Times: *"As I was born in London, took my degrees at Oxford, and am a member of the English bar, it is hardly correct to count me among 'the foreigners'. If my family name does not sound English, I need hardly remind you that I share this disadvantage with a large proportion of the oldest families in England."* (The Times Commercial Supplement, 23rd Oct 1908). He was knighted in 1907, and created KCMG in 1919. He retired from the Diplomatic Service in 1920 and died in 1961.

Sir Francis Charles Oppenheimer in 1900

Charles Lambert (1814-1887), tobacco manufacturer, is listed at No. 1a in the 1851 Census and in BCG, 1857. His father, Charles (I) Lambert, was a tobacco manufacturer, who also ran snuff mills in Effingham, Surrey. In 1834 Charles (II) Lambert entered into a business partnership with Charles Butler, establishing Lambert and Butler, cigar makers at 38, St John Street, Clerkenwell. In 1836 they opened additional premises in Drury Lane. The business grew steadily over the ensuing decades and established Charles (II)'s reputation as the finest judge of cigar tobacco in London. In 1842 Charles (II) married Ann (née) Brooker. The 1851 Census finds Charles (II) living with Ann in Russell Square with two daughters aged one and three, and two servants. By 1861 the family is living in leafy Battersea with three sons, three daughters and five servants. During the 1860s Lambert and Butler expanded rapidly under the partnership of Charles's eldest son, Charles Edward (I) and the son of Charles Butler, Charles junior. By 1870 the total amount of capital invested in the company had grown to £87,200, only a little less than that of its most serious rival W.D. & H.O. Wills. Charles (II) died in 1887 aged 73. Despite merging with Imperial Tobacco in 1903, the brand name Lambert & Butler is still going strong today, due to Imperial Tobacco not owning the trademark on the original name.

Other early occupants of No. 1a include: (1a) Jesse Cato (BCGs, 1829-34. *"Mrs Cato"* remained at No. 1a until at least 1846. She was also listed in the SDs, 1841-42). Jesse Cato was one of nine children. He and his wife, Sarah, married on 26th December 1836 (The Lady's Magazine, 1836), but he barely survived another year, dying at No. 1a on 19th January 1838, aged 61/2; Alexander Stewart, dental surgeon (RBB, 1858); Hyman Abraham Abrahams Esq. (SDs, 1861-1862); Rev. Robert Henry Augustus Bradley, MA, perpetual curate of the church of St Peter, Regent Square from 1874 (to 1905?), is listed at No. 1a in the SDs, 1875-93, with his MA suffix from 1881.

2 - Dr Henry Shuckburgh Roots MD (1785-1861), physician, lived at No. 2 for at least two decades and died there in 1861. He is listed in BCGs, 1840-57, in the SDs, 1841-61, and in the RBB, April 1858; although the 1844 College of Physicians Directory lists his home address as No. 42 (home to *"Sir C. Marshall"* for much of the time Roots is listed at No. 2 in the 1840s and therefore presumed to be a typing error). Henry, whose father George was also a doctor, became a Fellow of the Medical and Chirurgical Society (later the Royal Society of Medicine) in 1819. By 1853 he was consulting physician to St Thomas's Hospital, London. He found fame within his profession as a pioneering advocate of plastic surgery. In the course of his work at St Pancras Infirmary, he came across a hideously deformed shoemaker, whose nose had been eaten away by the mercury treatment then used as a 'cure' for syphilis.

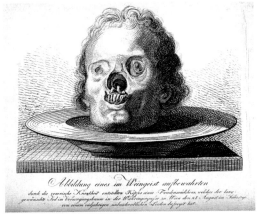

Medical drawing depicting the type of facial deformity caused by syphilis © Wellcome Images

Despite the fact that anaesthetics had not yet been invented, the patient was given a skin graft by a local doctor, and survived. An article by Henry Shuckburgh Roots in the Lancet (1823) describes how he tried a number of treatments for an enlarged thyroid in a 19-year-old girl, including the regular application of leeches to the thyroid. Eventually, after attending a talk by Dr Roget, who recommended the use of iodine to reduce the size of the thyroid, he successfully applied this remedy and subsequently reported his results.

Other early occupants of No. 2 include:
William Harvey (BCG, 1808); Dr Wilkinson (BCGs, 1820-34); Joseph Levy (SD, 1862, and listed as "Joseph Moses Levy" in the ABCCG, 1871); William Latham (SDs, 1878-82); and Nathaniel Harris (SDs, 1886-94).

3 - Sir Felix Booth, 1st Baronet (1775-1850),
was a wealthy gin distiller and promoter of Arctic exploration. He was the third and youngest son of Philip Booth, Esq. of Russell Square. Deborah Colville (A Tale of Two Squares, UCL Project) states that Felix lived with his family at No. 3 from 1808 to 1820, although he is listed at No. 3 in BCG, 1808, and is joined by "Miss Booth" from 1820 to 1824.

The Booth family were established wine merchants as early as 1569. They moved from the north-east of England in 1740 to establish their Booth's Gin distillery in London. Felix Booth launched his own brand of

gin in 1790 and his original recipe (a domestic gin in the London Dry style) was in use until production stopped around 2006. In 1832, Felix bought the site of the old Ophthalmic Hospital in Albany Street, Regent's Park as a site for his distillery, and in 1840 he went into partnership with William Grimble to produce vinegar from the spirit left over from the manufacturing process. The venture was unsuccessful so they turned to the more conventional method of vinegar brewing. King William IV gave the Royal Arms to Booth's Gin in 1833 and from then on the gin was sold under the strapline 'King of Gins'. Booth's built the Red Lion Distillery after World War II to replace the long-established distillery in Turnmill Street, which had been badly damaged in the war. The name was taken from the pre-1936 name of Britton Street or from the original Red Lion tavern, which occupied the corner of Red Lion Street and Clerkenwell Green, just north of the distillery site, before the creation of Clerkenwell Road. The lion is still used as an emblem by the Booth family and appears on all bottles and other merchandise. Note the use of the Royal Arms and red lion in the full page advert for Booth's Gin which appeared in the 25th May 1907 edition of Illustrated London News, which also includes the Turnmill Street address at the bottom.

One of the last industrial buildings of architectural quality to be built in the area, it had only a short

Full page advert for Booth's Gin in the
Illustrated London News, 25th May 1907

life, being closed in the 1970s, but not demolished until c.1990. Felix also financed John Ross's 1829 expedition to find the Northwest Passage. The Boothia Peninsula and Gulf of Boothia are named after him. Booth's connection with the successful expedition was rewarded with a baronetcy in 1835. He served as Sheriff of London in 1828 and was elected a Fellow of the Royal Society in 1834.

Other early occupants of No. 3 include:
William Hammond (1799-1861) is listed in BCGs, 1834-57, SDs, 1841-62, and RBB, April 1858. His eldest son, *"William A. Hammond jnr."*, is also listed in BCG, 1857 and in SDs, 1861-62. William Hammond (Snr) and his wife, Sophia, had produced four children prior to moving into No. 3, including William Amadee (1814-1877), Charles (b.1817), Sara Maria and George Dighton (both born 1818 and therefore probably twins); Stephen Olding (SDs, 1878-94).

4 – Early occupants of No. 4 include: James Walker (BCG, 1808); Thomas Roberts (BCGs, 1820-1824); Mrs Roberts (BCG, 1829); Robert Child (BCG, 1834, and only Mrs Child, 1840-42, Mrs Child and R.J. Child, solicitor, 1843-46, and Mrs Child and Robert John Child, Snr (SDs, 1841-42); Dr S.J. Goodfellow (RBB, April 1858); Rev. Robert Cooper Black, MA (SD, 1862); M. Drayson (ABCCG, 1871, and Michael Drayson, SD, 1878); Thomas Pearson (SDs, 1882-90); *"Mrs Levesion"* (sic- SDs, 1892-93); (Alexander Leveson (SD, 1894).

5 – Rev. Frederick Denison Maurice MA (1805-1872), Church of England clergyman, theologian and founder of Christian Socialism and the Working Men's College as its practical expression (the first one being in Red Lion Square in 1854). Generally known as F.D. Maurice, he lived at No. 5 from 1856 to 1862 (Chancellor, 1907). *"Here rising nearly always at six o'clock, he would take his habitual cold bath; and from breakfast-time till his frugal dinner at 6.30, he was almost invariably engaged in dictation to Mrs. Maurice, pouring out floods of words which found their ultimate expression in the Encyclopaedia Metropolitana; in his Ancient, Mediaeval, and Modern Philosophy, or in one of the numerous books or articles which he produced in such quick succession."* (Chancellor, 1907). He is listed in BCG, April 1857, the RBB, April 1858, and SDs, 1861-62. Maurice had become the leader of the so-called Christian Socialists in 1848. In 1853 he published his *Theological Essays* which led to his forced resignation from King's College, where he had been Professor of English Literature and History since 1846. Interestingly, a chair at King's College,

the F.D. Maurice Professorship of Moral and Social Theology, now commemorates his contribution to scholarship. A year later he was appointed Principal of St. Mary's Hall, Queen Square and Professor of Moral Philosophy at Cambridge in 1866, a post he held until his death on 1st April 1872. Maurice's activism and personality generated a range of opinions, with Julius Hare considering him *"the greatest mind since Plato"* and Charles Kingsley *"...the most beautiful human soul whom God has ever allowed me to meet with."* Conversely, John Ruskin thought him *"... by nature puzzle-headed and indeed wrong-headed."*

F.D. Maurice in the 1860s
© National Portrait Gallery, London

Sir John Hall (1779-1861), ship broker and Hanoverian Consul General, lived at No. 5 from at least 1820 to 1829 (BCGs). John Hall experienced a life-threatening event on 10th November 1820, which was recorded in, *"The Proceedings of the Old Bailey (Central Criminal Court), 10th January 1821 - First Middlesex Jury, before Ld. Chief Baron Richards"* as follows: *"JOSEPH WOOTTEN (aged 19) and WILLIAM BULLOCK (aged 22) were indicted for feloniously assaulting John Hall, Esq. on the King's highway, on the 10th of November, at St. Giles in the Fields, putting him in fear, and taking from his person, and against his will, one watch, value 20 l.; one ribbon, value 6 d.; two seals, value 2 l., and one key, value 2 s., his property."* Both men were charged with the offences of *"Violent theft"* and *"Highway robbery"* and they were both found guilty and sentenced to death. John Hall's lucid description of the traumatic event was recorded verbatim by the court : *"JOHN HALL , Esq. I am the Hanoverian Consul General. On the 10th of November, a little after five o'clock in the evening, I was walking up Drury-lane; on arriving opposite Charles-street, and passing near the north-east corner, I was near a house which was shut up - I received a push on my right side, and thinking somebody meant to pass, I turned aside, and got into Charles-street; immediately on my arrival there, a person stood close in front of me, and I received a violent blow on my head, which, from the position in which I stood, must have been struck behind me, or on my side - it cut a hole in my hat, and my head bled considerably. I have the scar still, and shall carry it to my grave. Immediately on receiving the blow, the man in front cried out 'Halloo! where are you pushing to?' and at the same instant my watch was snatched from my fob - it was a gold horizontal watch, capped and jewelled; the dial plate, instead of the usual figures, had my name and the date, 1808, in Roman characters; a ribbon, two seals, and a key were fixed to the watch. On my receiving the blow, and the snatch at my watch, I was staggered for a moment, then made a plunge at the man who took the watch, and he endeavoured to lay hold of me, but I fell with the effect of the blow with my hand down on the pavement, and my back against the house. I immediately jumped up to pursue the man whom I saw with the watch in his hand. I believe the man who cried halloo to be the man who took it, but am not certain; he ran up Charles-street, I immediately got up and attempted to pursue him, but had not got above three or four steps before some person in the street made a blow at me, which I warded off. I got into Drury-lane, some persons came round, and said 'What is the matter, you are all over blood?' I went into a shop, found myself covered with blood, which streamed down all over my face. I enquired for a surgeon, a boy came into the shop, and gave me information. I went home, was confined to my house fourteen days, and was under a medical man's hands for three weeks. The effects of the blow raised the scalp, and injured one of my arteries - the surgeon feared I should have had a locked jaw. When I recovered, I went and found the boy out, and went with him to the Coach and Horses, Belton-street, St. Giles's - I did not go into the house - the officers brought the prisoners out. The boy was waiting in a coach in Broad-street, St. Giles's. The prisoners were taken into a public-house in Holborn, the boy was sent in and came out again. I stood in the passage, and saw there were about thirty persons there. This was about half-past ten o'clock on Saturday evening. In consequence of what the boy said we took them to Bow-street."*

John Hall had recovered sufficiently by 16th May 1821 to undertake an extensive interview as expert witness to a committee of the House of Lords conducting an enquiry into *"Foreign Trade (Silk and Wine Trade)"*. He introduced himself to the committee, describing his profession as *"Ship Broker"*, adding *"… and I hold the office of Hanoverian Consul General in London"*. An official bulletin released by St. James's Palace in March, 1831 reads: *"The King was this day pleased to confer the honour of Knighthood on John Hall, Esq. Consul General for Hanover, Knight Commander of the Royal Hanoverian Guelphic Order."* 'Orange Boven', the title of the caricature of Hall, is a reference to his diplomatic work in relation to the positioning of the Orange family as rulers of a new state powerful enough to resist France, after a proposed marriage between the Prince Regent's daughter and the young Prince of Orange had fallen through.

03.3.14 Sir John Hall - 'Orange Boven' caricature
© National Portrait Gallery, London

Other early occupants of No. 5 include:
Robert Williams (BCG, 1808); John Teasdale (BCG, 1834-46, and SDs, 1841-42); James Rymer (SD, 1865); Rev. Robert James Simpson (SD and ABCCG, 1871); William Kynaston (SDs, 1875-78); Eugene Monteunis (SDs, 1879-81); Frederick Gordon & Thomas William Smith (SDs, 1882-83); Walter Henry Wilkin (1842-1922) is listed in the SDs, 1884-93. He is listed as Alderman Sir Walter Henry Wilkin in 1894, being Sheriff of London 1892, Lord Mayor of London 1895, and Master of the Worshipful Company of Broderers.

6 - Dr George Darling (1779/80-1862),

Scottish physician. No. 6 was his home and medical practice from 1823 until he died in 1862. He served as a surgeon with the East India Company before first settling at 29 Brunswick Square from 1815 to 1823, where he practised as a physician in partnership with the more accomplished Dr Neil Arnott MD, FRS (1788-1874), physician extraordinary to Queen Victoria, inventor (Arnott's Stove) and public health reformer. Darling is listed at No. 6 in BCGs, 1824-46, and in SDs, 1841-1862. Dr George Darling and Rev. Thomas Darling are listed in the RBB, 1858. *"Miss Darling"* is listed alone in the ABCCG, 1871, and SDs, 1865-93. George Darling was associated with a number of artists, including David Wilkie, Benjamin Haydon, Thomas Lawrence and Francis Chantrey, as both physician and friend. However, his main claim to fame was probably *An Essay on Medical Economy*, which he wrote anonymously. In it he boldly outlined the need for medical reform as regards the education, practice and status of medical practitioners, as well as anticipating many of the changes that were later to take place in the profession. He was also noted for making bread using sodium bicarbonate rather than yeast and for publishing his findings in which he argued, somewhat ahead of his time, that brown bread was more nourishing than white. George Darling died at No. 6 on 30th April 1862.

The above Mayoral robe and hat were presented to the Museum of London by its former owner Sir Walter Henry Wilkin.
Below: Wilkin's appointment as Lord Mayor of London

Nov. 9, 1895   THE COLONIES AND INDIA   17

THE NEW LORD MAYOR OF LONDON.

SIR WALTER HENRY WILKIN, J.P.

George Darling, by G. Zobell, 1855 © Wellcome Library

Other early occupants of No. 6 include:
John Horney (BCG, 1808); "William Phillimore, coun (sic)" (BCGs, 1820-21); Thomas Cotton (BCG, 1823).

7 – Early occupants of No. 7 include: Thomas Jervis (BCG, 1808); John Cox (BCGs, 1820-24); Mrs and Miss Cline (BCG, 1829); Lt. Gen. Robert Bell (BCGs, 1834-44, and General Robert Bell in SDs, 1841-42); Thomas Musgrave (BCG, 1845); Edward Hawkins (BCG, 1846); and Charles Ford, solicitor (BCG, 1857, RBB, 1858, ABCCG, 1871, and SDs, 1861-82). Charles Ford died on 15th January 1873 leaving £353,000 (*The Spectator* 15th May 1883) - equivalent to £36M in 2016; Julius Levy (SDs, 1886-88); Thomas Hill (SD, 1890); William Cole (SD, 1892); Augustus Dimmer (SD, 1894).

8 - Emmeline Pankhurst (1858-1928), feminist campaigner and founder of the Women's Social and Political Union in 1903, moved to No. 8 in 1888 with her husband Richard Pankhurst (1835/6-1898), barrister, and three of their five surviving children at the time: i.e. feminist campaigners **Sylvia Pankhurst** (1882-1960), **Christabel Pankhurst** (1880-1958) and **Adela Constantia Mary Pankhurst Walsh** (1885–1961), suffragette and pacifist.

Adela Constantia Mary Pankhurst Walsh c.1908

No. 8 is listed in the name of "Richard Marsden Pankhurst" in the SDs, 1890-93. They moved to middle-class Russell Square shortly after the death of their four-year-old son, Francis, from diphtheria, which Emmeline attributed to the poor conditions of the neighbourhood they left. Richard was also hoping the move would help him pursue a parliamentary career. The house was registered in the name of Frederick Pilkington until 1889. It is likely the family were occupying part of the house to begin with and acquired the entire house after the birth at No. 8 of their last child, Harry Francis, 1889 (*ODNB*). They remained at No. 8 until 1893, with a certain Harry Markham Caldwell being listed there in the 1894 SD.

Emmeline Pankhurst   Richard Pankhurst in 1879

At eighteen, Adela became the youngest of the early members of the Women's Social and Political Union (WSPU) formed by her mother in October 1903, and her enthusiastic campaigning led to arrests and prison terms. Adela has received little attention in British suffragist history, although she had a colourful career in Australia where she fully demonstrated the radical tendencies and organisational acumen she had inherited from her mother.

Emmeline Pankhurst founded the Women's Social and Political Union (WSPU) in 1903, five years after her husband died. It was set up as an all-women, suffrage advocacy organization dedicated to "deeds, not words." The group became known for physical confrontations: its members smashed windows and assaulted police officers. Pankhurst, her daughters, and other WSPU activists were sentenced to repeated prison sentences, where they staged hunger strikes to secure better conditions. As Pankhurst's eldest daughter Christabel took leadership of the WSPU, antagonism grew between the group and the Government. Eventually the group adopted arson as a tactic, and more moderate organisations spoke out against the Pankhurst family. In 1913 several prominent individuals left the WSPU, among them Pankhurst's daughters Adela and Sylvia. Emmeline was so furious that she *"…gave [Adela] a ticket, £20, and a letter of introduction to a suffragette in Australia, and firmly insisted that she emigrate,"* in which she complied. The family rift was never healed. Sylvia became a socialist.

In 1999, *Time* magazine listed Emmeline as one of the 100 Most Important People of the 20th Century, stating: *"…she shaped an idea of women for our time; she shook society into a new pattern from which there could be no going back."* Although her work is recognised as a crucial element in achieving women's suffrage in Britain, she was widely criticised for her militant tactics, with some historians disputing their effectiveness. She died on 14th June 1928, only weeks before the Conservative government's Representation of the People Act (1928) extended the vote to all women over 21 years of age on 2nd July 1928. Emmeline made their Russell Square home into a

Emmeline Pankhurst speaking at a rally in Trafalgar Square © National Portrait Gallery, London

Sylvia and Emmeline Pankhurst campaigning for Votes for Women

Emmeline Pankhurst being arrested outside Buckingham Palace © National Portrait Gallery, London

centre for grieving sisters, attracting activists of many types, including US abolitionist William Lloyd Garrison, Indian MP Dadabhai Naoroji, socialist activists Herbert Burrows and Annie Besant, and French anarchist Louise Michel. She took pleasure in decorating the house – especially with furnishings from Asia – and clothing the family in tasteful apparel. Her daughter Sylvia later wrote: *"Beauty and appropriateness in her dress and household appointments seemed to her at all times an indispensable setting to public work."* Their art-furnished double drawing room provided a useful gathering place for conferences of the Women's Franchise League, a society aimed at winning the vote for women. The most lavish of these conferences, held over three days in December 1891, was illustrated in *The Graphic* and reproduced 40 years later in *Our Mothers* (ed. Alan Bott & Irene Clepahane), a book owned by Virginia Woolf and consulted by her when writing *Three Guineas*.

CONFERENCE OF THE WOMEN'S FRANCHISE LEAGUE IN RUSSELL SQUARE

The Graphic 12.12.1891 - meeting in the Drawing Room of 8 Russell Square

Christabel Pankhurst was regarded as Emmeline's favourite child and worked tirelessly in support of her mother for nearly 15 years. Sylvia noted in 1931: *"She was our mother's favourite; we all knew it, and I, for one, never resented the fact."* As co-founder of the Women's Social and Political Union (WSPU), she directed its militant actions from exile in France from 1912 to 1913. In 1914 she supported the war against Germany, after which she moved to the United States, where she worked as an evangelist for the Second Adventist movement. Christabel was perceived by

her comrade Emmeline Pethwick-Lawrence as embodying an entirely new kind of womanhood: *"Christabel cared less for the political vote itself than for the dignity of her sex…to her the means were even more important than the end. Militancy to her meant the putting off of the slave spirit."* Christabel died on 13th February 1958, at the age of 77, sitting in a straight-backed chair. Her housekeeper found her body and there was no indication of her cause of death.

By 1914 **Sylvia Pankhurst** had had many disagreements with the route the WSPU was taking. While the WSPU had become independent of any political party, she wanted an explicitly socialist organisation tackling wider issues than women's suffrage, aligned with the Independent Labour Party. She had a close personal relationship with anti-war Labour politician Keir Hardie. In 1914, she broke with the WSPU to set up the East London Federation of Suffragettes (ELFS) which, over the years evolved politically and changed its name accordingly, first to the Women's Suffrage Federation and then to the Workers' Socialist Federation. She founded the newspaper of the WSF, *Women's Dreadnought*, which subsequently became the *Workers' Dreadnought*. It organized against the war, and some of its members hid conscientious objectors from the police. The WSF continued to move leftwards and hosted the inaugural meeting of the Communist Party (British Section of the Third International). In the early 1930s, Pankhurst drifted away from communist politics, but remained involved in movements connected with

Christabel Pankhurst © National Portrait Gallery, London

anti-fascism and anti-colonialism. After the post-war liberation of Ethiopia, she became a strong supporter of union between Ethiopia and the former Italian Somaliland, and MI5's file continued to follow her activities. In 1948, MI5 considered strategies for *"muzzling the tiresome Miss Sylvia Pankhurst"*. Pankhurst became a friend and adviser to the Ethiopian Emperor Haile Selassie and followed a consistently anti-British stance. She moved to Addis Ababa at Haile Selassie's invitation in 1956 with her son, Richard, and founded a monthly journal, *New Times and Ethiopia News*, which reported on many aspects of Ethiopian life and development. She died in Addis Ababa in 1960, aged 78, and received a full state funeral at which Haile Selassie named her *"an honorary Ethiopian"*.

Although there were divergent views within the women's movement about the validity of the use of violence and civil disobedience, of which Emmeline Pankhurst was a keen advocate, it was the autocratic proclamation by Emmeline Pankhurst at a conference in September 1907 that eventually caused the movement to split and heralded the formation of the Women's Freedom League, which had its home at the Minerva Club, 28a Brunswick Square from 1907 to 1961.

Sylvia Pankhurst © National Portrait Gallery, London

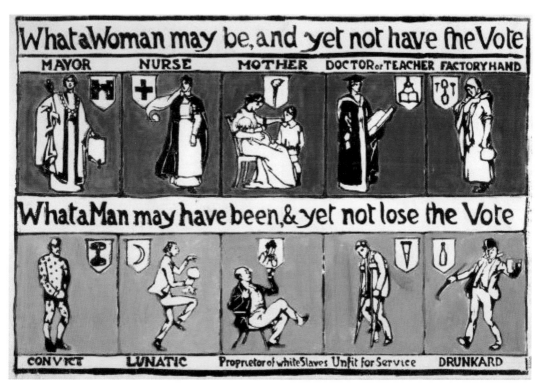

Votes for Women poster

Frederick Thomas Pilkington (1832-1898) was a Scottish architect, practising in the Victorian High Gothic revival style. He was an architect in Edinburgh from 1860 to 1883, concentrating on churches for the Free Church of Scotland, where worship focused not on a nave and altar, but on the pulpit and the 'Word of God'. He developed a new style of church building which accorded with the fashionable Gothic style but was adapted for the worship needs of the Free Church of Scotland. In 1867 he went into partnership with John Murray Bell (1839-1877) to form Pilkington & Bell, with Bell providing the structural know-how and Pilkington providing the design flair. Frederick's interest in the Scottish business declined and with the commission for the Army and Navy Hotel in London (completed 1882), the family and the practice were moved to Russell Square, his home being initially at No. 8 from 1886 to 1889 (SDs) and then at No. 24 from 1895, from where he ran his business (the SD, 1895, also lists Ernest Cropley Pilkington, architect, who is also listed at No. 24 in WRB, 1897). His firm's involvement in the construction of several buildings in the vicinity of Russell Square will be of particular interest to residents of those buildings, which include Ridgmount Gardens and 28-36 Rosebery Avenue. He died in Pinner in 1898. Brighton Palace Hotel and Barclay Church, Edinburgh, are contrasting buildings illustrating Pilkington's versatility.

Other early occupants of No. 8 include:
John Iggulden (BCGs, 1824-46,
and SDs, 1841-42);
Cyrus Slater (RBB, 1858, ABCCG, 1871,
and SDs, 1861-78);
Alfred Seaton (SD, 1882);
Harry Markham Caldwell (SD, 1894).

Hotel Russell

Doll, Fehr and Magnoni create the luxuriant exterior Charles Fitzroy Doll produced his final designs for the Hotel Russell in 1898, which James Stevens Curl (2006) describes as "…a luxuriant essay in the François Premier style, based on the Château de Madrid, Paris (1528–1785), clad in thé-au-lait (tea with milk) terracotta…", although it is described by certain publications in 1900 as the "German renaissance style". Doll engaged the sculptor Henry Charles Fehr (1867-1940) to model the four life-size statues of British Queens who look down from above the front entrance in Russell Square; from left to right (opposite) - Elizabeth I (1558-1603), Mary I (1553-1558), Mary II (wife of William III, 1689-1694), and Anne (1702-1714). Four of the hotel's suites are named after three of these queens, with Queen Victoria replacing one of the Marys, thus avoiding the potential confusion which two suites named after Mary would certainly have caused.

Brighton Palace Hotel

One of the earliest postcards of Hotel Russell, c.1900 © CLSAC

Fehr also provided the two seated knights flanking the sculptural decorations above the large figures denoting the year in which work commenced on the building - 1898 - and the adjacent green, fish-scale tiled towers. He also modelled the busts of the four British Prime Ministers who had served up until the time the hotel was built, which can be seen on the Guilford Street elevation - from left to right in the photograph on page 149: Lord Salisbury (Robert Arthur Talbot Gascoyne-Cecil, 9th Marquess of Salisbury), Lord Derby (Edward George Geoffrey Smith Stanley, 14th Earl of Derby), William Ewart Gladstone, and Benjamin Disraeli (Lord Beaconsfield). Fehr also designed the terracotta decorations featuring plentiful 'putti' (chubby male children) and the other allegorical figures in the columns and walls, as well as the ornate, cast-iron lamp standards at the hotel entrances. Fehr's stone carver at Hotel Russell was the highly skilled Carl Domenico Magnoni (1871-c.1950), *"…an anarchist refugee under constant surveillance by agents of the Italian state"* (Cormack 101). W.J. Neatby, Doulton & Co's chief architectural designer, was commissioned to create a frieze around the Hotel Russell with the Coats of Arms of numerous countries associated with the British Empire, which amounted to a quarter of the world at the time.

The resplendent centre-piece of Hotel Russell, with the 'Four Queens' watching over the main entrance

Opposite: Henry Charles Fehr's twin towers with seated knights, and examples of his 'putti' and allegorical figures Fehr's ornate, cast-iron lamp standards and ornate decorations around the Bernard Street entrance have stood the test of time

'society' press of the day, most notably *The Illustrated London News*, *The Graphic* and *The Sphere*. Messrs. Maple and Co's interior design and furnishing work was singled out for praise: *"The resources of the great establishment of Messrs. Maple & Co., who have more experience in hotel equipment than any other firm in the world, have been drawn upon for the furnishing of this latest of modern London hotels, which should count for a good deal in its favour."* (THE SPHERE, 9th June 1900). *The Illustrated London News* (16th June 1900), in a half-page feature about the opening of the hotel, added: *"Internally, it is one of the most beautiful and perfectly arranged hotels in London, and one of the finest examples of Messrs. Maple and Co's work. Their decoration is the perfection of good taste, and their furniture affords the acme of comfort."* The article also praises the *"…gorgeous marble entrance…luxurious winter-garden…handsome dining rooms…and…spacious reading, smoking, and billiard rooms, all fitted in a style to make visitors as comfortable as possible."* The article goes on to praise the artistic lighting, the *"Teleseme apparatus"* in each room for summoning waiters, and even the *"fire-prevention appliances"*.

The Graphic (16th June 1900) was particularly taken by the *"magnificent banqueting hall with an arcaded gallery for the orchestra..."*. Surprisingly, the en-suite bathrooms attracted hardly any attention, despite the Russell being the first hotel in London to feature them.

Frederick Hotels Limited organised a massive press campaign leading up to, and including, the grand opening on 2nd June 1900 (Derby Day), which was reinforced with regular advertisements in the 'society press', a selection of which are shown here. *The Illustrated Sporting and Dramatic News* of 16th June 1900, whilst praising the building in general, paid particular attention to the use of marble in the *"handsome dining room"* overlooking Guilford Street, with its exquisitely marbled walls and *"…a fine example of the work of Angelica Kauffmann…"* over the canopied fireplace. It is probably no coincidence that Ms Kauffmann's work also adorned the walls of the former Bolton House, which was later demolished to make way for the extension of Doll's Imperial Hotel. The article was illustrated with photographs of a reading room and a private sitting room in preference to the grander rooms featured in the article. The liberal application of rare marbles, sourced from around the world, was another admired feature, especially the Pyrenean marble staircase which would have provided a certain 'wow-factor' for arriving guests.

Porters and doormen posing for the camera outside the main entrance in 1900

Advert in the *Illustrated London News* 2.6.1900 - Opening day

The Graphic 9.6.1900 - 'Hotel Russell opened last week', half-page spread

The Sphere, 9.6.1900 photo of Hotel Russell's Winter Garden

Titanic connection

The ill-fated RMS Titanic`s first-class dining room, which Doll also designed, was inspired by his design of the hotel's recently refurbished restaurant, previously named Fitzroy Doll's, and renamed Tempus Restaurant. The original marble and chandeliers can still be seen. The RMS Titanic was a British passenger liner that sank on her maiden voyage in the North Atlantic in the early morning of 15th April 1912, after colliding with an iceberg during her maiden voyage from Southampton to New York. She was carrying 2,224 passengers and crew, more than 1,500 of whom lost their lives, making it one of the deadliest commercial peacetime maritime disasters in modern history. The largest ship afloat at the time it entered service, it was the second of three Olympic class ocean liners operated by the White Star Line, and was built by the Harland and Wolff shipyard in Belfast with Thomas Andrews as her naval architect. Andrews was among those lost in the sinking. The White Star Line had a direct commercial link with Hotel Russell, which was specifically targeting the trans-Atlantic market, with adverts such as the one illustrated. Other adverts, such as the one in *The Graphic*, were clearly aimed at affluent 'home' customers. The hotel's website reminds its guests that *"The hotel is home to 'Lucky George', a resident bronze dragon who sits atop the 2nd floor stairs. Fitzroy-Doll, one of the most renowned architects of his time, had two dragons moulded: one went to Hotel Russell….the other is today 2.5 miles beneath sea level in the Atlantic Ocean aboard the remains of RMS Titanic."*

RMS Titanic's first-class dining room

Tempus Restaurant & Bar - Doll's inspiration for the first-class dining room on the Titanic

'Lucky George'

George A. Riley's Hotel Russell postcard to Mr H.C. Grant in Massachusetts, USA, dated 23rd July 1907

EUROPE'S MOST CONGENIAL AMERICAN HOMES

The Hotel RUSSELL LONDON

Annually growing in the esteem of best American families. Delightfully situated, on high ground overlooking the verdant lawns and well-wooded grounds of Russell Square Gardens. (Guests have access to these grounds.) Within easy reach of all places of amusement, public buildings, in the very centre of the town, close to the leading railway termini and British Museum, yet enjoying a quiet situation well removed from the noisy traffic.

The bedroom accommodation at the Hotel Russell is luxurious in the extreme, probably without equal in Europe.

THE HOTEL GREAT CENTRAL AND WHARNCLIFFE ROOMS—LONDON

The magnificent terminus hotel, in conjunction with the Great Central Railway, the direct route to Stratford-on-Avon, the Penn County, Sulgrave Manor, the ancestral homes of the Washingtons; Nottingham, the centre of the Dukeries; Manchester and other great commercial centres of the North. **Cuisine is world-famed. Well-disciplined service.**

Other Hotels of the Famous Frederick Group comprise:

THE ROYAL PAVILION HOTEL, at FOLKESTONE, on the main route from London to Paris, adjoining the harbor landing stage.

THE HOTEL BURLINGTON, DOVER, the finest hotel on the Dover-Calais route to Paris and commanding a position overlooking the whole sweep of Dover Bay.

THE SACKVILLE HOTEL, at BEXHILL, the most elegant hotel at the daintiest watering place on the South Coast.

THE HOTEL MAJESTIC, at HARROGATE, the leading hotel at this the most fashionable of English Spas annually becoming more popular with the travelling American.

THE HOTEL METROPOLE, at WHITBY, well-known as the "Harrogate after-cure resort" Hotel.

Tariffs, Illustrated Descriptive Brochures free from

TOWN & COUNTRY BUREAU, Dept. 109, 289 Fourth Ave., NEW YORK CITY

1907 advertisement in the New York press

Advert in *The Graphic* aimed at the affluent 'home' customer, showing the dome and the spire in 'Tuscan' tower

Advert in *The Sphere*, 14th May 1904

Dome and spire 'lost' to the Luftwaffe

During World War II the hotel sustained some damage, most notably on 23rd April 1941, following which the then General Manager, Mr Tugel, commented that *"…several guests had suggested that the windows in the Billiard Room should be bricked up, in the same way as had been done to the Drawing Room windows."* The large dome which once crowned the building, and the spire which once stood on top of the 'Tuscan' tower on the south-east corner of the hotel overlooking Guilford Street, were both lost in a later raid. They can be seen in photographs accompanying the articles and adverts which appeared in many of the early newspapers. The Russell was the only hotel in the Frederick Hotels group not to be commandeered by the War Office during the War.

Investing to conserve

Hotel Russell was Grade II* listed by English Heritage on 3rd December 1970, the highest designation of any building in the square. When the hotel and catering magnate Charles Forte acquired the hotel in the 1970s, he spent £1M on restoring the listed façade (equivalent to £9.4M in 2016). Principal Hotels acquired the hotel from Forte in 1999, and carried out additional works in 2005. Extensive modernisation proposals were contained in planning and listed building applications to Camden Council in 2015. The architect's appraisal accompanying these proposals reads: *"The walls of the Entrance Hall are still clad in a mixture of pink and red Italian marble, with the space divided into three by grey marble round-arched arcades on grey marble columns with gilding. The frieze and spandrels feature extravagant plaster-moulded female figures of Proto-Art Nouveau character, whereas the plasterwork on the ceiling is coffered in a Jacobean Revival design; stylistically contrasting with the hanging chandeliers and limited use of stained glass. On the floor is a broken mosaic featuring the zodiac symbols that surround a 'winking' sun. This is considered to have been installed sometime in the early twentieth century."*

A specialist stone preservation consultant's report on the external condition of the building states that *"…the three elevations are in a reasonably good condition given the age of the building. The Fire Skin (a hard thin vitreous unglazed skin formed of a surface concentration of fine colloidal clay particles), which forms a protective surface on the terracotta, has*

Close-up of the upper floors of Hotel Russell, c.1905, showing the fish-scale tiles on the dome that was destroyed in World War II

Repairs outside Hotel Russell following a bomb which fell on 14-15.9.40 © CLSAC

Entrance Hall today, featuring Italian marbles and mosaic floor with 'winking sun' surrounded by signs of the Zodiac

Side view of main stairway

View from foyer to Tempus Bar

been widely damaged or removed on the Russell Square elevation due to previous robust or unsuitable cleaning." This explains the slightly lighter tone on the Russell Square elevation.

Noteworthy patrons

Considering the past prominence of Hotel Russell, it is surprising to find so few literary references to either the hotel or its guests. Alan Hollinghurst refers to the Russell in *The Swimming Pool Library* (1988), in which he renames it *"the Queensbury"*. There was a report in *The Times* on 20th April 1915, headed *"Charge of Shooting Hotel Waiter"*, in which a hapless *"French waiter"* working at the hotel, named Daniel Spieser, was shot in the arm by a *"young mine accountant named Alexander Cinamon"*, who was staying at the hotel. When charged with feloniously and maliciously shooting Spieser, Cinamon replied, *"That's not murder, is it?"*. He claimed in his defence to be suffering from some kind of fever picked up on the *"West Coast"*. T.S. Eliott used to regularly take his secretary and later wife, Valerie Fletcher, to the hotel for drinks after work, when they both worked at Faber & Faber at 24 Russell Square (see entry for No. 24 in chapter 4). Virginia Woolf wrote in *A Passionate Apprentice*, *"1st March 1905"*, p.245, *"We dined at the Hotel Russell…where Nessa upset her coffee over her dress."* Virginia's novel *Night and Day* was set in Russell Square.

Ornate marble stairwell

Vanessa Bell and Virginia Woolf

In 1933, nuclear scientist and 1918 Nobel Prize winner, Fritz Haber (1868-1934), was exiled from Nazi Germany. He came to London where he stayed at Hotel Russell, while his co-exile, Leo Szilard (1898-1964), a Hungarian physicist who had been working in Berlin for the past decade, stayed at the more affordable Imperial Hotel. They both played key roles in developing a new generation of scientific super weapons, although Haber was at the end of his career and died the following year (see section 1 of this chapter for more about Slizard and a photograph of Haber). The hotel today is a popular venue for a myriad of events, conferences, meetings, parties and wedding receptions, as it has been from its inception in 1900.

The Hotel Russell's first wedding reception held on 7th October 1902 - Alfred John Miller married Susan Julia Redmond

Ola and Samuel's wedding reception in more recent times

The 'Old Lady' has withstood the ravages of time, with her extravagant exterior still largely intact and her prominence in Bloomsbury's greatest Georgian square immutable.

Hotel Russell, June 1899

Hotel Russell, January 2016

A View of Hotel Russell from the roof of Senate House

Artistic view of Hotel Russell from the roof of Russell Square House

Morton Hotel Site

The Morton Hotel, which stands on the opposite side of Bernard Street to the Hotel Russell, and overlooks Russell Square from its prominent position in the north-east corner of the square, occupies the site of the original houses numbered 1 and 2 Woburn Place (No. 1 being a grander house than its neighbours, according to William Faden's 1813 map). The ground floor of the building has been continuously occupied by a bank from inception. The first bank to trade there was The London Joint Stock Bank Limited, managed by Alfred McGregor Hughes, according to its first entry in the SD, 1900 (there is no entry for 1898-99, when the hotel would have been under construction). The Morton Hotel was also first listed in 1900, with William Watson Suttie as manager. The photograph of the Morton Hotel, taken c.1903, shows the terrace of Georgian houses numbered 3-15 Woburn Place (named after the Woburn Estate, the principal seat of the dukes of Bedford) and the original houses in Bernard Street still intact. Many of these houses were functioning as boarding houses and apartment blocks by this time. There appears to have been a malfunction with the "MORTON" sign, but the name of the bank can just be made out on the fascia.

Morton Hotel c.1903 © Brian Girling

Morton Hotel, 2015; 03.3.79 Morton hotel postcard c.1910

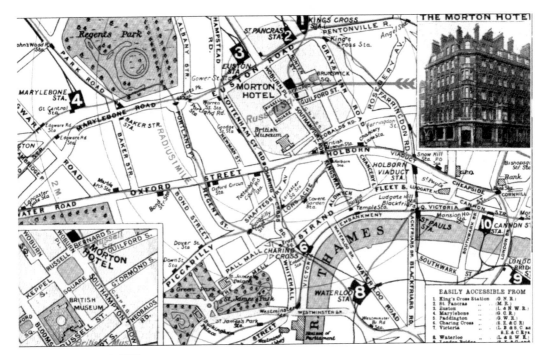

Morton hotel postcard c.1910.

Richard Walduck, Director of Imperial London Hotels Ltd, informed the author that they bought the hotel in 1970-72. It functioned as a staff hostel for the Imperial group for some years until it was refurbished and re-launched as a Bloomsbury Group themed 'boutique' hotel in 2013. The 1910 postcard highlighted the central location of the hotel on the map of London, and its close proximity to the British Museum. Note the two crosses of St John on the hopper at the top of the rainwater pipe.

Crosses of St John on the Morton's rainwater hopper

Richard Walduck believes that the hotel was named after an early Bloomsbury actor and theatre impresario named Morton. Three possibilities have been investigated, but none of them can be directly linked to the Morton Hotel or Bloomsbury. They are Cavendish Morton (1874-1939), actor, photographer and film director; a Mr Morton who performed

regularly at the Haymarket Theatre in 1792-1803; and the most likely candidate, Charles Morton (1819-1904), music hall and theatre manager.

Charles Morton, by Elliott & Fry, 1904
© National Portrait Gallery, London

Born in Hackney, builder of the first purpose-built tavern music hall, the Canterbury Music Hall, in Lambeth in 1852, he became known as the Father of the Halls. The 700-seat Canterbury became so popular that he demolished it and built a 1,500 seat hall on the same site, which opened in 1856. He went on to build The Oxford Music Hall in New Oxford Street, as a competitor to the nearby Weston's Music Hall, opening on 26th March 1861. In 1877,

Canterbury Hall

The Oxford Music Hall

James Cowles Prichard

he became the manager of the Alhambra Theatre, in Leicester Square. The theatre was destroyed by fire in December 1882, but it re-opened on 18th October 1884, with Morton in charge. Morton announced his retirement in 1891, but in 1892, he was persuaded by the Newson-Smith Syndicate to take over the failed Royal English Opera House. He re-opened it as the Palace Theatre of Varieties, with a programme of variety theatre and continued to manage the theatre profitably until his death in 1904.

A totally unrelated possibility is that the hotel was named after the ill-fated Thomas Morton (1813-1849), an accomplished surgeon who lived at 7 Woburn Place in the 1840s whilst working at University College Hospital (UCH). A succession of professional disappointments contributed to his tragic death by suicide at his home on 30th October 1848, which was seen as a great blow to the prestige of the college. His senior colleague at UCH, Samuel Cooper, whose daughter Morton had married, also lived at No. 7.

**Notable early occupants
of 1-2 Woburn Place include:**

James Cowles Prichard (1786-1848), English physician and ethnologist, lived at 1 Woburn Place, where he died of pericarditis in the night of 22nd-23rd December 1848. He was among the first to assign all the human races and ethnic groups to a single species. He was also responsible for the conception of moral insanity (psychopathic personality) as a distinct disease. He received his early education at Bristol as well as his early acquired knowledge of European and Oriental languages. After attending St Thomas's Hospital, London, he went to the University of Edinburgh, where he took his MD in 1808. Settling in Bristol in 1810, he was appointed physician to St Peter's Hospital in 1811 and to the Bristol Infirmary in 1814. His *Researches as to the Physical History of Man* (1813) was expanded into a five-volume work (1836–47). In his classic *Natural History of Man* (1843), he concluded that there was but a single human species. His *Eastern Origin of the Celtic Nations* (1831) established the Celtic languages as a branch of the Indo-European family of languages. He was elected a fellow of the Royal Society in 1827.

Abraham Mocatta (iii) (1797-1880), a not particularly distinguished member of the important Mocatta family of bullion dealers and brokers founded in the 17th century, is listed at No. 2 in the SD, 1841. The Mocatta family dominated the London bullion market for most of the 18th century and continued to have an influential role until the 1950s.

Russell Square, east side, 1929

| Russell Square east side today

Chapter 4

The North Side

It was after James Burton had successfully completed the construction of the south and west sides of Russell Square between 1800 and 1802 that James Gubbins, the Bedford Estate's surveyor, instructed three contractors for the north side of the square – Henry Scrimshaw, David Alston, Jr, and Thomas Lewis - to mirror Burton's designs for the south side, which had been exhibited at the Royal Academy. On the instructions of the Duke of Bedford, the 16 houses on the north side were adorned with the same terracotta decorations which were applied by Charles Fitzroy Doll to the houses on the south side in 1899 (See chapter 1 for photograph of Nos. 17-20 prior to the 1899 terracotta adornments). The north side comprises two separate terraces, numbered 9-16 from Woburn Place to Bedford Way (formerly Upper Bedford Place), and 17-24 up to Thornhaugh Street (formerly Upper Montague Street). Nos. 21-24 are the only surviving original houses.

Nos. 9-16

These eight houses which formed the eastern terrace, between Woburn Place and Bedford Way, were demolished in two phases, firstly to make way for present day.

Russell Square House (Nos. 9-12), and secondly for the construction of present day **Bloomsbury Mansions** (Nos. 13-16), the latter site, together with No. 12, having been designated a *"Clearance area"* after World War II, although it hadn't sustained bomb damage.

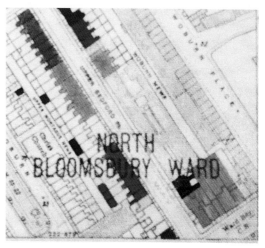

Bomb Damage map showing the *"Clearance Area"* covering Nos. 12-16, coloured green

Nos. 21-24 (r-l), the only surviving Georgian houses on the north side of the square

Nos. 9-12 (r-l), with a Russell Square House development sign on the roof of the single storey Barclays Bank building on the right, c.1939 © CLSAC

1934 Buick Series 90, convertible coupé, auctioned in 2009

The distinctive car in the 1939 photograph, above, is a 1934 Buick Series 90, convertible coupé (34-96C). It was registered in London in 1935, according to the number plate, BMX 67 (MX being allocated to number plates in the London area in December 1934). Sotheby's auctioned the above renovated version of the car in 2009 for $187,000, describing it as "The Holy Grail of early Buicks" - the only Buick accepted as a 'Full Classic' by the Classic Car Club of America.

Both of these buildings have interesting histories, according to *Streets of Bloomsbury & Fitzrovia* (1997). Russell Square House, completed in 1941, was originally intended as an extension for the Royal Hotel, Woburn Place (just visible on the right of the c.1939 photograph). However, it was immediately commandeered as a hostel for US servicemen, then became the headquarters of the Ministry of Information, prior to its relocation to Senate House. It was understandably listed as *"Russell Square House"* in the SDs from 1942, with no indication of its true occupants until after the War. The Paymaster General's Office was moved here in 1947, whereas the adjacent site (Nos. 13-16) remained vacant until 1952, when a new building was erected there and integrated with Russell Square House - the join is barely visible, except perhaps to the trained eye. The Ministry of Health (MoH) occupied this building from 1955, when it became the Department of Health and Social Security (DHSS), and later the Department of Health, which also fully occupied Nos. 13-16 by the 1980s and remained there until 1995. The basement of the original MoH building housed physics laboratories for testing new hospital equipment and instruments. Planning permission was granted on 24th July 1997 to convert Nos. 13-16 into luxury, managed leasehold apartments overlooking the gardens, with a relatively small quantity of obligatory social housing tucked away at the rear. The private element of the block was named Bloomsbury Mansions, their most famous former resident being the actor, producer and comedian Ricky Gervais.

Russell Square House (right) adjoining Bloomsbury Mansions (left) today

Cornerstone Russell Square House 1941

The original No. 9 went missing from the SDs from 1907 onwards (presumed to have been demolished), whilst Nos. 10-16 remained in place, but only until 1939, when the development of Russell Square House was announced in *The Observer* newspaper (19th March 1939) in an article titled *"Russell Square Changes – North Side To Go"*, which read *"… on Lady Day next the work is due to start."* It was completed in 1941 and first appeared in the SD, 1942. No. 9 reappeared as part of the massive Royal Hotel development, which was under construction in the 1927 photograph and opened in 1928, when it also first appeared in the SD, occupying the entire west side of Woburn Place. The terrace of Georgian houses on the east side of Woburn Place (right) would be replaced by the monolithic Russell Court a few years later.

Royal Hotel, Woburn Place, nearing completion, 1927

Royal Hotel postcard, c.1930

The Beatles stayed at the Royal Hotel when they first came to London from Liverpool in 1961, in search of a recording deal with Decca Records, which they didn't get because one of the Decca Directors believed that groups were on the way out and solo singers were the 'in-thing'. They were also turned down by Columbia Records (part of EMI) and the rest is history, as they say.

The Beatles (l-r) - John Lennon, George Harrison, Paul McCartney and original drummer Pete Best in 1961

The new No. 9 was initially a low-rise building, first occupied by Barclays Bank, but renumbered No. 8 by 1939, and incorporated into Russell Square House in 1942. Barclays Bank was still there when the Royal National Hotel replaced the Royal Hotel and National Hotel (on the east side of Upper Bedford Place – now Bedford Way) in 1974, and remained there until 1990/91, when it relocated to 73 Russell Square, below the President Hotel. It was soon replaced by a Post Office/Bureau de Change. The National Hotel, which occupied the entire terrace of original Georgian houses, boasted a Rifle Range, Swimming Bath and Dutch Garden among its attractions (see postcard).

National Hotel, Upper Bedford Place (now Bedford Way), 1950 © Brian Girling

National Hotel postcard;

National Hotel 'attractions' postcard

Here is Woburn Place

9 - John Stevenson Salt (1777-1845), barrister, banker and landowner, lived at No. 9 from at least 1820 to 1845 with his wife Sarah Stevenson, granddaughter of William Stevenson, founder of Stevenson's Bank in Stafford in 1737. Members of the Salt family remained in residence until at least

William Salt

1890, according to official records: BCGs, 1820-45, list *"John S. Salt"* at No. 9, and *"Mrs S. Salt"* in 1846, the year after John had died. The SDs, 1841-42, list *"John Stevenson Salt"*. The RBB, 1858, lists *"George Salt"* and *"The Misses Salt"*. The *"Misses Salt"* continued to be listed in the SDs until at least 1882, with *"William Salt"* joining them in BCG, 1857, and *"Thomas Salt jnr., Esq., M.P. for Stafford"* appearing in 1862. *"Miss Salt"* was listed alone in 1886-90. Stevenson's Bank

was established at Cheapside, London, in 1788. John became a partner in the bank, which in 1801 was renamed Stevenson and Salt. In 1867 it merged with Bosanquet & Co. and later with Lloyds Banking Company. John and Sarah had 10 children, one of whom was the antiquary

William Salt (1808-1863), who made many bequests to the British Museum. From the early 1830s, William devoted much of his spare time to antiquarian pursuits, with a primary interest in the County of Staffordshire, where in 1872 the William Salt Library was established in a house given by his nephew, Thomas Salt MP. The collection has since been greatly augmented by gifts and purchases. In his memory, the William Salt Archaeological Society was established at Stafford in 1879, with the object of editing and printing original documents relating to the county of Stafford in a series of volumes of *Collections for a History of Staffordshire*. The society remains in existence as the Staffordshire Record Society. The *Morning Post* (London) carried a notice of John's death on 18th August 1845: *"On the 16th inst., at his residence, No. 9, Russell-square, John Stevenson Salt, Esq., aged 70."* The William Salt Library was threatened with closure by the County Council in 2014, but was saved in 2015 after a successful campaign, which resulted in it being designated as a £4M one-stop Archives Centre for Staffordshire.

William Salt Library

Walter Hazell (1843-1919), was Chairman of Hazell, Watson and Viney for 50 years - a printing and publishing company with works in Aylesbury, which operated from 1839 to c.1991.

Walter Hazell MP is listed at No. 15 in the SD, 1895, and in WBB, 1897 (see No. 12, below). Walter Hazell MP and Wilberforce Ernest Hazell, architect, are both listed in the SDs, 1899-1902, but only Walter Hazell appears in BCGs, 1903-04. He is listed as Walter Hazell JP in 1905-06.

Hazell, Watson and Viney's printing works in Aylesbury

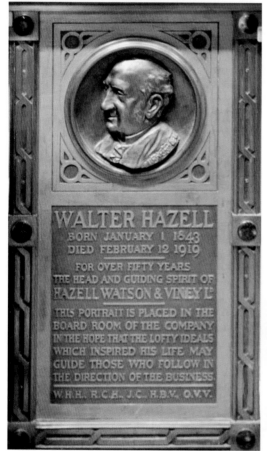

WALTER HAZELL
BORN JANUARY 1 1843
DIED FEBRUARY 12 1919

FOR OVER FIFTY YEARS
THE HEAD AND GUIDING SPIRIT OF
HAZELL WATSON & VINEY Lᴰ

THIS PORTRAIT IS PLACED IN THE
BOARD ROOM OF THE COMPANY
IN THE HOPE THAT THE LOFTY IDEALS
WHICH INSPIRED HIS LIFE MAY
GUIDE THOSE WHO FOLLOW IN
THE DIRECTION OF THE BUSINESS

W. H. H. R. C. H. J. C. H. B. V. O. V. V.

Portrait of Walter Hazell in the company's boardroom

as progressive. *Hazell's Magazine,* which appeared from 1886, was one of the company's first in-house publications. The company grew after World War I as part of the Hazell Sun group of companies, and in 1963 became the British Printing Corporation, which was one of the most influential printing and publishing organisations in Britain up until it was taken over in 1981 by Maxwell Communications Corporation. He served as Mayor of Holborn in 1911-12. The Walter Hazell Charitable and Educational Trust Fund still provides support to employees and past employees of the printing trade in Buckinghamshire and Berkshire, and to their spouses, widows, widowers and children and any other financial dependents.

Other early occupants of No. 9 include:
Henry Benjamin Barnard (1837-1895) and Walter Henry Barnard (SDs, 1892-95). Standing 6 feet 6 inches, *"W.H. Barnard",* as he is listed in WRB, 1897, was exceptionally tall for his time. He was also a keen cricketer, playing for the Kent 2nd eleven. Barnard Bros & Co., Metal Merchants, was a long-standing family business, trading at 149 Leadenhall Street in the City of London.

10 - Horace Horne (d. 1894), architect, and his wife Hannah lived at No. 10. Their better known son, **Herbert Percy Horne** (1864-1916), architect, art collector and art historian, was born here on 18th February 1864 (*ODNB*).

Entering the business in 1863, Walter launched the *Illustrated Photographer* and *Amateur Photographer,* and also printed the *Marylebone Mercury,* the *East London Observer* and the *Bucks Independent.* As well as his leading role in the company, he was a social reformer and Women's Suffrage supporter who wrote a number of pamphlets on social issues. He was also Liberal Member of Parliament for Leicester between 1894 and 1900, and was instrumental in introducing an employees' sick fund in 1874, one of many such welfare schemes that marked his company

Herbert Percy Horne

He made important designs for textiles and wall-coverings for the Century Guild (see samples), but the work with which his name was most closely associated was the editing of the *Century Guild Hobby Horse* which he shared with Mackmurdo.

Wallpaper designed by Herbert Percy Horne, c.1882

This finely printed quarterly magazine of art and literature ran, with gaps and a change of title, from 1884 to 1894. Its layout, from the issue of January 1888 onwards, was something of a milestone in British graphic design, presenting type, paper, and illustrations as a coherent whole. Meeting him in 1888, Bernard Berenson admired the range of Horne's talents and thought he might become William Morris's successor, *"the great man of the next generation"* (E. Samuels, Bernard Berenson, 1979). W.B. Yeats praised his knowledge and taste; and both Arnold Dolmetsch, the pioneer of the revival of early music, and the artist Lucien Pissarro – two Frenchmen struggling to establish themselves in London - had reason to be grateful to Horne for his early support. His *Alessandro Filipepi Commonly called Sandro Botticelli, Painter of Florence* survives today as one of the standard works on Botticelli. Fritz Saxl, lecturing in London in 1944, described Horne as *"…the most accomplished historian of art whom this country has ever produced"* (Saxl, 332). In 1911, Herbert purchased the fifteenth-century Palazzo Corsi in Florence, although he didn't actually move in until 1915, by which time he was seriously ill and often confined to two small, plain rooms at the very top, where he was part host, part caretaker of the riches on the floors below. He died at the palazzo on 14th April 1916, having bequeathed the building and its contents to the Italian state. It is now open to the public as Museo Horne.

William Hay is listed at No. 10 in BCGs, 1808-29, but only Mrs Hay is listed by 1834. William's death was announced briefly in *The Lady's Magazine*, 1830, under March deaths: *"On the 11th, at his house in Russell-square, William Hay, Esq., in his 88th year."* His will, held by the National Archives, is dated 29th March 1830. Obituaries for his two sons, which appeared in *The Gentleman's Magazine*, October 1811 and *The Naval Chronicle*, Jan-July 1812, respectively, tell of their tragic and untimely deaths within six months of each other: *"In Portalegre, serving with the army under Lord Wellington, Ensign Alexander Hay of the 50th regiment, eldest son of William Hay of Russell-square"* (died of) *"inflammatory fever"* as a result of his extreme exertions in the Portuguese heat, followed by the loss of his youngest son, Thomas, on 21st April 1811, whilst serving as a midshipman on board the Galatea frigate, aged 17. *"His remains were interred at Kidgeree on the Hoagley River."* On a brighter note, his daughter, Eliza, married *"…William Henry Sykes esq, capt. Bengal army"* at St George's Bloomsbury on 1st April 1824. Mrs Hay died at No. 10, aged 87, on 31st March 1839, according to her obituary in *The Gentleman's Magazine* of 1839.

Interior of Museo Horne in Florence

Other early occupants of No. 10 include:
Mrs Duff and Alexander Black (BCGs, 1840-42, but only Alexander Black in 1843-46, and in the SDs, 1841-42, BCG, 1857, and the RBB, 1858); John Rowland Gibson, surgeon (SDs, 1861-93); Alexander Philip Levy Tebbitt (c.1849-1902) (SDs, 1894-1903, WRB, 1897, and BCG, 1903, and only *"Mrs Tebbitt"* appears in the SD, 1904). There were no entries for No. 10 for 1905-07, with Bain & Longinotto, physicians & surgeons, taking up residence from 1908, renamed Longinotto, Bain & Hill in 1909, and Longinotto & Hill in 1910. Michael Joseph Longinotto, physician & surgeon, is the only occupant listed in 1912-20; No. 10 had multiple occupants in 1939, prior to being demolished to make way for Russell Square House.

11 - George J. Stodart, renowned reproductions engraver, with 29 portraits currently held by the National Portrait Gallery. His occupation is described as *"Gentleman"* in *The Gazette*. Michael Faraday wrote to George Stodart on 28th May 1838 regarding his subscription to the London Orphan asylum, which he had belonged to since 1818. A footnote in *The Correspondence of Michael Faraday, Vol 2, 1832-1840* states that George Stodart was the son-in-law of James Stodart (1760-1823), surgical instrument maker, who is listed in BCGs, 1808-24. Mrs Stodart and George Stodart are listed in BCGs, 1829-34, but George is listed alone in 1840-57, RBB, 1858, and SDs 1841-78. Here are two contrasting subjects which illustrate his range of skills as an engraver.

Other early occupants of No. 11 include:
"William Gill, J.P., surgeon/physician, M.R.C.S.", then *"F.R.C.S.",* is listed in SDs, 1882-1905 and in WRB, 1897. He is joined briefly by James Bussell Withington, surgeon, in 1894-96; Surtees Sumner, M.D., physician, is listed in 1912-20; *"Misses Newman"* are listed in 1930, but *"Miss Newman"* alone in 1939.

John Winston Spencer Churchill, Duke of Marlborough, KG, engraved by George J. Stodart © National Portrait Gallery, London

Portrait of Thomas Tooke

12 - Thomas Tooke (1774-1858), economist and writer on currency and political economy, lived at No. 12 with his wife Priscilla and their three sons. *"J. Tooke"* is listed in BCG, 1808, with Thomas Tooke listed in 1820-1824, and only his younger brother William Tooke (see below) in 1829-46, in the SDs, 1841-42, and the RBB, 1858, confirming that Thomas had moved to Richmond Terrace with his wife and children by 1829, leaving William behind at No. 12.

Mary Wollstonecraft Shelley & Percy Bysshe Shelley, engraved by George J. Stodart, 1853 © National PortraitGallery, London

Thomas gave evidence before committees of both Houses of Parliament on the resumption of cash payments by the Bank of England and was one of the earliest supporters of the free trade movement. He retired from active business on his own account in 1836, but was governor of the Royal Exchange Assurance Corporation from 1840 to 1852. He also served several terms as chairman of the St Katharine's Docks Company and was an early director of the London and Birmingham Railway. After his death in 1858, the Statistical Society endowed the Tooke Chair of Economics at King's College London and a Tooke Prize.

William Tooke © British Museum

Caricature of Thomas Cooke titled *A Near Miss*
© National Portrait Gallery, London

William Tooke (1777-1863), MP (Truro, Cornwall, 1832-1837), FRS, lawyer, politician, writer, President of the Society of Arts and co-founder of the Society for the Diffusion of Useful Knowledge, moved in with his brother at No. 12 around 1829, the year he was first listed in BCG, in which he continued to be listed until at least 1857. He was also listed as *"William Tooke, Esq., F.R.S., F.R.S.L."* in SDs until 1862, the year before he died. *"Arthur William Tooke, esq., M.A."* is listed in the SD, 1865 and ABCCG, 1871.

William was born in St Petersburg, Russia, where his father was chaplain to the factory of the Russia Company at St Petersburg. He came to England in 1792 to take up articles with a firm of solicitors in

Gray's Inn. Chancellor informs us that William Tooke was an acquaintance of Crabb Robinson (No. 30), who asked Tooke to buy him a share in the London University. They later served together on the Committee of University College and he was its treasurer until 1841. The *Oxford Dictionary of National Biography* states that William died at No. 12 on 20th September 1863.

Sir Francis Flint Belsey (1837-1914), JP, corn merchant and social reformer, lived at No. 12 from 1901 to 1914, when he died. He is listed in SDs, 1901-14, and in BCG, 1903. He is first listed as *"Sir Francis Flint Belsey J.P."* in 1910, having received his knighthood from the King on 13th December 1909. He stood as a Liberal candidate for the parliamentary seat of Faversam in 1885, but lost to the Conservative candidate, Herbert Thomas Knatchbull-Hugessen. He tried again the following year in Rochester, where he was already an Alderman, but with a similar result. He was chairman of the Sunday School Union Council, for whom he wrote several books, including *The Sunday School Red Book: a Manual of Instruction... for Superintendents* and *The Teacher's Red Book: Brief Hints...for Sunday School Teachers*.

Other early occupants of No. 12 include: John Henry Wellby (SDs, 1878-90); Mrs De Knevett (SDs, 1892-95); William Beattie (SD, 1896); Thomas Barnes-Williams (WRB, 1897, and SDs, 1897-98); John Lowles MP (SD, 1900); the Young Men's Christian Association Metropolitan and Provincial headquarters extended its premises into No. 12 from No. 13 in 1915, where it remained until at least 1920 (see below). From at least 1930 to 1939, No. 12 housed the Consulate-General of Republic of Paraguay, prior to the building making way for Russell Square House.

13 - Charles Edward Mudie (1818-1890),

publisher and founder of Mudies Circulating Library, is listed at No. 13 in the RBB, 1858, and in the SD, 1861, and with the *"F.R.G.S."* suffix in 1862.

He first set up his bookshop in Southampton Row in 1840, and in 1842, he began lending books to the young gentlemen at the University of London, charging subscribers one guinea per year for the right to borrow one volume of a novel at a time. This proved so successful that in 1852 he decided to sell books to the wider public and moved his *"Select Library"* to larger premises at 509-511 New Oxford Street, at its junction with Museum Street, which was a short stroll south from Russell Square, and just beyond the British Museum. He expanded into premises at 20-21 Museum Street in 1860.

Mudie claimed to have 120,000 volumes in circulation with a million more in reserve, serving 20,000 subscribers and making 1,000 exchanges per day. As an aside, Mudie's Library is mentioned in the H.G. Wells classic, *The Invisible Man: "We crawled past Mudie's, and there a tall woman with five or six yellow-labelled books hailed my cab, and I sprang out just in time to escape her, shaving a railway van narrowly in my flight. I made off up the roadway to Bloomsbury Square, intending to strike north past the Museum and so get into the quiet district."* The library had an immense influence on the book trade during the 19th century and by 1890 it had approximately 25,000 subscribers (Gerard 216). This large number of patrons meant that Mudie had *"…substantial control over the publishing trade, since his libraries bought a large percentage of the books they sold, purchasing an estimated 7.5 million books over the course of the century"* (Jacobs, *Circulating*). Mudie's also played a part in the success of novels: *"A listing in Mudie's selection had become one of the best advertisements for any novel…"* (Griest).

Charles Edward Mudie

Mudie's Library, 509-511 New Oxford Street

Mudies Select Library illustrated in *LondonSociety*,
1869 Vol. 16, No. 95

Mudie's continued to grow, opening branches in York, Manchester and Birmingham, and continued into the

1930s, when the rising number of government-funded public libraries offering similar services at a much reduced rate eventually took their toll and forced its closure. Mudie is listed at No. 13 in the SD, 1861, the year that he came close to bankruptcy due to a combination of over-expansion, the extravagant costs of renovating his New Oxford Street premises, and competition from other lending libraries. 1861 was also the year he bought almost the entire first edition, and most of the second, of Charles Dickens' *Great Expectations*. He was rescued by a consortium of publishers, who lent him money and supported his business until he returned to solvency in 1864. His business was floated on the stock market as a limited company in the same year, with Mudie retaining half the shares and overall control of the business, while providing his rescuers with a stake in the firm. By the 1870s, the firm was once again pre-eminent in the distribution and supply of literature.

Sir George Williams (1821-1905), founder of the YMCA, lived at No. 13 with his wife, Helen, from 1879 until his death in 1905. He is listed in the SDs from at least 1881 until he died in 1905, appearing as *"Sir George Williams"* in 1895 (the year after he was knighted) and in WRB, 1897. He was finally listed in BCG in January 1903, with *"Lady Williams"* continuing to be listed in the SDs, 1906-07. Appalled by the terrible conditions in London for young working

Exchanging books at Mudie's subscription library, 1901

Portrait of Sir George Williams
© National Portrait Gallery, London

Entrance lobby of Sir George Williams' house in 1907, with his portrait displayed © English Heritage

Sir George Williams' Study, 13 Russell Square, 21.7.1907
© English Heritage

13 Russell Square in 1906 © English Heritage

Council Chamber 13 Russell Square in 1907 © English Heritage

men, Williams gathered a group of his fellow drapers together to create a place that would not tempt young men into sin. That place was the YMCA, which he founded in 1844. *"The house in Russell Square was naturally a rallying-point for all those interested in this great work, and deputations as well as individuals from all parts of the globe were wont to wait on Sir George at No. 13."* (E. Beresford Chancellor, 1907).

He received his knighthood from Queen Victoria in 1894, the 50th anniversary of the birth of the YMCA, the headquarters of which was established at No. 13 in 1908. He was commemorated by a plaque on the site of his former home and by a stained-glass window in the nave of Westminster Abbey. He was buried in St. Paul's Cathedral. The YMCA now boasts over 58 million members in 119 countries worldwide.

Commemorative plaque to Sir George Williams on the site of former 13 Russell Square

Swinton Colthurst Holland (1777-1827), entrepreneur and son of Samuel Holland and Anne Swinton, is listed at No. 13 in BCGs, 1820-24, and in the list of members eligible to vote at the April 1926 Annual General Meeting of the United Company of Merchants of England trading to the East Indies. Swinton is praised by John Chapple in *Elizabeth Gaskell: The Early Years* as *"…an energetic man of affairs who would have brought more than a breath of the wider world to the peaceful life of a woman who lived in a little rural town. Swinton had begun business at Liverpool, gone to the United States for two years in 1800, travelled extensively in Italy, attempted to set up his own business in Venice and finally entered into a partnership with the American Consul at Trieste, a Mr Riggin. In April 1803…Swinton…was already on his way to becoming very rich in his own right, a partner in the once great financial firm of Baring Brothers, a man able to give advice on a national level."* He died on 27th December, 1827 in Roehampton, Surrey.

Other early occupants of No. 13 include:
George Trower (BCGs, 1829-34); George Baker (BCGs, 1840-46, and SDs, 1841-42); Henry Lewis Raphael (SD, 1865); John Baker (SD and ABCCG, 1871); Henry Gaisford Gotto (SDs, 1878-79); The Young Men's Christian Associations (YMCA): National Headquarters occupied the building from 1908 until at least 1930, sharing the premises with the Soldiers' Christian Institute/Association in 1914-15 and various professional organisations thereafter.

14 - Louisa Starr Canziani (1845-1909), the only child of a merchant and banker of 14 Russell Square, is listed at No. 14 as *"Miss Louisa Starr, artist"* in the SDs from 1876 to 1886, when *"Enrico Canziani, civil engineer"* is also listed. Her father, Henry Starr, is listed in the SDs, 1864-79 and in the ABCCG, 1871.

Her parents originated from America and she was born in London, living at No.14 when she became a copyist at the British Museum. She *"…painted out of love for the subject, having no need to work for a living. At the age of 14 she was allowed to study at the sculpture gallery of the British Museum."* (Sara Gray, *The Dictionary of British Women Artists*). She became a student at the Royal Academy in 1860, when she was just 16, and showed her first work there in 1866. Although her speciality was portraiture, she won a gold medal at the Royal Academy for history painting in 1867 and by 1876 she had shown 17 paintings there, being the first woman to do so. *A Gallery of her own: An annotated Bibliography of Women in Victorian Painting* makes a barbed remark about Louisa's accolade: *"Louisa Starr's David Brought Before Saul… received the Royal Academy School's gold medal for 'best historical painting' in 1867. Starr's success is proof that the Academy acted wisely in admitting women to its schools, but it remains impossible for women thus trained to become full members in the Academy."* Apparently the painting had caused her difficulty due to the lack of a model, but the local milkman obliged and the painting was completed. A lithograph of the painting

Louisa Starr's *David Brought Before Saul*

Lithograph of *David Brought Before Saul* – ILN

was published in the *Illustrated London News*. In 1882 Louisa married her cousin Francesco Enrico Canziani, a civil engineer in Milan, Italy who travelled regularly to see her in London where she earned her living as an artist. Thereafter Louisa signed her works with her married name, having signed *"L Starr"* up until then to conceal her female identity. Her attitude to life and work continued to be assertive and uncompromising. For example, she removed the *"and obey"* from the marriage service, and it was decided that she would continue to live and work in London, with Enrico being the one to move. She stated her position in a letter to Francesco, *"In all your plans you must not forget that I am an artist at bottom, and that you cannot change it."* Although Francesco settled in London,

he visited Italy at least three times a year to look after his business interests. They had one daughter, Estella Canziani (1887-1964), who became an equally prominent and successful artist. Louisa showed a total of 68 works at the Royal Academy which she continued to do up to her death in May 1909. In 1875 her *Tired Governess* was highly praised and was engraved by the *Illustrated London News*, 4th January 1908. She exhibited at major galleries and institutes in Britain and at the Chicago World Exposition in 1893. Her painting *Sintram and His Mother* was included in the 1905 book *Women Painters of the World*. Her portrayal of the children of wealthy clients who commissioned her to paint portraits of their beloved children were exceptionally appealing.

Tired Governess, engraving by *ILN* ©V&A

Louisa Starr Canziani's *Sintram and his Mother*

Kathleen (d.1946) and Marianne (d.1943), the Daughters of Samuel Gurney Sheppard, 1888
© Russell-Cotes Art Gallery and Museum, Bournemouth

Two Little Home Rulers: The Honourable Dudley Gladstone Gordon and the Honourable Archie Gordon, 1890
© The National Trust for Scotland

Harold Walduck (1872-1957), Bloomsbury hotelier, is listed at No. 14 in SDs, 1910-25. Harold became a 'force majeur' within the London hotels industry after taking over the running of the Bedford Hotel in Southampton Row from his father, Thomas Henry Walduck, in 1896. He went on to build a mini-empire of 10 hotels straddling the Southampton Row-Woburn Place corridor, providing the right modern accommodation, in the right central location at the right no-frills price, to meet the mass travel demand made possible by the new railway era in the mid-to-late 19th century. It is no coincidence that the promotional material published by Imperial London Hotels Ltd in the 1930s, titled *"9 LONDON HOTELS 3000 ROOMS"*, features a map illustrating the central location of its hotels and their close proximity to the mainline railway termini dotted along the north side of the Euston Road. Harold died in 1957, aged 85, with his specific contribution to the development of London hotels being acknowledged in Encyclopaedia Britannica, 1968.

Imperial London Hotels Ltd is still very much a family business today, although of the nine hotels shown on the 1930s map, only the

Harold Walduck by courtesy of the Walduck family

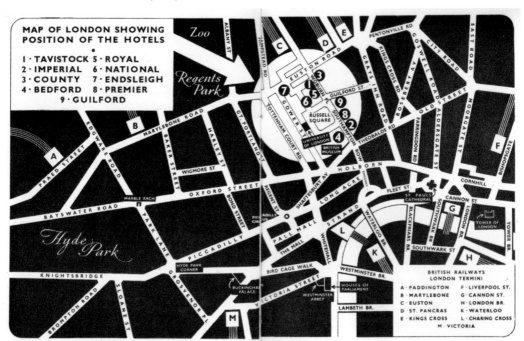

IT will be seen from the above Map that all our hotels are very well placed for reaching the City, West End and the Northern Railway Termini.

There are buses running along Euston Road, Woburn Place and Southampton Row, and Russell Square Underground Station on the Piccadilly Line is close by.

Taxis are practically always available and will take you to the City or West End in a matter of minutes.

The University of London, British Museum and British Medical Association Headquarters are within easy walking distance.

Tavistock, County and Bedford remain, and the Royal and National Hotels were replaced by the Royal National Hotel from 1969, since when it has become possibly the largest hotel in London, with 3,600 bed spaces and 1,600 rooms. The Endsleigh Hotel closed when the site was redeveloped to provide the Friends Meeting House in 1927, and Fitzroy Doll's flamboyant Imperial Hotel was replaced by a modern building in 1966, shortly after the President Hotel had replaced the Premier and Guilford Hotels (for more details, see chapter 3, parts 1 and 2). Other hotels included the Raglan (staff hostel) and Lincoln Hall in Bedford Way, both disappearing with the arrival of the Royal National.

Other early occupants of No. 14 include:

John Trelawny (BCG, 1808) is listed as a Governor of the Northern Dispensary (1813-14), when Sir Samuel Romilly was a Vice-President. He was also listed as a Contributing Member to the Society for the Encouragement of the Arts (1804-08). His obituary in *The European Magazine and London Review*, Vol. 73, 1818, states that he died at Tottenham on 19th December 1818, aged 59; Miss Barclay (BCG, 1820-24); Rev. Dr G. Shepherd (BCG, 1829-46, and SDs, 1841-42). He is listed in *The Gentleman's Magazine*, 1836, under *"Gazette Promotions"* for 1st September *"…as Metropolitan Commissioner of Lunacy during the space of one year"*; Nathan Wetherell (1808-1887), barrister (BCG, 1857, RBB, 1858, and SDs until at least 1863), was also a cricketer with amateur status associated with Cambridge University (1828-31), making his first-class debut in 1828. He and his wife, Susan, had three daughters. They lived previously at Great Coram Street (1941 Census). The 1871 Census shows them living at Pashley House in Ticehurst, Sussex. Susan died in 1879 aged 74 years at Ticehurst. In 1881 Nathan was still living at Pashley House, with his widowed daughter Susan Darby, together with her butler, ladies' maid, housemaid, kitchen maid, nurse, and page. He died at Pashley House on 7th February 1887 aged 78 years; Edward John Chance, surgeon (SDs, 1887-95); Charles James Wallis (WRB, 1897, and SDs, 1898-1902); Albert Berl Salmon (SDs, 1903-08); Henry Alexis Chodak Gregory M.C. physician & surgeon and Mrs Hazel Haward Chodak Gregory M.D. physician & surgeon (SDs, 1926-27).

15 – James Deacon Hume, (1774-1842), Secretary of the Board of Trade (1828-40), economics writer and advocate of free trade, lived at No. 15 for many years with his wife Frances (Ashwell, née Whitehouse) and their many daughters in the early nineteenth century (ODNB). J.C. Hume and I.D. Hume were listed separately at No. 15 in two editions of BCG, 1829, with I.D. Hume alone being listed until 1834, although J.D. Hume is correctly listed in the 1831 Rate Book, with the quintessentially Civil Service job title *"Comptroller Inwards and Outwards"*. James was awarded compensation for the enslaved people on La Fortune estate in Grenada, as owner-in-fee having originally been a trustee, arising from his marriage to Frances, who was the widow of Charles Ashwell of the Island of Grenada, according to an opinion of Law Officers concerning the La Fortune estate in 1811. In 1822 he conceived the idea of consolidating customs law, and was given three years' leave to realise this project. Some 1,500 Acts dating back to Edward I were reduced to 10 Bills, which received royal assent in 1825. In 1815 Hume published a protectionist tract on the Corn Laws, but he later became a strong advocate of free trade. Richard Cobden recalled a discussion at the Political Economy Club, to which Hume was elected in 1834. Most speakers were opposed to Hume's views. He retorted: *"Gentlemen land-owners, you have your landed estates, they are secured to you by law, you may fence them round and exclude all intruders, why are you not content with the possession of your property, why do you attempt to invade the property of the labourer by interfering with his right to exchange the produce of his own toil for the produce of other lands?"* (Badham, 159). According to *The Life of James Deacon Hume, Secretary of the Board of Trade*, 1895, Hume lived in Russell Square for 10 years. *"As he walked to, so he walked from, the Board of Trade to his residence in Russell Square, and Mrs. Hume was requested, on no account, to wait if he should fail to arrive at the expected time. He passed his evenings within his domestic circle, and if he was not fatigued, as was often the case latterly, he joined cheerfully in conversation, forgetful alike of the events, or of the labours of the day. Sometimes, and it was almost a habit, he would walk up and down the room for half an hour, with his hands lodged in the recesses of his pockets, talking as he walked, and pausing now and then, in order to express himself more deliberately. But when the hour of retiring arrived, and his family had one and all disappeared, unfortunately, as has been already mentioned, he was not accustomed to do likewise; for he indulged in the injurious practice of devoting an undue portion of the night to reading and writing, or to matters connected with official duties. And as he who would rise early must go to bed betimes, it will not be anticipated that he was, in the usual sense of the words, very frequently 'up with the lark'."*

On retirement Hume moved to Reigate, Surrey where he died of apoplexy at Great Doods House on 12th January 1842.

Great Doods House in 1821

Other early occupants of No. 15 include: John Bate (BCGs, 1808-24). He was a Governor of the Asylum for the Deaf & Dumb in 1821, and a member of The Society of Ancient Britons in 1815. He was a Member of the United Company of Merchants trading in the East Indies in 1825, and Governor of the Northern Dispensary in 1813-14. He was a life member of the Society of Arts. He was also an Alderman of the City of London; David Hunter Esq. (SDs, 1841-42, BCG, 1842); Mrs Whipham (BCG, 1846); Joseph Turnley (BCG, 1857, RBB, 1858, and SDs, 1861-62); Robert John Dobree (ABCCG, 1871, SD, 1878 and Mrs Dobree, SD, 1882); Mrs Dupree (SDs, 1886-87); Walter Hazell MP (SDs, 1889-98, when he was joined by Wilberforce Ernest Hazell, architect). He moved to 9 Russell Square, where he is listed in the various directories from 1899 to 1906

(see No. 9, above); John Henry Lile (SDs, 1899-1914).

16 - Horatio Porter MA (1861-1918), architect and Mayor of Holborn (1911-12), shared No. 16 with *"F.W. & Hill Porter"* in 1892-1908 (SDs). They were also all listed in WRB, 1897, with only *"Horatio Porter M.A., architect"* being listed in 1909-15. Horatio was the son of Sarah and Frederick (F.W.), whom he succeeded as Surveyor to the Clothworkers' Company. He was also a Member of the Board of Works for St Giles District (1897-1900). He died in London on 29th July 1918.

Other early occupants of No. 16 include: W. Page (BCG, 1808); A. Reid (BCGs, 1820-24); S.I. Capper (BCGs, 1829-34); Horatio Nelson Davis Esq. (BCGs, 1840-46, and SDs, 1841-42); Samuel Angel, architect and surveyor to The Clothworkers' Company in the City of London (BCG, 1857), and Samuel Angell, architect & William Angell jnr (RBB, 1858); Frederick William Porter (1821-1901), architect and successor to Samuel Angell as surveyor to The Clothworkers' Company (SDs, 1861-78). In October 1848 Frederick married Sarah Moyle in Liverpool. Although he appears in the Dublin directories until at least 1853, he had moved to London by 1849, when he and W.A. Boulnois exhibited a design

| Upper Bedford Place from Russell Square, c.1908, showing parts of Nos. 16 (right) & 17 (left)

for a county lunatic asylum at the Royal Academy; F.W. Porter, architect and surveyor and Mrs Moyle (ABCCG, 1871); Frederick William Porter, architect (SD, 1878), joined by Samuel Hill, architect (1879-86), then Samuel alone until 1890, then F.W. Porter & Hill, architects (SDs, until 1908) and Horatio Porter MA (SDs, 1893-1918); The Incorporated Insurance Industry Unemployment Insurance Board took up residence in 1924, followed by the grandly named World Association for Adult Education and its associated bodies in 1930-39, with no entries after that, the building being within the designated *"Clearance area"*.

Here is Bedford Way, formerly Upper Bedford Place.

Nos. 17-24
Nos. 17-18 sustained serious bomb damage near the end of World War II, although the houses were not cleared until much later, in conjunction with Nos. 19 and 20 (currently a gap site), to make way for the construction of the Queen's Award winning Charles Clore House, designed by Sir Denys Lasdun and

completed in 1975. The Institute of Advanced Legal Studies moved from 26 Russell Square into this brand new building at 17 Russell Square, and remains there today alongside the Institute of Education, which occupies the full extent of the west side of Upper Bedford Place. The building was officially opened by the Chancellor of the University of London, Queen Elizabeth, the Queen Mother, on 1st April 1976. The University of London's Master Plan published in 2015 has earmarked the gap site at Nos. 19-20 to be filled with an appropriate building that will be sympathetic to the original Georgian terrace.

The Bomb Damage map (see chapter 5) shows No. 17 coloured purple and No. 18 coloured dark red, categorising them respectively as *"Damaged beyond repair"* and *"Seriously damaged; doubtful if repairable"*. There are consequently no entries for Nos. 17-19 in the 1945 street directory. Nos. 17 and 18 were primarily occupied by the intriguingly named Ancient Order of Foresters Friendly Society from 1922 to 1944, when the Colonial Centre took over No. 17, having presumably been commandeered by the Government. Another interesting war-time occupant

Nos. 19-24 (r-l), c.1939 © CLSAC

The Institute of Advanced Legal Studies, Charles Clore House today, with gap site to its left

of No. 17 was the National Federation of Postal & Telegraph Clerks (1939-41). Photographs held by the Imperial War Museum (IWM), collectively known as *Colonial Centre – Everyday Life at the Colonial Club, 17 Russell Square - 1944*, would have been taken shortly before the building sustained bomb damage, although it was still not repaired or cleared five or six years later, according to the post-war photograph showing the buildings in c.1950 behind the Holborn Borough Council vehicle.

A barrage balloon can be seen floating ominously in the background of the photo of Mr D.A. Thomas (law student) and Miss Rosamund Harding (student teacher) from Sierra Leone as they enjoy the view from the sunny balcony of the Colonial Centre, viewed towards Hotel Russell. The other IWM photos taken around the same time show the reception clerk at Colonial Centre, Alfred Stanismore (from British Honduras), outside the entrance to the building giving directions to Mr Colley (a student of journalism from Gambia) and Mr Magzaka (a medical student from South Africa), both of whom would soon be engaged in war work. The interior photo shows Stanley Carter playing the piano at a Saturday night dance at the Centre, organised by the League of Coloured People. The New Zealand War Contingent Association Soldiers Club interestingly occupied nos. 17, 18 and 23 in 1918.

Early occupants of No. 17 include:
Illtid Nicholl (BCGs, 1820-34); Edward Leigh Pemberton (BCGs, 1840-46, SDs, 1841-42); Charles N. Wilde & Hon. Mrs Wilde (BCG, 1857, RBB, 1858, SDs, 1861-65, and ABCCG, 1871). An entry in *The County Families of the United Kingdom*, by Edward Walford, reads: *"Emily Thomasin Claudine, only daughter of the 1st Lord Truro (by his first marriage), married 1837, her cousin C.N. Wilde Esq. – 17 Russell-square WC"*; James Macdonald FSA Scot. (SDs, 1878-82, and only Mrs Macdonald in 1883-88); Robert William Dibdin (SDs, 1890-95 and WRB, 1897). Dibdin was a Member of the Board of Works for St Giles District

| Bomb damage to Nos. 17-18 (r-l), c.1950 © CLSAC

Two Sierra Leonian students enjoying the view from a balcony of the Colonial Centre at No. 17

Jamaican Women's Auxiliary Air Force (WAAF) volunteers dressed in their 'English' coats leave The Colonial Centre 17.2.43 all © IWM

Stanley Carter plays the piano at a Saturday night dance at the Colonial Centre

and Commissioner for Public Libraries and Museums (1897-1908); Edmund Meredith Crosse DL (SDs, 1902-16); The New Zealand War Contingent Association Soldiers' Club were there in 1918, also occupying Nos. 18 and 23.

Early occupants of No. 18 include: C. George Thornton (BCGs, 1808-24); Thomas Beckwith (BCG, 1829, and only Mrs Beckwith, 1834-40, and SD, 1841); J.T. Bell (BCG, 1842-46); Charles Berkeley, solicitor (BCG, 1857, RBB, 1858, and SDs, 1861-65 and only Mrs Berkeley in 1871-88); Miss Berkeley (SDs, 1889-1901, and WRB, 1897); Thomas Parker (SDs, 1902-04); Joseph Mawson (SD, 1905); Henry Wilson Young (SDs, 1906-10); John and Lady Congrave (SDs, 1915-16); Ancient Order of Foresters (SDs, 1922-44).

19 - George Richards (bap. 1767, d. 1837), poet and wealthy Church of England clergyman, died at No. 19 in 1837. His wife survived him and is listed as *"Mrs George Richards"* in the SDs, 1841-42, and BCGs, 1840-44. The renowned writer and essayist, Charles Lamb (1775-1834), knew George at school, referring to him as *"a pale, studious Grecian"*. Richards graduated BA in 1788, MA in 1791, and BD and DD in 1820. In 1790, when he took holy orders, he was elected to a fellowship at Oriel College, where he remained until 1796. In 1791 he published *An Essay on the Characteristic Differences between Ancient and Modern Poetry*. Also in 1791, George Simon (Earl Harcourt), gave anonymously a prize for an English poem, *The Aboriginal Britons*, which Richards won, and the donor of the prize became his lifelong friend. The poem was printed separately and in sets

The Colonial Centre's Reception Clerk, Alfred Stanismore, gives directions to two of his guests

of *Oxford Prize Poems*. It was called by Charles Lamb *"the most spirited"* of these poems, and lauded by Byron in *English Bards and Scotch Reviewers*. From 1795 Richards was rector of Lillingstone Lovel in Oxfordshire. In 1799 he was elected FSA, then appointed Bampton lecturer in 1800, and select

Rev. George Richards, 1828 © British Museum

preacher in 1804 and 1811. He married Anna Maria Parker of Oxford in 1796, and was from 6th October of that year one of the vicars of Bampton until 1824, when he was appointed to the more valuable vicarage of St Martin-in-the-Fields, Westminster.

There he erected at his sole cost a new vicarage, largely contributed towards the erection of the church of St Michael in Burleigh Street, Strand, and served for some years as treasurer of Charing Cross Hospital. He became a governor of Christ's Hospital in 1822, where he founded the Richards Gold Medal for the best copy of Latin hexameters. A satire arising from an incident on 26th March 1828 in the Vestry Room of St Paul's, which was an episode in a struggle against the autocratic Select Vestry, depicts eight of the Select Vestry of St Paul's, Covent Garden, dining in the Vestry Room, while the beadle blocks the doorway on the extreme right, saying, *"You can't come in now—the 'Select' are engaged."* A parson, identified as Dr Richards, is in the chair at the head of the table - mopping his bald head he says blandly: *"Don't be afraid of the viands, Gentlemen—although our fatigues are great, I hope we shall convince the parishioners we can do our duties at the table if we do not at the Board."*

Besides the works already noted, Richards published: *Songs of the Aboriginal Bards of Britain* (1792); *Modern France: a Poem* (1793); *Matilda, or, The Dying Penitent* (1795); *The Divine Origin of Prophecy Illustrated and Defended* (Bampton lectures, 1800); *Odin, a drama* (1804); *Miscellaneous Poems* (2 vols., 1804), the first

SELECT VESTRY COMFORTS.

| *Select Vestry Comforts*, satirical drawing, 1828 © British Museum

volume of which was dedicated to Lord Harcourt and the second to the Rev. William Benwell. Most of the poems which he had previously published were reprinted in this collection. Richards died at No. 19 on 30th March 1837, and was buried in a special vault in the churchyard of St Martin-in-the-Fields.

Other early occupants of No.19 include: I.C. Reeve (BCGs, 1808-24); Philip W. Wood (BCG, 1829); Charles John Smith and Misses Smith (SDs, 1861-65, RBB, 1858, and only Charles Smith in BCG, 1846); Mrs Johnson (ABCCG, 1871, SDs, 1871-1901, and WRB, 1897); No listings (1902-03); Henry Volckman (SDs, 1904-12); the World's Evangelical Alliance (British Organisation) occupied the premises along with variable tenants from silk weavers to ship builders from 1914 to 1944 (SDs), when it sustained bomb damage.

20 - Samuel Mills (1769-1847), textile merchant, property magnate, JP and philanthropist, lived at No. 20 from 1825, when *"Samuel Mills of Russell-square"* appears in the list of *Members of the United Company of Merchants of England trading to the East-Indies.* He was previously listed in 1796 in the *Members of Society for Promoting Christian Knowledge*, and he was Director of the Clerical, Medical, and General Life Assurance Co. *"Samuel Mills"* is listed in BCGs, 1829-46, and SDs, 1841-42. He married Mary in 1793 and they had four sons and one daughter: Thomas (b. 1794), Samuel Savage (b. 1796), John Remington (b. 1798), Maria (b. 1799) and Joseph (b. 1801). *"Settlement (monetary) before marriage between Samuel Mills weaver of Moorfields London, and Mary daughter of Thomas Wilson sen. gent., 1793"* (Norfolk Record Office). He qualified as a JP *"June 30, 1812"* (LMA). He was also a Governor of Christ's Hospital School. In 1806, he founded, with other Christian philanthropists in the City of London, The Hibernian Society for Establishing Schools and Circulating the Holy Scriptures in Ireland. Its local executive was in Sligo, Ireland, where Samuel was sent by the Society in 1807. Samuel bought Tolmers Park in Newgate Street Village near Hatfield in 1834, having previously acquired adjoining land in Cuffley. The estate passed to his son, **Thomas Mills**, who was MP for Totnes, and then to his other son, John Remington Mills, also an MP (for Wycombe). Thomas Mills and Miss Mills are listed at No. 20 in BCG, 1857, and the RBB, 1858. Miss Mills and Miss King are listed in the SDs, 1861-78.

Early occupants of No. 20 include: William Anderson (d. 1825), broker (BCGs, 1808-23). Identical notices in three editions of *The Gentleman's Magazine* announce *"At Highwood-hill, the wife of*

William Anderson of Russell-square, a son…" on 21st August 1807, 2nd October 1808, and 19th August 1811, respectively. Highwood Hill was an exclusive 'resort' in Barnet frequented by well-to-do Georgians. The *Annual Register*, Vol. 64, 1822, announced: *"At Hendon, William Mackenzie esq. 3rd dragoons, to Justina, third daughter of William Anderson of Russell-square."* William was a Governor of the Northern Dispensary in 1813-14; Frederick William Price (SDs, 1886-88). William died at Highwood Hill on 16th February 1825 (*The Gentleman's Magazine*, January-June, 1825); James William Wolfe (c. 1842-1913) and his wife, Agnes Elizabeth, lived at No. 20 from 1892 to 1912 (SDs and WRB, 1897). *"Mrs Wolfe"* alone is listed in the SDs, 1914-20, which confirms that William lived there until he died on 17th September 1913 (Notice to creditors: *The London Gazette*, 19.12.1913). He was a Member of the Board of Works for St Giles District (1897-1900), along with various other 'Gentleman' residents of Russell Square; Pitman's College shared the building with the British Association for Commercial and Industrial Education during World War II. No. 20 became a 'gap site' after the completion of Charles Clore House in 1975 and has remained as such to the present day. However, the University of London's 2015 Masterplan earmarked this *"unsightly piece of Bloomsbury"* for improvement with, *"A new infill building…to extend the Georgian terrace whilst respecting the character of the terrace and of Lasdun's Grade II* listed IOE building."* This implies that the new building is unlikely to replicate the design of the original terracotta clad building which once stood on this site.

No. 21 (left), with the gap site at former Nos. 19 and 20 and the Institute of Education occupying the site of former Nos. 17 and 18

The University of London's *"indicative view"* of their proposed new building to fill the gap at Nos. 19 and 20 © UoL

21 - Sir Samuel Romilly (1757-1818), law reformer and pioneer of the abolition of slavery, lived at No. 21 with his wife Anne and their children from 1803 to 1818, taking the first 99-year-lease on the newly built house (*ODNB*). He is listed in the only available BCG, 1808. Born in London, the son of a Huguenot watchmaker, Romilly entered Gray's Inn at the age of 21. On the accession of the 'Ministry of All the Talents' to office, he was offered the post of Solicitor General. Sir Samuel's many reforms included (whilst living at No. 21) in 1808, the repeal of the Elizabethan statute which made it a capital offence to steal from the person and, in 1814, the abolition of hanging, drawing and quartering. He also opposed the suspension of the Habeus Corpus Act, publishing *Observations on the Criminal Law of England* (1810). He tragically committed suicide at his home in his sixty-second year by slitting his throat on 2nd

Peter Mark Roget, 1867

186 | Sir Samuel Romilly by Sir Thomas Lawrence
© National Portrait Gallery, London

Friend at Hand public house in Colonnade, 1903 © CLSAC

November 1818, three days after the death of his wife, which was said to have unhinged his mind. He died despite the best efforts of his nephew Peter Mark Roget (famed for compiling Roget's Thesaurus), who slept in the same room due to concerns about Sir Samuel's mental state. Having sat up with his uncle all night, Roget was replaced by Sir Samuel's teenage daughter Sophie, whom Samuel persuaded to leave the room so that he was free to take his own life.

A report on the inquest in *The Times* (4th November 1818), which was held in the pub in the Colonnade off Bernard Street on 3rd November, reads: *"The utmost anxiety prevailed in the neighbourhood, and gloom pervaded every countenance"*. A certain C. Maybrey, surgeon, residing nearby in Great Russell Street, was sent for at 2pm: *"On entering the bed-chamber, he found Dr. Roget leaning over the deceased, who was on the floor; the servants were supporting him. The deceased held in one hand a sheet of paper, and a pen in the other, and appeared making an attempt to write."* Another surgeon, John Knox, also of Great Russell Street, was sent for at 2.30pm: *"He examined the body, and found a large wound in the upper part of the throat, which had completely severed the wind-pipe. The blood had then ceased to flow, as also circulation in the wrist; respiration continued in an imperfect state until 3 o'clock."*

Sir Samuel did not live to see the realisation of his humane efforts, which resulted in the abrogation of the death penalty for such trivial offences as petty theft. Although he made a large fortune at the Bar, his *Memoirs* suggest that it was at the expense of his happiness: *"...though by nature gifted for the delights and comforts of a domestic circle, and for the intercourse of social life, he saw little of his family or of his friends."* (*Life of Sir Samuel Romilly*). Creevey, wrote of the sad event to Hon. A.G. Bennett in the following month: *"I must advert to the great calamity we have all sustained in the death of poor Romilly. His loss is perfectly irreparable. By his courageous and consistent public conduct, united with his known private worth, he was rapidly acquiring an authority over men's minds that, had his life been spared a few years, would, I think, have equalled, if not surpassed, even that of Mr. Fox."* (*The Creevey Papers*, Vol. I) An ornate bronze tablet commemorating Romilly's residence at No. 21 was installed on the front of the building in 1919, but only after the previous owner (in 1904) had opposed its mounting due to the perceived stigma surrounding Romilly's death.

Russell Square - where Sir Samuel Romilly lived from 1803 to 1818

Commemorative tablet to Sir Samuel Romilly at 21 Russell Square

Other early occupants of No. 21 include:
George Moravia (BCG, 1820); A.A. Mieville (BCGs, 1821-34). The *Monthly Magazine*, June 1803, lists the marriage of A.A. Mieville of Bernard Street to Miss Mary-Ann, third daughter of James Browne Esq. of Brighton. The *Gentleman's Magazine*, June 1830, lists the marriage at St George's Bloomsbury of J.L. Mieville Esq. of Brunswick Place to Mary-Ann, eldest daughter of A.A. Mieville Esq. of Russell Square. A.A. Mieville is also listed in *The Lancet*, 4th December 1824, along with an impressive collection of 'the great and the good', as both Director and Trustee of the Clerical, Medical and General Life Assurance Society, 32 Great Russell Street. A notice in *The Gazette* refers to the company of A.A. Mieville and Co, stockbrokers, being dissolved by mutual consent on 5th August 1837. Andrew Amadec Mieville and John Henry Barlow are named as partners in this company; John Petty Muspratt (BCGs, 1840-46, and SDs, 1841-42); George Smith (BCG, April 1857, RBB, 1858, SDs, 1861-62, and ABCCG, 1871. Mrs George Smith is listed alone in the SDs, 1878-1882); Alfred Draper (SDs, 1886-93, and listed as *"Alfred Cribb Stennings Draper JP"* in 1894-1901, and in WRB, 1897, also in SDs and BCGs until 1905, with Mrs Draper listed alone in 1906 and 1907). Alfred's carpenters & joiners partnership was dissolved by mutual consent on 19th March 1859 (*The Gazette*). *"It was in this house that Irish playwright* **Oscar Wilde**

(1854-1900) spent his last evening in London on the 19th May 1897, before leaving for France under the alias Sebastian Melmouth; he never returned to the United Kingdom." (Gary Powell, *SQUARE LONDON*, 2012) It has not been possible to establish a link between Oscar and the Drapers, who were living at No. 21 at the time; Leslie Stuart (SDs, 1910-12); The National Amalgamated Union of Shop Assistants, Warehousemen and Clerks occupied the building in 1914-15; The Belgian News Fund (BNF) is listed at No. 21 in the 1918 SD, although a hand-written letter dated 24.8.1915, on its headed paper, states *"Information Bureau: 55 Russell Square, London, W.C.",* and describes the organisation as *"A newspaper for the Belgian Soldiers and refugees".* The President of BNF is indicated on the headed paper as *"MGR. DE WACHTER – Auxiliary Bishop to His Eminence Cardinal Mercier",* which fits with No. 55 being occupied by the Catholic Association at the time.

22 - Thomas Porrett Hayes (1772-1850), solicitor, is listed in *The Gazette* as living at 22 Russell Square, and as *"T. Porrett Hayes, sol."* in BCGs, 1845-46. He died in 1850, which explains why his wife, Frances, whom he married in Dorset in 1801, is listed as *"Mrs Porrett Hayes"* in BCG, 1857, and in the RBB, 1858, then as *"Mrs Hayes"* in the SDs, 1861-62. Thomas was a Governor of the Asylum for the Support and Education of the Deaf and Dumb Children of the Poor in May 1821. The *"Will of Thomas Porrett Hayes, Gentleman of Russell Square, Middlesex",* proved on 13th December 1850, and held at the National Archives, makes reference to his various properties: *"I give my dwellinghouse in Russell Square & the Coach house and stable held therewith and also my one third share in the Conservative Clubhouse in Saint James's Street unto my dear and affectionate Wife Frances Isaac Hayes."* After setting aside various sums from £100-500 for close relatives, he left *"...to my present Coachman Footman Cook and housemaid Emily Ettridge (if severally living with me at the time of my decease) the sum of nineteen pounds nineteen shillings".* He also left £500 to his Clerk in his chambers in Bedford Row. The records of compensation claims for slaves freed on the St Mary's, Bellfield Estate, Jamaica state that a *"...letter from Thos Porrett Hayes dated 30/07/1835, Bedford Sq, as agent for Thomas Forrest, alludes to 135 negroes claimed by Edward Hyde East and a further 113 on the same estate belonging to Thomas Forrest."* The claim lodged on 27th July 1838 related to compensation of £2,261 0s. 2d. for the release of 113 enslaved individuals, equivalent to £228,361 in 2016.

John (Giovanni Batista) Ortelli (1830-1898), Italian businessman, banker and philanthropist, is listed at No. 22 as *"J. Ortelli"* in WRB, 1897, and in the SDs, 1897 to 1898, the year he died, as John Ortelli. *"Mrs Ortelli"* is listed alone in the SDs, 1899-1912 and as *"Mrs John Ortelli"* in BCG, 1903. The 1851 Census lists 49 Hatton Garden as the address of Defendente Ortelli & Co., with Defendente being described as a looking glass manufacturer and his 20-year-old brother-in-law, John, son of Antonio, as the resident manager. The Small Edition of the Post Office Directory lists Defendente Ortelli & Co at 49 Hatton Garden as a maker of barometers, looking glasses and thermometers.

Example of a typical Ortelli & Co barometer dial

Defendente and John (in Italy he was called by the anglicised version of his real Christian name) were granted naturalisation as British citizens in 1853. Having received some of his education in England, John's fluency in English stood him in good stead in later years. In 1860, Defendente ended the partnership and went home to Italy, leaving John to build up a formidable business empire in London, where he became a great philanthropist, until his death in 1898. *"He carried on the looking glass business, but he is also described as a merchant and had fingers in several pies, from furniture to banking. His great work, (which was) centred on the poor, the sick, the trafficked and the uneducated of the growing Italian Colony in London, was continued by his wife, Angiola (Primavesi), until her death in 1912. The couple had no children of their own but adopted a young girl, always known as Minnie, who married one of her father's business friends and then had an affair with the grandson of Fedele Primavesi, eventually running off to Paris with him … In three generations, the Ortellis had done amazingly well for themselves in London, and elsewhere - they had significant interests in Argentina. Today, their names live on in the numerous barometers that they signed, but their story is entirely bound up with that of the late 18th-Century immigrant barometer*

sellers who established the Italian community in Britain that we know and take for granted today." (Jean Hood) Inside the badly deteriorated Ortelli family vault at St Mary's RC Cemetery, NW10, is an inscription which reads: *"In memory of Commendatore John Ortelli (late of Hatton Garden). Born 1830, died 1st Nov. 1898, buried in Appiano, Italy. Founder of the Hospital for Italians in Queen Square, WC, President of the Italian Night School, first Associate of the Italian Benevolent Society, an ardent lover of his country and admirer of England and a true friend to the poor."* An ornate plaque on the corner of the Italian Hospital commemorates John Ortelli's benevolence which funded the construction of this attractive building in 1898.

The Italian Hospital, Queen Square today

Plaque commemorating John Ortelli's benevolence

Footnote: The Italian Hospital, 40-41 Queen Square, WC1, operated as a hospital from 1884 to 1990. The *Ospedale Italiano* was founded in 1884 by the successful Italian businessman, Commendatore Giovanni Battista (John) Ortelli, who had become aware of the language difficulties faced by his compatriots in London hospitals. The Commendatore donated two houses in Queen Square which were later demolished and a new building erected in 1898.

THE GRAPHIC
AN ILLUSTRATED WEEKLY NEWSPAPER
SATURDAY, JANUARY 5 1889

THE FIRST ITALIAN HOSPITAL IN LONDON—QUEEN'S SQUARE, BLOOMSBURY

Front page feature in *The Graphic* illustrated weekly newspaper, January 5th 1889

The main wards were in the front of the building, with smaller ones at the back along with single rooms for private patients or cases that needed to be isolated. For infectious cases, there was a separate block at the back of the building, with its own bathroom and kitchen and bedroom for the nurse in attendance. The Hospital chapel was at the top of the main building, with a corridor past it leading to the flat roof, where convalescent patients could play games and enjoy the fresh air. The Hospital had a large passenger lift, as well as a service lift for food to be sent from the kitchen to the wards. The Sisters of St Vincent de Paul, with their distinctive uniforms, provided the nursing care. While preference was given to Italians, the Hospital treated any needy person - almost half its patients were British - and it became a respected medical facility, attracting highly qualified staff. Funds for the Hospital were raised from subscribers in Britain and Italy. In 1910 the Hospital was extended when two houses behind it were acquired. During World War I, the Hospital was affiliated to the Fourth London General Hospital, with 60 of its beds reserved for sick and wounded servicemen. In 1933 a group of British Fascists endowed a bed at the cost of 1,000 guineas (£1,050) dedicated to Il Duce, Benito Mussolini, who sent a telegram acknowledging the gift as *"...proof of the friendly spirit of cooperation which unites the people of the two countries"*. The Governors of the Hospital were lay members, unlike most other voluntary specialist hospitals, and this sometimes led to friction between management and the clinical staff. In 1935, the entire medical staff resigned because they felt doctors were being appointed without suitable qualifications. Friction appeared again in 1937, this time between the British and Italian Governors. The Italians insisted on having more control and the British resigned in protest. The Hospital, with 53 beds, was forced to close in 1941, when Italy entered World War II. It re-opened in 1946 with 48 beds, but did not join the NHS in 1948 and continued as an independent hospital. The Hospital played an important part in the Italian community - the 'Little Italy' of Clerkenwell - but the establishment of the NHS in 1948, the changing needs of the community, and the running expenses, all combined to make its upkeep difficult. Financial problems forced its closure in 1990. The Grade II listed building was sold and the revenue used to begin a charity entitled The Italian Hospital Fund (renamed the Italian Medical Charity), whose aim is to continue to financially assist patients of Italian nationality or descent. The Hospital for Sick Children in Great Ormond Street acquired the building and it is now used as offices and as hostel accommodation for parents whose children are patients of the Hospital. It was renamed the Italian Building.

23 - Alexander John Gaspard Marcet

(1770–1822), Swiss-born physician and chemist of Huguenot descent, and his wife, Jane Marcet, science author, took a house here shortly after they married in 1799, and brought up three of their four children at No. 23 - two daughters, Louisa and Sophie, and one son, François (1803–1883), who became a distinguished physicist (*ODNB*).

Alexander wrote a letter to Malthus from this address on 23rd December 1809, which included the following reference to No. 23: *"If you should favour us with a call when you come to London, you will find us in Russell square (No. 23), a place far less remote from your usual residence than that in which you did us the honor of visiting us 2 or 3 years ago."* (The Rev. Thomas Robert Malthus FRS [1766-1834] was an English cleric and scholar, who was best known for his hugely influential theories on population growth.) During the political disturbances in Geneva, following the French Revolution, Alexander was indicted for serving in the National Guard and, after the fall of Robespierre in 1794, he was banished from Switzerland for five years, with his boyhood friend Charles Gaspard De La Rive. Together they studied medicine at Edinburgh, and graduated MD on 24th June 1797. Marcet attended meetings of the London Medical Society and, discovering dissatisfaction among the members, became a founder member in 1805 of the Medico-Chirurgical Society of London, of which he was Foreign Secretary until his death in 1822. On 2nd June 1808 he was elected a Fellow of the Royal Society, and in the following year he took charge of a temporary military hospital at Portsmouth for troops suffering from a virulent fever contracted during the expedition to capture Flushing and Walcheren, from which he too suffered an attack. In 1817 Marcet published his most important and original work, *An Essay on the Chemical History and Medical Treatment of Calculous Disorders*. He retired from the staff of Guy's Hospital on 10th March 1819, after inheriting a large fortune from his father-in-law. He had paid a short visit to Geneva in 1815 and he returned in 1821, intending to live there. He was warmly received and was made both a member of the representative council and an honorary professor of chemistry, sharing lectures with his friend De La Rive. In 1822 he returned to England to settle his affairs prior to moving permanently to Geneva, but while visiting Edinburgh he suffered an attack of *"gout of the stomach"* (Munk, Roll). He returned to London, and was attended by William Babington and Astley Cooper, but he died at Babington's home in nearby Great Coram Street on 19th October 1822. He was survived by his wife, who died on 28th June 1858.

Other early occupants of No. 22 include:
Henry Martin (BCGs, 1808-20); Richard Stainforth (BCGs, 1821-23); Willoughby Rackham, Gentleman of Lincoln's Inn, who was appointed a member of the Society of Gentlemen Practisers in the Courts of Law and Equity (Great Britain) on 25th April 1803. He is listed at No. 22 in BCG, 1824. His death *"at Russell Square"* in March 1825 was considered worthy of a mention in the *Annual Register of World Events*; Samuel Platt, barrister (BCGs, 1829-43, and SDs, 1841-2); Edward Saunders (ABCCG, 1871, and SD's, 1878-82); Frank Statham Hobson (1851-1896), land agent, is listed in SDs from 1886 to 1895, when he died, aged 44. He and his wife Emma, who died in 1921, had eight children; The Royal Historical Society & Historical Associates occupied the building in 1915-30 (SDs); the Institution of Heating and Ventilating Engineers and the National Association of Heating, Ventilating & Domestic Engineering Employers shared the building in 1939-41 (SDs), replaced by the Holborn District Register Office in 1942-45 (SDs), probably as a refuge from bomb-ridden Holborn.

Alexander John Gaspard Marcet © Royal Society of Medicine

Bird's Eye View of The London Docks – Illustrated London News, 27.9.1845

Lansdowne Bridge over the Indus at Sukkur, completed 1889

Howrah or Jubilee Bridge in 1945

Sir Alexander Meadows Rendel, KCIE

(1828-1918), civil engineer, lived at No. 23 from 1904 to 1916 (SDs). He was the engineer of the London Dock Company in 1856, responsible for Shadwell Basin, the Connaught Tunnel and the Royal Albert Dock.

He was also responsible for the Albert and Edinburgh Docks in Leith, and for Workington Dock and Harbour. Other docks designed by him included those at Kirkcaldy, Llanelli, Milford, and Workington. In 1857-58 he was consulting engineer to the India Office, the East India Railway and other Indian railways, and was a member of the Commission to determine narrow gauge for Indian Railways in 1870. He was responsible for the construction of many thousands of miles of railway and for bridging many of the great Indian rivers, notably the Upper Son Bridge of Patna, the Alexandra Bridge over the Chenab, the Lansdowne Bridge over the Indus at Sukkur which, when it was completed in 1889, was the largest cantilever bridge in the world. He went on to design the Hardinge Bridge over the Ganges, the Empress Bridge over the Sutlej and the climax of his bridge-building career, the Howrah or Jubilee Bridge, which allowed trains to cross the Hooghly River near Calcutta. It was opened by the Viceroy on 21st February 1887, the year Rendel was knighted.

He was also consulting engineer to the strategically important Uganda Railway, reaching Lake Victoria ahead of the German competition. Other notable railway projects were the Egyptian Light Delta Railway and the Mexican Railway. His youngest surviving brother, Hamilton Owen Rendel, designed and supervised the installation of the steam driven, compound condensing pump engines, hydraulic accumulators and hydraulic machinery which first operated the bascules of London's iconic Tower Bridge. Alexander died at 51 Gordon Square on 23rd January 1918. Wealth at death: £96,015 18s. 8d. (equivalent to £6M in 2016).

Leila Margaret Rendel (1882–1969), social worker and children's campaigner, spent many of her early years at the house of her grandfather, Sir Alexander Rendel, when he lived at No. 23 (see above). After a short career as a teacher, then inspector of schools, she founded her own nursery at Cartwright Gardens, St Pancras, in 1911, and for the next 58 years ran a community that was to influence the lives of thousands of children and establish standards in residential care that were followed by many other pioneers. The nursery was surrounded with pictures by Randolph Caldecott and she took his name for her community. (Might Randolph have

Illustration by Randolph Caldecott

been related to Andrew Caldecott who lived next door at No. 24 in the 1840s? - see below) Leila was the moving force behind a great many of the mid-twentieth-century developments in the treatment of disturbed and difficult children. With the financial help of the Nuffield Trust in 1947 she set up the first experimental reception centre in England, to assess the most appropriate placement for children who came into care, a project later developed by many local authorities. Throughout the following years, the Caldecott Community served as a powerhouse of ideas for the better understanding of children and their needs, and the inspiration always came from Leila Rendel. She held three firm principles for dealing with young people. She maintained first that it was essential to give children continuity in their relationship with adults, and for them to receive appropriate affection from those adults. Second, she believed in integrating freedom and order within her community. Finally, she maintained that it was essential to recognize the individuality of each child and find an identity that might have been lost. Children recognized the love that Leila intuitively gave them, but also that there were necessary boundaries. She gave evidence to the Curtis Committee, set up in 1945 to examine the changes that needed to be made in looking after deprived children. As a result, children's departments were established by local authorities, and it was not surprising that she was then asked to be a member of the Home Office advisory council on child care. Her contribution to working with children was recognized in 1948 when she was appointed OBE.

Footnote about Randolph Caldecott (1846-1886): Caldecott was a British artist and illustrator, who greatly influenced the illustration of children's books during the nineteenth century. He moved to London from Manchester in 1872, where he remained for seven years, spending most of them in lodgings at 46 Great Russell Street, opposite the British Museum. While there he met and made friends with many artistic and literary people, among them Dante Gabriel Rossetti, George du Maurier (who was a fellow contributor to *Punch*), John Everett Millais and Frederic Leighton. His abilities as an artist were promptly and generously recognised by the Royal Academy. Two books illustrated by him, priced at a shilling each, were published every Christmas for eight years. He also illustrated novels and accounts of foreign travel, made humorous drawings depicting hunting and fashionable life, drew cartoons and made sketches of the interior and exterior of the Houses of Parliament. He exhibited sculptures and paintings in oil and watercolour in the Royal Academy and galleries. The Caldecott Medal, which has recognized the best illustrators in children's literature since 1938, was named in his honour.

Randolph Caldecott

Lilian Lindsay CBE, FSA (1871-1960), the first female dentist to qualify in Britain, lived with her dentist husband, Robert Lindsay, at No. 23 - she from 1920 to 1935, and he until his death in 1930. *"...Robert Lindsay became first dental secretary of the British Dental Association (BDA) in 1920 and they moved into a flat at headquarters in Russell Square, London"* (ODNB). The **British Dental Association** is listed in the SDs, 1920-33.

Here are two examples of the front pages of Caldecott's popular 1 shilling book

Boardroom of the British Dental Association, 23 Russell Square, 1919-20 © English Heritage

Lilian was the third of eleven children born to parents James and Margaret Murray. She was educated at the Camden School for Girls, and won a scholarship to the North London Collegiate School, where she rejected the encouragement of her head teacher to become involved in the teaching of deaf children, instead commencing a three-year apprenticeship with a dentist. After passing the preliminary examination for registration as a dental student, she applied to enter the National Dental Hospital and School on London's Great Portland Street. Her application was refused on grounds of gender though, and it was suggested that she instead apply to the Edinburgh Dental Hospital and School. Her application to Edinburgh was accepted and she graduated LDS (Hons), RCS Ed. in 1895. As well as practising, she took an active interest in dental politics and the advancement of the dental profession and oral health. She supported her husband, Robert, whom she had met in Edinburgh, in becoming the first Dental Secretary to the British Dental Association in 1919. After the couple had retired from practice she dedicated her energies to the establishment of the BDA's Library and Museum at their headquarters at 23 Russell Square and published an array of papers. With the move from its first headquarters at 19 Hanover Square to larger premises at 23 Russell Square in 1919, plans were made to allocate space for a BDA library. A report on the new offices at a Representative Board meeting on May 16th 1919 states that, *"On the ground floor is a large room – 28ft by 20ft, suitable for a library and reception room, and accommodation for offices."* In the event the library ended up in a smaller area on the second floor of the building. Lilian was made honorary librarian. Following Robert's death, Lindsay served for more than 20 years as Sub-Editor for the British Dental Journal and became the first female BDA President in 1946..
There is a detailed description of the history of the

Lilian Lindsay on the occasion of the presentation of her doctorate from Edinburgh University 1946 © BDA Museum

BDA on their excellent website, which refers to the unveiling of an English Heritage plaque to Lilian on 17th April 2013 at her childhood home at 3 Hungerford Road, Islington, where she lived from 1872 to 1892.

Lilian Lindsay in 1960

Today, the Lindsay Society aims to promote interest, study and research into the history of dentistry. It brings together members of the dental profession, historians and other interested people to research and discuss the history of dentists and dentistry. Each year the society hosts the Lilian Lindsay Memorial Lecture at the BDA conference. The BDA moved to larger premises at 13 Hill Street in 1935 and then again in 1967 to its current home in Wimpole Street. The library was named the Robert Lindsay Library and later, on Lilian Lindsay's retirement, the Robert and Lilian Lindsay Library.

Lilian Lindsay in the first BDA library at Russell Square © BDA

Sir Alfred Thomas Davies, CBE, DL, JP
(1881-1941) is listed at No. 23 in the SDs, 1939-41,
sharing the house with Film Booking Offices Ltd.
He was an underwriter, foreign carrier and merchant
and a Conservative Party politician. Educated at
London Polytechnic, he was Conservative Member
of Parliament for Lincoln from 1918-24. He was
a member of St Pancras Borough Council from 1913-
1919, and Mayor of St Pancras for 1931-32. He was
awarded the CBE in 1920 and knighted in 1931. He
was a Municipal Reform Party member of the London
County Council, representing St Pancras North
from 1931-37. He was also honorary colonel of the
19th London Regiment (St Pancras) from 1934-36.

Sir Alfred Thomas Davies, 1921
© National Portrait Gallery, London

Other early occupants of No. 23 include:
S.N. Cowley (BCGs, 1820-34). He married a Miss
Anistian at St Giles Church in 1805 (*The Universal
Magazine*, 1805). Key family events occurring during
their time at No. 23 include: their fourth son, Philip,
died, 5th September 1825 (*The London Magazine*),
another son, John Christian, left Harrow School in
1826 (*Harrow School Register*), their daughter, Harriett
Sophia, is married at St George's Bloomsbury on 3rd
April 1830, their eldest daughter, Emma, is married
in 1834 (*The Court Magazine*), their daughter, Anne

Matilda marries at Marylebone on 2nd May 1934
(*The Gentleman's Magazine*). Shortly after the family
moved from No. 23, a tragic event was recorded in
The Gentleman's Magazine, July-December 1835: "At
Gibraltar, Ensign Charles Cowley, 59th Reg. youngest
son of S.N. Cowley, esq. of Park Crescent. On board his
Majesty's ship Caledonia, off Zante, Lieut. Harris R.N. He
challenged one of the midshipmen to go inside the main
rigging into the main top as soon as he would go outside.
When two-thirds up, he lost his hold and fell on the deck
upon his head, and fractured his skull in several places."
Five years later, a notice in *The Gazette* announced
that Merchants & Scotch Factory, a business in which
"*Samuel Norman Cowley*" was a joint partner, was
dissolved; John Edward Todd (BCGs, 1840-45, and
SDs, 1841-42); William H. Smith, solicitor (BCG, 1846);
Henry Young, solicitor, and Francis Young (BCG, 1857,
and RBB, 1858), the SDs list Henry Young Esq and
Henry Robert Young Esq in 1861, Henry Young Esq.
in 1862, and Charles Waring Young in 1878, with
Mrs Henry Young alone in the ABCCG, 1871. Henry
was the "*...son of Jonathan Young and Mary Waring,
(1778-1845), illegitimate daughter of 11th Duke of
Norfolk... On his marriage to Maria Fladgate in 1823,
Henry Young was described as of the Inner Temple and
of Essex Street. In 1851 Henry Young solicitor was living
at 23 Russell Square with wife Maria aged 50, 4 sons
(3 involved in the law, the 4th at Balliol Oxford) and one
daughter.*" (UCL Project); William Thompson (SDs,
1882-1903, and WRB, 1897) - not to be confused
with William Marcus Thompson, who lived at No. 30
at the same time. He is listed at No. 23 in the available
electoral registers for 1891, 1898 and 1902. The 1891
census states: "*23 Russell Square - William Thompson
(65), auctioneer, b. Lancs., Sophia Thompson (illeg), wife, b.
Yorkshire, Edith W Thompson (35), unmarried daughter, b.
Middx, + 5 female servants*", and the 1901 census gives:
"*23 Russell Square - William Thompson (76), widower,
retired auctioneer, b. "Lee", Edith W Thompson (38),
unmarried daughter, b. Holborn, + 4 female servants.*"
William Thompson of 23 Russell Square appears in the
1902 membership list of the Zoological Society and
in documents at the Wellcome Library, which list him
as a Member of the Board of Works for the St Giles
District (1897-1900). Also present at the opening of
Endell Street Baths in 1902 was a Holborn Councillor,
William Thompson (address not given).

24 - T.S. Eliot, OM (1888-1965), essayist, publisher, playwright, literary and social critic - *"one of the twentieth century's major poets"* (Bush, Ronald. *T.S. Eliot's Life and Career, American National Biography*, 1999), worked as a Director of publishing firm **Faber & Faber** in a second floor rear room at No.

T.S. Eliot in his office at No. 24

24 from 1925 until his death in 1965.
Thomas Stearns Eliot is possibly best known for creating *Possum's Book Of Practical Cats*, as well as modernist masterpiece *The Wasteland*, and he was awarded the Nobel Prize in Literature *"...for his outstanding, pioneer contribution to present-day poetry"* (Stockholm, 1948).

American by birth, he became a British citizen in 1927. Much has been written about his disastrous marriage to Vivien Haigh-Wood, whose increasingly bizarre behaviour he endured until she was committed to a mental asylum in 1932. On one occasion she was said to have poured a tureen of hot chocolate through the letter box of his office door at No. 24, fearing that he was starving and imprisoned inside. She would march up and down the pavement outside the offices, wearing a sandwich-board which proclaimed *"I am the wife that T.S. Eliot abandoned."* He frequently escaped her eccentric visitations by fleeing down the fire escape. It was here at the age of 68 that Eliot proposed to his second wife, Valerie, who was 38 years his junior.

Richard Adlington summed up Eliot's achievement in his biography of Ezra Pound: *"... in the enormous confusion of war and post-war England, handicapped in every way... by merit, tact...and pertinacity he succeeded in doing what no other American has done — imposing his personality, taste, and even many of his opinions on literary England."* Nicholas Murray reminds us in his very readable *Real Bloomsbury* (2010) that Sir William Empson, the writer and critic who is commemorated with a Marchmont Association blue plaque at 65 Marchmont Street, was strolling across Russell Square one day when he met T.S. Eliot on his way to the Faber building. Empson asked Eliot about a preface he had written in an anthology of poems

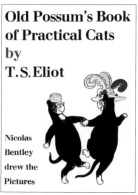

Old Possum's Book of Practical Cats front cover

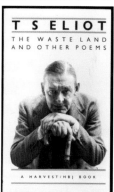

The Wasteland & other Poems front cover

The Faber building in the 1950s

by Ezra Pound in which he stated that a poet should be constantly writing, preferably at least one poem a week. Eliot replied: *"Taking the question in general, I should say, in the case of many poets, that the most important thing to do…is to write as little as possible."* A brown Camden Council commemorative plaque provides a permanent reminder that T.S. Eliot worked at 24 Russell Square for Faber & Faber, although many other notable poets also worked there, including **W.H. Auden**, **Ted Hughes**, **Louis McNeice** and **Stephen Spender**, who was also awarded the Nobel Prize for Literature, as well as serving as Poet Laureate.

Commemorative plaque to T.S. Eliot at 24 Russell Square

(l-r) Louis McNeice, Ted Hughes, T.S. Eliot, W.H. Auden and Stephen Spender at a gathering in the Faber building in 1960

Although Faber & Faber now occupy rather elegant premises on the corner of Montague Street and Great Russell Street, No. 24, now occupied by the University of London, is still affectionately known as The Faber Building and the street directories in 1943-45 list **Geoffrey Faber** as resident there. The Geoffrey Faber Memorial Prize is a British literary prize established in 1963 in tribute to Geoffrey Faber, founder and first Chairman publisher of Faber & Faber

Sir Frederick Morris Fry (1851-1943), KCVO 1919, CVO 1913, MVO 1911, barrister and benefactor, lived at No. 24 from 1900 to at least 1920. He married Edith Headley in 1910 and they had two daughters. *"Frederick Morris Fry"* and *"Miss Fry"* are listed in SDs for 1900-03, with only *"Frederick Morris Fry"* listed in 1904-18, with the titles *"M.V.O."* appended in 1912, *"C.V.O."* (Commander of the Royal Victorian Order) from 1914, and *"K.C.V.O."* in 1920. Queen Victoria established the Royal Victorian Order in 1896, allowing her to bestow junior and personal orders of knighthood directly to an empire-wide

Sir Frederick Morris Fry, 1919
© National Portrait Gallery, London

Africa. Unfortunately for him, fashions changed within a decade and one of his ostriches died. Although the business was on its last legs, he was still keen to know the reason for the demise of the unfortunate bird, which turned out to have had a diamond stuck in its throat. After locating the area where the ostrich had found its carboniferous lunch, he made a very quick fortune, came home, bought Buchan Park, Pease Pottage, West Sussex. It was a palatial estate of over 1,000 acres, complete with tenants, a home-farm for fresh produce, a separate stable block for carriages, lakes for fishing, woods stocked with reared pheasants and a walled garden that would employ six men to furnish the house with flowers, fruit and vegetables. There in 1882 he built a grand Jacobean-style mansion (named Buchan Hill) as home for his wife, Emily (m. 1867), and her sister, their two sons, two daughters and ten servants, according to the 1891 census. The mansion is described in Mark Girouard's *The Victorian Country House* as *"Large and florid, and everything that a Victorian manor should be; in a cheerful combination of hot red brick and yellow sandstone, with a large tower, fancy gables, much early Renaissance ornament and an external top floor loggia (for use as an orangery), and baronical fireplaces, a minsterel's gallery, oak carving, and embossed leather walls and rich panelling to the heart's content in the interior."* The heavily-tinted picture of Buchan Hill was taken about 25 years after it was built.

community for personal services. He was called to the Bar at Inner Temple in 1873 and was a Member from 1898 of the Council (and 1898–1942 of the Distribution Committee) of King Edward's Hospital Fund for London (Hon. Secretary, 1907–11 and 1914–21). He was also Past Master of the Merchant Taylors' Company, Member of the Court of the Sons of the Clergy Corporation, sometime Treasurer, Member of the Council of the City and Guilds of London Technical Institute. He was responsible for the publication of: *A Historical Catalogue of the Pictures, Herse-Cloths, and Tapestries at Merchant Taylors' Hall*; *An Illustrated Catalogue of the Silver Plate on the Merchant Taylors' Company*; *The Windows of Merchant Taylors' Hall*; *The Charters of the Merchant Taylors' Coy.*

Philip Feril Renault Saillard (1839-1916), wealthy merchant and entrepreneur, lived at No. 24 from at least 1878 to 1916. "*Mrs Saillard*" and "*Philip Saillard*" are listed in the SD, 1878, and only "*Philip Saillard*" in 1882-89. He pursued many interests and enterprises, one leading to his appointment as Master of The Worshipful Company of Makers of Playing Cards, for which he had his portrait embossed on the Ace of Spades.

In the 1870s, there was a boom in ostrich feathers, used for elaborating the hats and corsages of ladies of the period. Saillard, always the entrepreneur, seized the opportunity to set up an ostrich farm in South

Saillard's portrait on the Ace of Spades

Buchan Hill, Crawley.

Buchan Hill, Crawley, 1907

Cottesmore School, moved in and is still operating today, but as a boarding prep school for boys and girls aged four to thirteen.

Other early occupants of No. 24 include:
William Nanson (BCG, 1820); William Lettsom (BCG, 1821); William Groom, solicitor (BCGs, 1823-9); W.S. Warwick (BCG, 1834); Andrew Caldecott Esq. (BCGs, 1840-46, and SDs, 1841-42); Henry Hewetson (BCG, 1857, RBB, 1858, and SDs, 1861-65); Mrs H. Hewetson is listed alone in the ABCCG, 1871; Frederick Thomas Pilkington, architect (SDs, 1890-93, joined by Ernest Cropley Pilkington, architect (SDs, 1894-98), with only F.T. Pilkington, architect, being listed in WRB, 1897, even though he had moved to No. 8 in 1895 (see above). A certain William Groom Esq., Vestreyman of St George's Bloomsbury, is also located here, according to the UCL Bloomsbury Project.

Philip and Emily eventually had a total of seven children (five boys and two girls) between 1868 and 1881, although the last three children sadly died at eight, thirteen and twenty-seven years old, respectively. Philip died in 1916 and his widowed daughter continued to live at Buchan Hill until 1925. For several years it stood empty until, in 1931, Upland House School, a boys' prep school, moved there from Epsom. During World War II it was occupied by Pearl Assurance, but in 1946 another boys' school,

| Rear view of the south side of Russell Square in 1971 with No. 24, known as the Faber building, in the foreground

Footnote: The smart car which is parked outside No. 24 in the 1939 photograph on page 181 has been identified as a 1935 Rolls Royce Phantom III with a distinctive 'crocodile roof'. A search of the car's registration number, EXC 194, revealed that its first owner was Rudolph Meyer and that it is still 'on the road' and available for hire from Clouds Wedding Cars in Lancashire as a wedding car, named 'Grace'. It has recently been valued by Bonhams Auctioneers at £260,000. The man with the peaked hat facing the entrance to the Faber building would appear to be a chauffeur waiting for the arrival of his passenger, which we can speculate was Geoffrey Faber or any one of his celebrated colleagues who frequented the offices, such as T.S. Eliot, W.H. Auden, Ted Hughes and Stephen Spender. It might, of course, be none of the above, but instead the official vehicle of Sir Alfred Thomas Davies, who lived next door at No. 23.

Rolls Royce Phantom III, parked outside No. 24, c.1939

Rolls Royce Phantom III Reg. EXC 194, now operating as a wedding car named 'Grace'

The three distinct terraces on the west side of Russell Square today

Chapter 5

The West Side - featuring Senate House

The west side of Russell Square is divided into three distinct terraces, numbered from north to south: Nos. 25-30 (Thornhaugh Street to former Keppel Street); Nos. 31-37 (former Keppel Street to Montague Place); and Nos. 38-43 (from Montague Place to Montague Street). All the above street names are derived from members of the Bedford family, whose family name is Russell. Thornhaugh Street is derived from when the manor of Thornhaugh in Northamptonshire was brought into the Russell family by the marriage of Anne Sapcote to John Russell, 1st Earl. Keppel Street is named after Elizabeth Keppel, who was sister-in-law to the 4th Duke and mother of the 5th and 6th Dukes. Montague Street is named after the 1st Duke of Montagu, who married the step-sister of Lady Rachel Russell.

Nos. 25-29 (r-l) and the Institute of Chemistry building at No. 30 on the left

Nos. 25-30

The houses numbered 25-29 in the northern terrace are probably the least altered of James Burton's original buildings, and are Grade II listed by English Heritage, along with their railings and the sole surviving gas-lamp holder at No. 27. The fluted Doric half-columns either side of their double doors are a particularly attractive feature. Nos. 25-28 are now interconnected and occupied by the University of London's Birkbeck College – School of Social Sciences, History and Philosophy (which also occupies No. 30). The Pears Institute for the Study of Anti-Semitism shares No. 26, with No. 29 now housing The Weiner Library for the Study of the Holocaust and Genocide. Burton's original house at No. 30 was replaced by the incongruous and somewhat austere Institute of Chemistry building in 1915.

Keppel Street, which once ran between Nos. 30 and 31, connecting Russell Square to Malet Street, was closed by order of Parliament (1928) in preparation for the construction of Senate House, the centrepiece of a massive University of London scheme originally intended to stretch from Montague Place to Torrington Place (see section on Senate House, p.215).

Fluted Doric half-columns and original gas-lamp holder outside No. 27

The route of former Keppel Street which ran between Nos. 30 and 31 Russell Square

Brunei Gallery

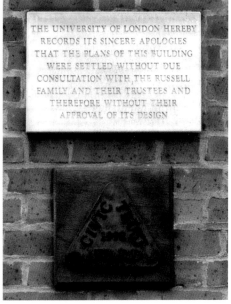

'Complementary' plaques on the Brunei Gallery wall

Brunei Gallery, SOAS – University of London

Positioned at the north-west corner of the square, between Nos. 24 and 25, the Brunei Gallery hosts a programme of changing contemporary and historical exhibitions from Asia, Africa and the Middle East, with a view to presenting and promoting cultures from these regions and to be a student resource and public facility. It is the newest building in the square, designed by Nicholas Hare and built in 1997, and is part of the School of Oriental and African Studies (SOAS), whose main building is a few metres to the north. The 'Birkbeck study' (2004) asserts that the building "... *uses Georgian proportions and scale to harmonise with its surroundings but at the same time makes a telling play of modern materials and structure to announce its twentieth- century creation."* On the flank wall, facing Russell Square, are two small plaques which speak volumes about the nature of land ownership and good taste. When the land on which the University now stands was purchased by the University in 1926, a proviso was included that any significant alteration in the buildings, or in the uses to which they are put, had to be agreed with the Russell family. Due to an oversight by the University, no such agreement was sought or obtained in relation to the Brunei Centre, which gave rise to the very public apology which appears on the upper plaque installed by the University in 1997. However, the lower plaque, which was installed by the Civic Trust a year later, has been interpreted by some as a barely concealed snub to the Bedford Estate's perceived claim to be the sole arbiter of good taste.

No such confusion arose in relation to the original SOAS building, about which there is an interesting World War II story. When war with Japan first broke out at the end of 1941 Britain had been woefully unprepared, not least because almost no one in Britain could speak Japanese. The only place that taught the language was SOAS, so they devised an 18-month course for bright sixth-formers with a flair for languages. They were called the 'Dulwich Boys', after their school, Dulwich College, and many of them went on to be key players in the post-war relationship between Britain and Japan. The SOAS centenary celebrations were launched in February 2016 with an event featuring the 'Dulwich Boys', such was their influence on the development of Japanese studies at the school.

SOAS building, 1943

Four 'Dulwich Boys' posing outside the SOAS building

Rev. Charles Jollands © National Portrait Gallery, London

25 - Charles Jollands (c.1765-1845), is listed in BCGs, 1829-46 and SDs, 1841-42. The *"Will of Charles Jollands of Russell Square, Middlesex"*, held by the National Archives and dated 28th November, 1845, indicates that he was living at No. 25 when he died, leaving £40,000 in funds and property (equivalent to £4.4M in 2016) to his four sons, including Rev. Charles Jollands (c.1802-1866), whose portrait is held by the National Portrait Gallery, London.

Henry Druit Phillips (?-1917), Master of the Worshipful Company of Makers of Playing Cards, 1896-7, is listed at No. 25 in SDs, 1894-1901, and in WRB, 1897. He is then listed at 48 Russell Square in 1902-16. A notice to his creditors in *The Gazette*, 29th March 1918, describes him as a retired solicitor and that he died on 15th May, 1917. Senate House Library lists *Playing-cards of the world: catalogue of the collection of the Worshipful Company of Makers of Playing cards and cards owned by the Guildhall Library, City of London*, where the collection has been deposited since the initial donation in 1908 by Henry Druit Phillips. He is listed in the Playing Card Makers Company's *List of the Master, Wardens, Court of Assistants, Officers, and Livery of the Company* as *"Junior Warden"*. In 1903 he published the *Catalogue of the Collection of Playing cards of various Ages and Countries: formed by Henry D. Phillips (Master of the Worshipful Company of Makers of Playing cards, 1896-7)*, also referred to as 'Father of the Company'.

Ace of Spades playing card bearing the name of H.D. Phillips

Other early occupants of No. 25 include: Mrs Hill (BCGs, 1820-24); James Easton (BCG, 1857, RBB, 1858, and James Easton Sr Esq, SDs, 1861-71. James C.E. Easton is listed in the ABCCG, 1871); Robert Howard Shepard (SDs, 1878-86); there were no listings for No. 25 in 1887-89; in the SD, 1890, Gaisford Gotto is listed at 25A, with George Dibley at 25, where he remained until 1893; No. 25 took on a new lease of life from 1908, when the *"London Biblewomen and Nurses' Mission"* (LBW&NM) moved in, joined in 1910 by the *"Ranyard Nurses' Institute"*. The Nurses' Mission remained until 1915, with only LBW&NM in 1916

and only the *"Ranyard Mission"* from 1918 to 1939. The original home of the Institute of Advanced Legal Studies (IALS) was opened at 25 Russell Square on 11th June 1948 by the Lord Chancellor, Viscount Jowitt, supported by leading members of the University and many distinguished members of the legal profession. With the rapid expansion of the Institute's Library, the shelf space at No. 25 was full in 1949, not helped by the age and condition of the house which restricted shelving to the outside walls. To meet the extra need the Institute expanded into the ground floor and basement of the adjoining house, No. 26, in 1949-1950.

26 - William Roxby Beverly (1810-1889), scenery painter, lived here with his wife Sophia and their children. He is listed as *"William Roxby Beverly, artist"* in the SDs, 1862-87. His brother, the actor Henry Roxby Beverly (see below), died here in 1863, while another brother, actor and stage manager, Robert Roxby, also died here on 25th July 1866, after a long and painful illness. William John Lawrence considered William Roxby Beverly second only to Clarkson Stanfield among British scene-painters of the 19th century (*Dictionary of National Biography*). The theatres he worked in ranged from the Theatre Royal in Manchester to London's Adelphi, Princess's, Lyceum, Drury Lane and Covent Garden Opera House. Beverly also painted to exhibit, with watercolour being his preferred medium. He showed at the Royal Manchester Institution in the 1820s and 1830s, and again in later life. Between 1865 and 1880 he exhibited 29 pictures at the Royal Academy, most of them seascapes. After 1884, failing eyesight led Beverly to stop working. He died in Hampstead on Friday, 17th May 1889. Rev. William Bramley-Moore, who occupied No. 26 after William, informed Chancellor that the ceilings of the first floor rooms were painted by William.

Misty morning, harbour mouth by William Roxby Beverly, 1866

Henry Roxby Beverley, (1796–1863), actor, acquired some reputation as a 'low' comedian, with his father's active encouragement. His first real success came in October 1838, when he replaced John Reeve at the Adelphi, and the following month he played the role of Newman Noggs in *Nicholas Nickleby*. He subsequently appeared in *Oliver Twist, Jack Sheppard* and other melodramas, and made a name for himself performing the principal characters in *The Dancing Barber* and other farces. In September 1839 he became the manager of the Victoria Theatre. Like his father, he died at No. 26, on Sunday 1st February 1863.

Robert Roxby (c.1809–1866), actor. After performing in provincial theatres, Robert appeared in London in 1839 at the St James's. In 1843 he took the Theatre Royal, Manchester, where he played many leading parts in comedy. He was for some years in London at the Lyceum or Drury Lane, and was stage manager of Drury Lane for eleven years. He acted much with Charles Mathews, and was with him and Madame Vestris at the Lyceum from 1847 to 1855. This was his brightest period. In October 1855, at Drury Lane, he played *Rob Royland* to the *Mopus* of Charles Mathews in *Married for Money*, an adaptation of Poole's *The Wealthy Widow*. The following year at Drury Lane, Robert supported Mrs Waller, an actress from America and Australia. In March 1858 he was the original *Lord George Lavender* in Stirling Coyne's *The Love Knot*. He played original parts again in 1860, in Fitzball's *Christmas Eve, or, The Duel in the Snow*, founded on Gérome's famous picture, and as the first Hardress Cregan in H. J. Byron's burlesque *Miss Eily O'Connor*. In January 1863, while stage manager at the Princess's Theatre, he was seriously burnt while fighting a fire on the stage, in which two girls in the pantomime died. On the first appearance in London of Walter Montgomery in that

Mr. SLOMAN, as Jemmy, and Mr. BEVERLY, as Jerry.

John Sloman and Henry Roxby Beverly by Piercy Roberts

Henry Roxby Beverly in *Nine to One*, in which he played all nine characters © British Museum

house as Othello, in June 1863, Roxby was Roderigo. At the close of the year he was again at Drury Lane, where, in April 1864, he played in *An April Fool* by Brough and Halliday.

Other early occupants of No. 26 include:
Benjamin Hawes (BCGs, 1820-29), wealthy Lambeth soap-boiler, was the father of Sir Benjamin Hawes KCB, MP (1797-1862), Whig politician and advocate for the arts, who lived at 36 Brunswick Square in 1834-47. The soap works stood opposite the Temple and was a prominent London landmark; Thomas Leach Esq (BCGs, 1840-46); Mrs Warren (BCG, 1857, and RBB, 1858); Mrs Wickens (SD, 1887); Herman Klein and Maclaine Klein (SD, 1890); Rev. William Bramley-Moore MA (SDs, 1892-1918 and WRB, 1897); The British Scientific Instrument Research Association occupied the premises from 1920 to at least the end of World War II, with the overflow from the IALS library in the ground floor and basement from 1950 (see above).

27 - Early occupants of No. 27 include:
James Dunlop (BCGs, 1820-42, SDs, 1841-42, and Mrs Dunlop in BCGs, 1843-46); J.M. Corrie (BCG, 1857, and RBB, 1858 - also listed as John Malcolm Corrie Esq in SDs, 1861-65); Robert Vigers (ABCCG, 1871, and SDs, 1871-82); Thomas Henry Woods (SDs, 1886-1900, and WRB, 1897; William Howard (SDs, 1902-4); No. 27 was not listed for two years, most probably because it was being refurbished for the arrival from 1907 of the Licensed Victuallers' Central Protection Society of London Ltd, which remained there until 1949. The Society is considered to be the most effective British retail trade organisation of the 19th and 20th centuries (*Alcohol and Temperance in Modern History*, by Jack S. Blocker, David M. Fahey, Ian R. Tyrrell); The Institute of Commonwealth Studies is listed at No. 27 from 1949; the building is now occupied by Birkbeck College.

28 - Sir Charles Abbott (1762-1832),
1st Baron Tenterden, later Lord Chief Justice of the King's Bench (1818-32), Foundling Hospital Governor, and Vestryman of St George, Bloomsbury, lived at No. 28. He is listed as *"Sir C. Abbott, Lord Chief Justice K.B."* in BCGs, 1820-1824 and as *"Lord Tenterden"* in 1829-34. Despite his humble beginnings as son of a Canterbury barber, he rose to the highest position in the English legal system and became an authority on mercantile law, his book *Law relating to Merchant Ships and Seamen*, published in 1802, being a text book on the subject. Although he was criticised by his contemporaries for his ill-temper and often surly manner, the normally critical Charles Greville described

Sir Charles Abbott, 1st Baron Tenterden

him as *"a remarkable man"* (and that) *"his elevation did great credit to the judgment which selected him... He was a profound lawyer, and appears to have had a mind fraught with the spirit and genius of the law, and not narrow and trammelled by its subtleties and technicalities."* Lord Tenterden, in distinctive legal garb, features in a political cartoon titled *"A Mayday Garland for 1820"*.

As Lord Tenterden he was a 'high Tory' in politics, opposing Catholic emancipation and telling George IV that such a concession to the Catholics would be a breach of his Coronation Oath. He also opposed the Reform Bill, which he felt would vest all the power of the state in the House of Commons and give the power of returning a majority of that house *"to a class of persons far below the middle class of society"* (Hansard 3, 1832, 398). He died at No. 28 on 4th November 1832. His last words, sitting up in bed, and making a motion as if dipping his pen in an inkstand, were, *"Gentlemen of the Jury, you are discharged."* (Polson, 1.360). At his own request, he was buried at the Foundling Hospital, London, of which he was a Governor, on 10th November 1832. An extract from the notice of his funeral arrangements posted in *The Times*, 8th November 1832 reads: *"Lord Tenterden was desirous of avoiding unnecessary pomp, and on this subject he expressed a desire, in his will, that he may be buried as a 'private gentleman', and not as a 'public officer'; in conformity with which desire his Lordship's family mean to proceed."*

"A Mayday Garland for 1820"

Sir William Elias Taunton (1773–1835), judge, lived briefly at No. 28, where he died suddenly on 11th January 1835 (Rate Book, Michaelmas 1834, and *ODNB*). He was born at Oxford, the eldest son of Sir William Elias Taunton, Town Clerk of Oxford and Clerk of the Peace for the county, and his wife, Frances, daughter of Stephen Grosvenor, sub-treasurer of Christ Church, Oxford. After an accomplished academic life at Westminster School and Christ Church, Oxford, (he graduated BA in 1793 and MA in 1796) he was admitted student of Lincoln's Inn in 1794, and called to the Bar in 1799, joining the Oxford circuit. In 1801 he became a Commissioner of Bankrupts, and in 1806 succeeded Charles Abbot (the previous occupant of No. 28) as Recorder of Oxford. On 10th October 1814 he married Maria, youngest daughter of Henry William Atkinson, provost of the Company of Moneyers. He was created King's Counsel in 1821 and elected a bencher of his Inn in 1822. In 1830 he was appointed a justice of the King's Bench, and was knighted five days later. Taunton soon in his career acquired the reputation of a black-letter lawyer (Foss, *Judges*, 9.96). As an advocate he was a somewhat dull and slow speaker who, however, *"made the monotony of his voice impressive and used his sluggishness as a power"* (*Law Magazine*, 13, 1835). He was survived by two sons and four daughters.

Sir William Elias Taunton

A VIEW taken from the TOWN HALL OXFORD.

Caricature of Sir William Elias Taunton as Recorder of Oxford

Sir John Voce Moore, 1898-99
© National Portrait Gallery, London

Sir John Voce Moore (1826–1904), businessman and Lord Mayor of London, lived at No. 28 from at least 1886 until he died in 1904. He was listed as *"John Voce Moore"* in the SD, 1886, and as *"Sir John Voce Moore, Knt [Alderman]"* in 1895-1904 and WRB, 1897.

Born in Stockport in 1826, the son of James Moore, he founded a tea-trading company at age 22 and retired as the senior partner of Moore Brothers Tea Merchants. He was a member of the Loriners Company and served as Alderman for Candlewick ward from 1889 to 1902. Whilst serving as Sheriff of the City of London for 1894, he also served as Deputy Lieutenant for Kent and was knighted the same year for his distinguished service connected with the opening of Tower Bridge. He was elected Lord Mayor of London for 1898, aged 72 and died on 11th February 1904. He had married Eliza in Cambridge in 1847, but she died in 1890, with their daughter, Mrs John King-Farlow performing the role of Mayoress, according to the *Sacramento Daily Union* of 20th November 1898. Their sons took on Moore Brothers, tea merchant, in which Sir John had been the senior partner.

Other early occupants of No. 28 include:
W.S. Marshall (BCG, 1840); Charles Skipper (BCGs, 1842-57, RBB, 1858, ABCCG, 1871, and SDs until 1882) Charles Skipper was born in 1798 and married Elizabeth Rippen in 1833. He was Magistrate for Essex, Middlesex and the City of Westminster, also Magistrate and Deputy Lieutenant for Tower Hamlets and Commissioner of the Lieutenancy of the City of London. His main residences were Great Blake Hall, Wanstead, Essex and 28 Russell Square, WC. (*The County Families of the United Kingdom*, Edward Walford). He died on 8th November 1883 at 3 Eastern Terrace, Brighton, Sussex (*The Gazette*, 11th January 1884) and was pre-deceased on 17th March 1878 by his son, Edward, who was a Lieutenant-Colonel in the Indian Army (*The London Gazette*, 5th April 1878). His other known children were Julia, Sidney Charles and Frederick, who attended Rugby School; No. 28 was unlisted from 1905 to 1909, from when it was occupied by Oscar Charles Selbach, motor car constructor and consulting engineer, until 1930. Oscar shared the building with the British Dairy Farmers' Association from 1915, who were joined by the Orconero Iron Ore Co. Ltd in 1920 and the National Fire Brigades Association in 1940, who all remained throughout World War II.

29 - Major (Sir) Percy Coleman Simmons
(1875-1939) was a World War I pilot officer with the rank of Major. He was also a member of the London County Council (LCC) for the City of London from 1919 and Chairman 1921-22. He represented St George's in the East on the London County Council, 1907-10, was Alderman, 1910-19, and Chief Whip, 1914-21. He stood twice as Conservative candidate in

1910 for the parliamentary seat of Tower Hamlets St George, first in the General election and then in a by-election caused by the incumbent Liberal MP, William Wedgwood Benn, becoming a Commissioner of the Treasury, which required him to seek re-election, but Sir Percy lost out on both occasions to Benn. He was a senior partner in the firm of solicitors, Simmons & Simmons and served surprisingly on the Glasgow University Improvements Committee. He also served on various LCC committees and led the fight for modernising the Thames bridges. He was knighted (KCVO) in 1922.

Sir Percy Coleman Simmons, 1929
© National Portrait Gallery, London

In the 1881 Census - 29 Russell Square, St George, Bloomsbury - Percy appears with his parents and siblings, "Henry John Simmons, 44, Costumier b. Strand; Fanny wife, 37, b. Brompton; Rose dau., 14, b. St Pancras; Nellie dau., 12, b. St Pancras; Charlie son, 10, b. St Pancras; Teddy son, 6, b. St Pancras; Maude dau., 3, b. St Pancras." There were at least six servants. Percy's father is listed as Henry Simmons, milliner and costumier, in the SDs, 1878-94, but only Bertram Simmons is listed in 1895 and only Mrs Simmons in 1896, and in WRB, 1897. Mrs Simmons, Percy Coleman Simmons and Edward Coleman Simmons appear together in the SDs, 1897-1901, with only Mrs Simmons and Percy Coleman Simmons listed until 1915. Percy is listed alone in 1916-18.

Other early occupants of No. 29 include:
George Cowie (BCG, 1820); George Brown (BCGs, 1823-29); George Meek (BCGs, 1834-46, and SDs, 1841-42); Samuel Beale (BCG, 1857, and RBB, 1858); William Ewings Esq (SDs 1861-71, and ABCCG, 1871); The London War Pensions Committee was listed in 1920-24; The Official Receiver in Bankruptcy occupied the premises from 1924 and during World War II.

30 - Henry Crabb Robinson FSA (1775-1867), lawyer and diarist, lived at No. 30 from 1839 to 1867, when he died at home. Henry was sharing the house from the time of his arrival in the Square, as he notes in his well-known *Diary* on 25th September 1839: "*I left my chambers in Plowden's Buildings, and went to my apartments in Russell Square, No. 30. I am to pay for this, my new domicile, £100 per annum. It gives me no vote, subjects me to no service. I have no reason to complain of my surroundings. Fellows has the second floor.*" Fellows was "**Sir Charles Fellows**, *the well-known traveller and archaeologist in Asia Minor, who discovered, among other things, the ruins of Tlos and Xanthus in Lycia. His collections are now in the British Museum, to which he left them on his death in 1860.*" (Chancellor, 1907). BCGs, 1840-43 list "*Dr Davison and H. Crabb Robinson, barrister*", with Charles Fellows also listed in 1844-46, but in 1857-58, Crabb Robinson was sharing the house with "*Francis Leach and John Henry Barrett, dentist*", but only Barrett in 1861-62, and only Crabb Robinson is listed in 1865.

Portrait of Henry Crabb Robinson
The Sphere, 19.10.1901

Henry Crabb Robinson's house, 30 Russell Square
The Sphere, 19.10.1901

Charles Fellows © National Portrait Gallery, London

Shortly after Henry's wealthy uncle died leaving him a legacy, he set off on a grand walking tour of Europe, which he spent mainly in Germany from 1800 to 1805, meticulously logging all his experiences and details of the people he encountered in his famous *Diary* (France was an impossibility due to the Napoleonic Wars). Henry was constantly in search of the new, visiting everything from mines to palaces and prisons to churches. He also met the leading poets and thinkers of his day, including J.W. von Goethe, Friedrich von Schiller, and J.G. von Herder. Dr James Vigus, in a talk given in Senate House Library on 29th October 2015, described Henry as *"…a political radical walker in the tradition of Rousseau"*, and an *"enormously influential figure"* in the field of German literature and philosophy, most notably through his essays on the philosophy of Immanuel Kant (1724-1804), still regarded as the central figure of modern philosophy.

Henry served as foreign correspondent for *The Times* (1807–09), becoming the first recognised war correspondent when he covered the Peninsular War (1808-09). He worked as a barrister on the Norfolk circuit from 1813 to 1828 and became involved in

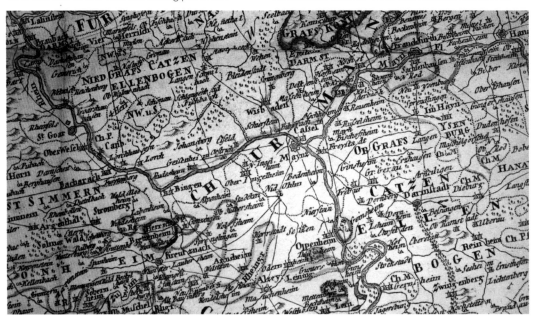

Extract from the map used by Henry Crabb Robinson whilst walking in Germany, with his routes marked in different colours

the anti-slavery campaign and in the founding of the University of London (1828) and the Athenaeum Club. He befriended William Blake, whose last years were fully reflected in Robinson's *Diary, Reminiscences and Correspondence*, published in 1869. His *Diary* contains lively portraits of central figures whom he knew in the English Romantic movement, such as Samuel Taylor Coleridge, Charles Lamb, Blake and William and Dorothy Wordsworth (see wording on his epitaph, below). His *Diary* also pays detailed reference to the comings and goings of residents in Russell Square and their busy social lives, including a detailed but garbled description of a dinner party *"...largely attended by actors, lawyers, and dramatists"* at 56 Russell Square, which was given by Macready after the first performance of *Ion*. Henry recalls that he *"sat by Miss Tree and near Miss Mitford".* (This was Mary Russell Mitford, a prolific and successful writer best known for penning *Our Village* and who was staying at No. 56 in 1836). He also recalls calling on John Walter the 2nd and his son, with whom he had a close personal friendship. An entry in Henry's *Diary* in 1846 reads: *"I called this morning on young John Walter's, who has taken a house on the opposite side of Russell Square, and I was induced to accept an invitation to join a family party there in the afternoon."* John, as editor of *The Times*, substantially increased the size and business of the paper by the inauguration of the Walter Press. In 1829, Robinson was made a fellow of the Society of Antiquaries (FSA). The touching inscription on his grave stone in Highgate Cemetery (near the grave of George Eliot) reads: *"Beneath this stone lies the body of HENRY CRABB ROBINSON...Friend and associate of Goethe and Wordsworth, Wieland and Coleridge, Flaxman and Blake, Clarkson and Charles Lamb. He honoured and loved the great and noble in their thoughts and characters. His warmth of heart and genial sympathy embraced all whom he could serve; all in whom he found a response to his own healthy tastes and generous sentiments. His religion corresponded to his life. Seated in the heart, it found expression in the truest Christian benevolence."*

William Marcus Thompson (1857-1907), journalist and barrister, is listed in SDs, 1882-1903, in WRB, 1897, and in BCG, 1903. Available electoral registers for 1898 and 1902 each have *"William Marcus Thompson"* living at No. 30. The 1901 census reads: *"30 Russell Square - William Marcus Thompson (45), barrister and journalist, b. Ireland, Mary Thompson (38), wife, b. Ireland, + cook & housemaid (both Irish)".* He was actually born at Londonderry, Northern Ireland and married Mary in 1888. They had one daughter who died in December 1907. He was

first a journalist on the *Belfast News Letter*, then the *London Standard* and as a journalist for *Reynolds's Newspaper* he wrote most of the leading articles as well as general contributions under the pseudonym of Dodo, becoming editor in 1894. He joined the bar in 1880, served as President of the National Democratic League, and was a Fellow of the Institute of Journalists. He was a powerful platform speaker, was elected to the London County Council as radical member for West Newington in 1895, but was defeated in his attempt to enter Parliament for the Limehouse division of Tower Hamlets in July of that year. He was largely responsible for the establishment in 1900 of the National Democratic League, of which he was the first President. He was a founder member and promoter of the National Liberal Club (1882), where his portrait by J.B. Yeats (1839-1922), father of W.B. Yeats, is on display.

William Marcus Thompson by J.B. Yeats
© National Liberal Club

He represented numerous Trade Unions and defended in many extradition and home political cases. William also maintained a strong radicalism and an aggressive sympathy with the Irish nationalists. His publications included: *Stories for the People; Democratic Readings from the World's Great Masters; Sweetness and Light,* and *Law for the People.* He later lived at 14 Tavistock Square, where he died of bronchitis and pneumonia on 28th December 1907.

Other early occupants of No. 30 include:
George Lyall (BCGs, 1820-24); Frederick Cox, Henry Baker and Thomas Birch (BCG, 1829); Dr Davison, Thomas Entwisle and John Entwisle (BCG, 1834); Nicholas Francis Davison, physician (SD, 1841, joined in 1842 by Nathaniel Nicholl Davison); Elijah Hoole, architect, and Robert John Chappell (SDs, 1878-83). Only Elijah made it into the ABCCG, 1871; James Jeffery (SDs, 1886-93). There were no further entries in the street directories for No. 30 until 1915, when the *"Institute of Chemistry of Great Britain & Ireland, Incorporated by Royal Charter"* was first listed, with *"Raphael Meldola, D.Sc., F.R.S.",* also listed as its President, although he died at his home at 6 Brunswick Square on 16th September of that year. The Meldola Medal, first awarded in 1921, was named in his honour by the Institute. The Institute of Chemistry was built in 1913-14 by Sir John Burnet, incorporating the seated figure of Joseph Priestley, the father of British chemistry, above the official entrance in former Keppel Street. The basement of No. 30 functioned as an air-raid shelter during World

Seated figure of Joseph Priestley above the official entrance to the Institute of Chemistry building

Raphael Meldola, by Solomon Joseph Solomon © National Portrait Gallery, London

War II, as evidenced by the sand bags in the photograph. The building is Grade II listed by English Heritage.

**Here is the 'rear' entrance
to Senate House,
formerly Keppel Street**

Senate House (University of London)

Senate House was designed by **Charles Holden** (1875-1960) and completed in 1937, from which time it has served as the administrative centre of the University of London. Holden, as architect to London Underground in the 1920s and 30s, is best known for his Piccadilly Line stations and St James' Park station, and for his War memorials in France and Belgium, which he created for the Imperial War Graves Commission.

Holden's headquarters for the Underground Electric Railways Company of London (UERL) at 55 Broadway (1929) bears a striking resemblance to the Senate House style and materials.Senate House was built in the first phase of an ill-fated grandiose scheme, originally intended to provide a new home for the University of London in the heart of Bloomsbury, on land bounded by Montague Place, Malet Street, Torrington Place and Woburn and Russell Squares.

Charles Holden

55 Broadway, 29th August 1930

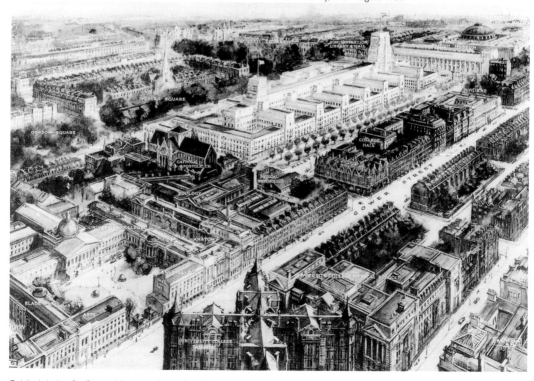

Original design for Senate House and associated buildings - *ILN* 21.1.1933

Although the University is often criticised by historians and conservationists for destroying much of Georgian Bloomsbury, it is a fact that many of the Georgian houses in Keppel Street and its associated Mews were built by less scrupulous builders than Burton and Cubitt and being so poorly built, had no value by the time their 99-year leases ran out in the early 1900s. Furthermore, the great swathe of land between Montague Place and Torrington Place was actually cleared by the British Museum as part of their earlier grand plan to improve the Museum's northern aspect.

Design for the northern approach to the British Museum, by Charles Fitzroy Doll, Surveyor to the Bedford Estate

The brief for the University development specified that it was to have at its centre a tower, "...to dominate the other buildings on and surrounding the site." (Karol and Finch, 1988). William Beveridge, as Vice-Chancellor of the University, who was instrumental in bringing the project to fruition, saw the University as one "...for the nation and the world, drawing from overseas as many students as Oxford and Cambridge and all the other English universities together", and he was adamant that "...the central symbol of the University on the Bloomsbury site cannot fittingly look like an imitation of any other University, it must not be a replica from the Middle Ages. It should be something that could not have been built by any earlier generation than this, and can only be at home in London. (the building) means a chance to enrich London - to give London at its heart not just more streets and shops... but a great architectural feature... an academic island in swirling tides of traffic, a world of learning in a world of affairs." It was Beveridge who had introduced the idea of the tower as early as 1928. The architect, he said, "...will think, I hope of at least one tower, with a great bell, a muezzin, calling the children of the University in all lands". He went further in a talk titled "My Utopia" which he gave to students in 1934, during the construction of Senate House, in which he suggested that on the 'Great Tower' there should be "...a great clock where eight mechanical deans of Faculties and fifty-five Senators dance each day at noon round a mechanical Chancellor." Whether spoken in jest or intended as a clear signal to prospective architects, this concept was not adopted by Holden, who had a singular vision of a monumental building devoid of external visual clutter. It may well have been the protracted early negotiations around the design of the building which led Holden to describe his remit at his appointment in 1931 as "a life sentence with hard labour". However, shortage of funds and the onset of World War II, meant that only the central tower of 19 floors, 210 feet (64 metres) high, and two of the wings of the original Senate House scheme were completed, thus providing Holden with an unexpected reprieve.

The completed building provided accommodation for the University's central administration and library. The library now occupies the fourth to the eighteenth floors, with the public areas of the library on the

| Charles Holden's drawing of the new University buildings, viewed from Bedford Square

fourth to seventh floors. It was the first large-scale building in the country to be heated by electricity, using an early form of storage heater, and as such was the first all-electric building, although there was an earlier plan to heat the building using the excess heat from Battersea Power Station, which instead went to heat the Pimlico Housing Estate, which is directly across the river Thames from Battersea. The original electrical equipment and control panels have been preserved in the basement of the building.

Although Holden opted for a traditional brick structure with load-bearing walls, the building was clad in Portland stone, the favoured material of London's more important buildings of the time, including the adjacent British Museum with its monolithic Ionic columns facing the University's site in Montague Place, previously widened to create a plaza for the Museum's Edward VII wing, which opened in 1914. For his part, Holden viewed Portland stone as *"…a stone identified with London for centuries and known to withstand the smoke and acid-laden atmosphere. The peculiar silvery beauty of its weathered surface may be said to be essential to the full realisation of the design."* He applied grey Cornish Granite below the first-floor level, and Travertine Marble was used throughout the public areas and staircases. Holden also designed many of the internal fittings, which still survive. *"Holden had long promoted controversial sculptors like Jacob Epstein, but he appears to have bowed to conservative opinions rather than risk difficulties elsewhere. The statues' plinths still remain on either side of the tower, nevertheless."* (20th Century Society). Holden's attention to detail is reflected in the attractively painted inscriptions on the rainwater hoppers at the top of the drain-pipes on the south and north wings of Senate House, reflecting their respective dates of completion. He also enthusiastically supported the invitation to the art schools in London to design and paint ceilings and walls, a surviving example of which can be viewed in Chancellor's Hall on the first floor of the North Wing (see photo).

The original electricity control rooms are preserved in the basement of Senate House

A View down the Senate House tower's stairwell

South Wing east side

South Wing west side

North Wing

Rainwater hoppers

Chancellor's Hall first-floor North Wing with mural depicting the distribution of the University across London in the 1930s

The inscription on the foundation stone laid on the west side of the base of the tower by King George V reads: *"This stone was laid by His Majesty King George V on the twenty-sixth day of June 1933 in the twenty-fourth year of his reign Her Majesty Queen Mary being present on the occasion."* The University has a grainy film of the ceremony, which was a very grand occasion, attended by 3,000 people, including Prime Minister Stanley Baldwin, the Archbishop of Canterbury and representatives of education from all over the world. The King and Queen arrived in a horse-drawn carriage and first inspected a guard of honour. There was a procession of men in mortar-boards and ermine gowns. During the ceremony the King packed and buried a casket containing, among other artefacts, newspapers of the day, a programme of the event, and a 1933 penny, one of only about eight that were minted. The Royal Mint had decided that no pennies were needed for the currency that year and so the only pennies minted were for burying under buildings, plus one or two for museums. A tragic accident occurred on 28th November 1936, when a group of University officials, led by the Principal, Sir Edwin Deller, went out to inspect the work in progress. Suddenly, without warning, a skip being pushed by a workman overhead accidentally fell down and hit them. All were rushed to University College Hospital, where two days later, Deller died of his injuries.

| George V laying the foundation stone at Senate House on 26th June 1933

Foundation stone

When the building was eventually unveiled in 1937 it was criticised by conservatives for being too different, and by modernists for being too traditional. However, opinions of the popular press and the general public were universally favourable, with the *Manchester Guardian* comparing Holden to Wren and Barry, and the *Daily Sketch* claiming that modern architecture in concrete had seldom achieved anything more outstanding. Functionalist architect Erich Mendelsohn wrote to Holden in 1938.

View south of the Senate House site, c.1935, with a remnant of Keppel Street on the left

Senate House's Malet Street elevation, close to completion on 15th March 1937

that he was *"…very much taken and … convinced that there is no finer building in London."* However, *Streets East of Bloomsbury* (1997) reminds us that more critical views came to be voiced later, citing Pevsner's unfavourable comparison with Holden's Underground stations (which he admired), Evelyn Waugh's *"grim mass of masonry"* critique and Max Beerbohm's *"bleak, bland and hideous"* lambasting. Nikolaus Pevsner also found the building baffling in its *"strangely semi-traditional, undecided modernism."* Others have described it as Stalinist (Jenkins, 2005), or as totalitarian due to its great scale (Karol, 2008).

'Egyptianate' entrance hall

In a more conciliatory vein, historian Arnold Whittick described the building as a "…*static massive pyramid … obviously designed to last for a thousand years*", but he thought "…*the interior is more pleasing than the exterior. There is essentially the atmosphere of dignity, serenity and repose that one associates with the architecture of ancient Greece.*" This impression is reflected in the contemporary photographs of the recently refurbished 'Egyptianate' entrance hall, and 'Art Deco' foyer and functional spaces illustrated here. It is worth noting that Crush Hall, with its monumental quality, polished travertine walls and deliberately unpolished travertine floor, was designed by Holden with University ceremonies in mind. The grand staircase was originally part of a formal processional route through the first-floor rooms of the senior University officers, such as the Vice-Chancellor, to the Great Hall (pictured above), which was never built. The site is now occupied by the Neo-Georgian Stewart House. The ceiling of Crush Hall is decorated with plane-tree motifs, symbolising London, and the first and last letters of world alphabets, reflecting the University's global reach. Notwithstanding the opinions of the professional architectural critics, the building was much admired by the general public, not least because it was seen as London's first 'skyscraper'. From its completion until 1957, it remained the second tallest building in London, intentionally built one foot lower than St Paul's Cathedral. It was also the tallest secular building in Britain and continues to hold its own in London's ever growing landscape of tall buildings, as can be seen from the photograph taken from the top of the 581 foot high BT (British Telecom) Tower.

library 1

library 2

library 3 – Three contrasting library/study spaces

Aerial view east, c.1937, showing Senate House towering over Russell Square

Apparently, it was not occupied immediately, since it swayed in the wind and the London County Council was worried about safety. Although the sheer scale of the building means that it towers over Russell Square, it was deliberately built with its back to the square, hence the unsatisfactory interrupted view from the square and untidy approach to the entrance, with its proliferation of delivery vehicles and miscellaneous builders' cabins. This might improve under the University's proposed Masterplan, which they were consulting the public about at the time this book was being written. However, this will be more than compensated for by their proposed restaurant with public viewing gallery at the top of the tower, and will fill the gap left by the recent closure of the Centre Point restaurant and viewing gallery and British Telecom's continuing reluctance to re-open the revolving restaurant near the top of their iconic tower. The three photos taken from the roof of the Senate House tower provide a flavour of what restaurant guests can expect for their money. In May 1938, Holden proudly

View east over Russell Square from the roof of the Senate House tower

View towards the City of London from the roof of the Senate House tower

View south from the roof of the Senate House tower

informed the Royal Institute of British Architects (RIBA) that *"...the base of the tower is the best bomb-proof shelter in London"*. As the wartime Ministry of Information with its 999 employees, it was hit nine times by bombs, although only damaged slightly, as evidenced by shrapnel 'wounds' on the tower. It was rumoured that it survived the Blitz because Hitler (no stranger to architecture built to withstand bombing) coveted Senate House as the Nazi party headquarters had he successfully invaded Britain. Another theory is that it was spared by the Luftwaffe as it provided a useful landmark for pilots navigating their way to the East End during the Blitz. Oswald Mosley, leader of the British Union of Fascists, also had designs on the building, in which he intended to house Parliament in the event of his taking power. A plaque on the roof of the Senate House tower commemorates its use by the Royal Observer Corps during World War II as a lookout point for enemy planes, and there is a War Memorial behind the staircase in Crush Hall. Also, observe how Beveridge Hall was used during the War as the press room for the Ministry of Information. Room 101, which was introduced in the climax of Orwell's *Nineteen Eighty-Four* as a torture chamber in the *"Ministry of Love"* (the three other Ministries were named *Peace, Plenty* and *Truth*), and in which prisoners were subjected to their own worst nightmare, fear or phobia, with the object of breaking down their resistance, has been respectfully preserved for posterity. However, Orwell

Beveridge Hall functioned as the press room for the Ministry of Information

Room 101

claimed to have named Room 101 after a conference room at the BBC's Broadcasting House where he used to sit through tedious meetings – another form of torture.

Senate House is probably best known as the model for George Orwell's *"Ministry of Truth"* in his best-selling book, *1984* (1949), and for Graham Green it was his inspiration for *"Ministry of Fear"* (1943), which was famously adapted for the cinema by Fritz Lang (1944). Orwell had worked for the Ministry of Information when it occupied the building during the War. Evelyn Waugh used it as a setting in *Put Out More Flags*, in which a 'lunatic' with a bomb ticking in a briefcase is referred from one department to another clutching his time bomb, with the building serving as a Kafkaesque symbol of the idiocy of bureaucracy. John Wyndham had Senate House as the last bastion of civilization in his *Day of the Triffids*. The Art-Deco interiors have been a popular setting for several movie 'block-busters' and acclaimed TV series, including *Jeeves and Wooster, Poirot, Foyle's War, Batman Begins, Blue Ice*, the 2010 film *Nanny McPhee and The Big Bang*, which is set during the World War II and features Senate House as the offices of the Ministry of War, the 2012 film *The Dark Knight Rises*, and, in 2014, *Jack Ryan*, starring Chris Pine and Keira Knightley. It is also a 'hot-ticket venue' during London Fashion Week and is a popular venue during each annual Bloomsbury Festival.

Royal Observer Corps plaque

| Ministry of Information official car leaving Senate House

Kevin Francomme reading on the roof of Senate House during the Bloomsbury Festival 2013

The building was listed as Grade II* in 1969. A £55-million refurbishment, which began in 2006, was the largest programme of works undertaken by the University since Senate House opened.

Nos. 31-37

These seven houses in the middle terrace were built by Burton in a deliberately grandiose style, with full height Ionic columns adorning Nos. 31, 34 and 37 (see 1939 drawing by Fletcher).

The west side of Russell Square by Kanslip Fletcher, 1939 © CLSAC

They were demolished in 1939 in preparation for the construction of the new University of London buildings, the foundation stone for which had been laid on the site of Senate House by King George V and Queen Mary in June 1933. The original plan was to build a massive, slab-sided university hall fronting Russell Square, but World War II intervened and the hall was never built.

Nos. 31-36 prior to being demolished in 1939

How the middle terrace between former Keppel Street and Montague Place might have looked if the Great Hall had been built

The site was shown as a designated *"Clearance area"* (with the houses still shown) on the London County Council's (LCC) Bomb Damage map, 1939-45, although it remained vacant until the 1980s, when the University of London eventually decided to construct Stewart House, which opened in 1982. Its façade was designed to match Burton's surviving houses, numbered 38-43, beyond Montague Place, no doubt at the insistence of Camden Council's Conservation Officers.

However, this nod of respect towards the Square's Georgian heritage was not unanimously welcomed at the time, with Charles Kean, Architecture Correspondent of The Times (21st November 1981), declaring: *"We are faced with a flabby, spineless and unattractive neo-Georgian reconstruction of a Russell Square that probably never was"*, and a letter in the Daily Telegraph (8th March 1982) which branded the building *"a miserable travesty, unworthy of its splendid site."* The University's 2015 Masterplan earmarked Stewart House for replacement: *"A high quality building is proposed to respect its important setting, facing Russell Square and Montague Place"*, a building which *"positively contributes to the Conservation Area"*, so the Neo-Georgian frontage will disappear, but may be replaced by a building which pays homage to James Burton's original design, according to the indicative view published by the University. No. 37 was demolished when Montague Place was widened in connection with the Senate House development.

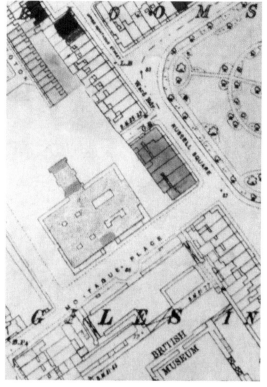

Nos. 31-36 are shaded blue, which denotes a *"Clearance Area"* on the LCC Bomb Damage map, 1939-45

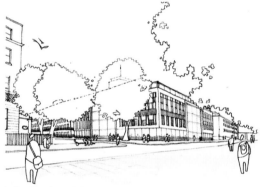

Indicative view of the replacement for Stewart House - University of London

Stewart House, July 2015

The revealed flank wall of No.36 faces Montague Place in 1935, with Senate House under construction behind

31 - Early occupants of No. 31 include: James Atkinson (BCGs, 1820-34, with Miss Atkinson the sole entry in 1840-43, and in SDs, 1841-42). William Tulloch joins Miss Atkinson in BCGs, 1844-45, and she is alone again in 1846. The Will of James Atkinson of No. 31 Russell Square, Middlesex, dated 17th December 1836, is held by The National Archives, Kew. His daughter's birth was announced in 1811. His wife, Caroline Porker, died in 1810, although there was a belated obituary dated 1st March 1813 in *The Gentleman's Magazine*; John Garford (BCG, 1857, RBB, 1858, SDs, 1861-62, and ABCCG, 1871); Ambrose Harmar (SDs, 1878-83, and Mrs Ambrose Harmar alone in 1886-1907); the English Church Union occupied the building from 1909 to at least 1930.

32 - John Capel (1767-1846), stockbroker and MP for Queenborough, moved from 8 Artillery Place in the City of London to 32 Russell Square in the 1810s, where he held a private concert in May each year. He is listed at No. 32 in BCGs, 1820-46, and in SDs, 1841-42. He was initially employed by John Bruckshaw, who worked as a stockbroker in the Royal Exchange and had premises at 96 Cornhill. Both men signed the London merchants' declaration of loyalty in 1795. At about that time they must have entered into a partnership, since from then on the firm is listed in the London directories as *"Bruckshaw and Capel, stockbrokers and lottery office keepers"*. They attended the first known meeting of the managing proprietors of the stock exchange at the *Antwerp* on 4th March 1801, and were instrumental in the regularization of the new financial institution established in Capel Court, Bartholomew Lane. John Capel was also one of the four stock exchange managers who supervised the establishment of a foreign dealing room in 1823. James Capel and Company was to become one of the leading stockbroking firms, with Capel remaining a partner until his death in 1846. (Also, see entry for James Capel, who lived at 40 Russell Square.)

Whilst resident at No. 32, John Capel made his first known venture into politics in May 1821, when he reluctantly stood in an Aldermanic by-election in Queenhithe, during which he was described as *"a rich and very charitable man"*. After a fierce three-day contest, and intensive scrutiny, he was defeated by 50 votes to 31. In 1825, although reluctant to stand for Parliament, he was persuaded to stand as an independent candidate at the urgent request of the freemen of Queenborough, who were suffering deplorable oppression at the hands of the Mayor, Thomas Young Greet. The Duke of Wellington complained at the time that the *"…under house officer at Queenborough is to set up a Member against the*

interest of the master general of the ordnance, and... is to be assisted by the secretary of state for the home department…"*, Robert Peel. *The Times* reported on 23rd July 1825 that *"Capel had strengthened his cause by generously treating the freemen resident in Queenborough and Dover with roast beef, plum pudding, speeches, harangues and music."* At the General Election of 1826 he stood as a Whig and in winning the seat he apparently showed his gratitude by kissing the freemen's wives and daughters. Wellington, again, was furious with the Treasury and Home Office for allowing subordinate officers to use their influence in support of Capel. The inhabitants were delighted with his victory, for which commemorative medals were struck. Detailed records of his parliamentary 'interventions' are found on the excellent *History of Parliament* website, including a reference to him voting against Catholic relief on three occasions between 1827 and 1829, and being *"opposed to the principle of the bill"* to emancipate the Catholics. He also presented petitions from the Foundling Hospital against the Lighting of Parishes Bill, and he was *"… in the minority for postponing authority to sell beer on the premises"*, 1st July 1830. His younger daughter, Sarah (bap. 30th May 1805), died on 2nd November 1822, and his elder, Mary Ann (bap. 24th April 1804), became the second wife of Sir Codrington Edmund Carrington, 2nd October 1830. Capel's first wife died in her 59th year on 18th December 1831, and sometime thereafter he married a Miss Frances Ralley. According to the cleric and author Richard Harris Barham, Capel, *"…a stockbroker of great worth as well as fortune"*, late in life married one of his first wife's friends (who Barham calls *"Miss Putley"*), an event *"…which occasioned a good deal of stock exchange waggery, not all of it of the most delicate description; some of the epigrams written on the occasion had point enough, but they will not bear recording"*. John Capel died in December 1846, in his 80th year, and was buried with his first wife and their younger daughter in the vault of St John's, Regent's Park. It is not known whether he died at No. 32, where he was still living in 1846.

Other early occupants of No. 32 include: Alderman Sir J. Musgrave, Bart (BCG, 1857, RBB, 1858, SDs, 1861-71, and ABCCG, 1871); Edward Tyer (SD, 1878); *"Isaiah Mark Marks"* (SDs, 1882-93); Charles F. Greenwood (SDs, 1894-1904, and WRB, 1897, Mrs Charles Greenwood, 1905-06, plus Arthur F. Greenwood, 1907-15. Mrs Greenwood was listed alone in 1916-18; The Student Christian Movement of Great Britain & Ireland occupied the building in 1920-39.

33 - Moses Mocatta (1768-1857),
a significant member of the Anglo-Jewish
family of bullion dealers and brokers, is listed
at No. 33 in BCGs, 1820-46, and SDs, 1841-
42 (Abraham Mocatta [3rd], a lesser member
of the Mocatta family, is listed at 2 Woburn
Place in 1841). The Mocatta family business,
founded in 1671 by Moses Mocatta (d.1693),
first sent gold to India in 1676, and became
broker to the Bank of England and the East
India Company in the 18th century. The firm
became Mocatta Goldsmid in 1779 and was
always run by a Mocatta or a Goldsmid until
1957 when it was acquired by Hambros
Bank, ending almost 300 years of business
as an independent entity. In 1973 Standard
Chartered Bank took over the controlling
interest, which was sold on to Bank of Nova
Scotia in 1997. Moses chose to retire in mid-
life from his position as partner at the bank
to devote himself to social and philanthropic
works and to study. His older son (of two),
David Alfred Mocatta (1806–1882), who
was an architect noted for his work for the
London, Brighton, and South Coast Railway,
lived and worked nearby at 32 Brunswick
Square from 1839 to 1846. The Mocatta
family dominated the London bullion market
for most of the eighteenth century and
continued to have an influential role until
the 1950s. Having accumulated wealth, the
Mocattas were inevitably attracted by other
areas of life, and played an important role in
the promotion of Jewish culture.

Benjamin Worthy Horne

Benjamin Worthy Horne (1804-1870),
coach proprietor, lived at No. 33 from at
least January 1857 (BCG) until he died here
in 1870 (*ODNB*). He is also listed in the RBB,
1858, and the ABCCG, 1871. Benjamin took
over his father's business when he died
in 1828.

By 1836 Benjamin was the second largest
coach proprietor (after William Chaplin), and
had 95 coaches, including five mail coaches,
leaving London every day. Horne was an
exceptionally aggressive competitor, and he
generally had sufficient resources to win any
contest. Harper described him as: *"...a tall,
lathy, irritable man, of eager face, quick, nervous
speech, and rapid walk, with something of a
military air in his alert, upright figure... Horne
must always expend his energies on the minor
details of his extensive business, and himself do
work that would have been better delegated to subordinates...
Up early, no day was long enough for him, and he economised
time by taking no regular meal until evening. He was generally
to be seen eating his lunch out of a paper bag as he swung
furiously along the streets... Although there was no keener
or more ruthless man of business... he was privately a
considerate and kindly man, helpful and charitable to those less
successful than himself."* (Harper, 2.221–2, 225). Benjamin
was aware by 1835 of the probability of coach businesses
being *"...annihilated by steam some few years hence"*, so
he joined up with his brother Henry and William Chaplin
in the firm of Chaplin and Horne which, in 1840, became
carrying agent to the Grand Junction Railway (later the
London and North Western Railway or LNWR), and was
also active on other railways. In 1858 Benjamin described
himself as the managing partner, and was constantly in and
out of the LNWR yards at Euston and Camden Town. He
also continued to run his coaches where they could still pay
their way, and in 1843, considered himself the largest coach
proprietor. His firm eventually merged with Pickfords. He
owned an estate at Highlands near Mereworth, Kent, as well
as his London residence at No. 33, where he died on 14th
April 1870, age 66. He was survived by his wife, Catherine
Larkin, with whom he had at least nine children.

Other early occupants of No. 33 include: William
Shephard (BCG, 1808); Charles Fellowes Pearson (SDs,
1878-83); George Stimpson (SDs, 1887-1905); Miss
Stimpson (SDs, 1906-39). No. 33 was demolished in 1939
to make way for the new University of London complex.

The Bedford Times, one of the last coaches to run, leaving the Swan Hotel, Bedford

34 - Early occupants include: Thomas Lewis (BCG, 1808); Mrs Horne (BCGs, 1820-24) – possibly related to Benjamin Worthy Horne, above; Robert Mitford (BCGs, 1834-46, and SDs, 1841-42); Jeremiah Pilcher (BCG, 1857, RBB, 1858, and SDs, 1861-65, and in 1871-78, Mrs Pilcher, Henry Drayson Pilcher and Arthur Pilcher); Henry Beyfus (SDs, 1882-89); Mrs John Stewart (SDs, 1892-1901, WRB, 1897). No. 34 then remained unoccupied until 1907, when the Auctioneers' Institute of the United Kingdom took up residence, followed by the Auctioneers' and Estate Agents' Institute in 1919; by 1930 the entire building was occupied by various bodies associated with the building trade, including the London Master Builders' Association and the National Association of Shopfitters.

35 - Sir Arthur Leary Piggott FRS (1749-1819), Whig lawyer, MP, Attorney General and Solicitor General, lived at No. 35 in 1808, when he was listed as *"Sir Arthur Piggott"* in BCG. He also lived at 11 Brunswick Square from 1809 to 1812. He was born in St Michael's parish, Barbados, the son of John Piggott of Grenada, and trained for the law at the Middle Temple, being called to the Bar in 1777. However, he commenced his legal career in Grenada, and in 1780 was appointed Attorney-General for the island. After returning to England in 1783 he maintained professional ties with the West Indian plantation community, regularly acting as their parliamentary counsel on the slave trade question. He went on to become Solicitor General to the Prince of Wales in 1783, but he was discharged in

1792 because of his membership of a radical reform group, the Society of the Friends of the People. As 'Old Pig' and the 'Learned Pig' he became one of the fathers of the Equity Bar. He was elected a Fellow of the Royal Society in 1787. Under the Whig administration of 1806 he was selected to be Attorney General, was knighted by the King and given a safe parliamentary seat at Steyning by the Duke of Norfolk. In the 1806 general election, the Duke found him a seat at Arundel, which he held until 1812, when he was returned for Horsham, sitting until 1818. In that year, he was again provided with the Arundel seat but died the following year.

Edwin Freshfield LLD, FSA (1832-1918), lawyer, is listed at No. 35 in the SDs, 1886 to 1908, and WRB, 1897. Freshfield family lawyers were partners in the City of London firm of solicitors which since 1800 has always used the Freshfield name in its title. Edwin, educated at Winchester College and at Trinity College, Cambridge, became a partner in the firm in 1858, and was the firm's senior partner from 1903 until 1918. In 1861 he had married Zoe Charlotte Hanson, daughter of J. F. Hanson, the Levant Company's representative in Smyrna. Edwin's marriage and his travels in that part of the world, which he first visited in 1854–5 after he left Cambridge, gave him a lifetime interest in Greece and the surrounding areas. He was awarded a doctorate from Cambridge for a treatise on the laws of the late Roman Empire. He and his wife had one son,

Edwin Hanson Freshfield FSA (1864–1948), who joined the firm in 1888 and came to live at No. 35. Like his father, he had considerable antiquarian and scholarly interests. Edwin Freshfield died on 1st September 1918. Edwin Hanson Freshfield retired from the firm three years later, and spent most of his retirement travelling in the Near East up until his death in May 1948. The firm continued to flourish under the leadership of Sir William Leese, brought in by Edwin Freshfield in 1906, and in the second half of the 20th-century it developed into one of the leading City law firms.

James Figgins MP (1811-1884) was a Conservative politician and Member of Parliament for Shrewsbury from 1868 to 1874. He was also a JP for Middlesex and Sheriff of London and Middlesex from 1865 to 1866. He is therefore listed as *"James Figgins M.P."* in the ABCCG, 1871, but not *"M.P."* in the SDs, 1871-82, even though he served as an MP until 1874.

James Figgins as Sheriff of London, c.1865

Other early occupants of No. 35 include:
Henry Budd (BCGs, 1820-46, and SDs, 1841-42); Major Usbourne (BCG, 1857, RBB, 1858, and SDs, 1861-65 – spelt *"Usborne"*); The Royal Photographic Society secured the lease on No. 35 in 1909, and occupied the building until 1939, when it was demolished to make way for the new University of London complex. The Society was previously at No. 66 (formerly Baltimore/Bolton House) from at least 1902, but it was forced to relocate when the Imperial Family Hotel acquired the building for its expansion.

36 – Dr William Saunders (1743–1817), physician, is listed in BCG, 1808, and he lived there until he retired from practice in 1814. He was born in Banff, Scotland, the son of James Saunders, physician. He was educated at the University of Edinburgh and graduated MD in 1765. He began practice in London about 1766, and gave lectures on chemistry with W. Keir at Red Lion Court, and *materia medica* at Guy's Hospital. He also lectured on medicine and in 1770 became the first in London to advertise clinical lectures. He is said to have made £1000 a year from his lectures, which he published. He was elected physician to Guy's Hospital in 1770, becoming a governor both there and at St Thomas's Hospital. He was appointed extra-physician to the Prince Regent in 1807, and was elected Licentiate of the Royal College of Physicians in 1769, and a Fellow in 1790, serving as censor four times. His publication on red Peruvian bark (1782), translated into French, German, and Latin, quickly led to the displacement of quilled bark in the treatment of fevers. In his Goulstonian lectures, which he afterwards published as *A Treatise on the Structure, Economy, and Diseases of the Liver* (1793), Saunders was probably the first English physician to observe that in some forms of cirrhosis the liver became enlarged and afterwards contracted. He also published, between 1768 and 1809, works on mercury, antimony, stones in the bladder, and mineral waters. On 22nd May 1805 Saunders was Chairman of the meeting which led to the formation of the Medical and Chirurgical Society and he was its first President. He resigned from Guy's Hospital in 1802, and retired from practice in 1814, moving from Russell Square to Enfield, Middlesex, where he died on 29 May 1817.

Robert Spankie (1774-1842), Scottish lawyer and *Morning Chronicle* editor, lived here from about 1832 until he died here in 1842 (*ODNB*). He is listed in the BCGs, 1829-42, and SDs, 1841-42, as *"Mr Serjeant Spankie"*, which reflected his professional status at the time.* *"Mrs. Spankie"* alone is listed in BCGs, 1843-46. Born in Falkland, Fife, Robert was the son of a Church of Scotland Minister. He entered the University of St Andrews but left without graduating, moving to London in about 1792. He became a reporter for the *Morning Chronicle*, rising to be the editor. He was noted for the unmatched speed of his handwriting and long remembered for a daring leap into the lobby of the House of Commons when a crowded staircase impeded the delivery of his report on a crucial division. In 1803 he left journalism and became a law student at the Inner Temple, and was called to the Bar in 1808. Following his marriage in 1813 to Euphemia

Inglis, daughter of an East India Company director, he pursued a legal career in India, becoming Advocate General of Bengal in 1817. He returned to England in 1823, due to illness, and resumed his legal practice from his home in Russell Square, becoming a Serjeant-at-Law in 1824 and a King's Serjeant in 1832, the same year that he was elected as one of two Members of Parliament for the new London constituency of Finsbury, which was enfranchised under the Reform Act 1832. Elected as Liberal, in Parliament he took a distinctly Conservative line, which lead to his defeat at the next election in 1835. He subsequently stood as a Conservative candidate at Bury in 1837, but without success. He continued his legal practice, becoming Standing Counsel for the East India Company. He died at No. 36 on 2nd November 1842, aged 68.

MR. SERJEANT SPANKIE.

Mr Serjeant Spankie by George Stead Veitch

*The Serjeants had for many centuries exclusive jurisdiction over the Court of Common Pleas, being the only lawyers allowed to argue a case there. At the same time they had rights of audience in the other central common law courts (the Court of King's Bench and Exchequer of Pleas) and precedence over all other lawyers. Only Serjeants-at-Law could become judges of these courts right up into the 19th century, and socially the Serjeants ranked above Knights Bachelor and Companions of the Bath. Within the Serjeants-at-Law were more distinct orders; the King's Serjeants (particularly favoured Serjeants-at-Law) and within that, the King's Premier Serjeant (the Monarch's most favoured Serjeant, and the King's Ancient Serjeant, the oldest).

Edward William Cox (1809–1879) was a lawyer, legal writer, publisher and wealthy landowner, described as *"the greatest entrepreneur of 'class' journalism"* (Research Society for Victorian Periodicals (1984), *Victorian periodicals review* - University of Toronto).

Edward William Cox – *ILN*

"In 1836 he married Sophia, daughter of William Harris, surgeon in the Royal Artillery; on 14 August 1844, he married Rosalinda Alicia (1822–1887), only daughter of J. S. M. Fonblanque, commissioner of bankruptcy. There was one son from each marriage: Edward Bainbridge Cox (1838–1922), barrister and Conservative MP for Harrow; and Harding Edward de Fonblanque Cox (1854–1944), who wrote extensively on sporting subjects. Little is known about Cox's activities until he reached his thirties, but thereafter he pursued a number of roles with determination and a flair for gaining public attention." (ODNB). After moving from Taunton to London he was called to the Bar in 1843. He is listed at No. 36 in BCG, 1857, in the RBB, 1858, in the ABCCG, 1871, and in the SDs, 1861-79, with *"J.P."* from 1865 and *"S.L."* from 1871. He is joined by *"Irwin Edward Bainbridge Cox"* from 1878. His periodicals, reports and textbooks led to his appointment as Serjeant-at-Law in 1868. *"Cox made his mark on Victorian society through a talent for publishing."* (ODNB). His publications include *The Field, Exchange & Mart, The Queen,* merged with *Ladies Paper* in 1863, the *County Courts' Chronicle,* and *Crockford's Clerical Directory. "Cox's national reputation was made as the founder and editor of the Law Times"* (ODNB),

which he produced for 25 years. Cox also set up his own newspapers, with mixed success. In 1871 he assisted William Crookes in his experiments into what Cox called *"psychic force"*. He was particularly interested in the psychological side of mediumship, which led him to establish the Psychological Society for Great Britain. On 15th November 1871, W.W. Harrison, the editor of the *Spiritualist* newspaper, had called for this to be established outside the Spiritualist belief, to encourage scientists to be involved. He wrote, *"It is thought desirable that most of the members of the society shall not be Spiritualists."* The Society came into being in 1875 but with Cox being the major driver of the project it ceased soon after his death in 1879. He bought swathes of land in his lifetime, including large landed estates, but his most quirky purchase must be the Serjeants' Inn in Chancery Lane, which he bought at auction in 1877 for £57,100 (equivalent to £5.9M in 2016) and reconstructed at Mill Hill (then Middlesex, now London, NW7), complete with the original stained glass windows from the hall and chapel at the inn. Cox kept a pack of hounds, which he and his son hunted with over what are now Golders Green, Hendon, Mill Hill and Hampstead Garden Suburb. Although his estate was declared as under £200,000, he owned at least as much again in landed property.

Arthur Addison Bright, J.M. Barrie's literary agent, is listed in BCG, 1903 and in SDs, 1904-06. Mrs Bright alone is listed in 1907-08. In May 1906, Bright was facing charges of misappropriating his clients' earnings, including £16,000 belonging to Barrie. He travelled to Switzerland, telling Barrie that *"the mountain air would give him sleep.."*, but he shot himself, being unable to face the humiliation of his imminent prosecution. Barrie, who was forced to travel to Lucerne to identify Bright's body, blamed himself for Bright's death, not having noticed that £16,000 of his own money had gone missing. He wrote a touching obituary for Bright in *The Times*, 1st June 1906, including the simple but moving statement: *"For many years he had been my most loved friend."*

Other early occupants of No. 36 include:
George Clay (BCG, 1820-24); Abraham Collins (SD, 1883); George Silke (SDs, 1886-1893); Abraham Cohen (SDs, 1894-1903, and WRB, 1897); William Thomas Smedley (SDs, 1910-12); *"Colonel William Robert Smith M.D., D.Sc., LL.D., F.R.S.E., J.P., D.L."* (SDs, 1914-30, with *"Lady Frances Smith J.P."* also listed in 1930); The Poetry Society is listed in 1939, the year No. 36 was demolished.

37 - Sir James Mansfield, SL, KC (1734-1821) was a British lawyer, judge and politician. He served twice as Solicitor General and was Chief Justice of the Common Pleas from 1799 to 1814.

The Right Hon Sir James Mansfield
© National Portrait Gallery, London

He is listed as resident of No. 37 in BCGs, 1808-21. As Chief Justice, he presided over the trial of John Bellingham, assassin of Prime Minister Spencer Perceval in 1812.

John Bellingham as he appeared at his trial in 1812

As a judge he was known for *"an ungraceful delivery and a husky voice"* (*Dictionary of National Biography*) and for his unsteady temper - easily exploited in court for the amusement of counsel rather than for the high quality of his judgments. However, a merchant, Joseph Minet, told Joseph Farington that Mansfield *"...preserved High Authority in the Court of Common Pleas by his superior knowledge of Law, which was such that in Chancery Lord Eldon was afraid of Him, & was glad to have him appointed to the Chief Justiceship..."* (Farington, *Diary*, 6.2428). He enjoyed shooting, and on circuit liked to rise at five *"to kill something before breakfast"* (*ODNB*). He resigned on 21st February 1814 due to ill health and died at No. 37, aged 87, on 23rd May 1821. A commemorative tablet was installed by his surviving children in St George's Church, Bloomsbury.

with a command of the German language qualifying him admirably for intelligence work..." (*ODNB*). He played an important role in laying the foundations for the remarkable success of Bletchley Park (the wartime home of the Government Code and Cypher School) in decrypting the German and Italian (Enigma) machine codes. *"Edward George Clarke QC"* is listed at No. 37 in the SD, 1886, with *"Sir Edward George Clarke QC, MP"* being listed from 1887 onwards, and in BCGs, 1887-93, and WRB, 1897. He is joined briefly by a certain **Edward Percival Clarke** (1872-36) in the 1898-1900 SDs. Percival, who is described as the eldest son of Sir George Clarke in various October 1936 newspaper reports of his sudden death from a heart attack in a West End hotel, became a prominent lawyer in the 1920s and '30s. He would have been the son of George's first wife, Anne, who died in 1881. The *Vanity Fair* cartoon of Sir George is signed by *"SPY"*. This is a strange coincidence, considering his sons chosen career, but *"SPY"* was actually the pen name of Leslie Ward (1851-1922) who, from 1873, produced some 254 portraits and was knighted in 1918.

Tablet in St George's Church commemorating Sir James Mansfield

Sir Edward George Clarke

Sir Edward George Clarke, QC, MP (1841-1931), lawyer and politician, lived at No. 37 from 1883 until 1901 with his second wife Kathleen. Their youngest son, **William Francis Clarke** (1883-1961), intelligence officer and wartime codebreaker, was born here on 22nd May 1883. He trained as a lawyer, but became a cryptographer, his *"...legal training combined*

Sir Edward Clarke is considered one of the leading advocates of the late Victorian era and whilst living in Russell Square he served as Solicitor General in the Conservative Government of 1886-92. His legal career included representing Oscar Wilde in his disastrous prosecution of the Marquess of Queensberry for libel, although he is thought to have made his name securing the acquittal of Chief

Caricature of Edward George Clarke -
Vanity Fair, 13th March 1880

Inspector Clarke, the acting head of the Detective
Department at Scotland Yard, on charges of
corruption. Three other, more junior, police officers
were convicted, and the detective division of the
Metropolitan Police was completely reorganised as
a result. He also represented Sir William Gordon-
Cumming, who sued five people for slander after
being accused of cheating at cards. The case was
notorious because the Prince of Wales, later King
Edward VII, had been banker during the game in
question. The Prince was called as a witness, and was
vigorously cross-examined by Clarke. Nevertheless,
Gordon-Cumming lost the case. Clarke was a staunch
supporter of the Church of England and, in 1894, had
built at his sole expense a church beside the river at
Staines, dedicated in honour of St Peter, and on his
retirement from the Bar he lived at a house called
Peterhouse which he had built adjacent to the church.
There he died on 26th April 1931 in his 91st year.
The following day, there appeared in *The Times*
a long obituary notice which he had himself written
and sent to the newspaper 18 years before with
a covering letter expressing the remarkable opinion
that an obituary notice of a man who has reached
old age should be written by himself.

Henry Hoyle Oddie, is listed at No. 37 in BCGs,
1823-1829 as *"Henry H Oddie"*, and is most likely
Henry Hoyle Oddie (1779-1847), son of Henry
Hoyle St Oddie (1744-1830), solicitor, philanthropist
and friend of the Rev. Samuel Parr, who died at
Barnwell Castle, Yorkshire. Henry was born in St
Clement Danes, London and married Georgiana
(1795-1862) on 3rd February 1813 in St Clement
Danes. One of their nine children, also named Henry
Hoyle Oddie (1815-1869), lawyer, landowner and
cricketer, conveniently named one of his daughters
Georgiana. There is a reference in *Recollections of the
character of the late Henry Hoyle Oddie*, by Henry
Hoyle Oddie, 1830, to Oddie senior being auditor to
the Montagu family, a role in which he was succeeded
by his son. There is an engraved portrait of Henry
Hoyle Oddie (senior) at the front of this publication.

Portrait of Henry Hoyle Oddie, 1830

William Lovejoy, auctioneer, surveyor and estate
agent, is listed at No. 37 in the SDs, 1871-79. There
is a report in *The Proceedings of the Old Bailey*, 19th
August, 1872, of a case in which two men, William
Hastings (23) and Sidney Elgar Pocock (18), were
convicted of *"Burglariously breaking and entering the
dwelling of William Lovejoy, and stealing there in three
cruet stands and other articles, value 350l., his property."*
They were both found guilty and given *"Seven years
penal servitude"*. William's son, Charles Walter Lovejoy,
who witnessed the offence, was cross-examined by
the Prosecutor: *"I am the son of Mr. William Lovejoy of
37, Russell Square—on Sunday, 14th July between 4 and
5 o'clock a.m, I had occasion to get up early, and heard
a noise down stairs and voices—I went down and saw
Pocock in the hall—I watched him a few minutes, and*

heard him say 'How shall we move these things?' and another voice said 'We had better take a cab'—I went upstairs put on some clothes, and went back and saw the prisoners folding up some clothes, and told them the best thing they could do was to go, they made no answer—they had some coats on belonging to the house—I kept my eye outside the door, and seeing a figure pass who I believed to be a policeman, I told them they had better go—I was talking to them five or six minutes—I had ample opportunity of observing their faces—I looked out at the door and saw a policeman there—I talked to them at the door half a minute, and suddenly called 'Police!' and 'Thieves!'—they ran away, and the policeman pursued them—the door opens into Montague Place, where it joins the square—the policeman came down Montague Place towards the square—I called my father, and in about five minutes Bell, the policeman, came to the house, and I went over it with him". The London Gazette, 10th July 1874, listed "William Lovejoy, 37 Russell Square" among the prominent people in London. His name appeared again in the same paper on 13th February 1880 in a notice posted by executors of his estate, which included his wife, "Ann Eliza Lovejoy of 37 Russell Square", having passed away on 12th January 1880. He is described as a partner in the firm "Warlters, Lovejoy, and Miles – Auctioneers, Surveyors, Valuers, House and Estate Agents". William was a member of the special jury which heard "The Great Convent Case; Saurin V. Star & Kenedy, Tried Before Lord Chief Justice Cockburn in the Court of Queen's Bench, February 1869." A summary of the case is given in the Preface to a transcript of the case by James Grant of 41 Guilford Street in 1869: "This was an action brought by a professed Sister of the Order of Mercy against the Mother Superioress and a professed Sister of the same order in the convent at Hull, to recover damages for assault, and conspiracy to drive her from the annoyances, and did deprive her of food and clothing, and of divers articles of her property; they also imprisoned the plaintiff to prevent her from attending the services, and made a false charge against her to the bishop, whereby she was exconvent and have her expelled from the order." It was in effect an action against Catholicism, as it existed at the time, and caused quite a stir in the national press.

Other early occupants of No. 37 include:
"George Parbury, esq., Mansfield House" (SD, 1842, and BCGs, 1842-43); Thomas Ellis (BCG, 1857, and Misses Ellis, SDs, 1861-65); Alfred Phippen Welch (SDs, 1881-83). The building remained vacant between 1901 and 1906, from when it was occupied by the Royal Institute of Public Health (until at least 1930) and the Universities of Glasgow & Aberdeen Conservative & Liberal Unionist Association, the latter being replaced by the Royal Naval & Military Musical Union in 1915-20. The site of No. 37 was lost in 1939 when the north side of the carriageway in Montague Place was widened as part of the University of London complex.

Here is Montague Place.
Nos. 38-43
These seven houses in the southern terrace, built by Burton in accordance with the 1800 agreement, are distinguished from his adjoining houses running down the west side of Montague Street towards the British Museum by a subtle change in the design of their front elevations.

View of Montague Place from the south side of Russell Square, c.1900 © CLSAC

Nos. 38-43 (r-l) and the west side of Montague Street, October 2015

The King Edward VII Galleries under construction. Painting by Frank Lishman, 1910 - BM

The opening of King Edward VII's Galleries on 27th June 1914

the King Edward VII Building, was completed (1906-14), although Museum ownership and the Burnet plan had changed the use of Nos. 38-43. Some of these houses acquired new names during the 20th century - No. 42 becoming Marylebone House and No. 43 Chalmers House. No. 38 sustained serious bomb damage in 1940/41 and so, to a lesser extent, did Nos. 39 and 40, and although none of this was indicated on the LCC Bomb Damage map, Nos. 38-40 were not listed in the Street Directories in 1942-4, which would suggest that they were not occupied and most probably undergoing repairs at the time. The United Nations Information Organization is listed at No. 38 in 1945, when 39 and 40 were still not occupied. No. 39 is only a façade, having been almost entirely rebuilt in 1962, when it was merged with No. 40. The Spiritualist Association, perhaps anticipating the bombings, built a robust air-raid shelter in the basement of No. 42, which escaped damage along with No. 43.

In 1895 the Trustees of the British Museum received a loan of £200,000 from Parliament to purchase outright all the properties surrounding the Museum. Architect

Sir John Burnet was commissioned to expand the Museum galleries to the new perimeter. Under this scheme, the houses on the west side of Montague Street and Russell Square, Bedford Square and Montague Place were to be demolished and replaced with vast colonnades leading to new galleries. In the event, only the Montague Place element of the scheme,

View west along the south side of Russell Square in 1955, showing No. 40 on the west side undergoing belated repairs following World War II bomb damage

In 1988, the British Museum's new department of Architectural & Building Services moved into Nos. 42-43 and the Education department was re-located to No. 38. Planning and listed building applications were submitted by the Museum in July 2015, which entailed the restoration and physical separation of 39-40 Russell Square and 8-11 Montague Street from the Museum so that they could be commercially let to the legal, financial and media sectors, with their entrances being restored onto Russell Square (they have provided laboratory space which has been privately accessed via the Museum since the 1980s). However, this was not registered by Camden Council, for reasons unknown. The Museum also declared its intention to apply the same treatment to a further six properties over the ensuing three to eight years, presumed to include Nos. 38, 41, 42 and 43 Russell Square.

38 – Helenus Scott MD (bap. 1758, d. 1821), East India Company military surgeon, opened a medical practice at No. 38 in 1817. *"Dr Scott"* is listed at No. 38 in BCGs, 1820-21, the year of his death.

He studied at Marischal College, Aberdeen, from 1773 to 1777 before studying medicine at Edinburgh from 1777 to 1779. He entered the service of the East India Company as a normal cadet, but, transferring to medical service, was commissioned as an assistant surgeon in January 1783, and served chiefly in the Bombay

Dr Helenus Scott, water colour in ivory miniature, 1820, attributed to Miss Sharpe

presidency. In 1787 the Bombay Medical Board chose him as apothecary to the hospitals of the region, and he became a member of the Bombay medical board in 1801 and President in 1806. He also worked as an agent for the local manufacture of gunpowder in Bombay, and spirits, from 1796. He was created MD by Marischal College in 1805. Scott retired from the East India Company in 1810, after 30 years in India, returning to England and, after some time attending medical lectures, began practice at Bath. On 22nd December 1815 he was admitted a Licentiate of the Royal College of Physicians, and in 1817 he moved to London and began to practise as a physician in Russell Square. Also in 1817, he contributed an interesting paper to the Transactions of the Medico-Chirurgical Society on the use in medicine of nitro muriatic acid, a substance he had tested by bathing in it for seven days running and assessing his own reaction to it. Scott used

it in a wider range of diseases than was customary, but its frequent use in the treatment of enteric fever and other illnesses originated in his advocacy of its merits. He published no other medical works, but while in India wrote a novel, The Adventures of a Rupee (1782). His extensive Indian connection and reputation in the treatment of hepatic disease soon gave him a large practice. He died on 16th November 1821 while on a voyage to New South Wales.

John Alliston (1781-1855) is listed at No. 38 in BCGs, 1834-46, and SDs, 1841-42. He is described as *"Lord of the manor"* of Chiddingstone in records held by Kent History and Library Centre. He was a *"Director for Life"* and Steward of the Humane Society, and was elected Member of the Royal Agricultural Society in 1842 (The Farmer's Magazine). His youngest daughter, Louisa Astley, was married at St George's Bloomsbury on 23rd September 1840 (The Gentleman's Magazine, July-December 1840)

John Alliston © National Portrait Gallery, London

Chester Cheston, Jr, (1799-1885), architect and surveyor for the Tyssen-Amhurst estate, the largest landed estate in Hackney, is listed at No. 38 in the 1878-79 SDs. Chester is cited in the St Mark's Conservation Area Appraisal (L.B. Hackney, 2008) as the person who was most probably responsible for devising the scheme for the estate, in which *"Many of the large houses and villas are of architectural merit, both in their overall design and in their architectural detailing. The estate was aiming for* a middle-class professional resident who saw Hackney as a desirable and convenient residential location for the City of London after the arrival of the railway in the 1860s." An entry for the Grade II* listed "CHURCH OF ST MARK, ST MARK'S RISE, E8" in the Historic England - Listed Buildings Register reads: "Evangelical church. Nave 1864-6 by Chester Cheston Junior. … Historical note: Cheston's original design for the tower was not executed but replaced by Blackburne's design when the tower was eventually built in 1880." One of the largest parish churches in London, it was nicknamed the Cathedral of the East. *Love Local Landmarks* (L.B. Hackney) also lists *"St Mark's Vicarage, Sandringham Road, E8… This imposing Victorian vicarage is located next to St Mark's Churchyard in Sandringham Road. Designed by the Tyssen-Amhurst Estate architect and surveyor, Chester Cheston Junior, it forms part of an important group, including the statutorily listed St Mark's Church (Grade II*), Church Hall (Grade II) and Verger's House (Grade II). St Mark's Church, which it serves, was built a decade earlier by the same architect."* The Hackney Society website says of his church in Dalston: *"…the enormous St Mark's (1866) by Chester Cheston Junior has been described as the 'wildest piece of Rogue Gothic ever conceived'."* Built by Dove Bros. of Islington, the imposing tower with gargoyles was added seven years later. However, the church had its early detractors, including its first Vicar, Joseph Pilkington, who described it as *"brutally ugly"* and in his 25 years he added most of the interior adornments: the font, lectern, organ, intricate oak screen and mosaics, pulpit, tower, eight bells, barometer and a chiming clock, as well as stained glass windows. *London Churches in Photographs* describes St Mark's as: *"A huge low church building by Chester Cheston (1862-66) not far from Dalston Kingsland station. The interior is little altered and is a stunning example of the more evangelical end of Victorian church design. The tower, completed by E.L.Blackburne in 1877-80, uniquely features an outdoor barometer."*

St Mark's Church, Dalston

Interior of St Mark's Church, Dalston

Chester's first wife, Emma Claudine, whom he married in 1864, died at Kensington in 1878. He married his second wife, Amelia, at Kensington in 1880, and they had one son, the artist, Charles Sidney Cheston (1882-1960). *British History Online* bluntly informs us that *"Charles Cheston, son and successor of Chester Cheston, ruined Lord Amherst of Hackney by embezzlement."*

Other early occupants of No. 38 include: William Everet (BCG, 1808); John Rawlinson, *"Vestryman of St George's Bloomsbury"* (Dobie, 1824, referenced by Chancellor, 1907), is listed in BCGs, 1823-29. The *Annual Register*, 1825, announced the marriage of Rev Andrew Irvine of Charterhouse to Rawlinson's eldest daughter, Eliza on 1st September 1825. *The Gentleman's Magazine*, 1823, announced a son born to Mrs John Rawlinson in Russell Square on 1st May; B.W. Powys, solicitor (BCG, 1857, RBB, 1858, and listed as *"Bransby William Powys, solicitor"* in the 1861-62 SDs and ABCCG, 1871). He was born in 1807 and died in 1886, married Eleanor Hoare in 1835, but she died in 1841 after having three children. He then married Catherine Blicke Archer in 1843, who gave him seven children before dying in 1869 (four sons and six daughters in all). He also lived at 78 Guilford Street, where his son, Rev. Horace Annesley Powys was born in 1850, and at an address in Bernard Street; Charles Park (SDs, 1882-90); Thomas Brookes Brown (SDs, 1892-94); Mrs Browne (SDs, 1895-98, and *"T.B. Browne"*, WRB, 1897); Joseph Wallace (SDs, 1901-10, and Mrs C. Leigh Hunt Wallace in 1914-15); the Union of the Four Provinces of Ireland Club occupied the building in 1939-40. No. 38 was not listed again until 1945, when it housed the United Nations Information Organisation.

39 - Early occupants of No. 39 include: Miss Ladbrooke (BCG, 1808); Thomas Rider (BCG, 1820); Miles Stringer (BCGs, 1823-34; Samuel Stiebel (BCGs, 1842-1846); Thomas Lambert (BCG, 1857, RBB, 1858, and SDs, 1861-62); Oswald Papengouth (SD, 1865); F. Picard (SD and ABCCG, 1871); Henry Augustus Deane (SDs, 1878-87)

Henry Augustus Deane, solicitor, as captured by a court artist 24.12.1856

William Floyd (SDs, 1889-99, and WRB, 1897); Henry de Meray (SDs, 1902-12, and only Mrs de Meray in 1914); Goldsmith Walters & Co., advertising contractors, occupied the building in 1915; the offices of the Register of Business Names is listed in 1918-20.

40 - Charles Grant (1746-1823), East India Company director, MP and philanthropist, lived at No. 40 from at least 1808, and he died there in 1823, being listed in BCGs, 1808-23, with only Mrs Grant listed in 1824.

Charles Grant

His father was a soldier in the Jacobite army of Prince Charles Edward Stuart. Charles's christening was a dramatic affair in which he was named after the Pretender and swords were clashed over his cradle dedicating him to the Prince's service. Shortly afterwards Charles's father, Alexander, was severely wounded at the battle of Culloden. He was forced into hiding and his property at Glen Urquhart was destroyed, leaving the family in great difficulty. In 1756 he joined a highland regiment raised for service in America and died in Havana in 1762. His wife had died in November 1758, leaving Charles and his four younger siblings orphaned. Thereafter, Charles's drive to improve the status of his family to what he felt was its rightful position underpinned his entire life. On 23rd February 1773, as Charles was about to embark for India, he married Jane (1755/6– 1827), the 17-year-old daughter of Thomas Fraser of Balnain. They had two daughters, Elizabeth (b. 1774) and Margaret (b. 1775), who both tragically died of smallpox within nine days of each other in 1776. He eventually left India because of worries about his family's health, by which time another five children had been born: Maria (b. 1778), Charles Grant (1778–1866), Robert Grant (1780–1838), Charity Emilia (Charamile; b. 1785), and Sibylla. Catherine Sophia and William Thomas (b. 1793) were born after the Grants' return to England.

Charles was elected to Parliament for Inverness-shire in 1802 and served as an MP until failing health forced him to retire in 1818. Motivated by his evangelical Christianity, he championed the causes of social reform and Christian mission, particularly in India. He served as Chairman of the British East India Company, and whilst he was a Member of Parliament he became an energetic member of the 'Clapham Sect', a group of social activists who spoke out about the moral imperative to end slavery. He was also a founding director of the Sierra Leone Company, a vice-president of the Church Missionary Society and of the British and Foreign Bible Society, and a pioneer of Sunday schools in Scotland. He continued to work loyally for the company until the day of his death, aged 77, from a heart attack at 40 Russell Square on 31st October 1823, after completing a full day's work in Leadenhall Street. The East India Company, in recognition of his 30 years of devoted service, commissioned a grand marble monument and lengthy inscription by Samuel Manning to be placed in St George's, Bloomsbury, where Charles was interred.

Monument to Charles Grant in St George's Church, Bloomsbury

Wilberforce thought him *"one of the best men I ever knew"*. James Grant of Bught considered him *"a man of great mental endowments"*, and his friend Lord Teignmouth wrote: *"Mr Grant's presence was imposing—perhaps repressive, and even alarming, in the estimation of some persons, even to members of his family, though he lived with them on the most affectionate terms. Mr Serjeant Stephen observed to me that he was, without exception, the most awful man he ever met with... My own recollections of Mr Grant are most pleasant. From no friend of my father did I receive more considerable kindness whenever the opportunity offered, and none did I ever find more gentle and un-appalling. Though much engrossed by state affairs, Mr Grant was fully capable of relieving the affliction of suffering friends."*

James Cholmeley Russell (1841-1912) was the eldest son of **James Russell** QC (1790-1861) and Maria, the daughter of the Reverend Robert Cholmeley. He was born at 40 Russell Square on 26th June 1841, some two years after his parents' marriage, and he was christened James Cholmeley, thus perpetuating his mother's maiden name. *"James Russell, barrister"*, is listed in BCGs, 1840-46. James Russell and Dr William Cholmeley are listed in the RBB, 1858. *"James Russell Esq"* is listed in SDs, 1841-42, with *"James Russell Esq., QC"* listed in 1861 along with *"William Cholmeley, Physician"*, who is also listed in 1862 alongside *"Mrs Russell"*. He is listed alone in 1863-68 and alongside James Cholmeley in 1871. James Russell died in 1861, so the court guides are not entirely accurate. The ABCCG, 1871 lists *"Mrs James Russell"* and *"Dr W. Cholmeley"*. His parents later had two further sons and five daughters. James Russell senior had a large chancery and bankruptcy practice and this may give a clue to his eldest son's future activities. In Easter 1855, at the age of 13, James Cholmeley Russell was sent to Harrow School, leaving in Christmas 1859 and going up to Magdalene College, Oxford as a Commoner. Here he remained until June 1864, graduating with a BA, 3rd class Moderations and 2nd class in Law and Modern History. During his time at Magdalene, Russell was a keen rifle shooter, and his granddaughter, Evelyn Pangman still has a number of pewter mugs awarded as prizes in shooting competitions. The signed photograph of Russell shown here is believed to have been taken c. 1859/60.

Signed photograph of James Cholmeley Russell, 1859-60

He went on to be a barrister, financier, property developer and railway entrepreneur. He was the Chairman and key shareholder of the North Wales Narrow Gauge Railways Company from which the Welsh Highland Railway Company ultimately emerged. In 1892, Russell was also involved in promoting a railway in London, between Royal Exchange and Waterloo. *The Engineer* magazine of 4th December 1892 stated: *"In addition to the intended Waterloo and City Electric Railway, it was also proposed to extend the London and South Western and London, Brighton, and South Coast Railways to a terminus in the City, for which purpose it is sought to incorporate a new company, consisting, among others, of the Hon. F. S. A. Hanbury-Tracy, Major John Eustace Jameson, Mr Campbell Praed, and Mr James Cholmeley Russell, with a capital of £2,700,000, divided into 270,000 £10 shares."* He also developed the Aldershot Lodge and Manor Estates in Surrey. He died at Longdene House, Haslemere, Surrey in 1912. A locomotive from the Welsh Highland Railway in North Wales, is named *Russell* after him.

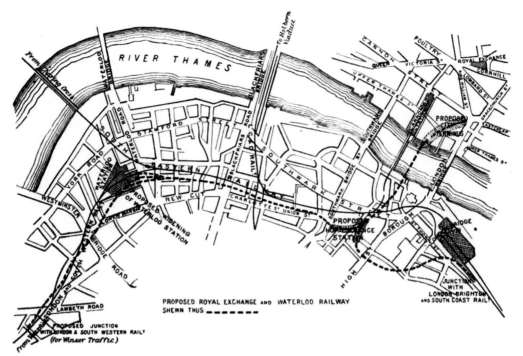

PROPOSED ROYAL EXCHANGE AND WATERLOO RAILWAY
SHEWN THUS ━ ━ ━ ━ ━

MAP SHOWING PROPOSED ROYAL EXCHANGE AND WATERLOO RAILWAY

Waterloo and Royal Exchange

James Capel (1789–1872), stockbroker and philanthropist, is listed at No. 40 in BCGs, 1829-34. He is also in the *Russell Institution Catalogue*, 1835. A notice in the obituaries in *The Gentleman's Magazine*, January 1840, which reads *"At Pisa, Mary, wife of James Capel, esq. of Russell-square"*, confirms his credentials as the famous stockbroker, James Capel.

James Capel first came to London to enter the office of his cousin John Capel, a registered bill-broker of 96 Cornhill, London and resident of 32 Russell Square (see entry above), but in 1806 James became a clerk in the office of Antrobus and Wood, stockbrokers. In 1813 he became a member of the London Stock Exchange, and a partner, at which time the firm changed its name to Antrobus, Brown, and Capel. In 1816 he was sworn a stockbroker as a member of the London Framework Knitters' Company, and in 1822 the name of his firm changed again to Marjoribanks, Capel, & Co., and again in 1837 to James Capel, Norbury, Trotter & Co., with James Capel as the senior partner. His son James Bury Capel was a partner in the firm by about 1844. The partnership was reconstituted in 1850 and again in 1864, when the firm became officially known as James Capel & Co. The early 19th century was a period of rapid development in the Stock Exchange. From 1824 to 1842 the number of companies quoted rose from 156 to 755. The stockbroking firm with which James Capel was associated was one of the principal dealers in government funds, but when foreign government securities also began to make their appearance in the London Stock Exchange, James Capel became a member of the Foreign Committee.

James Capel

In the 1840s, trading in these securities became increasingly difficult and the Spanish government proposed to repudiate its bonds. James had a pivotal role in resolving this difficulty when, as Chairman of the Spanish Bondholders' Committee, he persuaded both the London Stock Exchange and the Paris Bourse to suspend dealings in these bonds. Eventually, in 1852, the Spanish government was persuaded to give up this proposal and James Capel was presented with a piece of plate by grateful Spanish bondholders. By 1847 James Capel & Co., with five partners, was one of the two largest stockbroking firms in the London stock exchange. James became one of the trustees and managers of the Stock Exchange in 1843, and Chairman in 1853, when he oversaw the rebuilding of the premises of the Stock Exchange. He also became a member, and for 25 years Chairman, of the Stock Exchange Fund for Decayed Members. He became treasurer of the London Orphan Asylum at Watford and remained in this office for 18 years. Marion Mary Capel died in Pisa on 3rd January 1840, with James surviving until 18th November 1872. At the time of his death James Capel was the oldest member of the Stock Exchange and was described by a contemporary as: *"…a man of the strictest honour, untarnished reputation, exemplary in all business transactions, shrewd in his perceptions, keenly alive to the fluctuations of the market, clever at bargains for his clients, yet ever ready to act in a spirit of liberality in his dealings with his brother members of the Stock Exchange."* (Guildhall MS 15096).

Other early occupants of No. 40 include:
Robert Rutland Newman, solicitor (SDs, 1875-78, with only *"Mrs Newman"* appearing from 1879 to 1909. She is listed as *"Mrs R.R. Newman"* in WRB, 1897. Only *"Miss Newman"* is listed in 1910-20); the Land & Income Taxes (Office of) for St Giles-in-the-fields & St George's, Bloomsbury was listed from 1930 and shared the building with combustion engineers, an accountant and a firm of solicitors from 1939 to 1941, from whence it remained unoccupied, most probably due to bomb damage.

41 - Early occupants include: Samuel Marryat, barrister (c.1761-1828), is listed in BCGs, 1808-29. He is described in an obituary to his brother, Joseph, in *The Gentleman's Magazine*, 12th January 1824, as *"King's Counsel, equally eminent in his station of life…"*, and there is a record of him being assigned by Lord Tenterden (who lived at No. 28) as prosecuting counsel in a case of a *"pauper"* being sued for non-payment of debt. Mrs Marryat is listed in BCG, 1834. A notice of her death on 20th November 1839 (*The Gentleman's Magazine*, Jan-Jun, 1839) reads: *"In Russell-square,*

aged 80, Ann, relict of Samuel Marryat, esq. Kings Counsel."; George Barker (SD's, 1841-42, and BCG, 1842, which also gives 1 Gray's Inn square, presumed to be his place of business, indicating that he was in the legal profession); W.C. Harnett (BCG, 1857, and as *"William Chapman Harnett Esq, FSA"* in SDs, 1861-65); Robert Gray (SDs, 1871-92); William Blythe (SD, 1896); Edwin Snelling (WRB, 1897, and SDs, 1897-1904); Thomas William Conran (SDs, 1905-10); National Housing & Town Planning Council, and Richardson & Gill, architects (SDs, 1914-45, with Chas. Lovett Gill, architect, replacing Richardson & Gill in 1941).

42 - Sir Chapman Marshall (1786-1862), lived at No. 42 in the 1840s and 50s. He is listed at No. 42 in BCGs, 1834-46, and in SDs, 1841-42. The 1851 census records him there as *"Marshall"*, a 67-year old widower, being looked after by a housekeeper, cook, housemaid and coachman. He was a London grocer, knighted in 1831 after giving a particularly fulsome and loyal address to the King while serving as Sheriff of London. He also served as Lord Mayor of London in 1839-40.

Sir Chapman Marshall - watercolour on ivory pendant

Herbert Sefton-Jones, the eminent archaeologist, was listed at No. 40 in the SDs, 1907-10. He was a leading Quaker, patent attorney and world traveller, who actively promoted the League of Nations. He occupied the top-floor flat at the same time the house was occupied by Edward Matton, a Dutch coal merchant, and his family, and Alfred Kendrick (see below).

Alfred Kendrick was a renowned actor of the late Victorian and Edwardian age. The photo shows him (far right) in *The Scarlet Pimpernel*, which opened at London's New Theatre in January 1905.

"THE SCARLET PIMPERNEL"

J. BEAGLES & Co. E.C.

ELLIS & WALERY

MISS JULIA NEILSON, MR. FRED TERRY, MR. ALFRED KENDRICK.

The Scarlet Pimpernel

The Spiritualist Association of Great Britain

started renting No. 42 in 1930, following numerous stories of hauntings and poltergeist activity in the house. Regular séances were held, including at least one led by Helen Duncan, the notorious fake medium prosecuted in 1942, and the last person to be convicted in England under the 1735 Witchcraft Act. The photograph shows her materialising a 'spirit'.

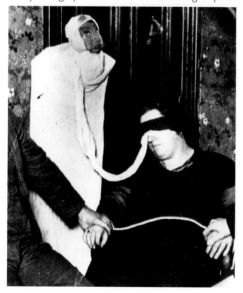

Helen Duncan materialising a spirit

The Football Association (FA) moved its

headquarters to No. 42 in 1910, from when it is listed in the SDs until 1929, along with its formidable Secretary, Sir Frederick Joseph Wall. These were years of expansion for the FA, as it organised links with foreign national football associations and oversaw changes in English football which led to the end of the dominance of northern teams in the Football League. There was of course no professional football played during World War I, and in 1915, the War Office commandeered the building, although the FA continued to be listed in the directories. Footnote: The FA is the governing body of association football in England, and the Crown dependencies of Jersey, Guernsey and the Isle of Man. Formed in 1863, it is the oldest football association in the world

The FA Crest, 2009

and is responsible for overseeing all aspects of the amateur and professional game in its territory.

Other early occupants of No. 42 include: William Mosse (BCG, 1808); Captain William Agnew (BCGs, 1820-24). He was a member of the London Institution for the Advancement of Literature and the Diffusion of Useful Knowledge. He is also listed in the 10th November 1825 Register of Members of the United Company of Merchants trading to the East Indies. His son, James, is listed as an alumni of the University of Cambridge in the flamboyantly named *Alumni Cantabrigiensis*; J.U. Farb (Boyle's Court Guide, 1829)

Warwick A Hackney, the property of James Christian Bell Esq, painted by A Cooper, 1816

William Agnew, 1880s © National Portrait Gallery, London

Mrs Aston and George Henry Aston, stockbroker (BCG, 1857, RBB, 1858, and in SDs, 1861-62, but only George in the SDs, 1865-83 and ABCCG, 1871); John Thomas Smith (SD, 1887); Edward De Matteo (SDs, 1889-90); Robert Daniel Dodson (SDs, 1892-99, WRB, 1897); the Marylebone Spiritualist Association shared the building with Frank William Hawken in 1939-44, and with the British Homeopathic Association in 1945.

43 - James Christian Clement Bell (1788-1871), merchant and Tuscan Consul-General, is first listed at No. 43 as *"James C. Bell"*, then *"James C.C. Bell"* in BCGs, 1820-46, and as *"James Christian Clement Bell, esq."* in SDs, 1841-42, and the 1851 census. Born in Dunkirk in 1788, Bell became a wealthy merchant. He married Jane Strangman at St Pancras, his local church, in 1825. The census shows they had at least two children, James junior and Alicia, and were looked after by a butler, cook, lady's maid, housemaid and footman. Mr Bell was active in mercantile affairs, corresponding with the Earl of Aberdeen about abolishing the slave trade. He had also been appointed Tuscan Consul-General (1838 -1871), which implies he traded with Italy. Tuscany was an independent grand duchy until 1859, so No. 43 enjoys the distinction of having served as a foreign embassy.

Less is known of Jane Bell, though in 1831 she was caught up in a scandal. Society doctor John St John Long was accused at the Old Bailey of murdering one of his patients, by not providing the proper treatment. After lengthy submissions by leading physicians, Long was found not guilty, thanks largely to a string of character witnesses, including Mrs Bell. She also supported worthy causes connected with her husband's interests, including a fund for the building of a hospital for sick sailors.

Augustus Henry Novelli MB Cantab. (1827-1887) is listed at No.43 as *"A.H. Novelli"* in BCG, 1857, as *"Augustus Henry Novelli"* in the RBB, 1858, and as *"Augustus Henry Novelli, esq."* in the SD, 1861. He was already an eminent and well-off member of the Royal College of Physicians when in 1852 his father died, leaving him a fortune of £50,000 (equivalent to £6.3M in 2016) from the family's business interests in Italy and the Middle East. Now a very wealthy man, Novelli gave up his medical practice at Middlesex Hospital and took over the family banking and trading business. With a country house in Aberystwyth and the family business trading out of London and Manchester, Augustus was doing very well, the 1861 census showing his family - wife, two daughters and a son - looked after by eight servants at No. 43. He used his money to buy influence and prestige in the world of the arts. He befriended Alfred Lord Tennyson and Charles Dickens, gaining a reputation as a man of exquisite taste and culture. He was a gifted pianist, commissioned works of art and was a prominent donor to worthy artistic causes. To the Pre-Raphaelite sculptor Thomas Woolner he was *"…one of the most fascinating men I have ever met, he has the soul of a poet with the profoundest comprehension of business in its minutest details"*. The Pre-Raphaelite Brotherhood, later known as the Pre-Raphaelites, was founded in nearby Gower Street. Novelli was the first to own, and may have commissioned, the painting entitled *'Fairlight Downs: Sunlight on the Sea'* by William Holman Hunt. He purchased it in November 1858 for £120.

Fairlight Downs, Sunlight on the Sea, by William Holman Hunt

He was also a close friend of James Brooke, the 'White Rajah', absolute ruler of Sarawak in the East Indies, who called Novelli *"Prince of British Merchants"*. However, an all-too public scandal engulfed the Novelli family in 1850 when Augustus's older brother Lewis died, leaving a widow, Harriet, and another brother, Alexander, as his executor. Alexander moved into Harriet's house and made no secret of his desire to marry her, even though she had rejected his advances. Then tragically one morning, the servants found Harriet's strangled body with her clothes all askew and, nearby, the body of Alexander, who had hanged himself. The relatives attempted to diffuse public interest by claiming insanity was widespread in the family, but the 'tabloid' press wallowed in sordid speculation. The scandal may have been the cause of another personal tragedy for Augustus, whose wife Helen went into labour prematurely and their daughter was still-born.

Sir John Braddick Monckton FSA (1832-1902), lawyer, civil servant and Town Clerk of the City of London (1832-1902), lived here in the 1870s. He is listed in the ABCCG, 1871, and the SDs 1871-75. In 1858 he married amateur actress Maria Louisa Long (1837–1920). His eldest son was Lionel John Alexander Monckton (1861-1924), who became Britain's most popular composer of Edwardian musical comedy in the early years of the 20th century, and who lived at No. 69 (chapter 3.2). His daughter, Mrs Augusta Moore, who wrote as Martin J. Pritchard, was a popular novelist of the period.

Sir John Braddick Monckton

Maria Louise, Lady Monckton, 1890
© National Portrait Gallery, London

Maria Emma Gray (1787-1876), conchologist and algologist (specialist in shells and algae), wife of **John Edward Gray** (1800-1875), naturalist, zoologist and keeper of the Zoological Department of the British Museum, died here in 1876 (*ODNB*).

John's family home was at 18 Burton Street from 1823 to 1826. They married in 1826 and moved to Blackheath. She was listed as *"Miss Gray"* in the SD, 1876. She greatly assisted her second husband in his scientific work, especially with her drawings. Between 1842 and 1874 she privately published five volumes of etchings, entitled *Figures of Molluscan Animals for the Use of Students*, and she mounted and arranged most of the Cuming collection of shells in the British Museum. She has two items – *Kobus Maria Gray* 1859 – in the collections of the Natural History Museum. John described and named many newly discovered species and transformed the British Museum's zoological collection into one of the most important in the world, corresponding with great pioneers

of science, including Charles Darwin and Michael Faraday. Figures of molluscs, by Maria Gray

Maria Emma Gray and John Edward Gray, 1863 © National Portrait Gallery, London

A medallion struck in honour of the Grays

Beryl de Zoete (1879-1962), ballet dancer, orientalist, dance critic, and dance researcher, lived in the top flat at No. 43 during the inter-war years. She is also known as a translator of Italo Svevo, the Italian writer championed by James Joyce. In the field of dance, she taught eurhythmics, investigated Indian dance and theatre traditions, and collaborated with Walter Spies on *Dance and Drama in Bali* (1937), which is still a standard reference for traditional Balinese dance and theatrical forms. In 1918, Beryl met **Arthur Waley** CH, CBE (1889-1966), a distinguished orientalist and poet, who was Assistant Keeper of Oriental Prints and Manuscripts at the British Museum. He earned both popular and scholarly acclaim for his translations of Chinese and Japanese poetry.

Beryl and Arthur formed a rather scandalous partnership; he was 10 years younger than she was, and living together unmarried was something shocking in the 1920s. However, the pair's relationship endured over many decades, albeit punctuated by two brief interludes of 'platonic unfaithfulness' in 1929 and 1943, when Arthur succumbed to the advances of Alison Grant, whom he eventually married weeks before his death in 1966 at the age of 76. Alison lived on to the next millennium, dying at the age of 100 in 2001. Her legacy could be said to be her personal memoir, *A Half of Two Lives* (1982), in which she explores her obsessive 40-year love for Arthur.

A Balinese dancer demonstrates dance positions for Beryl de Zoete

Arthur David Waley by Cecil Beaton, 1956
© National Portrait Gallery, London

Beryl de Zoete by Cecil Beaton, 1941
© National Portrait Gallery, London

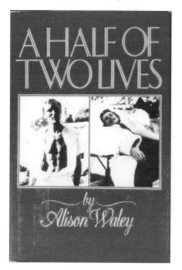

The writer James Cahill visited No. 43 in 1956 and wrote: *"I went alone to the meeting with Waley, who was living quietly in an upstairs apartment on Russell Square, with his long-time companion Beryl de Zoete. She was a specialist in Asian dance, and quite old by this time; she scarcely spoke, but sat by the stove wearing a cap with a green celluloid shade, reading. The flat was dishevelled and comfortable-looking, with a smell of wood smoke."* They associated with various members of the Bloomsbury Group, including John Maynard Keynes and Virginia Woolf. During the war, Arthur was employed as a censor at the Ministry of Information, vetting letters and telegrams written in Japanese. He found the work boring, and so relieved the tedium by writing to the senders of the letters criticising their sloppy handwriting and poor grammar. He left No. 43 when Beryl de Zoete died there in 1962 at the

Cover of the US edition of A Half of Two Lives by Alison Waley age of 82. E. Bruce Brooks praised Waley for being "…the great transmitter of the high literary cultures of China and Japan to the English-reading general public; the ambassador from East to West in the first half of the 20th century. He was self-taught, but reached remarkable levels of fluency, even erudition, in both languages. It was a unique achievement, possible (as he himself later noted) only in that time, and unlikely to be repeated." Waley was elected an honorary fellow of King's College, Cambridge in 1945, received the Commander of the Order of the British Empire (CBE) in 1952, the Queen's Gold Medal for Poetry in 1953, and the Order of the Companions of Honour (CH) in 1956.

Caricature of Arthur David Waley by Edmund Dulac, 1915

Other early occupants of No. 43 include: Charles Thompson (BCG, 1808); John Petty Muspratt, banker and director of the Hon. East India Company, who died at home in 1855; Richard Daniel Poppleton, well-to-do Yorkshire leather merchant, (SDs, 1878-82); Frederick Hill (SDs, 1886-99, listed as "Frederick C. Hill" in WRB, 1897); there were no further entries for No. 43 in the SDs until 1909, when the British Homeopathic Association (BHA) moved in, sharing the building with the London & Northern Tutorial College until 1914, when the latter was replaced by the South-Eastern Mounted Brigade (Territorial Force) and Girls' Realm Guild (1915), which served in Gallipoli in 1915. Also living there was **Myron Phelps**, a prominent American lawyer and campaigner for Indian independence, although better known as a promoter of the Baháí faith, translating the works of Abdu'l-Bahá, the second leader of Baháí, into English, which popularised Baháism in the West; the BHA was still there in 1939, sharing the building with the League of Nations Union (London Regional Federation), which promoted peace as the world slid towards another global conflict; World War II saw the arrival of several firms of solicitors, no doubt seeking the relative safety of Russell Square after the devastation inflicted by the Luftwaffe on the legal quarter in Holborn; the BHA remained until the end of the war, when the Jewish Fund for Soviet Russia appeared in 1945, followed by a gamut of horsey organisations, including the National Horse Association of Great Britain, the British Show Jumping Association, and the National Pony Society; 1958 to 1968 saw No. 43 host a variety of interesting tenants, including the HQ of Dairy Cream Products Ltd; the Bacon Society, which was devoted to the study of Francis Bacon the renaissance philosopher; the Educational Interchange Council, an educational charity which promoted links between schools and colleges around the world, best known for organising exchange visits for students across the Iron Curtain, hence the presence in the building in 1968 of the USSR Working Group on Youth Exchanges with the USSR.

Winter view of the west side of Russell Square today

Chapter 6

The South Side

South side from Montague Street (right) to Southampton Row, with incongruous 1960s development at Nos. 50-51 (corner of Bedford Place)

James Burton's designs for the south side of Russell Square were exhibited at the Royal Academy in 1800, thus confirming his credentials as an architect, as well as being widely regarded as late Georgian London's most ambitious and successful developer - responsible for much of its most characteristic architecture. This included large tracts of historic Bloomsbury, the villas and grand houses in and around Regent's Park and the elegant terraces in Regent Street. He went on to found and build the town of St Leonards-on-Sea in Sussex. The houses in the two south terraces were the only ones in Russell Square to be included in the original buildings agreement signed by Burton and the Duke of Bedford on 24th June 1800. With the notable exception of Nos. 50 and 51, all of Burton's houses on the south side survive today, albeit heavily disguised with the terracotta adornments added by Charles Fitzroy Doll in 1899 to 'match the standard' set by the newly built Hotel Russell on the east side of the square. The opportunity for the Bedford Estate to carry

out these 'improvements' arose because the original leases ran out in 1899, at which time thirteen of the seventeen houses on the south side had residents listed in the street directory. By 1900 there were only six residents listed, rising to eleven in 1901 and a respectable fourteen in 1902.

Nos. 50-51 (r-l) today. Lord Denman lived at No. 50

Nos. 44-51 (Montague Street to Bedford Place)

Nos. 44-51, c.1905 - courtesy of Brian Girling

The entry for Nos. 44-49 in the Register of listed buildings on the Historic England website states that these houses were listed on 28th March 1969 – too late for Nos. 50 and 51 to be afforded protection, but why did the Bedford Estate permit their demolition? The replacement office building, with one residential flat on the top floor, was granted planning permission by Holborn Borough Council in March 1963. The Bedford Estate archivist was unable to explain why Nos. 50 and 51 were singled out for demolition in 1962, even though they appeared to be in the same sound condition as the neighbouring houses in the 1955 photograph, and they were fully occupied by the Mineworkers' Federation of Great Britain and Gregg Publishing Co. Ltd, respectively,

Nos. 45 & 46 (r-l) showing superficial blast damage to top-floor windows caused by a bomb incident on the night of 15-16.10.1940 © CLSAC

The south side of Russell Square looking west in 1955, with Nos. 50 & 51 on the left-hand corner of Bedford Place

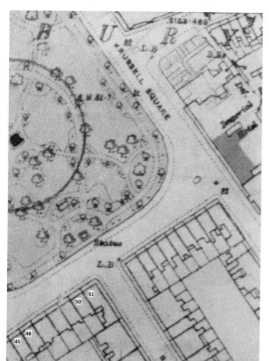

Bomb Damage map indicating no damage to the south side of the square

the 1890s electoral registers he is a voter in respect of his firm's premises in Hatton Garden. They eventually had 11 children, of whom Richard Davies Matthey (1858–1929) and Percy St Clair Matthey (1863–1928) subsequently entered the family business.

George's career was determined very early on, when an agreement between his father and Percival Norton Johnson, a family friend and business client, allowed for two of his father's sons to enter Johnson's business in Hatton Garden, Holborn, in return for the injection of new capital, believed to be about £10,000 (equivalent to £1.01M in 2016). Thus in 1838 Johnson, who at this time was refining gold, silver, and platinum on a modest scale, took on George as an apprentice. In 1845, George was put in charge of platinum refining, and it was due mainly to his persistent scientific endeavour over many years that the refining and fabrication of platinum was developed from a laboratory activity into a successful industrial enterprise.

He persuaded Johnson to participate in the Great Exhibition in 1851 - his display of platinum received a prize, but was outshone by a French competitor, who exhibited a large platinum still, used for the concentration of sulphuric acid. This spurred George to aim for pre-eminence in the platinum business. In the 1820s, significant platinum was found in the Ural Mountains in Russia. To begin with, this was subjected to an imperial monopoly, but in 1850 some mine owners there appointed George as their refiner and selling agent. Almost immediately, in 1851, he was taken into partnership by Johnson, and the firm became Johnson and Matthey. From then on Johnson began to relinquish control of the company's affairs, and on his retirement in 1860 Matthey became senior partner, one of the other two partners being George's younger brother, Edward. In 1891, George became the first chairman of Johnson Matthey & Co., a position he held until his retirement in 1909. Over the years, his acute business sense enabled him to see

throughout the war. Although the Bomb Damage map gives no indication of damage having been sustained by any of the houses on the south side of the Square during World War II, this cannot be totally relied upon, as illustrated by the photograph of Nos. 45 and 46 taken in 1940, which shows signs of superficial damage to the top-floor windows, suggesting that Nos. 50 and 51 might also have been affected, but not enough to justify their demolition.

44 - George Matthey (1825–1913), refiner, metallurgist, and founder of Johnson Matthey & Co., Hatton Garden, was baptised, aged one, at St Pancras Old Church on 14th May 1826, and lived with his family at No. 44 on 3rd January 1856 (the record of their son John Francis's baptism and his listing in BCG, 1857). In 1853, George married Charlotte Ann Davies, daughter of Richard Davies of South Hackney, where he lived prior to moving to Russell Square. Baptism records of three more children at All Saints, Gordon Square reveal that they also lived nearby at 3 Byng Place (at least 1862-67). In the 1871 census George is at Eastbourne and in

opportunities for the expansion of the platinum business and these he developed until both technical and commercial success were achieved.

Integral to his phenomenal success was the impression he made at the most significant international trade 'expos', most notably the Paris Universal Exhibition of 1855, and the Universal Exhibition in Paris in 1867. With the platinum business firmly established, George maintained mutually beneficial

George Matthey, aged 20, in 1845

contacts with the scientific community, playing an important role in the production of standard metres and kilograms in high purity iridium-platinum for the International Metric Commission. The engraving from the French magazine, *L'Illustration*, of 16th May 1874 shows George conducting the associated melting process to produce metric weights in conjunction with Henri Tresca, Professor of Mechanics at the *Conservatoire des Arts et Métiers* in Paris in 1874.

Engraving from the French magazine, *L'Illustration*, 16th May 1874

An eminent member of several scientific and technical bodies, he was active in the establishment of the City and Guilds Colleges at South Kensington and Finsbury. Elected to the Goldsmiths' Company in 1853, he became a member of its court in 1853, and served as prime warden in 1872 and 1894. Almost 150 years later, Johnson Matthey was still successfully engaged in the refining, fabrication, and marketing of gold, silver and platinum. In 1994–5, the company was the largest gold refiner in the world, and the sole marketing agent and joint refiner for Rustenburg Platinum Mines, the world's largest source of platinum metals. George died at Rosemount, his Eastbourne residence, on 14th February 1913.

George Matthey in later years

Other early occupants of No. 44 include: John Hanson (BCG, 1808, and Elizabeth, his third daughter's, marriage notice in *The Gazette*, 1808. *The Lady's Magazine* of 14th July 1808 announced the birth of a son to Hanson's daughter, *"The lady of captain Bogue…"*, at No.44); William Fox (BCGs, 1820-24); John Hanson (BCGs, 1829-40, and only *"Miss Hanson"* in 1840-46, and SDs, 1841-42). *The Gentleman's Magazine* had a notice of the marriage of William's fourth daughter, Anne, marriage on 6th June 1829; Alfred Waterhouse (RBB, 1858, ABCCG, 1871, and SDs, 1861-82, but only Mrs Waterhouse in 1886-87). Waterhouse, as *"…the proprietor of the large tea-dealing firm of Dakin & Company, was to have his home at 44 Russell Square, Bloomsbury, with his City office and shop at 1 St Paul's Churchyard, City, and his West End outlet at 119 Oxford Street, linked by telegraph, acquiring four instruments."* (distantwriting.co.uk); Arthur Lewis Leon (1855-1927) is listed in SDs, 1888-1897, and as *"Arthur Leon, L.C.C."* in WRB, 1897, reflecting his role as Alderman on the London County Council)

Arthur Lewis Leon

Francis Washbourne (SD, 1898); Percy Edward Sankey, solicitor and notary (SDs, 1901-30). Sankey is described in the National Archives as *"Well known Ramsgate Solicitor of 44 Russell Square"*. He was a member of the Sussex Archaeological Society and served on the Council of the Plainsong and Mediaeval Music Society; Intriguing occupants during World War II were the Fertilizer Manufacturers' Association and the International Superphosphate Manufacturers' Association, no doubt aligned with the 'dig for victory' campaign, or could they have been associated with something more sinister?

45 - John Meeson Parsons (1798-1870), art collector, lived at No. 45 from November 1869, where he sadly died four months later on 26th March 1870, leaving his valuable art collection to the National Gallery, the Department of Science and Art at South Kensington and the British Museum. His will stipulated that should the National Gallery not accept the whole gift, the Department would be entitled to the same right of selection. As the National Gallery chose only 3 oil paintings, including one by J.W. Turner, the Department selected 92 paintings and 47 watercolours, now held by the Victoria and Albert Museum. Parsons' varied career saw him become a member of the Stock Exchange, an associate of the Institution of Civil Engineers and, with his passion for railways, a Director and Chairman of the London and Brighton Railway Company.

Sheerness and the Isle of Sheppey (after J.M.W. Turner) c.1807–8, bequeathed by John Meeson Parsons 1870 © Tate

Oil painting, *Musicians An Old Man and an Old Woman*, Lucas van Leyden, Netherlands, bequeathed by John M. Parsons, 1870 © V&A

Michael Gunn lived at No. 45 when in London, where he divided his time with his Dublin home. He is listed at this address in the SDs, 1882-86. Gunn and Richard D'Oyly Carte (at No. 71) were close friends, Gunn serving as Carte's *"concert and dramatic agent,"* as well as being his *"silent partner."* Together they convinced Gilbert and Sullivan to create *Trial by Jury*, a new form of musical comedy which rapidly gained popularity in the United Kingdom and America. It was Carte's first important theatrical venture, and encouraged by its success, he found four backers, one of which was Gunn, and formed the Comedy Opera Company to produce the future works of Gilbert and Sullivan. This allowed Carte to lease the Opera Comique and to give Gilbert and Sullivan firm terms for a new opera, *The Sorcerer*, which was soon followed by *HMS Pinafore* in 1878. Family legend has it that during a tour that stopped in Dublin, Richard D'Oyly Carte obtained a loan from Michael without which he would not have been able to keep the partnership of W.S. Gilbert and A. Sullivan going. This is supported by a book of that time, *Old Days of Bohemian London*: *"From the minute Michael Gunn undertook to finance the Gilbert and Sullivan operas, impending disaster gave place to bustling prosperity."* In the summer of 1879, when Carte had left Gunn to manage his affairs in London, some of the other business partners tried to seize the scenery as well as performers to set up their own production of *HMS Pinafore*. Gunn wrote to Sullivan, who was away in France resting, that the rival directors were *"...seducing the male chorus by use of Champagne and promises of increased pay."* Carte maintained control as witness the fact that he continued with the production of *HMS Pinafore*, but now billed as *Mr D'Oyly Carte's Opera Company*. Gunn's wife, Bessie, invariably accompanied him to their *"fine old house on Russell Square".*

Bessie Gunn was born in Liverpool on 22nd July 1849, and at an early age went to America as a member of the burlesque troupe, the British Blondes, where her stage name was Bessie Sudlow.

Led by the famous English dancer, comedian, actress and producer, Lydia Thompson, it was one of the most popular entertainments in New York during the 1868-69 season at the Tammany Grand Theatre. What had begun as a six-month tour lasted six years. During both 1872 and 1873 she played the part of Dove Eve, an Indian Maiden, in *Scouts of the Plains*, which starred Buffalo Bill Cody as himself. While in Indianapolis, Cody proposed some sort of affair with her while on-stage! She responded by hitting him over the head with one of the war clubs lying about and when he fell to the floor, she sat on him until her anger

Bessie Sudlow

abated enough for her to leave the theatre, all of which was reported in the local press the next day. She continued her stage career in England as a comic opera soprano. Constantine Curran, who was born in Dublin in 1883, later wrote how *"...her glorious apparition in ballroom splendour remained long in the memory of our parents."* She also seemed to have had an extraordinary memory, as demonstrated on an occasion where she was called in at 24 hours-notice to play an unfamiliar role at the Gaiety Theatre. One of her co-actors recalled: *"She sang songs she did not know to tunes she had never heard, wedded to words improvised as she went along."* When the notices came out, she found herself famous. The opera was an English adaptation of *La fille de Madame Angot* that had achieved great success in Paris several years earlier. In 1876 she was the principal soprano for the touring Comedy Opera Company where she met Michael Gunn who was its manager at the time. They married in 1877, after which she made only one more appearance on the stage, although she kept the name Bessie.

Benjamin Greene (1780-1860) was the founder of Greene King, one of the UK's largest brewing businesses. He is listed at No. 46 in BCGs, 1840-57, RBB, 1858, and in SDs, 1841-61, although he is also recorded as dying at Russell Square in 1860.

Benjamin Greene

Benjamin Greene's first brewery at Bury St Edmunds

Born in Oundle and apprenticed at Whitbread, Benjamin Greene initially founded a brewing business with John Clark in Bury St Edmunds in 1801. He dissolved that partnership in 1806 and established a new venture with William Buck at the Westgate Brewery, which was to become Greene King. On the death of Sir Patrick Blake, 2nd Baronet ("Green's neighbour across the brewery yard" - ODNB) he became the executor and, on the subsequent

death of Sir Patrick's widow, the owner of two plantations on St Kitts and Montserrat in the West Indies. He went on to acquire further estates in his own right. In 1829 his eldest son, "...the immensely capable Benjamin Buck Greene (1808–1902) was sent out to St Kitts to run all these properties and consolidate the family's good fortune. On his return to England in 1836 he was managing and modernizing no fewer than eighteen estates (together producing one third of the island's sugar exports in the mid-1830s) and enjoying the greatest reputation as a planter." (ODNB). His new connections with slave owning, sugar production and molasses would colour his views for the future, so that when he acquired the *Bury and Suffolk Herald* in 1828 he took an ultra-conservative position opposing both the Reform Bill and the Slavery Abolition Bill. This position attracted much criticism and three libel actions. He was a supporter of the arts and in 1819 lent £5,000 to William Wilkins to build the Theatre Royal in Bury St Edmunds. He left Bury St Edmunds in 1836 and established with his son, Benjamin Greene & Son, West India Merchants and Ship owners, at 11 Mincing Lane, London. He died at No. 45 in 1860 and is buried at Highgate Cemetery. He was married twice, first in 1803 to Mary Maling and then in 1805 to Catherine Smith, with whom he went on to have seven sons and six daughters including: Benjamin Buck (1808 - 1902), Governor of the Bank of England, and Edward (1815–91), Conservative MP for Bury St Edmunds (1865-85) and Stowmarket (1886–91), who took charge of running the brewery.

Samuel Lyon de Symons (c.1788-1860), stockbroker and philanthropist, is listed at No. 45 in BCG, 1829. He was a major benefactor of the Jewish Free School (JFS), of which he became Treasurer. He also supported the Western Jews' Free School, the Jews' Infant School, and education projects in general. The son of Baron Lyon de Symons (1743-1813), he married Bella Barrow, daughter of Jacob Barrow and Gael Nunes. The name Lyon or Loew or Leb is an equivalent for the Hebrew name, Judah, on the basis of Jacob's blessing at the end of Genesis, where he compares his son Judah with a lion. Samuel died in 1860 at 9 Cumberland terrace, Regent's Park, where he had lived from 1851. He had one child, Fanny Louisa de Symons (b. 1819).

Other early occupants of No. 45 include:
Samuel Yate Benyon (1762-1822), Bencher of Lincoln's Inn, Attorney General of Chester and Vice-Chancellor of the Duchy of Lancaster, is listed in BCGs, 1808-21. He was sworn a Burgess of Shrewsbury in 1796; William Campbell (BCG, 1824). His minimalist obituary appears in the *Annual Register of World Events*, 1827, under 8th June: *"In Russell-square, aged 57, William Campbell esq. comptroller of the Legacy Duty new departments, and chairman of the Board of Stamps in Ireland."*; David Powell (BCG, 1834); Henry Goldstein (SDs, 1887-89); Francis Arthur Holman (SDs, 1890-1893); Charles Levy (SDs, 1894-99, and WRB, 1897); Charles Gordon (SDs, 1901-12, listed as *"Charles Wood Gordon"* in BCG, 1903, and SDs post-1903); Kennedy, Ponsonby, Ryde & Co., solicitors, occupied the building in 1914-20, renamed Tamplin, Joseph, Ponsonby & Ryde in 1930; The Anglo-German Academic Bureau was briefly there in 1939, although the building was not listed in SDs, 1940-45, most probably due to bomb damage sustained during the overnight incident on 15th-16th October 1940, in which Nos. 45-47 superficially damaged (see photograph, above).

46 - Sir George Sowley Holroyd (1758–1831),
judge, lived for a time at No. 46, being listed as *"Mr. Justice Holroyd"* in BCGs, 1820-29. He was called to the Bar in 1787, the year that he married Sarah Chaplin. They had fourteen children, only six of whom survived their father. An amusing anecdote is told by a certain Horace Smith about the efforts of his brother, James, to obtain a sworn affidavit on behalf of his father. James had a dinner engagement at a house next door to Holroyd's in Russell Square, so he decided to kill two birds with one stone and call on the judge to ask for his signature. Holroyd had just sat down to dinner when James knocked on his door, but he promptly left the table and swore the affidavit. On so doing he asked James what the emergency was that caused him to call on him at home. James fumbled for a good excuse and came out with *"The fact is, my Lord, I am engaged to dine at the next house-and-and-. "And, sir, you thought you might as well save your own dinner by spoiling mine?" "Exactly so, my Lord, but-. "Sir,"* (replied the irate judge), *"I wish you a good evening."* Holroyd served as one of the three puisne judges of King's

Bench with Ellenborough and then Charles Abbott, first Baron Tenterden, as his chiefs. He remained in office until the age of 70, when ill health forced his retirement on 17th November 1828. He died at his home in Hare Hatch, Berkshire, on 21st December 1831, *"…leaving his widow in less than comfortable circumstances"* (ODNB). Chief Justice Campbell proclaimed Holroyd's *"genius for the law"* (Campbell, 356) and Lord Brougham described him (on his memorial in Wargrave church) as *"…one of the most able, most learned, and most virtuous men that ever…adorned the profession of the law"*.

Sir George Sowley Holroyd
© National Portrait Gallery, London

Jeremiah Pilcher JP (1790-1866), is listed at No. 46 in BCGs, 1834-46, with the appendage *"Sheriff of London"* in 1843 only. He is listed in SDs, 1841 to 1842. He is noted for a complex case referenced as Pilcher v Rawlins in the Court of Chancery in 1872, which is often employed as a justification of the Torrens title system. It stemmed from a trust executed by Jeremiah on 23rd August 1830, involving a mortgage transaction entered into by his brother William Humphrey Pilcher, and was only resolved by the judgment of Lord Hatherley. As well as being a Justice of the Peace, he was a Sheriff of the City of London. After his death in 1886 his body was interred in St George's, Bloomsbury alongside his loving wife, Mary Rebecca (1803-1885), where a memorial tablet can be seen today.

Memorial tablet to Jeremiah Pilcher in St George's, Bloomsbury

Other early occupants of No. 46 include:

Abraham Favenc (BCG, 1808). He was a partner in the British Cobalt Smelting Company. The *"Will of Abraham Favenc of Boulogne sur mer, France…"*, dated 24th April 1845, is held by the National Archives, Kew. He was born on 15th February 1765 and christened at the Artillery-French Huguenot Church, Spitalfields, London. He was elected as an Upper Bailiff of the Weavers' Company in 1808, and was a Member of the Society of Friends of Foreigners in Distress; Alexander Isaacs (BCG, 1857, RBB, 1858, and SDs, 1861-62, with Mrs Isaacs alone in 1865); Henry Beyfus (1845-1889) is listed in ABCCG, 1871, and SDs, 1871-79). Beyfus is described in a Dissolution of Partnership Notice in *The London Gazette*, 3rd June 1879, as a diamond merchant. He and his wife, Jane, lived at 34 Russell Square until he died in 1889, aged 44. They had eight children; Edgar Horne (SDs, 1881-1894); Nathaniel Harris (SDs, 1895-1910, and WRB, 1897 and 1903); the Anglo-Continental Institute occupied No. 46 in 1915 and the University of London Officers' Training Corps from 1916 to 1939, but with no occupants being listed for the rest of World War II following bomb damage sustained on the night of 14th-15th October 1940, along with No. 45.

47 - Sir Samuel Morton Peto, 1st Baronet (1809-1889), entrepreneur, civil engineer and railway magnate, lived here with his second wife, Sarah, and their numerous children (four by his first wife who died in 1842 and eleven by Sarah) from 1845 to 1853 (*ODNB*). Sir Samuel is listed at No. 47 in BCG, 1845-46.

Sir Samuel Morton Peto © National Portrait Gallery, London

"Peto's omnibus, conveying family and servants (the sexes segregated) to worship in Bloomsbury, was a familiar Sunday sight between 1849 and 1873." (*ODNB*). As partner in the firm of Grissell and Peto, he managed construction firms which built many major buildings and monuments in London, including The Reform Club, The Lyceum, Trafalgar Square and Nelson's Column (1843), and the new Houses of Parliament, which made him a millionaire. They were also responsible for overseeing the vast infrastructure project of the London brick sewers. Another project was the Bloomsbury Baptist Chapel (1848), the first Baptist church with spires in London. Tradition has it that the Crown Commissioner was reluctant to lease the land to nonconformists because of their *"dull, spire-less architecture"*. Peto is said to have exclaimed, *"A spire, my Lord? We shall have two!"* The church had twin spires until 1951, when they were removed as unsafe. As a partner in Peto and Betts, he became one of the major contractors in the building of the rapidly expanding railways of the time. Adrian Vaughan, railway historian and Brunel biographer wrote: *"Peto was big in East Anglia and, with the willing co-operation*

of the Eastern Counties Railway Chairman, David Waddington, MP for Harwich, organised various swindles on the ECR shareholders. ECR money was used to improve Lowestoft harbour which was owned by Peto and Waddington and all the while the ECR's harbour at Harwich was neglected. Peto built chapels and supported orphanges and was a very good employer. He treated his navvies with the greatest care and they were the best paid workmen in the country."

Peto served for two decades as a Member of Parliament, first as Liberal Member for Norwich in 1847 to 1854, then for Finsbury from 1859 to 1865, and finally for Bristol from 1865 to 1868. During this time he was one of the most prominent figures in public life. He was guarantor to the tune of £50K for financing Joseph Paxton's Crystal Palace centrepiece of The Great Exhibition of 1851, but after his involvement in the insolvency of the London Chatham and Dover Railway in 1866 and the failure of the Peto and Betts partnership, his personal reputation as a trustworthy businessman was badly damaged and never fully recovered. In 1868, he had to give up his seat in Parliament, despite having the support of both Benjamin Disraeli and William Gladstone. After failed attempts to promote railways in Russia and Hungary and a small mineral railway in Cornwall, Peto died in obscurity in 1889.

Peto in later life

John Coxhead (1804-1882), merchant and banker, is listed at No. 47 in the SDs, 1861-82, in which year he died at No 47 on 13th August. He married Henrietta Laetitia Maddan, who was born in Jamaica c.1814 and who also died at No. 47 on 29th May 1885, which explains why only *"Miss Coxhead"* is listed in the SDs, 1883-86. They had seven sons and three daughters, one of whom became Brigadier-General James Alfred Coxhead. John Coxhead was one of the 22 survivors from the sinking of the Steam Packet *Rothesay Castle* which was wrecked in Beaumaris Bay, North Wales, on 17th August 1831, with the loss of 120 passengers. In 1835 he held a 'position of trust' in the firm Messrs Desgrand, Fordatue & Company, Merchants of the City of London. By 1848 he was a partner in the firm, which was then called Messrs Fordati, Coxhead & Company. By 1868 John Coxhead was a Principal of the firm which then became known as *"Messrs Coxhead, Goldsmid & Company, Silk Merchants, of 13 Old Jewry Chambers, London, EC"*.

Other early occupants of No. 47 include:
T. Greenwood (BCGs, 1820-29); Simon Fraser Pigott (BCGs, 1834-44, and SDs, 1841-42); William Jackson (BCG, 1857, and RBB, 1858); Thomas Perkins (SDs, 1888-94); Louis Spitzel (SD, 1896); Mrs Leighton (SD, 1898); Henry Sturt (SDs, 1901 to at least 1916); Cooper, McDougall & Robertson Ltd, sheep-dip manufacturers, occupied No. 47 in 1930-40, but the building was not listed in 1941-45, probably due to the bomb damage sustained in late 1940, which also affected Nos. 45 and 46 (see above).

48 - John Armstrong (1784–1829), physician, lived and died at his home in Russell Square. He is listed at No. 48 as *"Dr Armstrong"* in BCG, 1829. Armstrong built up a large practice and became a popular teacher of medicine. His works on fevers, founded on his own observations, were popular in Britain and America, but were overtaken by later discoveries. Armstrong himself changed his opinion of typhus, which he at first considered to be contagious but later attributed to a malarial origin. In treatment he was an ardent advocate of the antiphlogistic (counteracting inflammation) system, favouring the use of bleeding. A controversy with the Royal College of Surgeons, published by Armstrong as *An address to the members of the Royal College of Surgeons on the injurious conduct and defective state of that corporation with reference to professional rights, medical science, and the public health* (1825) arose from that body's attempt to discourage private medical teaching by refusing to accept certificates from anyone other than medical schools of the recognized hospitals. In 1828 failing health compelled Armstrong to give up teaching. A book, *On the Morbid Anatomy of the Stomach, Bowels and Liver* was left unfinished; this, and his *Lectures on the Morbid Anatomy, Nature and Treatment of Acute and Chronic Diseases*, were published after his death, of consumption, on 12th December 1829 at Russell Square. He was buried on 19th December at St George's, Bloomsbury.

Golding Bird (1814–1854), physician, moved to 48 Russell Square with his wife Mary Ann and their two daughters and three sons in 1850 (*ODNB*). *"Bird, Golding, FRS, physician"* is listed at No. 48 in the SD, 1852.

Golding Bird MD, 1840

Bird was a British medical doctor and a Fellow of the Royal College of Physicians. He became a great authority on kidney diseases and published a comprehensive paper on urinary deposits in 1844. He was also notable for his work in related sciences, especially the medical uses of electricity and electrochemistry. From 1836, he lectured at Guy's Hospital, a well-known teaching hospital in London, and published a popular textbook on science for medical students titled *Elements of Natural Philosophy*. Having developed an interest in chemistry while still a child, largely through self-study, Bird was sufficiently advanced to deliver lectures to his fellow pupils at school. He later applied this knowledge to medicine and did much research on the chemistry of urine and of kidney stones. In 1842,

he was the first to describe oxaluria, a condition which leads to the formation of a particular kind of stone. Bird was innovative in the field of the medical use of electricity, designing much of his own equipment. In his time, electrical treatment had acquired a bad name in the medical profession through its widespread use by 'quack' practitioners. Bird made efforts to oppose this quackery, and was instrumental in bringing medical electrotherapy into the mainstream. He was quick to adopt new instruments of all kinds. He also invented a new variant of the Daniell cell in 1837 and made important discoveries in electrometallurgy with it. He was not only innovative in the electrical field, but he also designed a flexible stethoscope, and in 1840 published the first description of such an instrument. A devout Christian, Bird believed Bible study and prayer were just as important to medical students as their academic studies, and he was responsible for founding the Christian Medical Association, although it did not become active until after his death. Bird had lifelong poor health and died at the age of 39. Bird's publications include: *Elements of Natural Philosophy; being an experimental introduction to the study of the physical sciences* (John Churchill, London, 1839); *Lectures on Electricity and Galvanism, in their physiological and therapeutical relations*, delivered at the Royal College of Physicians, in March, 1847 (Wilson & Ogilvy, London, 1847); *Lectures on the Influence of Researches in Organic Chemistry on Therapeutics, especially in relation to the depuration of the blood*, delivered at the Royal College of Physicians (Wilson & Ogilvy, London, 1848); *Urinary Deposits, their diagnosis, pathology and therapeutical indications* (John Churchill, London, 1844); *Case of Internal Strangulation of Intestine relieved by operation* (From *Transactions of the Royal Medico-Chirurgical Society*), with John Hilton (Richard Kinder, London, [1847]).

Early occupants of No. 48 include:
F. Robertson (BCG, 1808); Collin Robertson (BCGs, 1820-21); Alexander Turnbull, physician (listed as *"Dr Turnbull"* in BCGs, 1834-46, and as *"Alexander Turnbull, physician"*, in SDs, 1841-42); Dr E. Lloyd Birkett (BCG, 1857, RBB, 1858, listed as *"Edmund Lloyd Birkett, physician"* in SDs, 1861-90); Walter Sully (SDs, 1892-95); Thomas Borthwick (1835-1912) is listed in WRB, 1897, and SDs, 1896-1901). He moved next door to No. 49, where he is listed in 1900-10 (see entry, below); Henry Druit Phillips (d. 15th May 1917), solicitor, is listed in SDs, 1902-16; the British and London Poster Advertising Associations occupied the building from at least 1930 and throughout World War II.

49 - Sir John Barnard Byles (1801-1884),
barrister, judge and author of books on law and the
economy, is listed at No. 49 in BCG, 1857, and RBB,
1857 as *"Mr Serjeant Byles"* and *"Hon. Sir John B.
Byles, Justice of the Common Pleas"*, respectively. He
published an influential text on bills of exchange in
1829, commonly referred to as *"Byles on Bills"*. He
is even said to have named his horse *"Bills"*, so that
when approaching, people would utter *"Here comes
Byles on Bills"*. In 1843, he became a Serjeant-at-Law
and in 1857 he was appointed Queen's Serjeant. In
January 1858 he was promoted to the Bench and
was later made a Knight Bachelor and Justice of the
Common Pleas. In January 1873 he resigned as a
judge due to his failing health. He was a member
of the Privy Council for a short while until his death
on 3rd February 1884, aged eighty-two.

James Thomas Knowles (1806-1884), architect,
moved here to live with his younger son George
Knowles in 1876, following the death of his wife (George's
mother) Susannah. He is listed in the SD, 1882.

Sir James Thomas Knowles (1831–1908),
architect and editor, he was responsible for the
Victoria Station Hotel - originally named
The Grosvenor. Sir James, who worked in
partnership with his father, was also editor
of the *Contemporary Review*, 1870–77. He
associated with a number of the most interesting
men of the day, and in 1869, with Alfred Lord
Tennyson's co-operation, he founded the
Metaphysical Society, the object of which was
to attempt some intellectual rapprochement
between religion and science by getting the
leading representatives of faith and unfaith to
meet and exchange views. James, *"dignified"*,
"determined", and *"self-reliant"* (Metcalf, 19),
largely practised alone in the later 1860s. In
retirement, Knowles remained a dedicated and
active member of the RIBA Council (a record
of his activities may be found in *RIBA Transactions*,
47, 1884, and *The Builder*, 3rd May 1884).
He died at No. 49 on 23rd March 1884.

Design for the Houses of Parliament by James Thomas Knowles (1806-1884)

Sir James Thomas Knowles

James had an extensive
practice in building upper-class
houses in the Italianate manner.
He was evidently a practical
man who valued convenience,
*"...fitness in design...and
durability...in construction..."*
(*The Builder*, 15th June 1850).
He lost out to Sir Charles
Barry in the competition to
design the new Houses of
Parliament, in 1836, although he
went on to build the confident
and technically assured palazzo
at 15, Kensington Palace
Gardens (1854) and
together with his son,

The Grosvenor Hotel

Sir Thomas Borthwick, 1st baronet (1835–1912), meat importer, lived at No. 49 from 1900 to at least 1910. He is listed in SDs as Thomas Borthwick from 1900 until 1909-10, when he is listed as *"Sir Thomas Borthwick, bart"*. He also briefly lived next door at No. 48 from 1896 to 1899 (see entry for No.48, above, for duplicate directory entries for 1900/01). He worked his way up from apprentice butcher in the family business in Scotland to being the owner of Britain's largest meat dealerships. He was only twenty-two when he established himself as a livestock agent, and it was said that he could walk into a pen holding 500 or more sheep and tell the weight and value of any of them at a glance. He was later to become a judge at the Royal Agricultural Show. When refrigeration finally made it possible to bring meat to Britain from Australasia and Argentina, Borthwick was quick to recognize the possibilities in international trade in the product and by 1883 he was the selling agent for the New Zealand Loan and Mercantile Agency Co. Ltd. He opened meat depots in Liverpool, Manchester, Glasgow, and Birmingham, and in 1892 transferred the firm's headquarters to London, at the same time securing a stall in Smithfield. This was the real beginning of the large wholesale and distribution business that covered the major livestock products of meat, wool, and tallow. But the main business was meat, and Borthwick was a leading figure in promoting the trade, especially in experimenting with chilling (as opposed to freezing) techniques, which indirectly made him responsible for improving the quality of Australian beef. His eldest son, Thomas Borthwick (b. 1875), later Baron Whitburgh, went to Australia and New Zealand in 1904, where he purchased meat-processing works and established branch offices at Sydney, Melbourne, Brisbane, and Christchurch. That same year the firm became a limited company under the name of Thomas Borthwick & Sons Ltd, registered with a capital of £300,000. More meat works were added later, and the company continued to prosper until the early 1980s, and, together with the Vestey brothers, dominated the Australasian meat trade. At the time of his death, in 1912, Borthwick was still Chairman of Thomas Borthwick & Sons Ltd and a director of Lancashire Cold Storage Co. Ltd, Thames Cold Storage Co. Ltd, and Thomas Borthwick & Sons (Australasia) Ltd. The ODNB would have us believe that *"Weeks before he died he was named as baron in the birthday honours…"*, yet he appears as *"Sir Thomas Borthwick, bart"* in the 1909 street directory.

Strutt & Parker, surveyors, are listed at No. 49 in the SDs, 1915-45, and the Strutt & Parker website states that the firm remained in Russell Square until 1968. Strutt & Parker was founded in 1885 by two friends, Edward Gerald Strutt and Charles Alfred Parker, with their first office in Finsbury Circus, London. By 1896, Strutt & Parker managed 3,000 acres of land (1.5M today). In 1914-18, Edward Strutt advised the Board of Agriculture on national agricultural policy during the World War I. In 1934, despite the Stock Market crash, Strutt & Parker opened its second office in Lewes. When the firm celebrated its Golden Jubilee in 1935, with a dinner at the Holborn Restaurant, London, the firm employed some 50 staff. During World War II, Land Agency work involved a crash course in requisitioning large areas of land for military occupation, rationing of animal feeding stuffs, the destruction of woodlands and the control of the War Agricultural Committees. The management of estates was kept going by a handful of devoted people who worked 12-hour days seven days a week. 1955 saw a merger with Lofts & Warner, a rural estate agency, with the firm known for a time as Strutt & Parker Lofts & Warner. Under Mark Strutt's leadership in 1962-1979, the firm's activities became more diverse, reflecting changes in the world of property and business, forming a commercial division in 1967 and moving the Head Office to 13 Hill Street, London, in 1968. The last member of the Strutt family died in 1982. The following year, a programme of nationwide expansion was completed, with offices in Canterbury, Chelmsford, Cheltenham, Chester, Exeter, Edinburgh, Grantham, Harrogate, Ipswich, Norwich and Salisbury. The firm merged with Lane Fox in 2007, doubling in size to 50 offices. By 2011, Strutt & Parker had 800 staff working in over 45 offices around the UK and in 2012, it become the exclusive UK affiliate of Christie's International Real Estate, joining the world's leading network of luxury residential real estate specialists across 42 countries.

Other early occupants of No. 49 include:

J.T. James (BCG, 1808); James Cunningham (BCGs, 1820-24); Rev. A.M. Campbell (BCG, 1829); J.J. Leon (BCGs, 1834-44, also listed as *"Joseph Isaac Leon, esq."* in SDs, 1841-42); J. Stuart, solicitor (BCG, 1846); John Rouse Phillips (SDs, 1862-78, and ABCCG, 1871); Robert Carter (SD, 1895); Thomas Brooks Browne (SDs, 1888-90); Mrs. Carter (WRB, 1897, and SDs, 1892-99); *Charles Maud* (SD, 1914).

50 - Thomas Denman (1779-1854) – 1st Baron Denman, MP, Lord Chief Justice (1832-1850) and Counsel for Queen Caroline, lived at No. 50 with his wife, Theodosia, from 1816 to 1834. He is listed in Boyle's Court Guide, 1820-34 (as *"Common Serj. of the City of London"* in 1829 and as *"Lord Chief Justice of the King's Bench"* in 1834).

Thomas Denman, 1st Baron Denman
© National Portrait Gallery, London

Their son, **George Denman** (1819–1896), high court judge and politician, was born at No. 50 on 23rd December 1819. He was Thomas's twelfth child and seventh son. (The last of his 15 children, of whom 11 survived him, was not born until 1823.) George became Queen's Counsel in 1861. In May 1859, he was elected MP for Tiverton as Lord Palmerston's colleague, and held the seat until 1872, except for a short interval in 1865-66. The *Evidence Further Amendment Act* of 1869, popularly known as Denman's Act, was entirely due to his efforts. This allowed witnesses of no religious belief to affirm in place of taking the oath in courts of justice, so that parties who previously could not be heard could give evidence. *"Denman was popular on the bench, but was more*

distinguished as a graceful scholar than as a strong lawyer. He was said to have a fine presence and a beautiful voice." (ODNB). A plaque on the office building which replaced James Burton's original building (demolished in 1962), commemorates both men.

Thomas Denman distinguished himself by his defence of the Luddites and as Solicitor General he famously pleaded the cause of Queen Caroline before the House of Lords in 1820, and was at her death bed the following year. For this he was awarded the freedom of the City of London. He is credited in *The Creevey Papers* with saying of the Queen: *"If her Majesty is included in any prayer, it is in the prayer for all who are desolate and oppressed."*

Although Denman was a prominent anti-slaver, he prosecuted the rioters who were seeking parliamentary reform in 1832 and in November of that year, when he succeeded Lord Tenterden (who lived at No. 28) as Lord Chief Justice, he condemned the publisher of Shelley's complete works for blasphemy. His relentless efforts to bring an end to slavery exerted a great strain on his health. He died on 22nd September 1854.

While he was neither a great forensic lawyer nor a particularly gifted advocate, he earned and sustained a high professional reputation as *"a man of very pure honour"* and a champion of *"liberty and justice"* (*Life of Campbell*). This instinct was at the root of his political credo, as he told his friend Merivale in 1823: *"The greatest of all political evils I have always thought was... injustice deliberately perpetrated or wilfully persisted in by the state. Paramount...has ever been to my mind the question of parliamentary reform. The perpetual fraud upon the people, the audacious belying of the constitution, the shameless effrontery and cunning with which the multiform and outrageous abuse was at once avowed and concealed, the frightful small fry of peculation daily engendered in the huge midden of corruption, the license to degrade and oppress, the charter to demoralize and plunder the mass of our countrymen."*

William Revell Vigers, (1782-1848), merchant, is listed as *"R.W. Vigers"* in BCGs, 1840-46, and as *"William Revell Vigers, esq."* in SDs, 1841-42. He married Caroline Elizabeth and they had one son, Charles Kenneth Vigers (b. 1815). As Managing Director of the West Cork Mining Company, William represented the company in an appeal heard by the House of Lords in 1840. However, he is best remembered for being granted a patent on 7th July 1842 for the invention of *"…a mode of keeping the air in confined places in a pure*

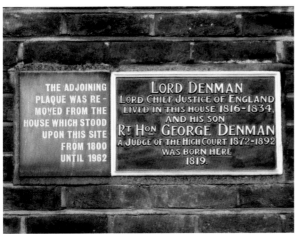

THE ADJOINING PLAQUE WAS RE-MOVED FROM THE HOUSE WHICH STOOD UPON THIS SITE FROM 1800 UNTIL 1962

LORD DENMAN
LORD CHIEF JUSTICE OF ENGLAND
LIVED IN THIS HOUSE 1816-1834,
AND HIS SON
Rᵗ Hᴼᴺ GEORGE DENMAN
A JUDGE OF THE HIGH COURT 1872-1892
WAS BORN HERE
1819.

and respirable state, to enable persons to remain or work under water and other places without a constant supply of fresh atmospheric air." (Mechanics Magazine, Vol. 40, by John I. Knight and Henry Lacey, 1844).

George Routledge (1812-1888), wealthy publisher, is listed at No. 50 in the SDs, 1861-89. Charles Harrison sold the lease on No. 50 to George Routledge on 8th May 1858. Routledge's first wife, Maria, the mother of their eight children, had died in 1855. Three years later, George married Mary Grace, with whom he had two children. Mary, who is listed as *"Mrs Routledge"* in the SDs, 1890-97, died in 1898.

George Routledge © National Portrait Gallery, London

George Routledge set up in business as a retail bookseller with his brother-in-law W.H. Warne as assistant, and in 1836 published his first (unsuccessful) book, *The Beauties of Gilsand* (a guidebook), moving to 36 Soho Square in 1843. Around this time Routledge was convinced that there were a great many readers who were unwilling or unable to spend even five or six shillings for a book, but they might be willing to pay cash for volumes costing just 1 shilling or 1 shilling and 6 pence. W.H. Warne was taken into partnership and the 'Railway Library' of cheap reprints of works of fiction began in 1848 with a bookstall at Euston Station. Similar outlets soon sprouted throughout the country. W.H. Warne's brother, Frederick Warne, was taken into partnership and the firm of George Routledge and Co was founded in 1851, relocating to 2 Farringdon Street in 1852, when the firm published Harriet Beecher Stowe's *Uncle Tom's Cabin*. Founded on the success of cheap editions of works

of fiction, the firm rapidly expanded into the reprint market, catering for the growing literate population of the Victorian age. Routledge and Co opened a New York branch in 1854. Robert Warne Routledge, George Routledge's son, entered the partnership in 1858 and the firm was restyled Routledge, Warne & Routledge. W.H. Warne died in 1859. In 1862 *Every Boy's Magazine*, edited by Edmund Routledge (George Routledge's son), was started. The firm entered a contract with Lord Tennyson in 1863. Frederick Warne left the firm, Edmund Routledge became a partner, and the firm was renamed George Routledge and Sons, relocating again to 7 The Broadway, Ludgate, in 1865. Routledge and Sons' publications included Kate Greenaway's *Under the Window* (1878), her first *Almanack* (1883), and *Morley's Universal Library* (1883). Frederick went on to set up his own publishing firm, which later published all sorts of children's books, including Beatrix Potter, to whom Frederick's son Norman was engaged, but he tragically died a few weeks later.

A Liberal in politics, George was appointed successively a county magistrate, a deputy lieutenant and a high sheriff. In 1887 he retired, having published 5,000 titles, an average of two volumes each week. In October 1888 he developed blood poisoning and had his leg amputated by the renowned Joseph Lister, the developer of antiseptic surgery. Routledge died on 12th December 1888 at 50 Russell Square, leaving an estate worth at least £80,000 (equivalent to £9.5M in 2016) in addition to extensive real estate holdings. Routledge and Sons was reconstructed under Arthur E. Franklin of Keyser & Co. banking house, in collaboration with William Sonnenschein and Laurie Magnus, in 1902. The firm of J.C. Nimmo Ltd was taken over by Routledge & Sons in 1903. Cecil A. Franklin entered Routledge & Sons in 1906. Kegan Paul, Trench, Trübner & Co. were incorporated with Routledge and Sons to form Routledge and Kegan Paul Ltd. in 1912.

Other early occupants of No. 50 include:
R. Crafton (BCG, 1808); G. Herbert Kinderley (BCG, 1857); Isaac Levy (SDs, 1899-1918, and records of the Central Synagogue); Universities Bureau of the British Empire and American University Union in Europe are listed in 1920-30; The Mineworkers' Federation of Great Britain occupied No. 50 for a substantial period, including during World War II, during which the building escaped harm, but it was inexplicably demolished in 1962 and replaced with an unremarkable office block, to the detriment of the original Burton terrace (see photograph - p.251).

George Edmund Street by Samuel A. Walker

51 - George Edmund Street (1824-1881), *"The most eminent practical exponent of the art of architecture and an author of no mean eminence. (ODNB),* lived here from 1862 to 1870, and is listed in the SDs, 1863-68. Though mainly an ecclesiastical architect, he is perhaps best known as the designer of the Royal Courts of Justice, in the Strand, London. *"A principal shaper of the architectural style later called 'High Victorian', he was also one of the most thoughtful architectural writers of his day."* (ODNB).

Street was apprenticed firstly, to an architect in Winchester, and secondly, to Sir George Gilbert Scott in 1844. Just four years later, Street left to establish his own practice, initially in Wantage, Oxfordshire and eventually in London. Scott's influence is shown throughout Street's work, as Street tended to favour the Gothic style. The Royal Courts are a good example of Gothic reticence – but this may be because they were completed by his son, A.E. Street, and Arthur Blomfield, after Street's death, with the benefit of 3,000 drawings left by Street when he died. An article in *The Builder* which perversely described the building as *"a deformity and an eyesore"*, is reputed to have driven him to an early grave before it was even completed. The Courts were formally opened on 4th December 1882 by Queen Victoria, in the presence of the Lord

| Royal Courts of Justice, c.1902 © *Victorian Web*

Chancellor, the Prime Minister and other dignitaries. The building cost about £75,000 and the site about £1,450,000 (equivalent to £8.25M and £159.5M respectively in 2016).

Considered by many to be one of the greatest Gothic architects in Europe, Street trained William Morris and his colleague Philip Webb and was warmly praised by Ruskin. Street also undertook considerable commissions abroad, including churches in Rome, Constantinople, Geneva, Lausanne and America. In addition to designing 260 buildings, he published books, including *Brick and Marble Architecture in Italy* (1855) and *Some Account of Gothic Architecture in Spain* (1865). He was awarded the Royal Gold Medal in 1874, was elected Professor of Architecture at the Royal Academy and was President of the Royal Institute of British Architects at the time of his death. As a highly revered architect, he was awarded the rare status of being buried in Westminster Abbey, near his old friend and former employer Sir Gilbert Scott. His only son, Arthur Edmund Street (d. 1938), oversaw the completion of many of his works.

James Ware. Stipple engraving by H. Cook, 1839, after M. Bro.
© Wellcome Library, London

James Thomas Ware (1817-1902) MRCS, FRCS, General Surgeon, lived at No. 51 in 1857-62. He was the eldest son of Martin and Anne Ware. His grandfather was James Ware, FRS (1756-1815), the surgeon and ophthalmologist, considered one of the founding fathers of modern ophthalmology. He was also founder of the Society for the Relief of Widows and Orphans of Medical Men in London. *"Martin Ware, oculist"* is listed alone in BCGs, 1842-46. Martin is joined by *"Charles Tayler Ware Esq., James Thomas Ware, oculist & surgeon, & Martin Ware, jnr., Esq."* in 1857 and in the RBB, April 1858. All four are listed in the SDs, 1861-62. Martin was one of eight children of James and Ursula, of whom six survived, including Martin who became an eye doctor, like his father, and later edited some of his father's works. Another son John was an eye doctor also, and for a while shared a practice with Martin. A third son Rev. James Ware (1790-1855) was rector of Wyverstone. Martin Ware junior (1818-1898), was co-founder of the Ragged Boy Shoeblack Society (National Archives), and Patron of the Royal Society of Musicians (1843).

James first entered St Bartholomew's Hospital as a student in 1835. He became House Surgeon and in later life a Governor of the Hospital. He studied in Berlin, Paris, and Vienna, and subsequently lived on the family estate at Tilford House, where he acted unostentatiously as a country gentleman and benefactor. Before 1842 there was no such thing in the country as a convalescent home, and being struck by the need for fresh air and treatment after

discharge from hospital - particularly in the case of a poor girl whose leg had been amputated in St Bartholomew's Hospital - he founded, with the aid of friends' subscriptions, the Metropolitan Convalescent Institution, which opened homes at Walton, Broadstairs, and at Highgate. Ware took an active part in the management of the Institution, was one of the surgeons from 1840, and later a Vice-President. In 1883 he met with an accident to his knee from which he did not recover completely and for the last two years of his life was bed-ridden. He died at Tilford on July 30th, 1902. He married Ursula, daughter of Robert Maitland, of Barcaple, Kirkcudbrightshire, but left no children, and with him ended the direct line of succession of a family of benevolent surgeons.

Other early occupants of No. 51 include:
Sir George Pauncefort (BCG, 1808). The only known reference to Sir George, which is repeated in all the society magazines published in 1808, was that he died on 24th August of that year, *"Suddenly, at his house on the West Cliffe, Brighton after taking a ride to the Devil's Dyke, about four o'clock on Wednesday August 24, Sir George Pauncefort, Bart. of Russell-square, London, aged 56 years. The body of the deceased was opened by Mr. Barrett, in the presence of Dr. Hunter, when the cause of his dissolution became apparent in a cancer which had destroyed a part of his stomach."*; Philip Wood (BCGs, 1820-24); Walter Learmonth (BCGs, 1829-40, and SDs, 1841-42); Alfred Jay (SDs, 1875-78);

Joseph Levy (SDs, 1882-99, and WRB, 1897); Alfred
Hessell Tiltman, architect (SDs, 1900-04); William
Albert Owston (SDs, 1905-09); No. 51 was not listed
again until at least 1930, with Gregg Publishing Co.
Ltd occupying the building during World War II. The
building was demolished in 1962 to make way for
a modern office block on the combined site of Nos.
50 and 51 (see above).

Nos. 52-60 (Bedford Place to Southampton Row)

The rare historic photograph of the south side of
Russell Square (Nos. 52-60 only), which appeared in
Pictorial London in 1896, shows how James Burton's
original houses looked prior to Charles Fitzroy Doll's
'improvement' works in 1899, which introduced the
terracotta cladding we see today. Three of the original
houses which pre-dated the development of Russell
Square can also be seen in the distance. They too
were duly 'Dolled-up' to reflect the aspirations of the
Bedford Estate. 'To Let' and 'For Sale' signs are visible in
the 1900 photograph of Nos. 55-57, which, together
with the improvement works, helps to explain why
these houses were not listed in the street directories
around that time.

52 - Early occupants include: William Bell
(BCGs, 1808-24); Bury Hutchinson, solicitor and
Clerk of the Distillers' Company (BCGs, 1829-34).
He was a Vestryman of St George's Bloomsbury in
1829. The birth of his daughter was announced in
the *London University Magazine*, 1830. His death on
20th November 1834 at his other house in Bromley
was announced in the *Asiatic Journal*. His widow,
Catherine, re-married in 1839, and his eldest daughter,
Maria Theresa, married in 1840 (*Asiatic Journal*, 1839

Nos. 52-60, on the right , viewed east in 1896, prior to the 1899
'improvement' works - *Pictorial London*, 1906

Nos. 55-57 (r-l) in 1900

and 1840); Henry Newark (BCGs, 1840-42, and SDs, 1841-42); P. Phené (BCG, 1844); Mrs Green (BCG, 1845, joined by Thomas Leach, 1846); Henry Wakefield, surgeon (BCG, 1857, RBB, 1858, and SD, 1861, with Mrs Wakefield alone in 1862); Edward Brayley (ABCCG, 1871, and SD, 1878); Lewis John Martin Mason (SDs, 1881-83); Isaac Abrahams (SDs, 1888-90); Edward Ward (SDs, 1892-99). E. Ward and G.H. Sawtell were listed in WRB, 1897; No. 52 was not listed in 1900-07; Arachne Club is listed at Nos. 52 & 60 in the SD, 1908, and renamed the Argyle Club in 1909. It was only listed at No. 52 in 1911-16 (see No. 60 for details of this establishment); Queen Mary's Hostel for Nurses (SDs, 1918-19); McNeill F. & Co. Ltd, felt manufacturers, occupied the premises from at least 1930 and throughout World War II.

53 - Early occupants include: John Towgood (BCG, 1808); Nathaniel Winter (BCGs, 1820-24): Colin Macrae (BCG, 1829); Dr Pardoe (BCGs, 1840-44, and listed as *"George Pardoe, physician"* in SDs, 1841-42). Mrs Pardoe is listed alone in BCG, 1845; Mrs. Webb (BCG, 1846); Thomas Richard Harrison (BCG, 1857, RBB, 1858, and SD's, 1861-65, and Mrs T.R. Harrison alone in the SD and ABCCG, 1871); Benjamin Winstone MD (SDs, 1878-1907, and WRB, 1897); Asher Isaacs (SDs, 1908-12, and Mrs. Isaacs alone in 1914-20); Ford, Michelmore, Rose & Wilkins, solicitors, moved to this address from Bloomsbury Square in 1923, and remained there until 1970, albeit with a temporary name change in 1930 when they were listed as Ford, Lloyd, Bartlett & Michelmore, solicitors. They shared the building with Ford, Harris & Co., solicitors during World War II, listed by their original name.

54 - Jonas Woolf, Jewish furrier, lived with his wife Rosetta (Rose Hyman) at No. 54 from at least 1879, the year their film producer son, **Charles Moss Woolf** (1879-1942), was born there on 10th July (ODNB). Jonas is listed as *"John Wolfe"* in the SDs, 1879-95, then correctly as *"Jonas Woolf"* in the 1897 WRB, but reverting to *"John Wolfe"* in the SDs, 1887-1903, and *"John Woolf"* in 1904-06, with *"Mrs Woolf"* listed alone in 1907-09, presumably following the death of Jonas.

Charles Moss Woolf

Charles Moss Woolf first worked in the family business in Aldersgate, followed by a stint at aircraft production in WWI. He made his first venture into film production in 1919 with two of his brothers-in-law – W. & F. Film Service - importing films from France and Germany and adding sub-titles. They also distributed some of Alfred Hitchcock's early films. Having established a successful distribution company, Charles turned to Hollywood and secured the rights to the early Tarzan films and Harold Lloyd's popular comedies. After being a dominant force in Gaumont Pictures and General Film Distributors, Charles persuaded J. Arthur Rank to buy out the Gaumont-British cinema chain. *"Woolf, as Rank's right-hand man, became the pre-eminent figure in the British film industry. His two sons, Sir John Woolf and James Woolf, followed their father into the film industry, their production companies Romulus and Remus Films being responsible for such highly successful films as Room at the Top (1959) and Oliver! (1968)."* (ODNB). Charles's career was cut short by his unexpected death on 31st December 1942 at University College Hospital, London, following an operation on a duodenal ulcer.

John Tidd Pratt, 1855 © National Portrait Gallery, London

John Tidd Pratt (1797–1870), barrister and influential civil servant, lived at No. 54 (BCG, 1846, and SDs, 1847-48). He was appointed as consulting barrister to the National Debt Commissioners in 1828, with an Act in that year giving him the duty of certifying the rules of savings banks, with further legislation in the following adding the certifying of the rules of friendly societies to his duties. *"The* enormous expansion of Tidd Pratt's official functions reflected growing national needs, but the way in which these were met - essentially the shape and form of a new government department - was largely due to the personality, vigour, and influence of the man himself." (ODNB). After Tidd Pratt's 41 years of public service, his death in 1870 inevitably raised the question of the future shape and form of an office which had been so closely associated with one man's personality and attitudes. A royal commission was appointed which reported in 1874. Describing Tidd Pratt as "...minister of self-help to the whole of the industrious classes", the Royal Commission on Friendly Societies observed that by the middle years of the 19th-century whether a man joined a savings bank, a friendly society, or a trade union, shopped at a co-operative store or bought his house through a building society, Tidd Pratt's certificate would follow him. The legislation arising from the Royal Commission's report built on, and extended, the work Tidd Pratt had accomplished and formed the basis for the state's relationship with self-help organizations well into the 20th-century. Tidd Pratt was the author of numerous legal manuals, and published on the law relating to savings banks (1828), friendly societies (1829), the poor (1833), and highways (1835). Active in London's cultural life, he was one of the founders of the Reform Club, a trustee of the Soane Museum, and a fellow of the Royal Society of Literature and of the Society of Antiquaries. The Institute of Actuaries made him an honorary fellow. He died at his home, 29 Abingdon Street, Westminster, on 9th January 1870.

Professor Henry Malden (1800–1876), classical scholar and prominent British academic, lived at No. 54 certainly from 1857 to 1871 (BCG, 1857, RBB, 1858, SDs, 1850-71, and ABCCG, 1871). He was Professor of Greek at University College London from 1831 until he died in 1876. In 1833 he agreed to become joint headmaster (with the Professor of Latin) of University College School, a post he held until 1842. He took an active part "...in promoting the compromise that led to the erection, in 1836, of the University of London as an examining body, and the incorporation of the Gower Street institution as University College." (DNB). He published in 1835 an essay On the Origin of Universities and Academical Degrees, which was written as an introduction to the report of the argument before the Privy Council in support of the application of the University of London for a charter empowering it to grant degrees. A Malden medal and scholarship, open to men and women, were established in 1878 by the subscribers to the Malden memorial fund. The medal, by M. Macphail, bears a portrait of Malden (Wroth, Engr. Personal Medals in Brit. Mus. 1887, p. 20), and there is also a portrait of him in University College, painted by Lawlor, and presented by the subscribers to the fund. He was a contributor to the Philological Museum, edited by Connop Thirlwall (1830), to the Classical Museum, edited by Dr Leonard Schmitz (1843-1850), and to the Transactions of the Philological Society. He also published in 1830 a History of Rome to B.C. 390 (Society for Diffusion of Useful Knowledge, 8vo).

| A painting of University College School, Frognal, Hampstead in the 20th-century

Professor Henry Malden, by U.J. Lawler © UCL Art Museum

Oscar Ludwig Levy (1867-1946), German Jewish physician and writer, now known as a scholar of Friedrich Nietzsche, whose works he first saw translated systematically into English, is listed at No. 54 in the SDs, 1910-18. He left the German Empire in 1894. He appears in the List of the Fellows and Members of the Royal College of Physicians, 1910 as a Licenciate (1895). Anthony Ludovici, one of his collaborators on the translation project, was a great admirer of Levy, whose preface in Ludovici's *Nietzshe His Life and Works*, 1910, included his address as 54 Russell Square, London, W.C. The 18-volume Nietzsche translation he oversaw appeared from 1909 to 1913. Subsequently his life was complicated by having to leave the United Kingdom and his medical practice despite his support for the British side against the Central Powers when World War I broke out. He went back to the German Empire in 1915 and then to Switzerland. Back in the United Kingdom in July 1920, he incautiously wrote a preface for an inflammatory political pamphlet by George Pitt-Rivers, *The World Significance of the Russian Revolution*, a denunciation of the dominant Jewish role in Communism, which led to his deportation as an alien in 1921. This quote from the Preface gives a sense of the outrage he caused at the time: *"We who have posed as the saviors of the world; we who have even boasted of having given it 'the' Savior; we are today nothing else but the world's seducers, its destroyers, its incendiaries, its executioners...I look at this world, and I shudder at its ghastliness; I shudder all the more*

as I know the spiritual authors of all this ghastliness..." He lived in the French Third Republic, before eventually returning again to the United Kingdom.

Oscar Ludwig Levy

Other early occupants of No. 54 include:
George Brown (BCGs, 1808-21). He was a Governor of the Northern Dispensary in 1813-14, and a member of the United Company of Merchants of England trading to the East Indies in 1826. His daughter's (Mary Frances) marriage was recorded in the *Annual Register of World Events*, 1830. *The Life of Major-General Sir Thomas Munro, Bart. and KCB*, refers to Munro having *"...kept up a constant and unrestrained correspondence* (with Mr Brown) *until the day of his death."* , regarding him as a special confidante; Thomas Yallop (BCGs, 1823-24) died at Hastings on 20th December 1824, aged 46 (*The Gentleman's Magazine*, 1824); John Johnson (BCG, 1829); Mrs Horne (BCG, 1834); Donald Mackay (BCGs, 1840-45, and SDs, 1841-42); Thomas Lumley (SD, 1920; The Central Employment Bureau for Women (CEBW) & Students' Careers Association occupied the building from at least 1930 to 1941, no doubt supporting the initial war effort in the absence of so many men defending the realm in World War II. The CEBW is reputed to have been the early mover in helping to establish the case for the right of women to work rather than be restricted to home and hearth; there were no further listings of No. 54 until 1945, when J.T. Davies & Sons Ltd, caterers, appeared.

55 - George Grossmith Snr, (1847-1912), comedian, writer, composer, actor, and singer, lived at No. 55 from 1902 to 1909, when he retired and went to live in Folkestone. He is listed at No. 55 in BCG, January 1903, and in SDs, 1903-10. E. Beresford Chancellor (1907) noted that at the time Grossmith was living at No. 55: *"Many notable people still reside in Russell Square, which seems to be again resuming its position as a fashionable locality. The legal profession is still largely represented, and to the legal has been added the theatrical, a combination which has become traditional"* Marion Sambourne's Diary, 1903, lists an appointment with Mrs G. Grossmith at 55 Russell Square on Wednesday 20th February from 4-7, presumably for tea: *"Went with Maud 3.30 Mrs Mayne's and Grossmith's deadly."*

decade of the 20th century. By the time George finally left the Savoy Theatre in 1889 his salary was said to be £2,000 a year (equivalent to £236,000 in 2016). Peter Morton's website states that in February 1882: *"George attends a dinner-party with the Prince of Wales, the first of several invitations."*, and on 12th November 1890: *"George entertains Queen Victoria at Balmoral."*

Despite his glittering career as an entertainer, George is probably best remembered as co-author of *Diary of a Nobody* (with his brother [Walter] Weedon Grossmith), a comic novel with illustrations by the latter. It originated as an intermittent serial in *Punch* magazine in 1888-89 and first appeared in book form, with extended text and added illustrations, in 1892. The 'Diary' records the daily events in the lives of a London clerk, Charles Pooter, his wife Carrie, his son

George Grossmith Snr © National Portrait Gallery, London

George Grossmith Snr as Ko-Ko in The Mikado (1885-1887)

George's performing career spanned more than four decades, during which he created 18 comic operas, nearly 100 musical sketches, some 600 songs and piano pieces, three books and both serious and comic pieces for newspapers and magazines. He is particularly noted for creating a series of nine memorable characters in the comic operas of Gilbert and Sullivan from 1877 to 1889, including Sir Joseph Porter, in *HMS Pinafore* (1878), the Major-General in *The Pirates of Penzance* (1880) and Ko-Ko in *The Mikado* (1885–87).

He became the most popular British solo performer of the 1890s and continued to perform into the first

Lupin, and numerous friends and acquaintances over a period of 15 months. Jim Holt, in his article *I Yield to Nothing* in the *New York Times*, 2nd July 2000 wrote: *"As much as I liked "Topsy-Turvy," Mike Leigh's movie about Gilbert and Sullivan, I did find one thing about it unsettling. Who was that diminutive, pallid, pince-nez-wearing and rather epicene actor in the D'Oyly Carte opera company, the one who was shown in his dressing room tearfully jabbing his needle-scarred forearm with a hypo full of heroin? After I noticed the other characters in the film address this fellow first as 'Mr Grossmith" and then as 'George', the penny dropped: Why, that must be George Grossmith -- the man who, after chucking his career with*

Gilbert and Sullivan, went on to write a book that I cherish above all others, a book that I have repeatedly rejoiced in reading, a book that has been my prop and stay in troubled times: 'The Diary of a Nobody' I am hardly alone in rating 'The Diary of a Nobody' a singular work of genius. From the time it was published in 1892 (with illustrations by George Grossmith's brother, Weedon), it began to collect enthusiastic admirers. Hilaire Belloc deemed it 'one of the half-dozen immortal achievements of our time…a glory for us all.' It was a favorite of T. S. Eliot and John Betjeman. Evelyn Waugh declared it to be "the funniest book in the world" and had his character Lady Marchmain read passages from it aloud to her family in 'Brideshead Revisited'."

George Grossmith died at his home in Folkestone in 1912, aged 64. Wealth at death: £19,628 19s. 6d (equivalent to £2.08M in 2016). His son, George Grossmith, Jr (1874-1935), with whom our George is often understandably confused, followed in his father's footsteps, becoming a famous actor, playwright and producer of Edwardian musical comedies. George senior received "…two silver bowls presented to him by [Gilbert, Sullivan and] Carte [and] the ivory baton with which he conducted the orchestra on the occasion of his said son's first appearance on the stage."

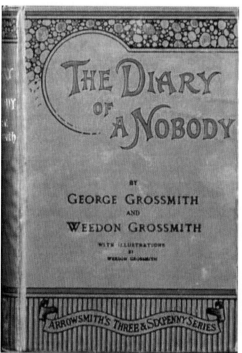

The Diary of a Nobody, 1st edition

George Grossmith Jnr on stage at the Gaiety Theatre

Weedon and George Grossmith (Snr), co-authored The Diary of a Nobody

William Groves (c.1809-1892), sculptor, is listed at No. 55 in the SDs, 1878-79. He was most active between 1834 and 1881. Born in Cripplegate, London, he was the son of a clerk, James Groves (born c.1780 in Bermondsey, Surrey). Groves entered the Royal Academy School c.1837 on the advice of J.T. Smith. He continued in practice in London until the 1870s. He married late and moved to Tunbridge Wells by 1881. In his later years he described himself as "living on own means". Whether this was the profits of his practice or another source of income is unclear.

Other early occupants of No. 55 include: Dr Snaw (BCG, 1808); Rev. I. L. Martin (BCGs, 1820-34); Mrs Dickinson (BCG, 1846); John J. Clark (BCG, 1857, RBB, 1858, and listed as *"John Jeffkins Clark"* in SDs, 1861-62); Frederick Pelasier (SD, 1865); Harris Talleman (SD and ABCCG, 1871); Thomas Briggs (SDs, 1882-83); Solomon Henry Apfel (SDs, 1887-93); Mrs Apfel (SDs, 1894-98, WRB, 1897); The Catholic Association occupied No. 55 in 1912/18, followed in 1920 by the Miners' Federation of Great Britain, which was joined in 1930 by The Travellers' Association of London, tourist agents; The British Psychological Society were there from at least 1939 to 1941; The Association for Planning and Regional Construction was briefly there in 1942, followed by Clay, Richard & Co., printers in 1943-45.

56 - James Lind (1736–1812), physician, died at No. 56 on 17th October 1812. It was the home of his son-in-law William Burnie (a manager of the Sun Life Assurance Society). *"Willm. Burney"* is listed in the 1802 Rate Book under *"East Wing, South Side"*, five doors west of the square's south-east corner with Southampton Row, i.e. No. 56. Lind went out as surgeon in an East Indiaman in 1766 and visited China. He accompanied Joseph Banks on his voyage to Iceland, in 1772. He reported several astronomical observations to the Royal Society, London, and a paper by him was read there in 1775. He was elected a Fellow of the Royal Society on 18th December 1777, and on 3rd November 1783 he became a Fellow of the Royal Society of Edinburgh. About the same time Lind apparently settled at Windsor, where he afterwards became physician-in-ordinary to the royal household. *"With his taste for tricks, conundrums, and queer things…"*, commented Fanny Burney, people were *"…fearful of his trying experiments with their constitutions, and think him a better conjuror than physician"*. In 1792 Joseph Banks recommended Lind as a useful member of Lord Macartney's embassy to the emperor of China. Banks said that Lind *"…is a man accustomed to Obedience & well acquainted with the Station of an inferior…"* (Gascoigne, 38). When the coffin of Edward IV was opened and examined at Windsor in 1789, Lind made an analysis of the liquid found in it. On one occasion Lind, according to Thomas Hogg, prevented Shelley from being consigned by his father to a private madhouse. Hogg's further statement that Lind was Shelley's *"Mentor in the art of execrating"* his father and George III can probably be dismissed, since Lind was devotedly loyal to the King. He lives in Shelley's verse as the old hermit in *The Revolt of Islam* and as Zonoras in the fragment *Prince Athanase*.

John Bardwell Ebden MLC (1787-1873) was an influential businessman and politician of Cape Colony, South Africa, who is listed at No. 56 in BCGs, 1820-23. He was born in 1787 in Suffolk, England, the son of John Ebden, an army surgeon, and Sarah Norman. He received little education, went to sea aged 16 in 1803, and travelled around the Torres Straits and China. On a second voyage, this time destined for India, he was shipwrecked off Cape Town. He received permission to stay at the Cape Colony in October 1806, and began work as a clerk in the Royal Naval Victualling Office. In 1808 he married Antoinetta Adriana Kirchmann, the daughter of an influential German immigrant businessman, and soon left his job to set up a wine merchant business, Ebden & Eaton. They had 12 children, but tragically two of them died as infants in South Africa (William Baynes – b.27.10.14, d. 10.9.1815, and Antoinette Mary Ann – b. 15.5.1816, d.4.2.1817), which might explain why they returned to England, where they settled at 56 Russell Square. Two of their sons were born at No. 56 - Alfred (b. 8.2.1820, d. 29.7.1908) and Henry Anderson (b. 15.6.1824, d. 14.6.1886). Alfred became co-founder of Dunell, Ebdon & Co, Port Elizabeth, South Africa, and Henry a respected surgeon (see below). They returned to South Africa in 1824, where John went on to dominate Cape Town commerce for over 60 years and became an unofficial member of the Cape Legislative Council in 1834. An ambitious and combative personality, he was known by the nickname *"the storm petrel"*, due to his reputation for frequently being in fights. He built Belmont (now St Joseph's College), Rondebosch, in 1836.

John Bardwell Ebden, 1849

This estate became his home and he lived there for the rest of his life. He founded the Cape of Good Hope Bank, of which he was President (1838-1873). He established the Cape's Commercial Exchange, which he chaired, and he was President of the Chamber of Commerce (1861-1873). John was one of the leaders of the renowned anti-convict movement, together with Cape Town Mayor Hercules Crosse Jarvis and Attorney General William Porter, even chairing it in 1849, when he abdicated his Legislative Council seat in protest. When the Cape received an elected parliament in 1854, John was elected to the Legislative Council (upper house) representing the Western Province. He held the seat until 1858. He died in 1873 and is buried in Cape Town.

Dr Henry Anderson Ebden (1824-1886), distinguished physician, surgeon, and son of John Bardwell Ebden (above), was born at No. 56 on 15th June 1824. He received part of his high school education at the South African College during 1838 and 1839. In 1845 he qualified as Doctor of Medicine (MD) and as a member of the Royal College of Surgeons of England (MRCS) at St Andrews, Scotland. Returning to the Cape Colony he was licensed to practise there as a physician, surgeon and obstetrician on 3rd September 1846. He provided free daily medical advice to the poor at a Cape Town pharmacy and published and edited the Cape Town Medical Gazette (from 1847), the first medical journal in southern Africa. Its aims were to provide a medium of publication for interesting local medical cases, promote communication and reduce discord among the colony's medical practitioners, and advance local medical knowledge. One of his editorials dealt with the introduction of ether as an anaesthetic at the Cape, which he and other medical practitioners and dentists at the Cape began experimenting with in April 1847.

Henry left the Cape for India at the beginning of 1848, where he worked for almost ten years in the Bengal medical establishment of the English East India Company. He was physician to the Indian rajahs of Rajputana and served throughout the so-called Indian Mutiny. Returning to the Cape in 1858, he opened a practice in Rondebosch, Cape Town, where he remained for the rest of his life. He also opened a small cottage hospital in Rondebosch and was particularly renowned for his ophthalmic work. Setting high standards of professional ethics and conduct, he was a very popular physician. He served on the Colonial Medical Committee from 1859, having been a member also in 1847. In 1862 he became its

president, a position he retained to his death. During the same year he became president of the Medical Board of Management of the New Somerset Hospital. He served on the Board of Medical Examiners, and was a member of council of both the South African College (1866 to about 1880) and the University of the Cape of Good Hope (1873 to 1885). From 1877 to 1878 he served on the first council of the South African Philosophical Society, and remained a member of the society for the rest of his life. In 1883 he became the first president of the (first) South African Medical Association, until his death in 1886 of pernicious anaemia.

Sir Thomas Noon Talfourd (1795-1854). The surnames Talfourd and Talford are used interchangeably in SDs, Rate Books and literature of the time, giving rise to confusion over Sir Thomas's actual address. The *Survey of London* and E. Beresford Chancellor (1907) place Sir Thomas Noon Talfourd at No. 67, whilst the *ODNB* has him at No. 56 *"in the early 1830s"*. The UCL Project repeats the *ODNB* reference. However, the Rate Books for St Giles & St George Bloomsbury, Book D, place *"Mr Sergeant Thomas Noon Talfourd"* at No. 56 by Michaelmas 1835. *"Mr. Serj. Talfourd"* is also listed at No. 56 in Boyle's Court Guide, 1840-46, and as *"Serjeant Talford"* in SDs, 1841-42. Although the Rate Books confirm that *"Mr Sergeant Thomas Noon Talfourd"* was still there on Lady Day 1845, by Michaelmas 1850 *"Mr Justice Thomas Noon Talfourd"* was living at No.67. He was presumably still resident there when he died in Stafford in 1854, as the ratepayer at No. 67 on Lady Day 1855 is his widow *"Lady Talfourd"*.

Sir Thomas Noon Talfourd

When Talfourd was residing at No. 56, Charles Dickens wrote an open letter from his address at 48 Doughty Street on September 27th 1837 *"To MR SERJEANT TALFORD, MP"* in the *Preface* to *The Posthumous Papers of the Pickwick Club, Vol 1* in which he dedicates the book to Talford in return for *"…the inestimable services you are rendering to the literature of your country, and of the lasting benefits you will confer upon the authors of this and succeeding generations, by securing to them and their descendents a permanent interest in the copyright of their works."* A fuller description of Sir Thomas's life and times is given in chapter 3.2, which deals with the site of Baltimore/Bolton House, later 66-67 Russell Square.

Mary Russell Mitford (1787-1855), author and dramatist, stayed at No. 56 on 26th May 1836 (Chancellor, 1907), where, buoyant after the success of *Our Village*, she attended a poet-packed dinner party given by Thomas Noon Talfourd. She wrote about the dinner party in a letter: *"Mr Wordsworth, Mr Landour and Mr White dined here. I like Mr Wordsworth…Mr Landor is a very striking-looking person, and exceedingly clever. Also we had a Mr Browning, a young poet, and Mr Procter and Mr Morley and quantities more of poets; Stanfield and Lucas were also there."* Mary's impression of Robert Browning that evening, and her feeling about his poetry, was described to Charles Boner in a letter of 22nd February 1847 (Yale): *"I … remember thinking how exactly he resembled a girl drest in boy's clothes—& as to his poetry I have just your opinion of it. It is one heap of obscurity confusion & weakness…I met him once as I told you when he had long ringlets…& when he seemed to me about the height & size of a boy of twelve years old—Femmelette—is a word made for him. A strange sort of person to carry such a woman as Elizabeth Barrett off her feet."* She met Elizabeth the following afternoon when mutual friend John Kenyon took the two of them sightseeing. In sharp contrast to her feelings about Robert, Mary was soon writing of Elizabeth: *"If events lead her to write on, & she be blest with life & health I have no doubt of her being the most remarkable woman that ever lived"*. Their special relationship continued until Mary's death, with Elizabeth writing more letters to Mary (around 500) than to any other one person. Brian Waller Procter, a.k.a. Barry Cornwall, lived firstly in Brunswick Square, then in Bedford Square and later in Southampton Row. Mary also attended a supper party called by Macready after the first performance of *Ion*, *"…largely attended by actors, lawyers, and dramatists"*.

Mary Russell Mitford © National Portrait Gallery, London

Mary was the only daughter of George Mitford, a dashing but irresponsible character whose extravagance (and gambling habit) compelled the family, in 1820, to leave their grand house in Reading (built when Mary, at the age of 10, won £20,000 in a lottery) for a labourer's cottage in the nearby village of Three Mile Cross. Thereafter, until her father's death in 1842, Mary struggled to provide for him and to pay his gambling debts out of her literary earnings. In 1810 she published *Miscellaneous Poems,* which was followed by five more volumes of verse, including *Watlington Hill* (1812) and *Dramatic Scenes, Sonnets, and Other Poems* (1827). Her narrative poem *Christina* (1811) was revised by Samuel Taylor Coleridge. She then turned to the theatre, with some success, most notably in the blank-verse tragedies *Julian* (1823) and *Rienzi*, the latter having 34 performances at London's Drury Lane in 1828. Her reputation, however, rests on the sketches, started in *The Ladies Magazine* (1819), that fill the five volumes of *Our Village* (1824–32). Based on her observation of life in and around Three Mile Cross, they catch the pleasant atmosphere of the English countryside and the quaintness of village characters. She published a further volume of sketches, *Belford Regis* (1835) and *Recollections of a Literary Life* (1852). Her work helped to establish the format of the realistic domestic novel of provincial life and continues to have appreciative followers today, including Digital Mitford, an active digital humanities project begun in April 2013, with the formation of the Mary Russell Mitford Society at the 18th and 19th century British Women Writers' Conference in Albuquerque, U.S.A.

Israel Abrahams (1858-1925) was one of the most distinguished Jewish scholars of his time, who wrote a number of enduring works on Judaism, particularly *Jewish Life in the Middle Ages* (1896).

Israel Abrahams

He is listed at No. 56 in SDs, 1878-82, whilst he was teaching at Jews' College in nearby Guilford Street, and also studying for his MA at the University of London. In 1902, he was appointed Reader in Talmudics (Rabbinic literature) at the University of Cambridge, a post he retained until his death. From 1888 to 1908 he was editor, jointly with the Anglo-Jewish scholar Claude G. Montefiore, of the *Jewish Quarterly Review*. Although of strict Orthodox upbringing, Abrahams was among the founders of the Liberal movement, an Anglo-Jewish group that stressed the universality of Jewish ethics, minimized ritual and custom, and originally eschewed Zionism. In *Jewish Life in the Middle Ages*, he concluded that there was no medieval period in Jewish history but that Christian medievalism had a lasting effect on the Jews, particularly in the sense of having deepened the process of Jewish isolation from the rest of society. Other important works include *Studies in Pharisaism and the Gospels*, 2 vol. (1917–24), and *Chapters on Jewish Literature* (1899), a survey of the period from the fall of Jerusalem in A.D. 70 to the death of the Jewish philosopher Moses Mendelssohn in 1786.

Charles Snewing, publican, veterinary surgeon and bookmaker, is listed at No. 56 in BCG, 1857, the RBB, 1858, and SDs, 1861-62. As a yearling, a thoroughbred racehorse named Caractacus (1859–1878) was bought for 250 guineas by the trainer William Day, acting on behalf of Charles Snewing. Caractacus went on to win the 1862 Epsom Derby, which was memorable for the large field (34 horses), and the winner being ridden by a 16-year-old stable boy, which led to Caractacus's near disqualification for an underweight jockey and a false start. Allegedly, the colt was named Caractacus because Snewing, whilst admiring a statue of the British chieftain Caractacus bound in chains at the 1851 Exhibition, is reported to have said: *"If ever I try a horse good enough I'll call him Caractacus, and win the Derby with him."* An unsigned photograph of Caractacus with owner, Charles Snewing, trainer Robert Smith and winning jockey, 16-year-old John Parsons, was recently sold at auction.

The 1862 Epsom Derby winner, Caractacus, with owner, Charles Snewing, on the left

Other early occupants of No. 56 include:
Mrs Williams (BCG, 1829); David Anderson, journalist (SDs, 1886-87); Miss Holly (SDs, 1889-90); Mrs. Foley (SDs, 1892-97, and WRB, 1897); Robert William Dibdin FRGS (SDs, 1899-1916), was also previously listed at No. 17 in the SD, 1895, and WRB, 1897; various elements of the Medical Practitioners' Union occupied much of the building from 1930 and during World War II, together with Sir William Brandford Griffith CBE, and Walter Sydney Vale in 1939, and Miss L.M. Brooks, OBE in 1941-45.

57 - Early occupants include: Hugh Atkins, Russia broker and underwriter (BCG, 1808). Notices relating to his bankruptcy appeared in several editions of *The London Gazette*; William Hoffman and J. Hoffman (BCGs, 1820-24); Edmund R. Daniell, legal writer and Secretary of the Royal Institution of Great Britain (BCGs, 1834-43, listed as *"Edmund Robert Daniell, esq."* in SDs, 1841-42); G.F. Bennet (BCG, 1844); Peter Poland (BCGs, 1845-46); George Clowes (BCG, 1857, and RBB, 1858). Between 1847 and 1852, Mrs Clowes gave birth to at least three sons at No. 57 (*The Spectator Archive*); John Hodge (SDs, 1861-78, and ABCCG, 1871); Charles Belton (SD, 1882); John Ramus (SDs, 1886-96); John H. Lile (SDs, 1897-98, and WRB, 1897); *"George Albert Hamerton, physician, MRCS, FRCS, LSA, LM, LRCP, MD (Hons) Brussels, 1878, DPH, RCPS, 1892"* (SDs, 1902- 20). *"Studied at St Thomas's Hospital; was Resident Medical Officer at the Lambeth Infirmary; Medical Officer of the Inland Revenue Office, Somerset House; to the Bow Street and to the Thames Divisions of the Metropolitan Police; Examiner for the Civil Service Widows' and Orphans' Fund; Medical Officer of the General Post Office Life Insurance, and of other insurance companies."* (*Plarr's Lives of the Fellows Online*, RCS). He died of pneumonia on 11th January 1920; National United Laundries Corporation Ltd occupied the building from at least 1930 and throughout the war.

58 - Early occupants include: Thomas Smith, barrister and MP for West Looe (1802-03), is listed in BCGs, 1808-29, although *History of Parliament Online* states that he appeared in various court directories as early as 1803 with *"MP"* after his name, and that he also disappeared from the law lists a few years later and died at Russell Square on 24th April 1831, aged 77; Charles William Tabor, banker and partner in Jones Loyd & Co. (BCGs, 1834-46, with Mrs. Tabor alone in 1857 and in the RBB, 1858). The 1841 census lists the occupiers of No. 58 as Charles, his wife, Jane, three children - Fanny Clifton Tabor (age three and born at No. 58), Elizabeth and Charles - five servants and a certain Richard Ayres. His Will is dated 1852; Daniel

Keane, lawyer and one time shareholder in the Tahiti Cotton and coffee Plantation Company Limited (SDs, 1862-71, and ABCCC, 1871); William Stebbing (1831-1926), scholar, barrister, and journalist for *The Times* for 30 years from 1868, is listed at No. 58 in the SD, 1878. In later life he reverted to his earlier scholarly passions (he was Fellow of Worcester College, Oxford), publishing several important works until 1926, when he died, aged 95

William Stebbing © Worcester College, University of Oxford

Philip Beyfus, solicitor and partner in Beyfus & Beyfus of 69 Lincoln's Inn Fields, is listed in the SDs, 1879-95, and WRB, 1897, with Mrs Beyfus alone in the SDs, 1896-99. Philip Beyfus died at No. 58 on 28th December 1894. His daughter, Blanche, was married eight days later to Daniele Piperno, second son of the Rev. J. Piperno. Henry Beyfus, Philip's business partner, lived at No. 34 and died on 24th January 1889; William Trigg (SDs, 1902-04); William Swan Sonnenschein (SDs, 1905-10), previously lived at No. 62 from at least 1895 to 1904 (see entry for No. 62); Robinson, Wilkins & Thacker, solicitors (SDs, 1914-18, minus Thacker in 1920 and until 1930); there followed a period of multiple-occupancy, after which the building was unlisted from 1940 to 1945. It is now combined with No. 57 to form De Morgan House, which is home to the London Mathematical Society, the major UK learned society for mathematics, and doubles up us a conference centre, making the most of its central London, *rus in urbe* location.

59 - Montague Richard Leverson (1830-1925), solicitor, is listed at No. 59 in the SDs, 1862-63. He was the son of a wealthy diamond merchant, Montague Levyson, who lived with his wife Elizabeth and two sons, James and Montague, at 18 Queen Square (listed in SD), which was a regular meeting place for radical political agitators of the time such as Victor Hugo, Louis Blanc and Guiseppe Garibaldi. It turns out that Montague Leverson was Esther Rantzen's great-grandfather, whom she innocently described as *"the black sheep of the family"* at the start of the *Who do you think you are?* TV programme which delved into her ancestry. Montague is usually described as a solicitor in the City of London, although he appears in the trade directories as a patent agent in Bishopsgate, remaining there until 1859, when he entered into partnership under the style Montague Leverson & Hawley, Patent Agents. The business appears to have been successful, and in 1854 he published his first work, *Copyrights and Patents, or property in thought.* However, in 1867, his career took a turn for the worse when he was alleged to have lost some of his clients' money and he fled the country before he could be brought to justice. A notice appeared in *The Times,* 27th March 1867, offering a £100 reward for information leading to the arrest of *"Montague Leverson, solicitor…of Jewish persuasion".* It said that he had been charged with fraud but that he had absconded, and was being sought by the City of London Police, having left his wife, Kate, and four children to fend for themselves. Based on typical fraud cases of the 1860s, Montague was likely to have been accused of stealing the equivalent of a quarter of a million pounds in today's money. Nine months later, another notice appeared in *The Times* (December 1867), still appealing for information about Montague's whereabouts, this time giving his latest known whereabouts as Paris.

Having escaped the hands of justice, Montague then fled to America, where he reinvented himself, first working as a lawyer in the 'Wild West', where he became a close confidant and business acquaintance of the famous cattle rancher John Chisum, who was the sworn enemy of the even more famous outlaw Billy the Kid.

He returned to Europe in 1872 where he obtained degrees at the University of Gottingen, returning to America where he again practiced as a lawyer and lecturer in political economy. Throughout 1874 and 1875 his letters on election law, public schools and other topics appeared in the Denver *Rocky Mountain News.* He even found time to draft a new state constitution. In 1879 he moved to California where he became a member of the State Assembly. After

Montague Richard Leverson in his 'Wild West' days, c.1872

tinkering with his CV, he took a medical degree and became a homeopathic doctor, returning east in 1893 where he graduated from the Baltimore Medical College. In the same year his book, *Thoughts on Institutions of the Higher Education* was published in New York, where he became very active in the Anti-Vaccination League.

But there was another dark secret going back to Montague's early life, when in 1848, aged 18, he was sitting in the parlour of the luxury family home in Queen Square playing with a gun which had a fatal design fault, which went off in his hand, shooting their 51-year-old parlour maid, Priscilla Fitzpatrick, in the chest as she was cleaning the windows. Contemporary newspaper reports describe Montague's horror, how he rushed to a nearby hospital to fetch help - but all to no avail. Poor Priscilla took ten painful days to die, and spent each day assuring anyone who would listen that the fatal shot had been an accident. There was a police investigation, and Montague appeared at Clerkenwell Magistrates Court, where he was bailed on personal recognizance of £500 and two sureties of £250, and he avoided prosecution, most probably because the coroner ruled that Priscilla's death was accidental. Newspaper reports describe the young man as being stricken with remorse.

The photo of Montague was taken 40 years after he fled England. He returned to England in his 80s and regained his nationality. He delivered a lecture under the auspices of the British Union for the Abolition of Vivisection at Claridges Hotel in Mayfair, London on 25th May 1911, although he is listed at 927 Grant Avenue in the New York directories for 1912. His wife had died 20 years earlier, while he was in America, and at 82 he married again to a 43-year-old teacher called Ethel Charlton. It has not been possible to find a record of his place or date of death, although he would appear to have been working on a paper when he died, which was completed in 1923 by Ethel D. Hume and published that year *"…founded on a manuscript by Montague R Leverson and others."*

Other early occupants of No. 59 include:
Mrs. Wilby (BCG, 1808); William Pratt, Esq., Vestryman of St George's Bloomsbury and Member of the United Company of Merchants of England trading

to the East-Indies (BCGs, 1820-42, and SDs, 1841-42); Joseph Collis (BCGs, 1844-57, RBB, 1858, and SD, 1861); Alexander Thompson (SDs, 1864-65); Dr James Andrew (SDs, 1868-71, and ABCCG, 1871); Peer Bukhsh (SDs, 1875-81); Lewis Michael Myers (SDs, 1882-89); Harry Courthope-Munroe (SDs, 1890-98, and WRB, 1897). There are no entries in the street directories until 1905, when Stanley Cook, dentist, is listed until at least 1920; the British Radio Valve Manufacturers' Association and their various offshoots occupied the premises from at least 1930 and throughout the war.

60 - Philip Hardwick (1792–1870), architect and surveyor, is listed at No. 60 in BCGs, 1829-46 as *"Philip Hardwicke"*, and in SDs, 1841-42, as *"Philip Hardwick"*. Other reliable references list him without an 'e' after Hardwick, including the *ODNB* and the 1851 census. He exhibited seven drawings at the Royal Academy between 1807 and 1814 and became surveyor to several important institutions and estates, mainly in London, including the Portman Estate and St Bartholomew's Hospital. His commissions for grand buildings in the City of London, such as Goldsmith's Hall and the City of London Club, established his reputation as a classical architect. *"Hardwick employed his liking for the masculinity of Doric brilliantly in creating the greatest monument of the railway age: the propylaeum fronting the London and Birmingham Railway terminus at Euston—the so-called 'Doric arch' (1836–8, £35,000; dem. 1961–2). This was modelled on the entrance to the Acropolis at Athens, only the noblest gateway of antiquity being symbolically appropriate for such an overwhelming achievement as the world's first long-distance railway."* (ODNB).

Hardwick's important commission for a new hall, council room, and library for the great legal focus, Lincoln's Inn, London, proved innovative and was much admired - the first conspicuous metropolitan building *"…in which the piquant possibilities of articulated Gothic composition were made strikingly evident"* (Hitchcock, 1.315). He also completed Lincoln's Inn Stone Buildings to the original Palladian design of 1774. He was admired for his unswerving probity and notable business efficiency - qualities reflected in his election as vice-president of the Institute of British Architects, being one example of many such honours. From about 1845 a spinal complaint confined his practice to such *"as could be followed in his own room"* (The Builder, 14th January 1871), although he was able to drag himself to committees, only gradually surrendering his offices and surveyorships before retiring from business in 1861. *"In the 1850s the Hardwicks had moved from bourgeois Russell Square to aristocratic 21 Cavendish Square, where*

GRAND ENTRANCE TO THE LONDON & BIRMINGHAM RAILWAY.
Drummond Street, opposite Euston Grove.

GROUND PLAN OF ENTRANCE TO THE LONDON & BIRMINGHAM RAILWAY.

Philip Hardwick's drawings for the grand entrance to the London and Birmingham Railway at Euston

THE GRAND ENTRANCE TO THE METROPOLITAN STATION OF THE NORTH WESTERN RAILWAY

Engraving of Hardwick's 'Euston Arch'

they enjoyed the services of a butler, footman, lady's maid, cook, and two housemaids." (ODNB). Suffering from heart disease Hardwick retreated about 1865 to Westcombe Lodge, Wandsworth, where, "helpless in body and infirm in mind" (ibid.) he died on 28th December 1870. Despite his significant professional career, "His life," wrote an obituarist, "was singularly uneventful" (The Times, 31st December 1870). He bequeathed his estate, sworn at £120,000 (equivalent to £12.96M in 2016), to his surviving son, Philip Charles Hardwick (1822–1892), who carried on the family business and attained a reputation as an architect, with an extensive country house practice, mainly from City contacts.

Arachne Club – "founded in 1905; Secretary 1909 Mrs Armstrong; election to membership was based on social references" (Elizabeth Crawford, The Women's Suffrage Movement - A Reference Guide 1866-1928). Mrs Armstrong and Rev. Henry Armstrong MA are listed at No. 60 in the 1906-07 SDs, followed in 1908 by the appearance of the Arachne Club, which is simultaneously listed at No. 52 (above). In 1909 it had changed its name to the Argyll Club, with "Miss A. Woods Sec." listed at Nos. 60 and 52. Likewise in 1910, but it was only listed at No. 52 in 1914 and not at all in 1915, thus reflecting the transient nature of such institutions. An article in the Los Angeles Times of 15th April 1906 describes the Archne Club as "…an institution which provides lady servants… They are all ladies by birth, the daughters of officers

and so on…the lady servant is a person of a strong individuality and no inconsiderable amount of mental culture and ingenuity. So by degrees there have been devised means whereby a lady can undertake all the drudgery of the household and yet remain beautiful." The writer, Dorothy Richardson, met Veronica Leslie-Jones (Veronica Grad/Amabel) at the Arachne Club in August 1906. According to the not very accurate John Rosenberg, Veronica was in digs there. Richardson had previously met Miss Moffatt (Moffat/Selina Holland) in 1905 whereupon they decided to share rooms. After a fortnight together in a newly converted flat in a "St. Pancras slum", they moved to Woburn Buildings, where Dorothy's stay was commemorated in 2015 by a Marchmont Association blue plaque at the renamed and renumbered 6 Woburn walk.

Other early occupants of No. 60 include:
John Winter (BCG, 1808); Francis Waskett Myers (BCGs, 1823-24); Charles Parker, Robert Hayes, F. Lowry Barnwell, Thomas E. Twisden and Charles Lewes Parker, solicitors (BCG, 1857, RBB, 1858, and SDs, 1861-78 as Hayes, Twisden, Parker & Co., solicitors, and simply Twisden & Co., solicitors in 1882-99); Alexander Denham (SDs, 1900-02). There are no entries in the SDs for No. 60 until 1905, when Miss Henslow is briefly listed prior to the Armstrong's' arrival (see above); Edmund Balding and Percy James Proud, dentists (SDs, 1914-45, joined by William George Burns MA, MB, gynaecologist, in 1939, and the National Federation of Credit Traders from 1940-45.

| Philip Hardwick

Dorothy Richardson

Sources:

Books & Pamphlets:

Michael Ainger, *Gilbert and Sullivan – A Dual Biography*, Oxford University Press, 2002

Sir J. Arnould, *Mem. of Lord Denman*, 1873

Rosemary Ashton, *Victorian Bloomsbury*, 2012

Professor Michael Ball, David T. Sunderland, *An Economic History of London 1800-1914*, 2002

Arthur H. Beavan, *James and Horace Smith…A family narrative based upon hitherto unpublished private diaries, letters, and other documents*, date unknown

Andrew Birkin, Sharon Goode, *J.M. Barrie & the Lost Boys*, 2003

Jack S. Blocker, David M. Fahey, Ian R. Tyrrell, *Alcohol and Temperance in Modern History*, 2003

John Britton, *Picture of London*, 1826

Edward C. Brooks, *Sir Samuel Morton Peto Bt: eminent Victorian, railway entrepreneur, country squire, MP*, Bury Clerical Society, 1996

Lady (Georgiana) Burne-Jones, *Memorials of Burne-Jones*

Ronald Bush, *T.S. Eliot's Life and Career, American National Biography*, 1999

E. Bruce Brooks, *Arthur Waley*, Warring States Project, University of Massachusetts

Camden History Society, *Streets of Bloomsbury & Fitzrovia*, 1997

G. Carter, P Goode, K Laurie, *Humphry Repton*, 1982

Old and New London: Vol. 4. Originally published by Cassell, Petter & Galpin, London, 1878

E. Beresford Chancellor, *The history of the squares of London, topographical and historical*, 1907

John Chapple, *Elizabeth Gaskell: The Early Years*, 2009

Sir Edward Clarke, *The Story of my Life*, 1918

Richard Clarke, Elizabeth McKellar, Michael Symes, *Russell Square a lifelong resource for learning*, FCE Occasional Paper 5, Birkbeck, University of London, 2004

Elizabeth Crawford, *The Women's Suffrage Movement - A Reference Guide 1866-1928*

George Frederick Cruchley, *Picture of London*, 1835

James Stevens Curl, *Doll, Charles Fitzroy, A Dictionary of Architecture and Landscape Architecture* (2nd ed.), 2006

James Stevens Curl and Susan Wilson, *The Oxford Dictionary of Architecture*, 3rd ed., 2015

Alzina Stone Dale, Barbara Sloan-Hendershott, *Mystery Reader's Walking Guide*, 2004

Ricci de Freitas, *Tales of Brunswick Square – Bloomsbury's untold past* – Marchmont Association, 2014

Charles Dickens, *Bloomsbury Bouquets*, 1864

Dictionary of South African Biography, Vol. 3, 1977

Rowland Dobie, *The history of the United Parishes of St Giles in the Fields and St George Bloomsbury*, 1829

John Bardwell Ebden: His Business and Political Career at the Cape (1806-1849), The Government Printer: Pretoria, 1986

Thomas Fairchild, *The City Gardener*, 1722 David R. Fisher, *The History of Parliament: the House of Commons 1820-1832*, 2009

Brian Girling, *Bloomsbury and Fitzrovia Through Time*, 2012

Mark Girouard, *The Victorian Country House*, 1979

A. Stuart Gray, *Edwardian Architecture: A Biographical Dictionary*, Duckworth, 1985

Sara Gray, *The Dictionary of British Women Artists*, 2009

J. Gurney, *The trial of Frederick Calvert (1768) – Memoirs of the seraglio of the bashaw of Merryland, by a discarded sultana*

Harleian Society, *Familiae minorum gentium, diligentia 1894-1896*, Vol. I

Charles George Harper, *Stagecoach and mail in days of yore: a picturesque history of the coaching age,1863-1943*, 1903

Eileen Harris, *Robert Adam on Park Avenue: The Interiors for Bolton House*

Statesmen of Time of George III, first series

Elree I. Harris & Shirley R. Scott, *A Gallery of her own: An annotated Bibliography of Women in Victorian Painting (Women's History & Culture)*, 1997

Christopher Hibbert, Ben Weinreb, *The London Encyclopaedia*, 3rd ed., 2008

Alan Hollinghurst, *The Swimming Pool Library*, 1988

Gerald Howat, *Learie Constantine*, 1977

Imperial London Hotels, *Notes on the History of the Imperial Hotels*, 1910

Imperial London Hotels, *THREE LONDON HOTELS* brochure, 1910

R. H. Inglis Palgrave (ed.), *The Life of James Deacon Hume, Secretary of the Board of Trade, Dictionary of Political Economy*, Vol. 2, 1895

L.J. Jennings, *The Croker papers*, Vol. 2, 1885

E. Karol and A. Finch, *Charles Holden: Architect 1875-1960*, 1988

Fanny Kemble, *Records of a Girlhood*, 1878

M. Levey, *Sir Thomas Lawrence*, New Haven and London: Yale University Press, 2005

London County Council (LCC), *Bomb Damage map, 1939-45*

Todd Longstafffe-Gowan, *The London Square*, 2012

J.C. Loudon, *H Repton, Landscape Gardening*, 1840

Anthony Ludovici, *Nietzsche His Life and Works*, 1910

Macaulay, *History of England*, 1685

Denis Mackail, *The Story of J.M.B.*, 1949

J.P. Malcolm, *Londinium Redivivum*, 1803

C.F.G. Masterman, *Frederick Dennison Maurice*, in series, *Leaders of the Church, 1800–1900*, London: A.R. Mowbray, 1907

Victor T.C. Middleton with the late Leonard J. Lickorish, *British Tourism – The Remarkable Story of Growth*, 2005

Houghton Mifflin ed., *Writings of Mrs Humphry Ward*, Vol. ii, 1911

The letters; with important additions and corrections from his own manuscripts selected and edited by the Rev. John Mitford, Thomas Gray & John Mitford, 1st January 1816

Joseph Morris, *Genealogy of Shropshire*, Vol. 3, p. 1304; Vol. 9, p. 4654

J.G. Morris, *The lords Baltimore (1874): A catalogue of the royal and noble authors of England, Scotland and Ireland…by the late Horatio Walpole, ed. T. Park*, Vol. 5, (1806), 278–82

Nicholas Murray, *Real Bloomsbury*, 2010

Frederick W. Nolan, *The Lincoln County War: A Documentary History*, 1931, revised 2009

L.B. Namier, *Powlett, Harry (1720–94)*

Frederick W. Nolan, *The West of Billy the Kid*, 1931, revised 1998

John Noorthouck, *A New History of London, including Westminster and Southwark*, 1773

Henry Hoyle Oddie, *Recollections of the character of the late Henry Hoyle Oddie*, 1830

Donald J. Olsen, *The growth of Victorian London*, Part 2, 1976

Donald J. Olsen, *Town Planning in London*, 1982

Revd Samuel Hadden Parkes, *Window Gardens for the People, and Clean and Tidy Rooms: Being an Experiment to Improve the Lives of the London Poor* (London: S.W. Partridge, 1864)

Nikolaus Pevsner,
The Buildings of England, 1951

Pevsner, N., *The Buildings of England: London Except the Cities of London and Westminster*, 1952

Pevsner, N. and B. Cherry, *The Buildings of England: London 4: North*, 1988

Pictorial London, 1896

Alfred Plummer, *The London Weaver's Company 1600–1970*, 2015

Gary Powell, *SQUARE LONDON – a social history of the iconic London square*, 2012

Humphry Repton, *An Enquiry into the Changes of Taste in Landscape Gardening*, 1806

M.C. Reed, *A history of James Capel & Co.*, privately printed, London, 1975

Nick Rennison, *The London Plaque Guide*, 4th ed., 2015

Research Society for Victorian Periodicals, *Victorian periodicals review*, University of Toronto, 1984

John Reynolds, Gill Davies, *One Thousand Buildings of London*, 2006

Richard Rhodes, *The Making of the Atomic Bomb*, 1986

John Richardson, *The Annals of London*, 2000

Henry Crabb Robinson, *Diary, Reminiscences and Correspondence*, 1869

N.A.M. Rodger, *The wooden world: an anatomy of the Georgian navy*, 1986

Samuel Romilly, *Memoirs of the Life of Sir Samuel Romilly: Written By Himself; With A Selection From His Correspondence: Vol. 2*, 2014

William D. Rubinstein, Michael A. Jolles, Hilary L. Rubinstein, *The Palgrave Dictionary of Anglo-Jewish History*, 2011

Marion Sambourne's *Diary*, 1903

W. Shugg, *The baron and the milliner: Lord Baltimore's rape trial as a mirror of class tension in mid-Georgian London*, Maryland Historical Magazine, 83, 1988

Piet Schreuders, Mark Lewisohn, Adam Smith, *The Beatles' London*, 1994

Mr John Thomas Smith, *A Rainy Day*, 1845 and 1861

Gavin Stamp, *Lost Victorian Britain*, 2010

John Strype, *Survey of London*, 1720

John Summerson, *Georgian London*, 1991

Richard Tames, *Bloomsbury Past*, 1993

William Makepeace Thackeray, *Vanity Fair*, 1847-8

The Lancet, 4th December 1824

John Timbs FSA, *Romance of London*, 1865

Edward Walford, *Old and New London*, Vol. iv, c.1800s

Edward Walford, *The County Families of the United Kingdom*, 1860

Mrs Humphry Ward, *A Writer's Recollection*, 1918

Alexis Weedon, *Hazell, Watson and Viney Limited*, in Laurel Brake, Marysa Demoor, Margaret Beetham, *Dictionary of Nineteenth-century Journalism in Great Britain and Ireland*, 2008

H.G. Wells, *The Invisible Man*, 1897

Virginia Woolf, *A Passionate Apprentice: The Early Journals 1897-1909*, 2004

Edmund Yates, *The Business of Pleasure*, 1879

Websites:

adb.anu.edu.au/biography/scott-helenus-2851

Ancestry.com

Architecture.com

Archiveshub.ac.uk

bbc.co.uk/whodoyouthinkyouare/new-stories/esther-rantzen/

bda.org

beginnings.ioe.ac.uk/index.html

Bloomsbury People blogspot

bmagic.org.ukpeople/+Louisa+Starr+Canziani

Bonhams Auctioneers' website

Britannica.com/biography/Mary-Russell-Mitford

Britannica.com/biography/James-Cowles-Prichard

british-genealogy.com/threads/79138-SIR-PERCY-COLEMAN-SIMMONS

Survey of London, British History Online

Browningscorrespondence.com/biographical-sketches/?id=944

Burlington Mag on-line Feb 1995 edition: *Robert Adam on Park Avenue: The Interiors for Bolton House*

Bylesfamilytree.com/sir-john-byles.asp

Camden.gov.uk - *History of Russell Square*

c20society.org.uk/botm/senate-house-bloomsbury-wc1/

Cottesmoreschool.com/about-cottesmore/history-the-house

Cricketarchive.com/Archive/Players/37/37911/37911.html

dia.ie/architects/view/4387/PORTER-HORATIO%23

Dictionary of National Biography:

George Simonds Boulger, *Gray, John Edward*, in Stephen, Leslie; Lee, Sidney, 1890 Sidney Lee, ed., *Beverley, William Roxby*, 1901

Sidney Lee, ed., *Hullock, John*, 1891

Malden, Henry Smith, Elder & Co., 1885–1900

Leslie Stephen, ed., *Caldecott, Randolph*, 1886

Tooke, William (1777-1863)

distantwriting.co.uk/privatetelegraphy.html

Epsomandewellhistory explorer.org.uk

ezitis.myzen.co.uk/italian.html

Genealogy.kirkpatrickaustralian.com/archives/

Genealogy.co.uk

Hackney L.B. website: *Love Local Landmarks*

Hackney Society website

Historic England's *National Register of Historic Parks and Gardens of Special Historic Interest*: historicengland.org.uk/listing/the-list

History of Parliament Online, David R. Fisher (ed.), 2009

Historyofparliamentonline.org/volume/1820-1832/member/capel-john-1767-1846

Historyofparliamentonline.org/volume/1790-1820/member/nicholl-sir-john-1759-1838

Historyofparliamentonline.org/volume/1790-1820/member/smith-thomas-1754-1831

Hotel Russell website

Imperial War Museum website

Inflation.stephenmorley.org

jeanhood.co.uk/later_ortellis.html

Kingscollections.org/catalogues/kclca/collection/b/10bi65-1

Land Use Consultants website

livesonline.rcseng.ac.uk/biogs/E000200b.htm

London Remembered website

London.wikia.com/wiki/Thomas_Henry_Brooke-Hitching

lafayette.org.uk/bro3794.html

london.wikia.com/wiki/Percy_Coleman_Simmons

math.boisestate.edu/GaS/british/composers/monckton.html

Medievalgenealogy.org.uk/sources/peerages.shtml

natgould.org/nathan_wetherell_1808-1887

discovery.nationalarchives.gov.uk

npg.org.uk

Onlinebooks.library.upenn.edu

Oxford Dictionary of National Biography, Oxford University Press, 2004:

H.F. Augstein, *Prichard, Jas Cowles (1786–1848)*

Elizabeth Baigent, *Booth, Sir Felix, first baronet (1775–1850)*

Anne Pimlott Baker, *Evans, Evan (1882–1965)*, May 2005

John D. Baird, *Gray, Thomas (1716–1771)*

James J. Barnes, Patience P. Barnes, *Routledge, George (1812–1888)*

G.C. Boase, Rev. Anne Pimlott Baker, *Parsons, John Meeson (1798–1870)*

G.C. Boase, Rev. Eric Metcalfe, *Tooke, William (1777–1863)*

David B. Brownlee, *Street, George Edmund (1824–1881)*

Forrest Capie, *Borthwick, Sir Thomas (1835–1912)*

William Carr, Rev. Eric Metcalfe, *Taunton, Sir William Elias (1773–1835)*

Penelope Carson, *Grant, Charles (1746–1823)*

R. C. J. Cocks, *Cox, Edward William (1809–1879)*

Verna Coleman, *Walsh, Adela Constantia Mary Pankhurst (1885–1961)*

N.G. Coley, *Marcet, Alexander John Gaspard (1770–1822)*

Thompson Cooper, Rev. Patrick Wallis, *Lind, James (1736–1812)*

W.R. Cornish, *Holroyd, Sir George Sowley (1758–1831)*

Ian E. Cottington, *Matthey, George (1825–1913)*

Phillip L. Cottrell, *Heath, John Benjamin (1790–1879)*

W.P. Courtney, Rev. Rebecca Mills, *Richards, George (bap. 1767, d. 1837)*

Alan Crawford, *Horne, Herbert Percy (1864–1916)*

Michael T. Davis, *Mansfield , Sir James (bap. 1734, d. 1821)*

Margaret Escott, *Nicholl, Sir John (1759–1838)*

Kurt Gänzl, *Monckton, (John) Lionel Alexander (1861–1924)*

Dorian Gerhold, *Horne, Benjamin Worthy (1804–1870)*

M.A. Goodall, *Knowles, James Thomas (1806–1884)*

Peter Gosden, *Pratt, John Tidd (1797–1870)*

H.G. Hanbury, Rev. H. G. Judge, *Stallybrass , William Teulon Swan (1883–1948)*

T.F. Henderson, Rev. Jonathan Harris, *Adams, William (1772–1851)*

T.F. Henderson, Rev. David Turner, *Calvert, Frederick, sixth Baron Baltimore (1732–1771)*

Christine Hillam, *Lindsay, Lilian (1871–1960)*

Arthur Jacobs, *Carte, Richard D'Oyly (1844–1901)*

Gareth H. Jones, Vivienne Jones, *Denman, Thomas, first Baron Denman (1779–1854)*

D.A. Johnson, *Salt, William (1808–1863)*

Tony Joseph, *Grossmith, George (1847–1912)*

Joseph Knight, Rev. Nilanjana Banerji, *Beverley, Henry Roxby (1796–1863)*

Joseph Knight, Rev. Nilanjana Banerji, *Roxby, Robert (c.1809–1866)*

Michael R. Lane, *Rendel, Sir Alexander Meadows (1829–1918)*

Michael Lobban, *Abbott, Charles, first Baron Tenterden (1762–1832)*

M.M. Macnaghten, Rev. H. C. G. Matthew, *Clarke, Sir Edward George (1841–1931)*

Joseph A. Maiolo, *Clarke, William Francis (1883–1961)*

Robert L. Martensen, *Wharton, Thomas (1614–1673)*

Anita McConnell, *Armstrong, John (1784–1829)*

R.A. Melikan, *Gibbs, Sir Vicary (1751–1820)*

R.A. Melikan, *Pigott, Sir Arthur Leary (1749–1819)*

R.A. Melikan, *Romilly, Sir Samuel (1757–1818)*

Norman Moore, Rev. Jean Loudon, *Saunders, William (1743–1817)*

A.J.A. Morris, *Cook, Sir Edward Tyas (1857–1919)*

Alexander Murdoch, *Wedderburn, Alexander, first earl of Rosslyn (1733–1805)*

Robert Murphy, *Woolf, Charles Moss (1879–1942)*

John Orbell, *Mocatta family (per. 1671–1957)*

Alexander Murdoch, *Wedderburn, Alexander, first earl of Rosslyn (1733–1805)*

W.B. Owen, Rev. Matthew Lee, *Thompson, William Marcus (1857–1907)*

M.H. Port, *Hardwick, Philip (1792–1870)*

M. H. Port, *Peto, Sir (Samuel) Morton, first baronet (1809–1889)*

Patrick Polden, *Spankie, Robert (1774–1842)*

June Purvis, *Pankhurst, Dame Christabel Harriette (1880–1958)*

June Purvis, *Pankhurst, Emmeline (1858–1928)*

Michael Reed, *Capel, James (1789–1872)*

Simon Rodway, *Rendel, Leila Margaret (1882–1969)*

Judy Slinn, *Freshfield family (per. 1800–1918)*

Martin L. Smith, *Benson, Richard Meux (1824–1915)*

Jane W. Stedman, *Burnand, Sir Francis Cowley (1836–1917)*

John Sutherland, *Ward, Mary Augusta [Mrs Humphry Ward] (1851–1920)*

Martha S. Vogeler, *Stebbing, William (1831–1926)*

David Waller, *Tennant, Gertrude Barbara Rich (1819–1918)*, May 2011

Patrick Wallis, *Scott, Helenus (bap. 1758, d. 1821)*

C.D. Watkinson, *Beverly, William Roxby*

Stanley Weintraub, *Buckle, George Earle*, H.C.G. Matthew and Brian Harrison, eds

R.G. Wilson, *Greene family (per. 1801–1920)*

G.S. Woods, Rev. P.W. Hammond, *Cokayne , George Edward (1825–1911)*

Oxfordindex.oup.com

Peter Morton's ancestry website

Plarr's Lives of the Fellows Online, Golding-Bird, Cuthbert Hilton (1848–1939)

Plarr's Lives of the Fellows Online, James Thomas Ware (Information kindly given by his nephew, A.M. Ware, MD Cantab., and grandson of Martin Ware)

Playing Card Makers Company, *List of the Master, Wardens, Court of Assistants, Officers, and Livery of the Company*

Richardrbeeman.com/ excerpts3.html

Royalcollection.org.uk/ collection/1078134/the-complete-peerage-of-england-scotland-ireland-great-britain-and-the-united

s2a3.org.za/bio/Biograph_final. php?serial=831

SarahYoung.com

sas.ac.uk/newsletter/autumn09/ simpson.html

Sculpture.gla.ac.uk

shadyoldlady.com

Sotheby's Auctioneers' website

Southafricansettlers. com/?cat=15&paged=4

archive.spectator.co.uk

Spiritualismlink.com/t1285-the-psychic-forc

stedmundsburychronicle.co.uk/ Chronicle/1813-1899.htm

Struttandparker.com/about-strutt-and-parker/history

Thegazette.co.uk/London/ issue/28321/page/9763/data.pdf

Theodora.com/encyclopedia/s2/ sir_edward_tyas_cook.html

The National Library of Wales online, Sir John Nicholl

Ian Chilvers (Ed.), *Lawrence, Sir Thomas, The Oxford Dictionary of Art and Artists*, Oxford University Press, 2009. Oxford Reference Online. Oxford University Press.

UCL Bloomsbury Project website

V&A website - fabric designs

Victorian Web

Burnand, Sir Francis Cowley, Who Was Who, online edition, Oxford University Press, 2014

Wikipedia.org/wiki/Frederick_ Calvert,_6th_Baron_Baltimore

Wikipedia.org/wiki/ Richard_D%27Oyly_Carte

Wikipedia.org/wiki/Benjamin_ Greene

Wikipedia.org/wiki/John_Voce_ Moore

Wikipedia.org/wiki/John_ Nicholl_(judge)

Wikipedia.org/wiki Harry_ Powlett,_6th_Duke_of_Bolton

Wikipedia.orgwiki/Alexander_ Wedderburn,_1st_Earl_of_ Rosslyn#

wikiwand.com

Newspapers & Periodicals:

Asiatic Journal, 1834

Asiatic Journal, 1839 and 1840

City Press, July 1863

Daily Telegraph, 8th March 1982

Holborn and Bloomsbury Journal, July 1863

Copeland Bowie, Inquirer, April 1920

Jewish Chronicle, 1869

Law Magazine, 13, 1835

London University Magazine, 1830

Los Angeles Times, 15th April 1906

Mechanics Magazine, Vol. 40, 1844

Monthly Magazine, June 1803

Morning Post (London), 18th August 1845

New Sporting Magazine, 259, July 1862

Penny Illustrated News, 18th July 1863

Public Advertiser, 1764

Sacramento Daily Union, 20th November 1898

St James's Magazine, 1878

The Builder, 15th June 1850, 3rd May 1884

The Court Magazine, 1834

The Daily Graphic, 13th September 1910

The Engineer (magazine), 4th December 1892

The European Magazine and London Review, Vol. 73, 1818

The Farmer's (magazine), 1842

The Gazette, 1808, 19th March 1859, 29th March 1918

The Gentleman's Magazine: 21st August 1807, 2nd October 1808,

19th August 1811, October 1811, 1st March 1813, 1823, 12th January 1824, January-June 1825, 1829, January 1830, July-December 1835, 1836, January-June 1839, January 1840, July-December 1840, 1934

The Illustrated London News, 27th September 1845, 23rd July 1864, 16th June 1900

The Illustrated Sporting and Dramatic News, 16th June 1900

The Lady's Magazine, 14th July 1808, 1830, 1836

The London Gazette, 10th July 1874, 5th April 1878, 3rd June 1879, 19th December 1913

The London Magazine, 1820, 5th September 1825

The Morning Chronicle, 25th October 1826

The Naval Chronicle, January-July 1812

The Observer, 19th March 1939

The Spectator, 10th September 1943

THE SPHERE, 9th June 1900

The Sydney Morning Herald, 1858

The Times: 4th November 1818, 23rd July 1825, 7th April 1827, 8th November 1832, 11th April 1848, 15th August 1854, 31st December 1870, 19th November 1872, 1st June 1906, 16th October 1911, 20th April 1915, 20th March 1928, 7th July 1928, 27th April 1931, 23rd August 1940, 18th April 1957, 2nd May 1960, 16th March 1971, 21st November 1981

The Times Commercial Supplement, 23rd Oct 1908

The Universal Magazine, 1805

Time (magazine), 1999

Archive Centres:

Camden Local Studies Library and Archives Centre

National Archives

Norfolk Record Office

Senate House Library

Sir John Soane's Museum

The Spectator Archive

UCL Archives

Wellcome Library

Maps: As referenced
in the respective chapters.

Other records:

Act of Parliament, 20th June 1800 (George III, cap. 50)

J.U. Farb, Alumni Cantabrigiensis

The Annual Biography and Obituary for the Year 1830

Annual Register of World Events: 1805, Vol. 64, 1822, 1825, 1827, 1830

The Director of Planning and Transport's decision letter of 14th November 1988 to the Chief Executive of L.B. Camden

Interpretive boards titled The Restoration of RUSSELL SQUARE GARDEN in Russell Square Gardens, L.B. Camden

Census returns (as mentioned in the text)

Records of the Central Synagogue

College of Physicians Directory, 1844

The Creevey Papers, Vol. 1

Electoral registers (as mentioned in text)

The Correspondence of Michael Faraday, Vol. 2, 1832-1840

GEC, Peerage, P. Watson, Powlett, Harry

Hackney L.B., St Mark's Conservation Area Appraisal, 2008

Hansard, 28th March 1825

Hansard, 16th May 1825

Harrow School Register, 1826

H.F. Clark, The Proposed improvements to Russell Square and Bloomsbury Square, report to Holborn Borough Council, 19th September 1946

London Squares Preservation Act, 1931

Records of a committee of the House of Lords conducting an enquiry into Foreign

Trade (Silk and Wine Trade), 16th May 1821

The Proceedings of the Old Bailey (Central Criminal Court), 10th January 1821

The Proceedings of the Old Bailey, 19th August, 1872

Records of the Prerogative Court, Canterbury, Tobago

Official Bulletin, St. James's Palace, March, 1831

Tate

Probate, CGPLA Eng. & Wales, 3rd May 1912, 25th April 1918

Gregory, R. A., Ferguson, A, (1941), Oliver Joseph Lodge, 1851-1940. Obituary Notices of Fellows of the Royal Society

RIBA Transactions, 1884

Royal Commission on Friendly Societies, Fourth Report, C 961, Appendix 1.22

Russell Institution Catalogue, 1835

Members of Society for Promoting Christian Knowledge, 1796

Register of members of the United Company of Merchants of England trading to the East Indies, 10th November 1825, 1875

University of London Masterplan, 2015

Richard Walduck, letter to the London Evening Standard, 25th October 1995

Russell Square, c.1963 © CLSAC

View towards Russell Square from the Centre Point viewing gallery prior to its closure in 2015